Beyond 1917

Beyond 1917

The United States and the
Global Legacies of the Great War

Edited by
THOMAS W. ZEILER, DAVID K. EKBLADH,
AND BENJAMIN C. MONTOYA

OXFORD
UNIVERSITY PRESS

OXFORD
UNIVERSITY PRESS

Oxford University Press is a department of the University of Oxford. It furthers
the University's objective of excellence in research, scholarship, and education
by publishing worldwide. Oxford is a registered trade mark of Oxford University
Press in the UK and certain other countries.

Published in the United States of America by Oxford University Press
198 Madison Avenue, New York, NY 10016, United States of America.

© Oxford University Press 2017

CIP data is on file at the Library of Congress
ISBN 978–0–19–060400–4 (hbk)
ISBN 978–0–19–060401–1 (pbk)

9 8 7 6 5 4 3 2 1

Paperback printed by Webcom, Inc., Canada
Hardback printed by Bridgeport National Bindery, Inc., United States of America

To Leah, Haley, and Rocio

Contents

Acknowledgments

The editors would like to thank the contributors to this volume, many of whom bore with us as we asked for repeated revisions to their chapters and other materials. We must single out James McAllister and Carrie Greene at Williams College for sponsoring the conference, "World War I Legacies" on April 18–19, 2014, out of which this volume arose. Their hospitality, organization, good cheer, and firm hand were essential to our success, and Williams was a perfect setting for academic interchange. The commentaries and discussions at each panel were so fruitful and exciting that we decided to move forward with this book. In addition to the authors, we wish to thank the following participants at that conference: Anthony Adamthwaite, Daniel Gorman, Gretchen Heefner, David Mayers, Nicole Phelps, and Anders Stephanson. Thanks also to the journal *Diplomatic History* for permission to reprint the articles from the September 2014 issue. Susan Ferber at Oxford University Press has overseen the production of this volume with her typical keen eye and wise advice. We certainly appreciate the support of our home institutions—the Department of History at the University of Colorado Boulder, and the Department of History at Tufts University. We were fortunate to have the timely support provided by the Faculty Research Awards Committee of Tufts University.

Contributors

EDITORS

Thomas W. Zeiler is Professor of History and Director of the Program in International Affairs at the University of Colorado Boulder. Recent publications include *Annihilation: A Global Military History of World War II* (2011). He is the former editor of the journal *Diplomatic History* and president (2012) of the Society for Historians of American Foreign Relations.

David K. Ekbladh is Associate Professor of History and Core Faculty in International Relations at Tufts University. His first book, *The Great American Mission: Modernization and the Construction of an American World Order* (2010), won the Stuart L. Bernath Prize of the Society of American Historians as well as the Phi Alpha Theta Best First Book Award. Articles of his have appeared in *Diplomatic History*, the *International History Review, International Security, World Affairs*, and the *Wilson Quarterly*.

Benjamin C. Montoya earned his Ph.D. at the University of Colorado Boulder in 2015. His dissertation, entitled *Risking "Immeasurable Harm": The Diplomacy of Immigration Restriction in U.S.-Mexico Relations, 1924 to 1932*, considers how American efforts to place a quota on Mexican immigration affected foreign policy between the two nations. He teaches for the Program in International Affairs and the Department of History at the University of Colorado Boulder.

CONTRIBUTORS

Michael Adas is the Emeritus Abraham E. Voorhees Professor and Board of Governors Chair at Rutgers University. His recent publications on comparative history have focused on great power military interventions in the post-colonial world, including a forthcoming book from Oxford University Press, *Everyman in Vietnam: A Soldier's Journey into the Quagmire*, coauthored with Joseph Gilch.

Christopher Capozzola is Associate Professor of History at the Massachusetts Institute of Technology. He is the author of *Uncle Sam Wants You: World War I and the Making of the Modern American Citizen* (Oxford University Press, 2008). He is a cocurator of "The Volunteers: Americans Join World War I," a public history project about American civilians who volunteered in Europe during and after the First World War.

John Milton Cooper, Jr., is E. Gordon Fox Professor of American Institutions, emeritus, at the University of Wisconsin-Madison. He is the author and editor of several books on the World War I era, and he served on the Editorial Advisory Committee to the Papers of Woodrow Wilson.

Lloyd Gardner is Professor Emeritus at Rutgers University. He is the author of over fifteen books in the field of American diplomatic history, including *Safe for Democracy: The Anglo-American Response to Revolution, 1913–1923* and, most recently, *The War on Leakers: National Security and American Democracy from Eugene Debs to Edward Snowden*.

Robert Gerwarth is Professor of Modern History at University College Dublin and Director of UCD's Centre for War Studies. He specializes on the history of political violence in late nineteenth and early twentieth-century Europe. His most recent monograph is *The Vanquished: Why the First World War Failed to End* (2016).

Akira Iriye is Charles Warren Professor of American History, emeritus, Harvard University. He has also taught at the University of Chicago, University of Rochester, and the University of California, Santa Cruz. His recent publications include *Cultural Internationalism and World Order* (1997), *International and Transnational History* (2014), and (as editor) *Global Interdependence: The World since 1945* (2013).

Julia Irwin is an Associate Professor of History at the University of South Florida. Her research focuses on the role of humanitarianism and foreign aid in twentieth-century US foreign relations. She is the author of *Making the World Safe: The American Red Cross and a Nation's Humanitarian Awakening*

(Oxford University Press, 2013) and is now working on a second book project, *Catastrophic Diplomacy: A History of U.S. Responses to Global Natural Disaster*.

Matthew F. Jacobs is Associate Professor of US and International History at the University of Florida, where he teaches courses on US–Middle East relations, the Vietnam War, US foreign relations, the world since 1945, and international studies. He earned his Ph.D. in history at the University of North Carolina at Chapel Hill in 2002, and his first book, *Imagining the Middle East: The Building of an American Foreign Policy, 1918–1967*, was published by the University of North Carolina Press in 2011.

Erez Manela is Professor of History at Harvard University, where he teaches international history and the history of the United States in the world. His most recent book, *Empires at War, 1911–23* (2014), coedited with Robert Gerwarth, has been translated into seven languages. His other books include the prizewinning *The Wilsonian Moment: Self-Determination and the International Origins of Anticolonial Nationalism* (2007) and (as coeditor) *The Shock of the Global: The 1970s in Perspective* (2010).

Michael S. Neiberg is the inaugural Chair of War Studies at the United States Army War College. He is the author of *Dance of the Furies: Europe and the Outbreak of World War I* (Harvard University Press, 2011), which the *Wall Street Journal* recently named it one of the five best books ever written about the war, and *The Path to War: How the First World War Created Modern America* (Oxford University Press, 2016).

Andrew Preston is Professor of American History and a Fellow of Clare College at Cambridge University. He is the author of *The War Council: McGeorge Bundy, the NSC, and Vietnam* (Harvard University Press, 2006) and *Sword of the Spirit, Shield of Faith: Religion in American War and Diplomacy* (Knopf, 2012), as well as the editor of four other books.

Katharina Rietzler teaches history at the University of Sussex, England. Her work has appeared in the *Journal of Global History, Diplomatic History, Diplomacy & Statecraft*, and *Historical Research*. She is currently completing a transnational history of internationalism and American philanthropy in the first half of the twentieth century.

Emily S. Rosenberg, a former chair of history at the University of California, Irvine, now emeritus, is the author of *Transnational Currents in a Shrinking World, 1870–1945*, a book published from her edited volume, *A World Connecting: 1870–1945* (Harvard University Press, 2012). Other books include *Spreading the American Dream: American Economic and Cultural Expansion,*

1890–1945; Financial Missionaries to the World: The Politics and Culture of Dollar Diplomacy, 1900–1930; and *A Date Which Will Live: Pearl Harbor in American Memory*. She has served as president of the Society for Historians of American Foreign Relations, and coedited the American Encounters, Global Interactions series for Duke University Press.

Dietmar Rothermund is Professor Emeritus of South Asian History at the University of Heidelberg, Germany. A member of the Royal Historical Society in London since 1988, he has published *Government, Landlord and Peasant in India* (1978), *India in the Great Depression* (1992), *India: The Rise of an Asian Giant* (2008), and *A History of India* (with H. Kulke) (sixth ed., 2016).

Klaus Schwabe is a retired professor of modern history at the Technical University—RWTH—at Aachen, Germany. His publications encompass international and German-American relations in the twentieth century, in particular in the era of World War I and the period of the Cold War. In 2011 a third printing of his history of America's foreign relations in the twentieth century appeared (*Weltmacht und Weltordnung*). At present, he is preparing a brief German-language biography of Jean Monnet.

Hatsue Shinohara received her doctorate from the University of Chicago and is a professor at the Graduate School of Asia-Pacific Studies, Waseda University in Tokyo. She is the author of *US International Lawyers in the Interwar Years: A Forgotten Crusade* (Cambridge University Press, 2012) and "Drift towards an Empire? The Trajectory of American Reformers in the Cold War," in *International Law and Empire: Historical Explorations*, edited by Martti Koskenniemi, Walter Rech, and Manuel Jiménez Fonseca (Oxford University Press, forthcoming).

Beyond 1917

Introduction

Legacies

David K. Ekbladh

World War I blasted scars in the earth and onto human societies but it also left indelible marks on our understanding of time. The conflict and the years that surround it now mark departures into sweeping eras as well of pivotal historical change. Staple concepts that divvy up recent epochs, such as the "long nineteenth century" and the "short twentieth century," hinge on that war. As the architect of those periods, Eric Hobsbawm, noted, "if there are dates which are more than conveniences for purposes of periodization, August 1914 is one of them."[1] For other influential scholars, the gestation of the modern world is bounded by the ominous date of 1914.[2] The importance of these dates is not limited to scholarship, however. In important respects, our understanding of the world today rests on the legacies of World War I.

A massively destructive and transformative event, the First World War left innumerable wounds in its wake. A sign that the war is something our present is compelled to understand, yet struggles to grasp, is that it is still passionately debated. What is not disputed is that a crisis brought by the assassination of an Austrian Archduke in Sarajevo in today's Bosnia (then a part of the Austro-Hungarian Empire) brought a collision of the European powers in the summer of 1914. The resulting conflagration led to a long struggle that eventually swept in empires, states, and peoples from North America, Africa, Asia, and the Middle East. The brutal intensity of the conflict, in part a product of the scientific and technological advances and the capacities of modern industry when bent to warfare, stunned participants at the time and still has the ability to shock in the present.

When the war officially ended on November 11, 1918, there were still aftershocks to endure. The peace hammered out at Versailles did codify a victory but it did not assure peace. In the years following the war many parts of the world were wracked by disease, dislocation, revolution, and civil war that were direct results of the conflict that began in 1914. For many the war and what followed became a catastrophic upheaval that marked a dramatic departure for states, societies, individuals, and the modern world itself.

That the First World War has become an integral milepost for human history is a reflection of the importance of the conflict, the forces that led to it, and the forces it unleashed. The legacies generated by the war left tension, pain, and sometimes hope but they have never been static. Rather, they have been a shifting set of experiences, lessons, interpretations, and costs left by an unparalleled global war. Generations have grappled with these questions, interpreting and reinterpreting their changing meanings that come with the passage of time. The influence of this activity extends/has extended far beyond the cloisters of academia. World War I remains a very real, and sometimes painful, fixture in contemporary global politics and society. Critical aspects of international affairs touch emotionally charged legacies that remain live wires. Just one gruesome segment of the war, the Armenian genocide, retained the power to generate moving commemorations as well as produce diplomatic sparks between states as the Great War's centennial progressed.[3]

The war itself was terrible enough. The Great War's clash of mass armies generated changes that still echo on today's battlefields. Unparalleled combat demanded innovations that brought the sustained use of rapid-firing artillery, poison gas, aircraft in combat (and the bombardment of civilians from the air), submarines, tanks, machine guns, and aircraft carriers as well as the modern medical techniques to patch, literally, scarred faces, mutilated bodies, and "shell shocked" psyches for which these innovations were responsible. Total war's influence reached far beyond the battlefield and bled into societies that had been fully mobilized for the struggle. Conscription, pacifism, militarism, humanitarian, and socialist movements reshaped politics within countries and global affairs during the war and for decades to come. Governments learned the value of modern propaganda techniques, both in print and in film. Societies were changed in far-reaching ways: women were emancipated in some countries and citizenship was fundamentally altered in many places.

Globally, aristocracy and monarchies went into decline. Empires were smashed. In Europe, Germany, Austria-Hungary, and Russia disintegrated under the demands of modern war and popular unrest. In the Middle East, the collapse of the Ottoman Empire was epoch-making. Those empires that survived—Great Britain, France, Japan, and the United States—were profoundly altered. So were whole continents. Europe, the Middle East, Africa, and Asia saw territories traded, boundaries redrawn, and new states emerge during the conflict and its aftermath, redrawing the cartography of international life in ways that can still be seen and felt today.

Of course, roots of an even more horrific conflict, the Second World War, lay, in part, in the First World War. Elements of the toxic conditions that led to that disaster were stirred up by the shockwaves of the Great War. In the war's wake, fascism and communism gained traction as movements; mass migration reshaped many regions; independence for places like Ireland, Turkey, and the Baltic states pointed to the Janus-faced power of nationalism; militarism in Japan and elsewhere became more palatable; and an influenza pandemic that still serves a chilling warning for disease outbreaks shook already trembling societies. Closer to home, even as there was a slowdown in the process of liberal globalization, the United States moved from a historical position from debtor to creditor, a condition that heralded the rise of Wall Street and American economic dominance. A widely accepted lesson of the war was that any peace would have to be worldwide. That set many on a mission to establish an international organization committed to collective security. That errand continues into the twenty-first century.

These are just some reminders that perhaps no conflict's legacies are more visible that those of the First World War. Its traumas are evident on all sorts of terrain, and not all are physical. Red poppies pop up around the globe for Remembrance Days in the Commonwealth of Nations to recall the human costs sustained by the British Empire. The long tradition of monument construction continues in the present. In 2014, France dedicated a massive new memorial to the war dead from across its former empire. Empire assured that places seemingly remote from the major theaters of action felt the war directly. British dominions like Australia and New Zealand sent large contingents that suffered fearful casualties relative to their populations. These losses served to solidify emerging senses of nationhood in both places and remain integral to national narratives. Australians marked the centenary of the war with a slew of exhibits and remembrances that even focus on specific battles. Just one segment of the 1916 Somme campaign, the Battle of Pozières where Australians played an outsized and bloody part, was honored in numerous ways. During commemorations in July 2016 a national prime-time television broadcast of the ceremony remembering those slain in France was matched by individual acts of placing fresh flowers at the alcove marking the campaign at the ANZAC monument in Sydney, the National War Memorial in Canberra, and elsewhere around the country. Investing the wider public in the memory of the war is a goal of these commemorations. To this end, one of the many New Zealand tributes included an imposing multimedia exhibit at its national museum in Wellington. Composed by Academy Award–winning director Sir Peter Jackson, it vividly focused on the individual experience of the grinding fighting at Gallipoli. As in other places, the distilled memory of the war no longer has much place for its cause and politics. The legacy that is offered audiences is one of the sacrifice and endurance of those who experienced the war. These images of the past then become a reflection of esteemed national characteristics that are seen as worthy of emulation in the present.[4]

International ceremonies now mark campaigns like Gallipoli where all sides recall the battles as a shared sacrifice and a critical moment in the national consciousness of not only New Zealand and Australia but also Turkey. Yet this commemoration cannot escape the pull of other political legacies of the war. Critics see it as a means for the contemporary Turkish state to evade the memory of the Ottoman Empire's mass killing of Armenians.[5]

In other places remembrance has been obscured or modified over time. This is true in the United States, where Armistice Day morphed into Veterans Day. The invented tradition of the president laying a wreath at the Tomb of the Unknown Soldier (Figure I.1) in Arlington National Cemetery is a reminder that even the ambivalent Americans have carved out space for commemoration of the sacrifices of the Great War and these actions have become part of the national culture. The war scratched its legacies on the United States, just as it did on Europe and other places. This volume touches on many of these consequences, and especially the long-term policy, political, social, economic, and cultural developments for the United States itself, and for the United States in the world after entry into the Great War in 1917 as well.

The war lives in the present in more subtle and subconscious ways. English speakers reflexively use phrases such as "over the top" or "no man's land," reminders that everyday lingo in a set of languages remains dotted by terms minted or given currency by the conflict. Perhaps one of the most enduring legacies is the very impulse for remembrance itself. A reflection of this desire is the popular and scholarly mobilization (including those called to the colors for this volume) that accompanied the centenary of the war. Activity on this front stresses the lively and ongoing debate about the cause, course, conclusion, and consequences of the conflict.

Yet legacies are not historically remote things; they were felt from the moment the conflict began and have shifted and been reinterpreted ever since. The essays in this collection demonstrate there is no single legacy of the First World War but an unstable set of lessons, interpretations, perceptions, and costs left by the conflict.

FIGURE I.1 Constructing a legacy of the Great War. An image of construction of the Tomb of the Unknown Soldier, taken by an unknown photographer on December 28, 1934. The tomb was built following World War I and dedicated on November 11, 1921. Additional work was completed on the memorial, which was opened to the public on April 9, 1932. US Army Photo.

Beyond 1917: The United States and the Global Legacies of the Great War explores both the consequences of the war for the United States (and the world) and American influence on shaping the legacies of the conflict in the decades after US entry in 1917. It enters the expectedly busy field of First World War studies from a sharp angle: that of the endgame, the consequences, the impact of the war—both immediately, medium-term (in the following few decades after its conclusion), and into the present. In a moment where the war is passing from living memory, the pressing power of its legacies remain apparent in the world today and understanding them remains a vital means to decode events in the present. The overall goal is to demonstrate the reach of the legacies of the First World War, both in and on history.

All authors were asked to deeply reflect on their field of expertise and how it applied to the subject of the legacies of World War I. The essays varied in intention and type but all represent thoughtful interventions—some specific to a topic or issue, others more broadly sweeping in historiography or scope. Some drew primarily on secondary works and primary sources, while others were essays. Governments and states were targeted by some contributors, while transnational actors and movements were the focus of some of the authors. A national focus preoccupied some authors, while others spread out geographically but relate their work to the United States and the legacies generated by the conflict. It should be noted that even in chapters in which the theme or coverage is global, the United States' role casts a shadow and comes under scrutiny. Themes were worked out beforehand to ensure originality and reflection with as little overlap as possible. Hence the contributions themselves suggest the disparate ways the war changed the world. In and of themselves, the perspectives offered herein are an expression of how, as Akira Iriye explains in his essay, the historiography of the war has changed as historians have reevaluated the world and who and what makes up its history.[6]

Of course, the legacies of the Great War have shifted and been reinterpreted constantly over the tumultuous twentieth century. Debates over Versailles and the settlements that followed continue as do the image of Woodrow Wilson and the ideas and institutions credited to him. Emily Rosenberg interrogates some of the received wisdom about the departures of Wilsonianism by drawing out the imperial views of Wilson and others, as well as the anti-imperial activism generated in parts of the US Empire. While the American Empire rode out the war, other empires were sundered by defeat and revolution. Matthew Jacobs outlines the calamitous collapse of the Ottoman Empire during the war and the rise of a new Middle Eastern state and imperial order that also brought the expansion of a regime of oil production and the rise of ardent nationalist movements. All assured that peace in the region would remain an aspiration over the century that followed. As the Ottoman and other empires fell and societies reeled, fears of the contagion of revolution, particularly its Bolshevik variant, ultimately reshaped US geopolitical strategy as Lloyd Gardner argues.

None of these dramatic transformations can be divorced from the crucible of the armed struggle. A rich and shifting military history of the conflict has long shown how mass armies grappled with each other and with new, terrible kinds of warfare. The road to military intervention and the experience of the war that Michael Neiberg and Michael Adas reconstruct, in their respective contributions, showcase how an unprecedented crisis altered how Americans entered and waged wars. As these themes are discussed over time, there has been increasing emphasis on other ways the war had profound and far-reaching political, economic, social, and cultural influences. As historians have widened their interpretive lenses, many facets of society, including many subordinate and subaltern groups, have been included in narratives about the conflict. Erez

Manela and Robert Gerwarth's chapter underlines how empire has returned as a central feature of analysis and it provides a fresh and inclusive view of the war as a transformative global event. Katharina Rietzler recovers how the early histories of the war, through the lens of the Carnegie Endowment for International Peace's voluminous *Economic and Social History of the World War*, were part of a longer struggle to shape the war's history and therefore its legacies. Those early clashes over its history, as John Milton Cooper recounts, contributed to the memory of the conflict and how it resonated in American society in the decades following the war.

The pull of memory remains a testament to how the conflict shocked peoples and societies in broad and intimate ways. The intensity of the war threw assumptions about race, gender, citizenship, and rights into flux in many places, fracturing societies in long-lasting ways. The United States was not immune. Christopher Capozzola shows how the demands of a world conflict reshaped not only who could be a US citizen but how they could become one. In an increasingly interconnected world Americans were aware that dislocation wrought by the war and its aftermath reduced many peoples to destitution. This suffering generated a remarkable international humanitarian impulse. The United States responded to this vast crisis with a zeal, as Julia Irwin recounts, that changed how the nation engaged the world. Religious ferment was part of this humanitarian urge as well as American society's general response to the war. It assured, as Andrew Preston describes, the conflict's inflection point for many American religious communities. Other articles of faith were transformed by the war. As Hatsue Shinohara explains, believers in the possibility of international law were shocked by the outbreak and severity of the war. The new international legal framework that emerged with the peace settlements and the Covenant of the League of Nations marked a decisive shift in crucial international norms. Despite these innovations, that the "war to end all wars" proved to be nothing of the sort is echoed in the work of Dietmar Rothermund and Klaus Schwabe. Indeed, a major reason the First World War is remembered and debated with such fervor is that it is seen as kindling the forces and individuals that ignited a second, even more destructive global conflagration just twenty years later.

It is a truism that every generation writes its own history. Over the course of a century the labors of several generations of scholars have provided a growing spectrum of interpretation, reminding us that the legacies of the Great War are a powerful fulcrum for grasping how history itself is altered over time. One scholar has described the memory of the war as a "long shadow."[7] As the contributions here reveal, this shadow has changed, and will continue to change, as the war is illuminated from new angles. But there is little chance the shadow will recede.

NOTES

1. Hobsbawm, *The Age of Empire, 1875–1914*, 6.
2. Bayly, *The Birth of the Modern World, 1780–1914*.
3. Yeginsu, "Turkey's Focus Is Elsewhere on Anniversary of Armenian Genocide"; Yardley and Sebnem, "Pope Calls Killings of Armenians 'Genocide,' Provoking Turkish Anger."
4. Gallipoli, *The Scale of Our War*, Museum of New Zealand Te Papa Tongarewa, Wellington, New Zealand.
5. *Al Jazeera*, "World Leaders Join Gallipoli Commemoration in Turkey."
6. Any single footnote on the historiography of the Great War is certain to be inadequate. What follows is merely suggestive. However, Benjamin Montoya, one of the organizers of the Williams College conference, has provided an extensive bibliography at the end of this volume. One of the best recent overviews is Horne, *A Companion to World War I*. See also Manela, *The Wilsonian Moment*; Knock, *To End All Wars*; Cooper, *Breaking the Heart of the World*; Fischer, *Germany's Aims in the First World War*; Steiner, *The Lights That Failed*; May, *The World War and American Isolation, 1914–1917*; Eksteins, *Rites of Spring*; Wall and Winter, *The Upheaval of War*; Winter and Prost, *The Great War in History*; Fussell, *The Great War and Modern Memory*.
7. Reynolds, *The Long Shadow*.

Timeline of World War I and Its Legacies

Benjamin C. Montoya

1914

June 28: Assassination of Archduke Franz Ferdinand in Sarajevo

September 6–8: Battle of the Marne

September 12: American Red Cross sends first relief ship to Europe

1915

February 10: United States issues note to Germany on "strict accountability" for submarines

March 28: British liner *Falaba* sunk by a German submarine; one American killed

April 28: American vessel *Cushing* attacked by German aircraft

May 7: British Cunard liner *Lusitania* sunk; 124 Americans killed

May 23: Italy declares war on Austria-Hungary

July 28: Beginning of US Marines' occupation of Haiti

August 19: British liner *Arabic* sunk by a German submarine; two Americans dead. Woodrow Wilson threatens to sever diplomatic relations with Germany

September 1: Germany's *Arabic* pledge that submarines will not sink liners without warning and will provide for the safety of noncombatants

October 5: German government "disavows" act of submarine commander in sinking of *Arabic*

1916

March 14: US Punitive Expedition enters Mexico, seeking Francisco (Pancho) Villa in response to cross-border raid on Columbus, NM, on March 9, 1916

March 24: French passenger steamer *Sussex* sunk; four Americans hurt

April 24–29: Easter Rising in Dublin, Ireland

May 4: Germany suspends U-boat campaign under *Sussex* pledge

May 16: US occupation of Dominican Republic; Britain and France conclude Sykes-Picot agreement, which divides Ottoman holdings in Middle East between the two nations in the event of victory over Ottoman Empire

May 31–June 1: Battle of Jutland

June 5: Arab Revolt against Ottoman Empire

June 16: Congress passes National Defense Act to increase regular army to 223,000 over a five-year period and strengthen National Guard to 450,000 men

August 29: Congress passes Philippine Autonomy Act, or Jones Act, promising independence to Philippines

October: US Naval Expansion Act establishes a three-year construction program

November 8: Wilson reelected

1917

January 22: Woodrow Wilson delivers "Peace without Victory" speech

February 1–3: Germany resumes unrestricted submarine warfare; United States breaks diplomatic relations with Germany

February 5: Congress passes Immigration Act of 1917

February 7: Punitive Expedition departs Mexico without apprehending Villa

March 1: Zimmerman Telegram becomes public

March 2: Congress passes Jones Act to provide citizenship for Puerto Ricans

March 8: February Revolution in Russia

April 6: Congress declares war on Germany

April 16 to May 9: Failure of Nivelle offensive on Western Front

May: Stationing of American destroyers in British Isles

May 18: Congress passes Selective Service Act

June 15: Congress passes Espionage Act

July to November: Battle of Passchendaele (Third Battle of Ypres)

August 10: US Food Administration established by executive order

October 24 to November 19: Italians defeated at Battle of Caporetto

November 2: Balfour Declaration on Palestine made public

November 5: Republicans gain control of US Congress

November 7: October Revolution in Russia

1918

January 8: Wilson announces Fourteen Points

March 3: Treaty of Brest-Litovsk

March 21 to July 18: German Spring Offensive in France; Spanish flu begins

May 16: Congress passes Sedition Act

May 22: Congress passes Travel Control Act

United States at War

May: One million US troops in Europe

June 1–26: Battle of Belleau Wood

June 4: American Second Division helps French army break German advance at Château-Thierry

July 4: Battle of Le Hamel

July 15 to August 6: Second Battle of the Marne

September 12: First strictly American offensive of the war launched at St.-Mihiel

September 26 to November 11: Meuse-Argonne Offensive

August 2: 8,000 US troops deploy with Allied contingent in Russia

August 8: Hundred Days Offensive launched

September 29: Bulgaria signs armistice with Allies

October: End of Arab Revolt against Ottoman Empire

October 4: German and Austrian governments appeal to Wilson for armistice

October 16: Immigration Act of 1918

October 30: Ottoman Empire signs armistice with Allies; Allied prime ministers accept Fourteen Points (with reservations) as basis of armistice with Germany

November: Beginning of Egyptian Revolution

November 3: German Revolution; Austro-Hungarian Empire signs armistice

November 9: German emperor abdicates; German Republic declared

November 11: German armistice

December 14: Wilson arrives in Paris

December 25: Wilson embarks on tour of Great Britain and Italy

1919

January 7: Wilson to Paris for peace conference

January 16: Eighteenth Amendment ratified

January 25: Paris Conference approves resolution for League of Nations and creates a commission to draft League Covenant; Commission on the Reparation of Damage established

February 3: First meeting of League of Nations Commission

February 6: Prince Faisal lobbies for independence for Arabic-speaking population of Middle East

February 14: Draft of League of Nations Covenant approved at Paris Conference

February 19–21: Pan-African Congress meets in Paris

February 25: Wilson creates American Relief Administration

March 1: March First Movement in Korea against Japanese rule

March 3: US Senator Henry Cabot Lodge publicizes "round robin" to defeat peace treaty

March 4: Wilson proclaims League Covenant cannot be separated from peace treaty

March 21: British Imperial government in India passes Rowlatt Acts

Spring: Spanish flu ends

March 27: British representative Lord Sumner seeks pensions in reparation bill

April 1: Wilson accepts British proposal to include pensions

April 4: Approval of German-Czechoslovak frontier

April 5: Germany held responsible for war and resulting damage ("war-guilt clause")

April 10: Approval of German-Polish frontier

April 11: League of Nations Commission recognizes Monroe Doctrine

April 28: League of Nations Covenant final draft

May 7: Draft peace treaty submitted to German delegation

June 28: Versailles Treaty signed

July: End of Egyptian Revolution

July 19: Cenotaph is unveiled in London

August 11: Weimar Republic in Germany established

November 19: US Senate rejects League of Nations clause

1920

March 19: US Senate rejects League of Nations clause again; final veto

April: US troops leave Russia

April 25: British Mandate for Palestine established

May–October: Iraqi revolt against British

August 10: Treaty of Sèvres

August 18: Nineteenth Amendment ratified

1921

May 19: Congress passes Emergency Immigration Act

July 2: Joint resolution of Congress ends war with Germany and Austria-Hungary

July 22: Rif guerrillas defeat Spanish colonial army in Battle of Annual

November 12: Washington Naval Conference

December 13: Four-Power Treaty

1922

February 6: Five-Power Treaty and Nine-Power Treaty

February 28: Egyptian independence

September 22: Congress passes Cable Act

October: Russian Civil War ends; occupation of Dominican Republic ends

October 28: Establishment of Fascist Italy

December 6: Irish Free State founded (renamed Ireland in 1937)

1923

June 15: American Relief Administration departs Russia

July 24: Treaty of Lausanne

October 29: Turkey declared an independent republic

1924

April 9: Dawes Plan

May 26: Congress passes Immigration (Johnson-Reed) Act

June 2: President Calvin Coolidge signs Indian Citizenship Act

1925

April 12: France intervenes in Rif War

July: Syrian Revolt against French rule in Syria and Lebanon

1926

February to May: Spanish and French forces crush Rif resistance

July: End of Syrian revolt

1927

February 10: Ligue contre l'Impérialisme et l'Oppression Coloniale founded

1928

March: Muslim Brotherhood established in Egypt

June: Kongo-Wara Rebellion

August 27: Kellogg-Briand Pact

1929

February 17: League of United Latin American Citizens founded in United States

June 7: Young Plan completed

October 29: Great Depression begins

1930

February 10: Yên Bái mutiny in French Indochina

March: Publication of Clark Memorandum

May 14: Republic of Syria

1931

End of Kongo-Wara Rebellion

Summer: End of Yên Bái mutiny

September: Japan occupies Manchuria; Great Britain abandons gold standard

1932

January 7: Hoover-Stimson Doctrine on Japanese aggression

January 29: Japan bombs Shanghai

October 3: Kingdom of Iraq declares independence

1933

January 30: Hitler becomes chancellor

March 4: FDR becomes president

March 27: Japan withdraws from League of Nations

April 19: United States abandons gold standard

November 16: United States recognizes Soviet Union

December: United States supports nonintervention resolution at Seventh Pan-American Conference

1934

April 13: Congress passes Johnson Debt Default Act

June: FDR abrogates Platt Amendment on Cuba

August 1: US Marines end occupation of Haiti

December 29: Japan leaves Washington Naval Treaty system

1935

August 31: Congress passes Neutrality Act

October 3: Fascist Italy invades Ethiopia

1936

February 29: Congress passes Neutrality Act revision

March 7: Nazi troops occupy Rhineland

July 17: Spanish Civil War begins

1937

April 6: Emergency Peace Campaign holds "No Foreign War Crusade"

May 1: Congress passes Neutrality Act revision

July 7: Marco Polo Bridge clash between Japanese and Chinese troops

1938

March 12: *Anschluss* between Nazi Germany and Austria

September 29: Munich Agreement on Czechoslovakia

1939

March 28: Spanish Civil War ends

April 7: Fascist Italy seizes Albania

September 1: Germany invades Poland; Second World War begins in Europe

September 3: Britain and France declare war on Germany

November 4: Congress passes Neutrality Act revision

1941

March 11: Congress passes Lend-Lease

June 22: Germany invades Soviet Union

August 14: Atlantic Charter proclaimed

November 17: Congress passes Neutrality Act revision

December 7: Japan bombs Pearl Harbor

December 8: United States enters Second World War

1942

February 19: FDR initiates deportation and incarceration of Japanese within United States

1943

May 18–June 3: Conference on Food and Agriculture (Hot Springs, VA)

1944

July 1–22: Bretton Woods monetary and financial conference establishes IMF and International Bank for Reconstruction and Development (World Bank)

August 21–October 7: Washington, DC (Dumbarton Oaks) conference on Peace and Security, planning for United Nations

1945

April 25: United Nations conference in San Francisco

May: Algerian uprisings against French colonial rule at Sétif and Guelma

May 8: World War II ends in Europe

June 26: United Nations Charter signed

July: Congress passes Bretton Woods Agreements Act

July 22: World Health Organization constitution signed

October 16–November 1: First Food and Agriculture Organization conference (Quebec City)

October 24: United Nations Charter enters into force

September 2: Japan surrenders, ending World War II

1946

April 20: League of Nations dissolved

1947

October 30: First negotiations under General Agreement on Tariffs and Trade (Geneva)

1948

April 7: World Health Organization established

May 14: State of Israel proclaimed

May 15: Beginning of Arab-Israeli War

August 23: World Council of Churches founded

1949

March 10: End of Arab-Israeli War

August: Fourth Geneva Convention establishes provisions for "Protection of Civilian Persons in Time of War"

1951

European Coal and Steel Community founded

1952

June 27: Immigration and Nationality Act of 1952 (McCarran-Walter Act), enacted in United States

July 23: Egyptian Revolution of 1952

1953

Agreement on West German World War I war debt payments (in 1995, the two Germanys unified and payment agreement reached; final payment ($94 million) was made October 3, 2010, to settle debt/reparation claim)

1965

October 3: Immigration and Nationality Act of 1965, or Hart-Celler Act, enacted in United States

1991

Collapse of Yugoslavia

2001

September 11 attacks

2011

February 27: Last American soldier to have served in World War I, Frank Buckles, dies at 110 years of age

NOTE

Besides the contributions within this volume, the following works were consulted to compile this timeline: George Brown Tindall and David Emory Shi, *America: A Narrative History*, 8th ed. (New York: W. W. Norton, 2010); Paul Johnson, *A History of the American People* (New York: HarperPerennial, 1999), 758–878; Martin Thomas, *The French Empire between the Wars: Imperialism, Politics and Society* (Manchester: Manchester University Press, 2005), 211–244; John Horne, ed., *A Companion to World War I* (Oxford: Wiley-Blackwell, 2010), 550–566; Walter LaFeber, *The American Age: US Foreign Policy at Home and Abroad, 1750 to the Present*, 2nd ed. (New York: W. W. Norton, 1994), 338–359; Thomas G. Paterson et al., eds., *A History of American Foreign Relations, Vol. 2, Since 1895*, 6th ed. (Boston: Houghton Mifflin, 2005); William R. Keylor, ed., *The Legacy of the Great War: Peacemaking, 1919* (New York: Houghton Mifflin, 1998), xii–viii, 164; Robert W. Tucker, *Woodrow Wilson and the Great War: Reconsidering America's Neutrality, 1914–1917* (Charlottesville: University of Virginia Press, 2007), xiii–xv; Thomas J. Knock, *To End All Wars: Woodrow Wilson and the Quest for a New World Order* (Princeton, NJ: Princeton University Press, 1992), 61, 74; Christopher Capozzola, *Uncle Sam Wants You: World War I and the Making of the Modern American Citizen* (New York: Oxford University Press, 2008), 96; George C. Herring, *From Colony to Superpower: US Foreign Relations since 1776* (Oxford: Oxford University Press, 2008), 367, 405–407, 504, 510; Ross A. Kennedy, *The Will to Believe: Woodrow Wilson, World War I, and America's Strategy for Peace and Security* (Kent, OH: Kent State University Press, 2009), 147; Alan Dawley, *Changing the World: American Progressives in War and Revolution* (Princeton, NJ: Princeton University Press, 2003), 291–292; Louis A. Pérez, Jr., *Cuba and the United States: Ties of Singular Intimacy* (Athens: University of Georgia Press, 1990); Robert Gerwath and Erez Manela, eds., *Empires at War, 1911–1923* (Oxford: Oxford University Press, 2014).

PART 1

Historians

Writing, Legacies, Memories

1

The Historiographic Impact of the Great War

Akira Iriye

How did the First World War affect the writing of history? Did historians begin to conceptualize history, in particular modern world history, differently after 1918? In view of the fact that this was understood (at that time and since) as the first "world" war, it would be relevant to ask if the global conflict held implications for the study and writing of history. There are many ways of examining the question, but this essay will focus on the question of periodization: Is World War I to be understood as part of contemporary history? Or does it belong to some other epoch? The issue is a historiographic one inasmuch as historians seek to understand the war (or any event) not in isolation but in the context of what preceded and what followed it.

To cite an example, in November 2013 the Institute of Contemporary History in Munich organized a conference on the war, indicating that from the institute's perspective the Great War belongs in contemporary history. *The Journal of Contemporary History* notes editorially that it publishes scholarly pieces on twentieth-century history, which would by definition include the war, although it says that its book reviews are limited to those that deal with post-1918 history. Such examples suggest that many historians continue to put the First World War in the larger framework of contemporary history. Others, however, have begun to question such periodization and sought to understand the Great War in the context of an earlier age.

Much, of course, depends on what one means by "contemporary" history. How different is it from "modern" history, or even from "ancient" history? To cite one example at random from the writings of a leading historian, Peter Gay, in reminiscing about growing up in

Nazi Germany, mentions "current politics and ancient (which is to say: Nazi) history."[1] So "ancient" would seem to mean not only the 1930s but also something negative, in contrast to "current" affairs. But in the same book, Gay recalls that when he went back to Berlin in 1961, for the first time since he had left Germany in 1938, "Contemporary history raw and ugly had caught up with me."[2] Here he seems to be referring to the Nazi past as part of "contemporary" history. The example here indicates the rather arbitrary, even contradictory, ways in which historians use adjectives such as "contemporary" and "ancient."

Nevertheless, it would help clarify the historiography of World War I if we examined whether historians have studied the war as an aspect of contemporary history or have tended to consign it to another era, ancient or not. This is important because how one conceptualizes a phenomenon like the Great War has a great deal to do with one's scheme of periodization. Does World War I fit the historical developments that are usually associated with the contemporary world? Or, on the contrary, was the war more a phenomenon that preceded the coming of the world that we call contemporary? These are important questions because they relate to how historians understand the legacy of the war, in other words, how they relate it to the world that exists today.

Not surprisingly, historians writing on the war for many decades after 1918 continued to write about it as a phenomenon of contemporary history. To them the "realities" of international affairs did not seem to change much in the wake of the war, which would soon be followed by another world war, which in turn could be seen as a prelude to the Cold War. This is the familiar geopolitical story, which for a long time was the basic framework in which contemporary history was comprehended. The bulk of historical writings on the Great War and its aftermath continued to note its geopolitical legacy, tracing the subsequent history of the world in terms of the changing vicissitudes of international relations that came after 1918.

It is to be noted that despite the Great War's obviously global dimension, it did not immediately trigger a scholarly movement to globalize the study of history. Internationalism, to be sure, returned with a new vitality and a sense of urgency after the war, when European intellectuals vowed never again to put their resources at the service of nationalistic ends.[3] They and their like-minded colleagues across the Atlantic and elsewhere became active participants in the League of Nations' efforts to promote "intellectual cooperation." But surprisingly little resulted from these efforts in the realm of historical study.

Scholarly history books as well as general surveys throughout the 1920s and the 1930s remained bound in their traditional methods and conceptual characterizations, with little innovative initiative taken in the direction of global history or of the history of interconnections. It may well be that even those who would have moved in such a direction were discouraged by what appeared to be the reappearance of old-style rivalries among the great powers that culminated in the Second World War, which simultaneously brought about a heyday of "realism" in the study of international relations.

To cite a few notable examples, we may all agree that William L. Langer's *European Alliances and Alignments* (1931) and *The Diplomacy of Imperialism* (1935) were among the most authoritative accounts of recent international relations written during the interwar years. Langer was a towering figure among diplomatic historians whose publications were notable because of the use of diplomatic documents in several languages (not including Russian, however) and the discussion of currents of thought that he gained from the press, on occasion even from literary sources. Reading his books, one learned a great deal about how European statesmen and the public viewed the world and how the great powers, in particular, formulated their approaches toward one another. All the same, the world described by Langer was one in which only European diplomacy mattered, defining the international order in the period leading to 1914. If the Great War had aroused the awareness of global connections, there was little evidence of such awareness in Langer's work. The non-Western areas of the world remained objects of Western expansion. Some parts of the world, such as Latin America and the Pacific Ocean (even Australia and New Zealand), were almost completely left out. In the well-known last paragraph in *The Diplomacy of Imperialism*, Langer wrote, "The basic problem of international relations [before 1914] was who should cut up the victims. In our own day we have learned otherwise and all this now seems long ago."[4] But such reflections did not lead him to alter the key conceptual framework for examining international relations.

Langer's best equivalent in the post–World War II historiography in international relations would be A. J. P. Taylor, whose *The Struggle for Mastery in Europe, 1848–1918* (1954) was required reading in most undergraduate courses dealing with modern European history. Although nine years separated their books, Langer and Taylor held to the same geopolitical focus in describing modern international relations. "The relations of the Great Powers have determined the history of Europe," Taylor wrote, and he added that his book "deals with them in the last age when Europe was the centre of the world."[5] By that, of course, he meant that Europe had since been replaced by the United States as the center of the world. Numerous books had already appeared on the theme of the rise of the United States as a great power, which remained the most influential conceptual framework for many years.

One can see this in such widely used surveys of US diplomatic history as those by Robert H. Ferrell, *American Diplomacy: A History* (1959), and Richard

Leopold, *The Growth of American Foreign Policy: A History* (1962).[6] These and other historians all saw the United States as having become a world power at the turn of the twentieth century but that the nation did not immediately replace the European powers in determining the shape of international affairs. That would come later, in the wake of the Second World War. As Ferrell wrote, "It might have been possible for the United States to have prevented what happened" in 1914, but the nation chose not to play the role of a great power, although in reality it was.[7] The question of how and when the United States came to play that role concerned a generation of diplomatic historians after the Second World War, indicating that this conflict, far more global than the Great War, still did not bring about a major historiographic transformation in understanding world history. Historians continued to follow Europeanist writings in conceptualizing world affairs in terms of power equations. Undoubtedly the postwar vogue of "realism" abetted such preoccupation with geopolitics.

In the geopolitical framework, little distinguished between the two world wars. Indeed, in the eyes of many writers, the end of one world war led inexorably to another global conflict. The year 1939 was essentially no different from 1914 in that sense. And even after the Second World War, historians continued to write about international relations in pretty much the same way as their predecessors had done. No new conceptualization was needed so long as one focused on power relations. Despite the fact that geopolitics had always been, and now even more so, a poor explanatory strategy to account for the bulk of human behavior, the realist historiography perpetuated its influence well into the post-1945 years. One can see this with the frequency with which the word "power" continued to be used in book titles. Starting with Howard K. Beale's *Theodore Roosevelt and the Rise of America to World Power* (1956) and all the way to as recent a book as Bruce Cumings's *Dominion from Sea to Sea: Pacific Ascendancy and American Power* (2009), many historians were preoccupied with the emergence and growth of American power in the world from the late nineteenth century into the twentieth, in Cumings's case into the twenty-first century.[8] They all tell virtually the same story, recounting how the United States steadily amassed its power and influence, a phenomenon that fits into the traditional story of "the rise and fall of the great powers." Paul Kennedy's *The Rise and Fall of the Great Powers* (1987), which was enormously influential when published, showed that even as late as the 1980s, the same geopolitical framework remained.[9]

To sum up, the Great War did not result in notable historiographic innovations, and historians continued to put the global conflict in the framework of the never-ending story of "the rise and fall of the great powers." In their view, then, World War I was very much part of contemporary history.

New perspectives on the study of world history, in particular international affairs, would seem to have emerged only toward the end of the twentieth century. During the 1980s and especially in the 1990s, historians began reconceptualizing international history, and indeed world history, by incorporating a number of nongeopolitical themes, such as globalization, human rights, environmental issues, cultural exchange, and migrations. Thanks to their work and that of those who came after them, it is now possible to throw much fresh light on World War I and on subsequent developments. In particular, the new and ongoing historiography enables us to put the war in the context of the history not just of international relations but of all these other themes.

A good recent example of an attempt at reconceptualizing modern world history through the theme of globalization is the volume edited by Emily Rosenberg, *A World Connecting: 1870–1945* (2012), which contains five long chapters by American and German historians. The contributors consider the growth of international networks as a key phenomenon of world history since the latter part of the nineteenth century.[10] In such a perspective, the Great War is seen as having disrupted the process of global interconnections without ever destroying them. As Rosenberg says, "The extension of transnational networks in science, health, entertainment, and a variety of other specific affiliations accelerated after World War I."[11] By choosing to present world history from 1870 to 1945 within a consistent conceptual framework, Rosenberg and her colleagues seem to be disputing the traditional, geopolitically defined chronology that sees 1914 as the major turning point.

Another contemporary scholar, C. A. Bayly, on the other hand, does seem to view 1914 as the key chronological moment, as indicated by the fact that his masterpiece, *The Birth of the Modern World* (2004), covers the period from 1780 to 1914.[12] Like Rosenberg and others, however, Bayly also sees the history of the modern world as having been notable because of the growing "interdependence" among countries and peoples. This interdependence, however, according to him, instead of producing a peaceful world order, instead internationalized violence, a perspective that is shared by other scholars writing on the history of globalization. In their interpretation, "the era of intensified and multifaceted globalization was ... brought to a rapid and abrupt halt by the First World War."[13] But most historians would view this abrupt halt as having been temporary and that at least by the 1950s globalization returned as a major theme of world history.

Other than globalization, historians have become increasingly interested in tracing such other themes as human rights, environmental issues, cultural exchange, and migrations as a way to restructure our understanding of nineteenth- and twentieth-century history, thereby putting World War I in a fresh conceptual framework. Davide Rodogno's *Against Massacre* (2012), for instance, focuses on European humanitarian interventions, both executed and aborted, in human rights abuses in the Ottoman Empire, thereby presenting a novel prehistory of the Great War.[14] Patricia Rosenfield's history of the Carnegie Corporation traces the growth of cultural internationalist initiatives by private foundations that went on during the war and throughout the rest of the century, thereby enriching our understanding of global history in the era of the Great War.[15] Xu Guoqi's *Strangers on the Western Front: Chinese Workers in the Great War* (2011) is not just another study of the war but is rather the other way round; it puts World War I in the long history of Chinese migrations.[16]

Many other examples can be cited to illustrate a clear trend among historians to get away from, or at least to go beyond, the geopolitical centrism in which the Great War as well as international history have been traditionally presented. The geopolitical perspective, after all, is a Eurocentric view of the past in which the great powers are pictured as the definers of the world at a given moment in time. It is not surprising, then, that the enrichment of the scholarly literature by penetrating new studies of the Islamic world, South Asia, the Pacific, and other regions has reshaped our understanding of modern history, including World War I. Recent works on such topics as South Asian cosmopolitanism, Islamic humanism, and transnational movements have served to decenter European history as the primary determinant of historical chronology. Put in the context of such themes as Islamic internationalism or transnational migrations, the conventional Eurocentric periodization that privileges dates such as 1914 would need to be reconsidered.[17]

The question of whether World War I is to be considered a phenomenon of contemporary history still remains, however. Even if we were to broaden our perspective on World War I and to bring in many nongeopolitical themes and extra-European regions and civilizations of the world into view, would we not continue to understand the war as part of contemporary history? For instance, if we added to our framework the theme of interconnectedness, as Rosenberg does, or brought in such considerations as human rights into our examination of the war, would that lead us to a different chronology? Or would we consider the war as well as the subsequent geopolitical developments, along with various nongeopolitical phenomena, as having been part of contemporary history? Put another way, even after we broadened our understanding of World War I by juxtaposing it with human rights, migrations, non-Western traditions, and other themes, would we still consider them aspects of contemporary history?

The question is important because if World War I and all other developments are part of contemporary history, we are by definition still living under the same circumstances. The world at the beginning of the twenty-first century, in other words, must be seen as much the same as the world that existed in 1914.

That, however, would not be the view of many "contemporary" historians. Those who write on recent and current world conditions tend to stress discontinuities, departures, and novel themes in history during the last several decades. Particularly notable have been historians of human rights. Samuel Moyn, Sarah Snyder, and Barbara Keys, among others, have emphasized the significance of the 1970s as having marked a major landmark in the meaning and practice of human rights.[18] Likewise, in the field of environmental history, John McNeill has noted that the awareness of environmental disasters as well as a global movement to do something about them emerged only in the 1970s.[19] In economic history, Eric Hobsbawm has noted the abrupt growth in the number of multinational corporations after the 1970s, a phenomenon that parallels the remarkable increase in the number of international nongovernmental organizations in that decade.[20]

What these examples suggest is that the world may have begun to transform itself significantly in the last decades of the twentieth century. This transformation may best be seen in the spectacular development of nongeopolitical phenomena. To be sure, all those phenomena had been there long before the late twentieth century. As alluded to already, globalization, human rights, and other developments that formed close ties among individuals and groups across nations were quite evident on the eve of the Great War. But it may also be recognized that nongeopolitical forces came to overshadow geopolitics in defining the world only in the 1970s and beyond. We may briefly sketch this transition.

As Rosenberg, Bayly, and others show, global connections were already in existence and were rapidly expanding at the end of the nineteenth century. But, compared to the contemporary world, those connections were more tenuous and were not sufficiently well developed in order to prevent international conflict. Even more crucially, if we examined the connections and networks in their economic, social, and cultural dimensions, we would have to recognize that those connections, albeit their universality, were fundamentally Western dominated and therefore did not signify equally shared or universally applicable networks. This is the major difference between the world described by those historians and today's world.

Economically, to begin with, the allegedly universal connections were dominated by Western Europe and North America till toward the end of the twentieth century. It was only during the 1980s that Asian countries—China, Japan, South Korea, and others—came to account for more than 10 percent of world trade, or more than 15 percent of the total gross national product of all countries. Although those countries were linked to the West, the Middle East, South America, and other regions, until the last years of the century the economic connections were not exactly multilateral. They were virtually unidirectional, goods going from East Asia to Europe and North America, and capital moving in the opposite direction.

Socially, one important indicator of global interdependence would be spontaneous and unrestricted interactions among people of diverse races and ethnicities. But the bulk of the world remained segregated till toward the end of the twentieth century, and so interracial social contact was very limited. People of different racial identities tended to live apart and did not mix. This was even truer of cross-border migrations, or the movement of people from one part of the world to another. To be sure, through the United Nations, refugees from wars and civil wars could find asylum in some countries willing to accept them, but as far as immigration was concerned, segregation was the rule, not an exception. At least until the 1960s migrants out of most Asian countries were not admitted as immigrants into the United States, Canada, Australia, New Zealand, or South Africa. These countries restricted immigration to only those originating in Europe or its outposts.

Such restrictiveness and segregation were not limited to the West, however. In many of the newly independent countries, often sharp lines were drawn between ethnic groups, and the conflict among them was endemic. The principle of "national self-determination" that was promulgated at Versailles more often than not produced ethnically defined national entities. As many historians have noted, this principle was exemplified by the exchange of populations between Turkey and Greece after 1923 in order to make Turkey more purely Turkish and Greece more purely Greek, away from the Ottoman "model" of diversity and cohabitation. The ethnicity rule remained key to the founding of most of the new states through the rest of the twentieth century.

The realities, in other words, belied the allegedly global networking of people. But segregation was not confined to ethnic groups. Till the last decades of the twentieth century, there were other divisions that kept people and communities of the world apart. Perhaps the most glaring example would be the segregation of the sexes. Prior to the Great War, New Zealand was the only country with universal suffrage. To be sure, women in Europe, North America, and elsewhere had been actively involved in humanitarian activities, ranging from alcoholic prohibition to drug control, and there were active political movements for women's right to vote in national elections. One may note in this connection that one of the causes that various women's groups promoted at that time was birth control, especially eugenics. As Matthew Connelly has shown, the concern with "improving the race" inherently divided the human race into two.[21] Those who were judged to be of less than average intelligence were considered to be inferior, objects of social policy to discourage them from producing more children like them. Just as the sexes were segregated, those with intellectual disabilities were set apart from "normal" human beings. Socially, therefore, we would have to conclude that the world in 1914 was not a fully interconnected one.

The same would be even more true of cultural connections. To be sure, thanks to technological innovations in the means of transportation and communication, cultural products in various parts of the world were coming into closer contact than ever before. Here, too, however, it needs to be noted that much of this contact took the form of Westernization of the non-Western parts of the world, not of interactions and exchanges among various regions of the globe. European and American products, ranging from food and clothing to art, literature, and music, crossed oceans and transplanted themselves in Asia, Africa, and elsewhere. Occasionally, a Western artist might go to the Middle East or the Pacific and become inspired by the encounter with indigenous art. Traditional Chinese and Japanese art would attract the attention of museumgoers in Paris, London, or Boston. But such instances did not amount to cultural encountering, not to mention cultural blending. Western art remained the basis for the training of art students all over the world.

In literature and music, such one-sidedness was even more pervasive. Western literary works were translated into so many non-European languages that at least to educated people everywhere there was a shared familiarity with the works of Shakespeare, Zola, Goethe, Dostoevsky, and many others. What non-Western writers could claim such universality? The literary traffic was decidedly unidirectional. The same was true of music, where "classical" works meant eighteenth- and nineteenth-century compositions as against twentieth-century works, not traditional Chinese, Indonesian, or African music. Musical education in modernizing countries entailed a familiarity with Western instruments, and people from all over the world went to Europe to study the piano, the violin, and other instruments. Already at the turn of the twentieth century, a Japanese novelist was bemoaning that his country produced nothing comparable to Western music. If Japan's own traditional music was too old-fashioned, but all its modern music was imported from the West, what would be the future of music in the country?[22] The same question undoubtedly arose in the minds of countless people everywhere.

If, then, the "world connecting" (that is, the world described in Rosenberg's volume) was not exactly a world of multilaterally interconnected economic, social, and cultural activities before 1945, did the situation change significantly after

World War II? To put it another way, is the contemporary world essentially a continuation of the earlier periods, or does it mark a departure from them? It would, of course, be impossible to be all-embracing in comparing these two periods, for undoubtedly there are things that have remained more or less the same through the twentieth century and beyond, whereas in other areas there have occurred profound transformations. In the framework of global connections, however, it may be noted that the world has become far more interconnected in the last three or four decades than ever before. Economically, as noted above, a fully globalized economy emerged only in the wake of China's decision around 1980 to open itself to foreign trade and investment, whereas in social relations, the human rights revolution of the 1970s was the major turning point. Culturally, what Petra Goedde calls "global cultures" came to interact with one another extensively during the 1970s.[23] Also in that decade, transnational movements to save the earth from "ecocide" began in earnest, and global concerns with "alternative energy" became intense after the Chernobyl disaster of the mid-1980s.

Humanity, in other words, has come to be seen in the context of encountering, interconnecting, coexisting, intermixing, and blending in various parts of the earth as well as in the framework of ecological survival in which all living things have a stake. The stress here is more on connection than on separation, more on interdependence than on mutual antagonism, more on cohabitation than on discrimination.

If these characteristics exemplify the contemporary world, it is clearly not the world that existed in 1914, or even in 1945. Both world wars were products of the precontemporary world. It would be wrong, therefore, to view the First World War as contemporary history. It was more like ancient history, something that took place when the globe was not sufficiently interconnected.

When did historical writings begin to go beyond traditional platitudes and to embrace the world as it became increasingly interconnected, developing new ways of looking at the past to reflect that awareness? It may well be that to most historians working and writing in the second half of the twentieth century, the two world wars and the Cold War were the fundamental reality and, therefore, that they had continued to focus on such conventional themes as the origins of wars, the nature of the modern state that had defined itself in geopolitical terms, and the tendency of most states to become more and more authoritarian in the process. But to frame their historical inquiry that way could blind scholars to other developments that were taking place right in front of their eyes, such as globalization, human rights, environmentalism, the rapid growth of nongovernmental organizations, and many others. Although these phenomena had become quite noticeable by the 1970s, most historians did not take notice of them till close to the end of the century.

To cite one example, in 1983 and again 1993, the Japan Foundation organized international symposia where historians and others from various parts of the world discussed what they considered to be significant themes and features of twentieth-century history. A number of scholars participated in both conferences, but quite remarkably, they and their colleagues presented drastically different perspectives on the history of the century. In 1983, their ideas were still couched in the framework of wars and the rise and growth of totalitarianism, and so the participants gave a rather pessimistic overview of the twentieth-century world.[24] Ten years later, however, when some of the same scholars were joined by others and met again to consider the same subject, they were now far more interested in, and attentive to, nongeopolitical issues, whether economic, social, or cultural. They spent much time discussing such topics as globalization, human rights, and environmentalism, as well as the future of religion, women's rights throughout the world, migrations, and new identities. In other words, the traditional concern with geopolitics was now pushed behind and virtually replaced by a fascination with an emerging world reality that seemed to be defined as much by individuals as by states, as much by economics as by politics, and as much by small countries as by the great powers. In other words, scholars were finally catching up with the real world and recognizing that the traditional nation-centric presentation of history needs to be augmented by fresh perspectives that paid equal attention to nongeopolitical themes and non-state actors.

Historical writings since the 1990s seem to reflect such a trend. In the study of international history, scholars have been paying greater attention to these themes and players. Even the Cold War, which till then had been treated almost exclusively in a geopolitical framework, has begun to be put in the context of nongeopolitical phenomena. For instance, Thomas W. Zeiler's *Free Trade, Free World* (1999) introduces the theme of economic globalization into the history of the early Cold War, while Sarah Snyder's *Human Rights Activism and the End of the Cold War* (2011) looks at its conclusion through a focus on human rights.[25] David Zierler's *The Invention of Ecocide* (2011) harnesses the history of environmental disasters as an important part of the geopolitical story.[26]

What these and other works show is that geopolitical hegemonism has been steadily challenged by other ways of looking at the past, which, combined together, has led to the emergence of transnational history as a new approach to the past. In the field of international relations history, the transnational history perspective adds many dimensions that have been hitherto obscured by the obsession with power-political questions. Instead of division and conflict among the major powers, the transnational perspective would stress cross-border connections throughout the world, among nations, religions, ethnicities, and other communities. Historians such as Bayly, Hobsbawm, and Rosenberg, all stress connections and networks and are therefore transnationally oriented scholars, and it is very likely that their footsteps will be followed by many others all over the world.

When a nongeopolitically oriented history of the twentieth century is written, therefore, there will be much stress on connections that remained even during wars and greatly strengthened in their aftermath. Nevertheless, it will have to be recognized that the kind of intimately networked world that exists today came about only in the last decades of the twentieth century. When historians come to recognize this, they would probably date the contemporary world from those decades, from the 1970s at the earliest, even later if the criterion of global interconnectedness were to be applied rigorously.

The key here would be the diminishing role of the state in human affairs. Since the 1970s, the nation-state has increasingly had to share its authority with nonstate actors, and nation-centric agendas have frequently been pushed aside by transnational concerns. The result has been that international relations, too, have changed their character, from state-centered preoccupations with national power and interests to issues that concern the whole world and all people. International relations today are less relationships among states than among nonnational groupings, be they religious, ethnic, or other identities or those concerned with global warming, endangered species, the rights of the handicapped, and many others. Under the circumstances, interstate conflicts of the sort represented by World Wars I and II are anachronistic. They do not fit into the human experiences of the age of global interdependence and transnational nexus.

In other words, the two world wars clearly did not belong in contemporary history. They were phenomena of the age that can best be understood as ancient history.

NOTES

1. Gay, *My German Question*, xii.
2. Ibid., 7.
3. Iriye, *Cultural Internationalism and World Order*, 56.
4. Langer, *The Diplomacy of Imperialism, 1890–1902*, 797.
5. Taylor, *The Struggle for Mastery in Europe, 1848–1918*, ix.
6. Ferrell, *American Diplomacy*; Leopold, *The Growth of American Foreign Policy*.
7. Ferrell, *American Diplomacy*, 429.
8. Beale, *Theodore Roosevelt and the Rise of America to World Power*; Cumings, *Dominion from Sea to Sea*.
9. Kennedy, *The Rise and Fall of the Great Powers*.

10. Rosenberg, *A World Connecting*.

11. Ibid., 6.

12. Bayly, *The Birth of the Modern World, 1780–1914*.

13. Held et al., *Global Transformations*, 422.

14. Rodogno, *Against Massacre*.

15. Rosenfield, *A World of Giving*.

16. Guoqi, *Strangers on the Western Front*.

17. See, among other works on these subjects, Bose and Manjapra, *Cosmopolitan Thought Zones*; Bennison, "Muslim Universalism and Western Globalization"; Dabashi, *The World of Persian Literary Humanism*.

18. Moyn, *The Last Utopia*; Snyder, *Human Rights Activism and the End of the Cold War*; Keys, *Reclaiming American Virtue*.

19. McNeill, *Something New under the Sun*.

20. Hobsbawm, *The Age of Extremes*, 277; Iriye, *Global Community*, 129.

21. Connelly, *Fatal Misconception*.

22. See Kafu, *Amerika monogatari*, 191.

23. Goedde, "Global Cultures," 537–678.

24. For a discussion of the 1998 and 1993 symposia on twentieth-century history, see Iriye, *Global and Transnational History*, 25–28.

25. Zeiler, *Free Trade, Free World*; Snyder, *Human Rights Activism*.

26. Zierler, *The Invention of Ecocide*.

2

The War as History

Writing the Economic and Social History
of the First World War

Katharina Rietzler

As public commemorations mark the centenary of the outbreak of the First World War, it seems remarkable to what extent the history and the memory of the war remain fragmented, characterized by heated debates on its causes, conduct, and moral purpose for the nations that fought in it. But is it even possible to write a "total history" of this total war? Clearly, the war meant different things to different people in different parts of the world. European patterns of remembrance show divergences. The American memory of the First World War, long assumed to be characterized by the desire to forget, has recently been reinterpreted as shot through with competing war stories.[1] While historians increasingly aim to transcend national war narratives, and emphasize transnational and global dimensions, some remain adamant that every nation needs its own war story.[2] The war was fought by entire populations, mobilized to an unprecedented degree. Interpreting its origins began to matter to audiences sensitized to official falsehoods by government propaganda and revelations of previously secret diplomatic correspondence. Governments intent on legitimizing their actions wrote the history of the war as it happened and after the battlefields fell quiet, they continued the war by other means, those of historical interpretation. Historians entered the debate, leading to controversies that split the profession. Soldiers and statesmen wrote their memoirs, army historians their official histories, and novelists fictionalized accounts of their wartime experiences. Many voices joined in the tussle over the meaning of the war.[3]

Among all these efforts, the Carnegie Endowment's *Economic and Social History of the World War* stands out. It was a private project, sponsored by an American philanthropic foundation, the Carnegie Endowment for International Peace, with an international roster of authors. Nothing quite like it had ever been attempted.[4] Today, its studies continue to provide benchmarks for historians working on the conflict.[5] In 152 volumes, published in the interwar years, the Carnegie Endowment attempted to write a comprehensive history of the war's impact on national economies. As a social history of the First World War, it pioneered the analysis of topics that have only become relevant to historians comparatively recently, such as public health, the role of women, and the experience of cities during the war.[6] It also predated the French *Annales* school, similarly dedicated to writing "total" history but from a rather different perspective. The *History*'s editors, the economist John Bates Clark and the historian-turned-international relations expert James T. Shotwell, emphasized the war's effect on civilians in a way that enabled readers to make international comparisons. Shotwell ensured that the international community of authors adhered to the tenets of the ideological project behind the Carnegie *History*: to show that war was not only an illegitimate but an unsound policy choice. He hoped that the lessons of the war, as it had been experienced across fifteen countries, would go on to shape and standardize social and economic policies in a world made insecure by the global reach of social problems.

This essay analyzes the "history wars" that ensued in the two decades after the First World War through the prism of the Carnegie *History*, and it charts the changing interpretations of the social and economic transformations that had been brought about by the war. The Carnegie *History* was the product of a transnationally constituted American internationalism with its roots in pre-war economic thought and the propaganda anxieties that came after, which gave the unearthing of "facts" about the war a heightened importance.[7] The United States nonmembership in the League of Nations, qualified by significant American participation in the League's so-called technical work, reinforced the Carnegie *History*'s focus on seemingly nonpolitical aspects of the war's history.[8] Within its transnational framework the Carnegie *History of the World War* could not escape a political-historiographical constellation that, in the 1920s and 1930s, was determined by the question of whether a neutral interpretation of the war was possible. By the end of the 1930s, however, the economic and social history of the war had transcended such narrow debates and opened up broader vistas on the responsibility of governments for the welfare of their citizens, the politics of international comparisons of social and economic data, and the social and economic foundations of peace and security. Thus, the Carnegie *History*'s meticulous analysis of the First World War contributed to a new style of international politics. Its legacy remains important today.

History's Laboratory

When John Bates Clark, a neoclassical economist, Columbia University professor, and first director of the Carnegie Endowment's Division of Economics and History, conceived what would become the Carnegie *History* in 1911, he envisioned a rigorous investigation of the economic dimensions of war. A known figure on the American internationalist lecture circuit, Clark argued that military expenditure should be diverted to pressing reform causes, from public health to environmental conservation, to take the wind out of the sails of socialist revolutionaries that promised international peace through transnational working-class solidarity.[9] Clark belonged to an international network of scholars and publicists, nurtured by his long-standing correspondence with leading liberal economists in Europe, such as Charles Gide and Alfred Marshall.[10] At a conference in Bern, Switzerland, in August 1911, he signed up fourteen European and two Japanese collaborators for a multivolume study on the relationship between war and economic life (see Figure 2.1). The project was designed to scientifically test the popular theories of Norman Angell, a British journalist and campaigner for the idea that, in economic terms, industrialized nations had nothing to gain from modern warfare.[11]

The war's outbreak in 1914 pushed Clark toward a bolder conception of his original project: a definitive economic history of the First World War. Although Clark acknowledged that an actual war was a "terrifically costly laboratory for the study of war," he regarded the conflict as an "incomparable" opportunity for data collection. Clark realized that wartime economic mobilization had an enormous impact on industrial organization and income distribution, and it was liable to change the course of an economy well into the postwar era. Massive government intervention in the economy might even introduce socialism through the back door. In December 1914, Clark asked his Columbia colleague James T. Shotwell to draw up a proposal for a history of the war designed to reveal the social and economic dislocations caused by armed conflict.[12]

Shotwell came with his own assumptions about how history should be written and how it should be deployed. Like Clark, he regarded the First World War as a "laboratory," a historical event that could be mastered scientifically in a way that would yield general insights into the nature of war.[13] Shotwell, who held a professorship in history, belonged to the "New History," which argued that historical scholarship had to shift its focus away from political and military

FIGURE 2.1 Scholars studying war in the Belle Époque, at the first meeting of the Carnegie *History* editorial board, Bern, Switzerland, August 1911. John Bates Clark Papers, Rare Book and Manuscript Library, Columbia University.

history and toward contemporary social and economic problems using explanatory models from the social sciences.[14] The New History shared its affinity for the social sciences and criticism of political history with other historiographical currents in Europe, some of which coalesced in the Annales movement in the late 1920s. But whereas the Annales historians aimed for a history that took a holistic view of human activity over a long period of time and produced its most famous works in medieval or early modern history, Shotwell was resolutely focused on the contemporary.[15]

According to the New Historians, the past had to be made useful to the present. During the war, this assumption encouraged scholars to become involved in propaganda. Shotwell was one of many American historians who responded to the call for patriotic service when the United States entered the war in 1917. As the chair of the National Board for Historical Service he endeavored to "mobilize the historical forces of the country." He also acted as a historical adviser to the Creel Committee, the United States' official propaganda agency.[16] Shotwell did not write any propagandistic pamphlets himself but neither did he question whether scholars in the humanities and social sciences compromised their integrity by doing so.[17] Yet his brush with American war propaganda sensitized Shotwell to the possibilities for distortion, and it arguably lay behind the pronounced empiricism he adopted when he began to work on the Carnegie *History*. If war was a laboratory, a unique event that provided the historian's raw material, then the data it produced had to be harvested before it could be distorted. As Shotwell explained to the head of the Carnegie *History*'s Dutch editorial board in 1920, "the question of securing and safeguarding the source material for subsequent historical work" was a priority, especially in the belligerent countries.[18] Precisely because the writing of the war's history had important policy implications for the postwar years, it had to be rooted in incontrovertible fact.

The "documentary moment" that followed the First World War was an auspicious time for Shotwell's project. Several national initiatives sought to document the history of the war and regarded themselves as laboratories for contemporary history. They included the Hoover Institution on War, Revolution and Peace at Stanford, created in 1919 with its comprehensive collection of private papers and informal publications, as well as the Imperial War Museum in London, opened in 1920. In the same year, the French Ministry of Public Instruction began to finance a library and document center dedicated to the First World War, the Bibliothèque de Documentation Internationale Contemporaine.[19] Its directors, Camille Bloch and Pierre Renouvin, also wrote volumes for the Carnegie *History*. Renouvin, who was sympathetic to the Annales school, would go on to reinvigorate the study of diplomatic history in France by underlining the importance of *forces profondes* in shaping international relations. Similarly, Henri Pirenne, the editor of the Belgian Carnegie series, headed Belgium's official effort to collect and classify material for a comprehensive archive relating to the war.[20] Sifting through the abundant documentary debris left by the war remained a preoccupation for historians and information professionals in the 1920s. This was reflected in the decision of several national Carnegie editorial boards to include bibliographical volumes.[21] The war's total nature raised fundamental questions about the sources for its history. Which materials should be regarded as sources, where should they be housed, and how should they be made accessible to the public? How were historians and archivists to cope with the abundance of material? Addressing these problems would be the first step to writing a comprehensive history of the war.

Many Carnegie authors enjoyed privileged access to source material. As Shotwell commissioned them in trips across Europe between 1920 and 1924, he enlisted as many wartime administrators as possible who drew on private papers and personal experiences. The Carnegie *History of the World War* was to be a history written not principally by historians but by men of war acting as eyewitnesses. Twenty-five authors had held offices in wartime cabinets and many more had administrative or political posts during the war.[22] They included William Beveridge, British food administrator in the war and subsequently permanent secretary to the Ministry of Food; Walker Hines, assistant director of the United States Railroad Administration; and Édouard Herriot, wartime minister of transport, public works, and supply, and future prime minister of France.[23] Shotwell also drew on expertise gained outside of government and recruited labor leaders, for instance the German social democrat Paul Umbreit and the British Fabian G. D. H. Cole, of whom Shotwell expected privileged access to trade union materials.[24] Sources, authors, and national editorial boards were all part of Shotwell and Clark's laboratory of history. By the mid-1920s, all ingredients were assembled and the first volumes had appeared or were in print.

Preemptive Historiography

With its emphasis on telling the story of the war by assembling documentary evidence in the most neutral way possible, the Carnegie Endowment moved in step with contemporary trends in what may be called historical diplomacy. The historian Erich Hahn has coined the term "preemptive historiography" in his analysis of German attempts to craft a narrative that refuted responsibility for the outbreak of the war.[25] But in a broader sense, preemptive historiography denotes preparing the ground for current and future political projects by interpreting the past, and this practice had many adherents in the 1920s.

The selective publication of official diplomatic documents in "colored books" had been used as a foreign policy tool by governments since the second half of the nineteenth century, usually to justify military action. During the First World War each belligerent published a colored book. In addition, authentic source material became one of the spoils of war. Shortly after invading Belgium, the German government published a selection of captured dispatches from the Belgian embassies in Berlin, London, and Paris to show that Britain's policies were to blame for the outbreak of war. Significantly, the edition included facsimiles, as if to underline the authenticity of the assembled material.[26] In 1917 the Bolsheviks published diplomatic correspondence from the Tsarist state archives, but for different purposes. Their revelations blamed the outbreak of the war on the imperialist powers, including Russia.[27]

Most belligerent states came to recognize the explosive potential of published archival documents in the international political battles of the postwar era, none more so than the Weimar Republic. The *leitmotiv* of German foreign policy in the 1920s was the revision of the postwar settlement, which focused on Article 231 of the Versailles Treaty, the so-called war-guilt clause. If it could be shown conclusively that Germany did not bear full responsibility for the war, the door to revision was open.[28] After the Armistice, revolutionary forces within Germany sought to put the blame on the country's old elites but these efforts soon stalled in the shadow of Versailles. Shortly after the treaty was signed in June 1919, the government authorized the publication of an official document volume on the outbreak of the war, a sanitized version of an earlier collection that had been collated by the socialist Karl Kautsky. Similarly, the German Foreign Ministry suppressed the final reports of a parliamentary inquiry into the causes and conduct of the war, and instead set up an entire industry of governmental and quasi-governmental institutions to disprove the so-called war-guilt lie.[29]

The Foreign Ministry coordinated what became a highly sophisticated propaganda campaign through its own war-guilt department but it also relied on the willing cooperation of German scholars. An eminent law professor, a theologian, and the former head of the library of the Prussian Parliament coedited one of the most successful projects under the umbrella of propaganda denouncing German guilt, a multivolume edition of German diplomatic documents from 1871 to 1914.[30] Published between 1922 and 1927, the edition was hailed as a milestone within Germany and abroad. It was not apparent at the time that the documents had been selected with the intention to support Germany's case for treaty revision. In the course of their archival work, conducted under the watchful eyes of the Foreign Ministry, the editors omitted and falsified critical documents, erased incriminating comments that Wilhelm II had scribbled on margins, and took documents out of their chronological context.[31]

Nonetheless, to all outward appearances, Germany mounted an earnest attempt to investigate the war's causes almost immediately after it was over. This put pressure on all other belligerents to do the same. The Carnegie Endowment translated both the German document volume on the war's outbreak and the proceedings of the parliamentary inquiry, prompting an American reviewer to muse in 1924 that "any honest effort to fix the responsibility for the war" would have to wait "until we have access to the archives of Great Britain and France."[32] The translation and publication efforts of agencies such as the Endowment encouraged a sense of entitlement to previously restricted information among reading publics, especially in Britain and the United States. In this competitive atmosphere Germany had managed, whether deservedly or not, to set a benchmark for archival openness in the post-1919 era.

Germany's perceived commitment to transparency was accentuated by the less impressive efforts of the Western democracies. Ramsay McDonald (incidentally a former member of the Carnegie Endowment's European advisory board) decided to open the British archives in 1924, resulting in the *British Documents on the Origins of the War*. Aristide Briand charged an archival commission with the sifting of the Quai d'Orsay archives in 1928 and the *Documents Diplomatiques Français* started to appear from 1930. Both series were political responses to Germany's opening wager in the war of documents and were similarly the fruit of tendentious editing practices.[33] The United States' official document collection, the *Foreign Relations of the United States* (FRUS) series, had fallen more and more behind before the war due to inadequate funding. By 1920 it was eight years from currency, an interval that would stretch to twenty in the course of the interwar period. Furthermore, the State Department initially withheld documents that detailed American involvement in the First World War before publishing them in separate FRUS volumes between 1928 and 1933, prompting the head of its Division of Publications, Tyler Dennett, to complain "we are today about the only great Government which has not given to the public its diplomatic correspondence of the war period."[34] Boasting of its good archival practice, the German Foreign Ministry even managed to send its chief war-guilt propagandist to the United States where he advised the Archives of Congress on document management.[35] In the 1920s, the demonstrable responsiveness to the demands of an informed public represented hard currency in the politics of international comparisons. They formed the backdrop to the writing of the Carnegie Endowment's *Economic and Social History of the World War*.

The Carnegie *History*, with its focus on the economic and social effects of the war, did not directly address the question of war guilt but it became nonetheless embroiled in the historiographical battles of the period. This was partly due to Shotwell's choice of collaborators. To lead the German board of editors, he chose none other than Albrecht Mendelssohn-Bartholdy, one of the editors of *Große Politik der Europäischen Kabinette*, Germany's official document collection. Mendelssohn-Bartholdy, a professor of international law at the University of Hamburg, was a liberal who believed in the revision of Versailles through international cooperation. At Shotwell's behest, he lobbied several German government ministries for access to their wartime files and "sold" the case for collaborating with the Carnegie project by claiming that it would be a highly valuable opportunity to present Germany's case to an American audience, the key propaganda target. Furthermore, and this mattered to a nation that sought to regain its place among the great powers after a catastrophic defeat, the German series of the Carnegie *History* would have the same status as the French and the British series.[36]

The German volumes of the Carnegie *History* slotted into the pattern of officially sponsored preemptive historiography but the collaboration was problematic. Although the ministries granted the Carnegie authors archival access, they also exerted censorship. Some volumes were written but never published.[37] This gave Shotwell a taste of the less salubrious side of Germany's effort to set the record straight through documentary evidence. He lamented that "the politicians were merely hurting Germany's case by refusing to open up the economic and social costs of war."[38] But Shotwell, who was not sympathetic to German revisionism, also knew how to retaliate, as in terms of public relations suppressing a publication was not a victory but a defeat. Shotwell made it known that censorship had happened, and it was reported in the media.[39] Fueled in part by Germany's efforts to demonstrate good archival practice in the 1920s and in part by the wartime experience with censorship, the reading public in the English-speaking countries had come to expect something of a right of information. The bold project of the Carnegie *History* further encouraged these expectations as it negotiated with the demands of governments, authors, and an imagined transnational public sphere.

A Transnational History?

James T. Shotwell was earnest in his desire to take the heat out of the "history wars" of the interwar period. This made him an interventionist editor who examined every single volume and criticized authors' manuscripts in detail to ensure that they would unambiguously demonstrate the disastrous social and economic costs of war. Shotwell was keenly aware that detailed accounts of wartime administration could well be misread as how-to manuals for future conflicts.[40] He suppressed publications that he felt were not conducive to postwar reconciliation, among them a history of Alsace-Lorraine favored by the French editorial board, and he demanded substantive cuts to other volumes, notably one on French prisoners of war.[41] These enforced silences were the price for a history that did not pander to revanchist demands and subverted the patterns of preemptive historiography. Together with his national editorial boards, Shotwell offered a perspective on the war that avoided questions of war guilt. Topics such as crime or public health directed the reader's gaze away from foreign ministries and battlefields and toward the plight of ordinary people.[42] By avoiding the question of responsibility for the war, and embracing a high level of facticity, the Carnegie *History* removed an element of contention. But did it offer an interpretation of the war that connected and even transcended national war stories?

To some extent it did. One American reviewer of the entire series remarked that "it is possible to follow a thread from one volume to another, picking one's way from country to country and from problem to problem, with constant enrichment."[43] The *Economic and Social History of the World War* was written for an international and principally English-speaking audience. While the Austrian, German, Italian, and French series appeared in their national languages, abridged versions and those volumes originally written in minority languages were translated into English. The structure emphasized the common experience of war. The deliberate inclusion of neutral countries—after all, the United States entered the war to defend neutrals' rights—as well as the existence of a Japanese series underlined the global reach of the conflict. For instance, the Netherlands was an important case study because, although nominally neutral and trading with both sides, economically and socially Dutch society came under severe strain due to the war. Afterward, "dislocated society had to resume its former equipoise."[44] War upset the natural order of things, and nobody profited.

The bulk of the studies fell within the broader field of economic history, covering trade, industry, commerce, finance, prices, and wages but also wartime industrial organization and its challenges in the form of strikes and forced and deported labor. Agriculture, in particular in Eastern Europe, forms another strand. Public health was an additional theme that fell outside the mainstream debate on the war's origins.[45] There are some regional and urban studies, providing small-scale histories of the war, and exploring the impact of warfare far away from the front.[46] Women in the war, not studied by professional historians for decades to come, appear in several volumes.[47] In general, the authors employed a dry, factual style, supported by figures and diagrams, which subtly conveyed the dislocating impact of war on the societies they described.

Food in the war was the subject of no less than eight individual volumes.[48] It had a special resonance with European audiences who had known deprivation and rationing but also with Americans, who voluntarily restricted their own consumption during the war, exported critical food supplies to Allied countries and donated millions of dollars for food aid. American food abroad showcased American humanitarian credentials and high living standards but could also be used for strategic advantage, for example in Herbert Hoover's relief mission to the Soviet Union between 1921 and 1923. As the scientific measuring of food enabled governments to master the human body and moral values such as self control became attached to eating, the war transformed attitudes toward food.[49] In the words of an American Carnegie author, war was "a very valuable course of education in the science of food values," both in the nutritional and moral sense.[50] For governments food became, as Nick Cullather has put it, "politically legible" and the Carnegie *History* enhanced this

legibility as it provided a set of data that outlined the mechanics of food production and distribution across eight national war efforts.[51] Beveridge's volume,
for instance, compared how much bread, meat, fats, and sugar were available
to civilians in Germany, Britain, and the Netherlands before and after the war
(he claimed the Dutch suffered the greatest reduction). The German history on
food in the war detailed conservation practices such as *Fletschern*, the vigorous
mastication of food to extract maximum nutritional value. The technique had
been invented by the American Horace Fletcher and it was promoted to com-
pensate for Germany's lack of an effective food policy in the face of Britain's
wartime blockade.[52] No reader could come away from reading one of the food
volumes without concluding that a scientifically managed food policy could
make or break a national war effort.

Such information represented valuable knowledge for the conduct of total
war. The study on feeding Austria-Hungary's population recognized that it was
unprecedented that over one hundred million people were forced to arrange
their lives as if in a "fortress under siege."[53] The facsimiles of Austrian ration
cards (Figure 2.2), which were included in the volume, visualized the reality
of food scarcity in a way that, significantly, avoided emotive images of individual suffering.[54] Instead, they coolly provided a practical model of how the
nutritional needs of a wartime population could be scientifically managed. In
its desire to eschew appeals to humanitarian or nationalist sentiment in favor
of facticity, the Carnegie *History* left itself open to multiple interpretations.
Certainly, war had a devastating impact on a people's well-being. However, in
a national crisis, governments ignored the welfare of their populations, which
could be measured accurately according to international standards, at their
peril. This lesson took on a new significance in the troubled 1930s when international organizations increasingly regarded research into problems of nutrition, food production, and food consumption as one of their core functions and
as intimately related to maintaining peace and stability. After the Second World
War, this concern took on even more intensity.[55]

The Legacy of the *Economic and Social History of the World War*

Although appreciatively reviewed, the Carnegie *History* never sold well. The
Carnegie Endowment's practice of donating it to large libraries across the
globe was partly to blame but a more important factor was the attrition of its
natural audience. When Shotwell pronounced the series concluded in 1937,
economic liberalism of the kind that John Bates Clark had originally promulgated, with government intervention as its *bête noire*, was discredited. John

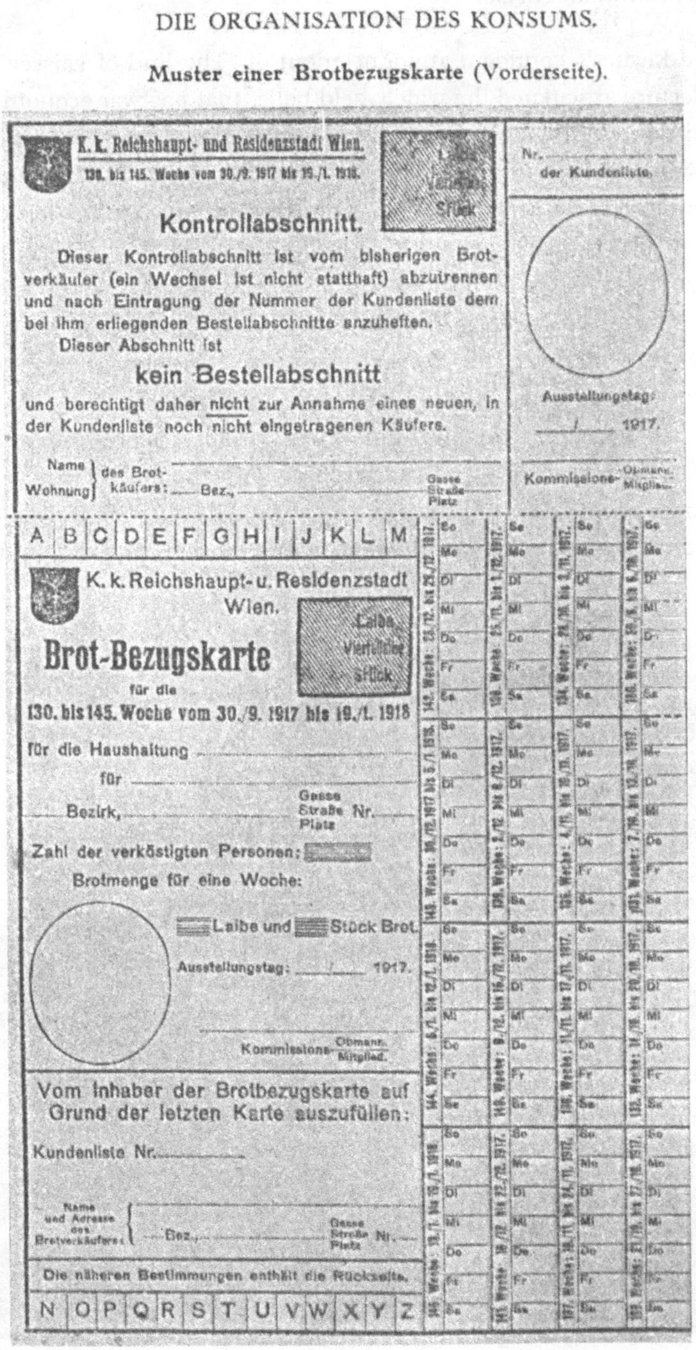

DIE ORGANISATION DES KONSUMS.

Muster einer Brotbezugskarte (Vorderseite).

FIGURE 2.2 Facsimile of a bread ration card for residents of Vienna (reproduced in Löwenfeld-Russ, *Die Regelung der Volksernährung im Kriege*, 346). The number of loaves, quarter-loaves, and even pieces of bread could be adapted according to the needs of each household. What this piece of visual evidence did *not* show was the impact of wartime malnutrition on individual human beings.

Maynard Keynes's confident announcement of "The End of Laissez-Faire" in a 1924 lecture articulated the widely held belief that postwar economies could only function well if governments intervened.[56] Under the impact of the Great Depression and the rise of economic nationalism, totalitarianism, and autarky, this view became entrenched as liberal governments embraced collectivist measures such as planning, not least in the New Deal.[57] The wartime experiments in the collective management of populations and economies served as templates for governments gearing up for conflict, certainly for those that sent in orders for volumes of the *Economic and Social History of the World War* to the Carnegie Endowment's Washington headquarters (see Figure 2.3).[58] As one reviewer suggested in 1939, "War-time socialization, it is only too evident, was put into effect by men who were not prepared for it and did not believe in it. We know now that they paved the way for men who did believe in it as an article of faith and for whom it provided the preparation. Socially and economically, we

FIGURE 2.3 James T. Shotwell, standing on the right, continued his efforts to use history in the cause of peace. Here he is in discussion at a UNESCO-sponsored seminar on "Education for a World Society," at Adelphi College, Garden City, New York, July/August 1948. An issue of the *UNESCO Courier* is visible on the desk. © UN photo, Department of Public Information.

are in the midst of a second world war. The Shotwell series was completed in time to be contemporary."[59]

Indeed, the year 1937 not only saw the completion of Shotwell's magnum opus but also the publication of Walter Lippmann's *The Good Society*, which attempted to reconfigure the embattled liberalism of an earlier generation for a new era. In the book, Lippmann acknowledged the failures of both laissez-faire and collectivism. His hypotheses touched a nerve among economists, historians, and philosophers who were skeptical of an all-powerful state but reluctantly accepted the need for selective intervention in the economy. Some of these intellectual trailblazers met at the 1938 Colloque Walter Lippmann in Paris, a seminar to discuss *The Good Society* and a landmark event in the history of neoliberalism.[60] These discussions echoed arguments put forward in the Carnegie *History*. One of Shotwell's closest collaborators, Albrecht Mendelssohn-Bartholdy, wrote his contribution, the "testament of a liberal," in exile after fleeing Nazi racial persecution in Germany. Among all the disastrous legacies that emanated from the First World War, Mendelssohn-Bartholdy argued, centralization was the worst, as it had made Hitler's totalitarian state and Germany's moral decline possible.[61] Even if a Second World War could not be avoided, now it was time to take seriously the lessons emanating from the First.

The Carnegie *History* was one of the missing links that transported the "documentary moment" of the immediate postwar period and with it the experience of the First World War, into the international social politics of the 1930s and beyond. Debates on the responsibility of governments for human welfare that previously took place in national contexts were increasingly internationalized as new players such as the League of Nations, the International Labor Organization, and transnational networks of technical experts and advisers advanced a new way of making international policies. It relied heavily on documentation, measurement, and a discourse that emphasized the link between improved living conditions, modernization, and security. Its techniques survived another war and became embedded into the developmental thinking of the Cold War era. In the 1930s, the pacifist impulse behind the Carnegie *History* was also discernible among officials in the League of Nations who hoped that a border-transcending focus on human welfare would redirect governments' energy away from preparing for military conflict.[62] The Carnegie *History*'s appeal to archival openness and transparency did not avert the conflagration of another war but, by asking probing questions about the kind of information governments should make available and what degree of openness would be in the public interest, it ensured that international data would become a crucial dimension of international politics.

NOTES

1. Winter, "Cultural Divergences in Patterns of Remembering the Great War in Britain and France"; Trout, *On the Battlefield of Memory.* See also Kennedy, *Over Here,* 218–230; and the essays in Snell, *Unknown Soldiers.*

2. On the importance of transnational perspectives, see Horne, "The Great War at Its Centenary." For the historical deconstruction of a national war story, see Reynolds, *The Long Shadow.*

3. Winter and Prost, *The Great War in History.*

4. Ibid., 8; see also a short overview based on the prefaces to the Carnegie *History* volumes by Chatriot, "Comprendre la guerre."

5. Broadberry and Harrison, "The Economics of World War I"; Gatrell explicitly endeavors to "rise to Shotwell's challenge" in his *Russia's First World War,* 3.

6. As addressed in Winter, *Cambridge History of the First World War.*

7. Kennedy, *Over Here,* 88–92; Gary, *The Nervous Liberals,* chapter 1; Carruthers, "Propaganda, Communications and Public Opinion."

8. Clavin, *Securing the World Economy,* 38–39; see also Rietzler, "Before the Cultural Cold Wars."

9. Clark, "An Economic View of War and Arbitration"; Ross, *The Origins of American Social Science,* 115–122, 143–145.

10. Clark Papers, box 2.

11. Barber, "British and American Economists and Attempts to Comprehend the Nature of War, 1910–1920"; Prudhommeaux, *Le Centre Européen de la Dotation Carnegie pour la Paix Internationale, 1911–1921,* 40; Ceadel, *Living the Great Illusion,* 91–103.

12. Quoted in Marchand, *The American Peace Movement and Social Reform, 1898–1918,* 165; Barber, "British and American Economists," 71–74, 79–80; see also earlier references to Clark's planned "laboratory study of war," in letter to family, October 7, 1911, Clark Papers, box 1.

13. Shotwell, preface to Mendelssohn-Bartholdy, *The War and German Society,* xi.

14. Novick, *That Noble Dream: The "Objectivity Question" and the American Historical Profession,* chapter 4; Josephson, *James T. Shotwell and the Rise of Internationalism in America,* 47.

15. Burke, *The French Historical Revolution;* on Shotwell's complex relations with key Annales scholars, see Harvey, "An American *Annales?.*"

16. "National Board for Historical Service." On historians and war propaganda, see Vaughn, *Holding Fast the Inner Lines;* Gruber, *Mars and Minerva.* On historians and peacemaking, see Nielson, *American Historians in War and Peace.* See also the useful overview by Rosenberg, "War and the Health of the State."

17. Josephson, *James T. Shotwell and the Rise of Internationalism in America,* 62–64.

18. Shotwell to H. B. Greven, February 11 and August 13, 1920, Shotwell, box 80.

19. Tesnière, "La BDIC dans le 'moment documentaire'"; Malvern, "War, Memory and Museums."

20. Renouvin, *The Forms of War Government in France;* Bloch, *Bibliographie méthodique de l'histoire économique et sociale de la France pendant la guerre;* Pirenne,

La Belgique et la guerre mondiale; Ministère des Sciènces et des Arts, *La Commission des archives de la guerre*; Shotwell, *The Autobiography of James T. Shotwell*, 140.

21. Jenkinson, *A Manual of Archive Administration Including the Problems of War Archive Making*; Leland, *Introduction to the American Official Sources for the Economic and Social History of the World War*.

22. Winter and Prost, *The Great War in History*, 111.

23. Beveridge, *British Food Control*; Hines, *War History of American Railroads*; Herriot, *Lyon pendant la guerre*.

24. Umbreit, *Der Krieg und die Arbeitsverhältnisse*; Shotwell to Cole, February 9, 1920, Shotwell Papers, box 56. Cole contributed two volumes to the British series: *Labour in the Coal-mining Industry (1914–1921)*; *Trade Unionism and Munitions*.

25. Hahn, "The German Foreign Ministry and the Question of War Guilt in 1918–1919," 47.

26. Auswärtiges Amt, *Belgische Aktenstücke, 1905–1914*; on the "colored books," see Taylor, *The Struggle for Mastery in Europe, 1848–1914*, 569–570. On archival theft, see Eckert, *The Struggle for the Files*.

27. Mombauer, *The Origins of the First World War*, 57.

28. Niedhart, *Die Außenpolitik der Weimarer Republik*; Steiner, *The Lights That Failed*, 59–63, 410–413, 610–611.

29. Montgelas and Schücking, *Die deutschen Dokumente zum Kriegsausbruch*; Herwig, "Clio," 90–91, 108–112.

30. Lepsius, Mendelssohn Bartholdy, and Thimme, *Die Große Politik der Europäischen Kabinette 1871–1914*.

31. Herwig, "Clio Deceived," 95–98; Heinemann, *Die verdrängte Niederlage*, 80–90.

32. *Outbreak of the World War. German Documents Collected by Karl Kautsky and Edited by Max Montgelas and Walther Schücking. Translated by the Carnegie Endowment for International Peace*; *Official German Documents Relating to the World War. Translated by the Carnegie Endowment for International Peace*.

33. Mombauer, *The Origins of the First World War*, 62–69; Clark, *The Sleepwalkers*, xxi–xxii; Gooch, *Recent Revelations of European Diplomacy*, 269, 344; for a comparative perspective on official document collections, see Zala, *Geschichte unter der Schere politischer Zensur*.

34. McAllister, Botts, Cozzens, and Marrs, *Toward "Thorough, Accurate, and Reliable,"* chapters 5 and 6, Dennett quoted on 129.

35. Heinemann, *Die verdrängte Niederlage*, 91.

36. Rietzler, "Philanthropy, Peace Research and Revisionist Politics," especially 67.

37. Ibid., 68.

38. Shotwell, *The Autobiography of James T. Shotwell*, 151.

39. *Sunday Mercury*, "152 Volumes of War History"; *Times of India*, "Post-war Germany."

40. Minutes of the twentieth meeting of the French editorial committee, May 31, 1922, 3–4, Shotwell Papers, box 63.

41. Minutes of the fifty-first meeting of the French editorial committee, November 24, 1925, 6; minutes of the sixty-first meeting of the French editorial committee, March 18, 1927, 4, Shotwell Papers, box 63. In the end, the book on prisoners of war was not published as part of the Carnegie *History*: Cahen-Salvador, *Les prisonniers de guerre*. Note, though, that Renouvin's contribution did antagonize pro-German interpreters of the war by comparing Germany's slide into military dictatorship with France's preservation of democracy (Renouvin, *The Forms of War Government in France*).

42. Hirschfeld, "Der Erste Weltkrieg in der deutschen und internationalen Geschichtsschreibung."

43. Binkley, "*Social and Economic History of the World War* by James T. Shotwell," quote on 631.

44. de Monchy, *Commerce and Navigation*, 162.

45. Mitrany, *The Land and the Peasant in Rumania*; Bernard, *La défense de la santé publique pendant la guerre*; Pirquet, *Volksgesundheit im Krieg*.

46. The French series contained several volumes on urban history. Winter and Prost, *The Great War in History*, 112; Jones, *Rural Scotland during the War*.

47. Lorenz, *Die gewerbliche Frauenarbeit während des Krieges*; Frois, *La santé et le travail des femmes pendant la guerre*.

48. Henry, *Le ravitaillement de la Belgique pendant l'occupation allemande*; Pinot, *Le contrôle du ravitaillement de la population civile*; Bachi, *L'alimentazione e la politica annonaria in Italia*; Skalweit, *Die Deutsche Kriegsernährungswirtschaft*; Löwenfeld-Russ, *Die Regelung der Volksernährung im Kriege*; Beveridge, *British Food Control*; Posthuma, *Food Supply and Agriculture*; Berngardovich Struve, *Food Supply in Russia during the World War*.

49. Veit, *Modern Food, Moral Food*, chapters 1 and 3; Cabanes, *The Great War and the Origins of Humanitarianism, 1918–1924*, chapter 4; Patenaude, *The Big Show in Bololand*.

50. Clark, *The Costs of the World War to the American People*, 47.

51. Cullather, "The Foreign Policy of the Calorie," quote on 338.

52. Beveridge, *British Food Control*, 317; Skalweit, *Die Deutsche Kriegsernährungswirtschaft*, 28; Veit, *Modern Food, Moral Food*, 40–41. On food and hunger in wartime Germany, see Davis, *Home Fires Burning*; Vincent, *The Politics of Hunger*.

53. Löwenfeld-Russ, *Die Regelung der Volksernährung im Kriege*, 356–357.

54. On suffering and spectatorial sympathy, see Halttunen, "Humanitarianism and the Pornography of Pain in Anglo-American Culture"; on the era of World War I, see Kevin Rozario, "'Delicious Horrors'."

55. Amrith and Clavin, "Feeding the World"; Clavin, *Securing the World Economy*, 165–179; Weindling, "The Role of International Organizations in Setting Nutritional Standards in the 1920s and 1930s"; on the science of hunger, see Vernon, *Hunger*, chapter 4.

56. Keynes, *The End of Laissez-Faire*; Burgin, *The Great Persuasion*, 1–8.

57. Ekbladh, *The Great American Mission*, 57–76.

58. Josephson, *James T. Shotwell and the Rise of Internationalism in America*, 110.

THE WAR AS HISTORY   53

59. Binkley, "*Social and Economic History of the World War* by James T. Shotwell," 632.

60. Denord, "French Neoliberalism and Its Divisions"; Burgin, *The Great Persuasion*, 58–67; Jackson, "At the Origins of Neo-Liberalism." See also the meticulously researched account by Walpen, *Die offenen Feinde und ihre Gesellschaft*, especially chapter 1.

61. Mendelssohn-Bartholdy, *The War and German Society*, 152.

62. Amrith and Clavin, "Feeding the World," 35; on the legacy of interwar thinking on Cold War modernization discourse, see also, e.g., Ekbladh, *The Great American Mission*; Cullather, *The Hungry World*; and Engerman, *Modernization from the Other Shore*.

3

The World War
and American Memory

John Milton Cooper, Jr.

"What's in a name?" asks Shakespeare's Juliet. The play's answer is, just about everything, as Juliet and her lover Romeo learn to their sorrow and finally at the cost of their lives. The same question and answer apply to the names given in different parts of the English-speaking world to the war that raged between 1914 and 1918. People in Britain and the nations of the Commonwealth soon started calling it "the Great War," and they have persisted in that usage even after the bigger war of 1939–1945.

It is easy to see why that name sticks in those parts of the world. You only have to visit the chapel of an Oxford or Cambridge college or drive through the center of a small Canadian town. The walls of the chapel and the obelisks in the town have inscribed on them long lists of dead from that first war, much longer than from the second war. Geopolitically, too, this earlier war marked a much bigger turning point for Britain and its empire: it marked the beginning of a rapid descent from a point still near the zenith of their prestige and power.

Fittingly, the year 2014—which marked the centennial of the war's outbreak—witnessed a medium-sized controversy in Britain in the press and politics about how to mark this anniversary. Some stoutly maintained that this war, like its successor, deserved to be celebrated as another in the line of examples of national heroism—another "finest hour." Others just as stoutly rejoined that this war needed to be deplored as an act of folly and hubris. Interestingly, the two sides did not follow predictable right/left lines; some of the strongest nay-saying voices belonged to conservatives, such as the latter-day celebrant of empire, Niall Ferguson. For Britons, then, this is still their Great War.

That name has never caught on in the United States. Before our intervention, Americans simply called it "the war in Europe." After intervention, there was no rush to pin a special name on the conflict, and it sometimes went by the "War of 1914–1918." For example, in 1937 a rare dissenting editorial voice derided the purportedly "permanent" Neutrality Act of that year as "an act to preserve the United States from intervention in the War of 1914–'18." That dissent appeared in the *New York Herald-Tribune*, and it was most likely written by the paper's chief editorial writer, Walter Millis. Two years earlier, Millis had published a widely read book, *The Road to War*, which retrospectively deplored intervention in the earlier war as an act of near-criminal folly. By 1937, however, Millis was emerging as a strong advocate for resistance to aggression in Europe and Asia, although he did not alter his views about the earlier intervention. Two months after the outbreak of the next war, he defended his newfound stance by publishing an article in *Life* magazine entitled "1939 Is Not 1914."[1]

Yet the most common name in America, even before that second global conflict, was "the World War." Theodore Roosevelt first used those words in 1915, but few others joined him for a while. Wider acceptance of this name came a few years later when, in the immediate postwar period, translations of German books and documents appeared, frequently using the terms "world power" and "world war." Those translations helped to plant the name firmly in this country's usage. Moreover, those two words dovetailed with Americans' national pride in conveying the idea that our intervention had transformed the conflict into something bigger and morally weightier.

Self-aggrandizement aside, this view has much to recommend it. Apart from the Bolshevik Revolution, nothing did more than US intervention to transform the nature of this war. Before 1917, it had been mainly the latest in the four-century-long string of European dynastic wars with far-flung ramifications owing to overseas maritime contact and colonization—albeit much bigger and deadlier.

True, there had been some exceptions and innovations on the part of both sets of European belligerents. Each side tried to ignite internal conflicts in their adversaries' backyards. The most noted of those efforts occurred in what was then called the Near East and in central and eastern Europe, Ireland, and Russia. The British hatched schemes to stir up revolts among the Arab subjects of Germany's ally, the Ottoman Empire, some led by the young archaeologist-turned-unconventional-warrior T. E. Lawrence. Likewise, the Allies encouraged separatist movements among the Slavic subjects of another of Germany's allies, Austria-Hungary. The Germans similarly plotted to incite anticolonial dissent among Muslims in British-dominated Egypt and Persia and more broadly in the jewel in the empire's crown, India. Before the Easter Rising of

1916, Irish nationalists got arms and money from the Germans, who transported the nationalist leader Roger Casement to Ireland in a submarine. The most famous exploit to undermine a foe came when the Germans facilitated the return to Russia, after the fall of the tsarist regime, of Vladimir Lenin, who played the leading role in the Bolshevik Revolution of November 1917.

Still, even before that revolution, with its radical and anti-imperialist outreach, the nature of this war was changing fundamentally. American intervention was transforming it into a truly world-altering event. Much of the transformation stemmed from the way both the president and a majority of his people sold themselves on the war.

Woodrow Wilson would later get blamed for having painted intervention in sweeping idealistic colors and having promised a brave new world of lasting peace and freedom. Speaking as someone who has spent quite a few years studying Wilson, I think such blame almost entirely misses the mark. The most famous words in his war address were "The world must be made safe for democracy."[2] Coming from perhaps the most punctilious stylist to occupy the White House, this use of passive voice had to be deliberate. Wilson wanted to underline the sense of limitation and multilateralism that he had already conveyed several times in this speech, and he was eschewing any notion of a single-handed American crusade. Likewise, the president's subsequent war aims statements, especially the Fourteen Points, were almost always circumspect.[3]

In April 1918, Wilson made his viewpoint crystal clear when he talked to a group of foreign journalists. He rejected what he scorned as "the language of braggadocio" and he insisted that he had "no desire to march triumphantly into Berlin." As earlier in the Fourteen Points speech, he laid down no general principle of "self-determination"—a term coined not by him, but by Britain's Lloyd George, and one that Wilson used only sparingly later in 1918. He drove home his basic point when he affirmed, "There isn't any one kind of government which we have a right to impose upon any nation. So that I am not fighting for democracy except for the people that want democracy."[4] The president also reminded his listeners that he was a disciple of Edmund Burke and therefore, by implication, immune to utopianism. Unfortunately, Wilson said those things off the record, and this statement would not see the light of print for another six and a half decades. If he had spoken publicly, he might have spared himself much misplaced calumny in years to come.

Still, Wilson did bear responsibility for the zealous, overreaching way this country went to war. Idealism was the coin of the realm in American political rhetoric of that day, especially among progressive reformers, who included not only Wilson but also his archrival Theodore Roosevelt and his bitter opponent over the war, Robert M. La Follette. The emotional climate of that decade—which seethed with domestic conflict over political, economic, and social reform and with ethnic and racial strife—almost certainly precluded a low-keyed, carefully calibrated approach to fighting this war. Also, as David Kennedy observed over thirty years ago in *Over Here*, the limited tools of compulsion available to the federal government required the Wilson administration to whip up popular fervor in order to gain voluntary compliance for such measures as military conscription, home-front rationing, wage and price controls, and economic mobilization. Progressive intellectuals such as Walter Lippmann and John Dewey joyously jumped aboard the war bandwagon as a means to advance cherished domestic reforms, but they soon recoiled in horror at the outbursts of mass hysteria, incidents of popular vigilantism, and official repression of free speech. As Kennedy notes, "The next reforming generation ... would hearken not to the buoyant optimism of John Dewey but to the sober voice of Reinhold Niebuhr, preaching in Augustinian accents the doctrine of human imperfection and the necessity of diminished hope."[5] Ironically, those accents characterized Wilson's frame of mind as he decided to enter the war. I want to return to this point at the end of this essay.

The contrast between Americans' attitudes toward and memories of the two world wars goes further. The second war would become America's "good war" at home because there was precious little dissent and therefore less perceived need for control of public opinion, although the government would once more practice censorship and resort to propaganda. That "good war" likewise witnessed one far larger and centrally directed violation of civil liberties—the forced removal and internment of thousands of citizens of Japanese descent. Much of the difference between the memories of the two wars also springs from the length and scope of American belligerency in them. This nation's time in arms during the first war lasted less than half as long as during the second. Likewise, this first war put less than half as many men and women in arms. An easy way to note the disparity in memories of the two wars is to visit the military section of the Museum of American History at the Smithsonian Institution or go into any store that sells military memorabilia and books. Both the museum and the store devote at least three-quarters of their space to the Civil War and World War II. The other wars divide up the remaining quarter, mainly in proportion to their remoteness in the past.

Perhaps just as important to the disparate memories of the two world wars is the contrast in their endings. The first war did not witness the triumphal march through Berlin that Wilson eschewed in 1918 but that the Red Army made in 1945, or the surrender ceremony aboard the USS *Missouri* in the Tokyo Bay that we staged that same year. If the first war had lasted longer, it would have looked more like the second war. The British were the great military innovators of the first war. By the latter part of 1918, they had begun to perfect the use of tanks and develop aircraft with further cruising ranges and substantial bombing capacity. The injection of massive numbers of American doughboys in the summer and fall of 1918 was already breaking the stalemate of trench warfare on the Western Front, and in the months to come their numbers, augmented by tanks and planes, could have restored the kind of war of movement that would spawn satisfying military memories of World War II. Sad to say, World War I ended too soon for the sake of future American nostalgia, and the sense of unconsummated combat would contribute to the fetish of "unconditional surrender" in World War II.

Lack of interest in America's other, "forgotten" wars is particularly deplorable in the case of World War I. This was the United States' first experience with fighting a big overseas war; as such, it provided the training ground at first for the people and subsequently for the ideas that would guide later American wars. The generation gap in the top ranks was wide enough to preclude the same men from holding major commands in both wars, with one exception. Douglas MacArthur led the "Rainbow Division" in World War I and all ground forces in the Pacific in World War II. How much the earlier experience shaped his later conduct I leave to others to judge. Of the top generals in the second war's European theater, only George S. Patton had seen combat in the previous conflict. Both Dwight Eisenhower and Omar Bradley were still training stateside in tank warfare when the Armistice came in November 1918. Easily the most important high-level carryover experience from one war to the next can be called "the education of George Marshall." As John J. Pershing's chief of staff and indispensable right-hand man, Marshall learned firsthand the challenges and pitfalls of such massive long-range operations and the intricacies of coalition warfare. The trials and tribulations of dealing with Allied commanders played a big part in Marshall's choice of the diplomatically gifted Eisenhower to be Supreme Commander in Europe twenty-five years later.

Neglect of World War I is doubly unfortunate because this conflict once loomed so large in public and political consciousness for "lessons" to be learned from it—a distinction it shares with the Vietnam War and the Iraq War. Hard as it may be to believe for most people who are old enough to be reading these essays, World War I for a while came to be repudiated even more thoroughly than either Vietnam or Iraq. That should not come as a surprise. From the outset, this war had a large number of opponents and a much bigger cohort of uneasy supporters.[6] Those numbers guaranteed that the war would have its naysayers even before the guns fell silent in November 1918. In many ways, the debate over the peace treaty and membership in the League of Nations served as a surrogate for argument over the wisdom and consequences of the war. The way that debate ended in sputtering deadlock and ultimate evasion of international commitments further dampened fond memories of this war. The decade of the 1920s featured mostly a benign amnesia toward the conflict, except among diehard dissidents such as La Follette and Oswald Garrison Villard and a rising cohort of academic historical revisionists.

Such quietude of memory ended abruptly with the 1930s. The miseries at home of the Great Depression incited veterans to demand early payment of promised bonuses, which had the effect of plunging the war back into the center of public consciousness. So did the investigation by the Senate subcommittee chaired by Gerald P. Nye of North Dakota into the possible influence of munitions manufacturers before intervention. In fact, the Nye Committee conducted a widely publicized fishing expedition into various alleged nefarious influences, mainly financial and propagandistic, on the events that led to intervention, and its hearings served as a sounding board for deploring and accusatory "revisionist" views. The Nye Committee helped make Millis's *Road to War* a best-seller and served to spawn several other books in the same vein. Nye garnered maximum publicity for himself and his committee by manipulating the press, as he repeatedly made sensational charges that subsequent hearings did not bear out—a technique that Senator Joseph R. McCarthy would copy in the 1950s.[7]

Equally important in inflaming memories of the war was the patent breakdown of international order in Europe and Asia; which aroused fresh fears of new wars. These influences spurred a swift, massive public and political reaction. Between 1935 and 1937, Congress passed the successive Neutrality Acts by overwhelming margins and to near-universal public applause. Nearly all the opposition on Capitol Hill and criticism from outside came from those who demanded more sweeping, embargo-style legislation. As the *Herald-Tribune* noted, the neutrality measures enshrined in law the ideas advanced twenty years earlier by opponents of intervention in the first war.[8]

Likewise, on Capitol Hill, observances of the twentieth anniversary of entry into World War I honored those members who had voted against the war resolution. It is worth pointing out that nothing similar happened in 1984 on the twentieth anniversary of the Gulf of Tonkin Resolution. Otherwise, Ernest Gruening and Wayne Morse might have statues in the Capitol. By 1937, George Gallup and Elmo Roper had begun to develop "modern" techniques for sampling people's views, thereby making it much easier and more reliable to gauge public opinion. That year, a Gallup poll found that 70 percent of respondents believed that it had been a mistake to enter the world war. That response may have partly reflected the way the question was worded, but it did accurately reflect the popular mood. Another indication of how things stood had come a year earlier during the 1936 presidential campaign. That contest had turned almost exclusively on domestic issues, which was to be expected, since the country remained in the throes of the Depression.

Still, with war clouds gathering in Europe and Asia, it does seem odd that neither major party nominee devoted any time to international matters—with one exception. Just once, one candidate did proclaim, "We are not isolationists except in so far as we seek to isolate ourselves completely from war."[9] The person who said that was not an arch-isolationist such as Nye or his fellow senators William E. Borah of Idaho or Hiram Johnson of California, but Franklin D. Roosevelt. This was a case of history repeating itself. In 1912, there had been only one reference to foreign policy in that year's momentous four-way presidential contest. It had come in a passing comment about the need for strong armed forces to enable Americans to play their destined, leading role in world affairs. It had come, not surprisingly, from Franklin Roosevelt's distant kinsman and his wife's uncle, Theodore Roosevelt. The upsurge of isolationism in the mid-1930s was of a piece with appeasement in Britain and elsewhere across the Atlantic. All were part of a one-sided transnational wave of disillusionment and buyers' remorse over the previous war and horror at the prospect of another such conflict.

Here in America, as elsewhere, the remarkable thing is how quickly this anti-interventionist tide receded. At the beginning of September 1939, as the next war was breaking out in Europe, *The Nation*, previously owned by the opponent of the first war and unrepentant isolationist Oswald Villard, stated approvingly, "We know already from numerous 'polls' that the majority of Americans would hope for the defeat of Germany.... We suspect that most Americans, once the issues become clear, will consider that it would be wiser to render what economic aid we can now than to wait until mere economic action will be powerless to maintain a barrier between us and a Europe under Nazi domination."[10] Shortly afterward, the person who probably wrote those words, the magazine's editor, Freda Kirchwey, beat Walter Millis to the punch by two months with a signed editorial identically entitled "1939 Is Not 1914."[11] By the same token, whereas in 1914 President Wilson had called upon Americans to be "neutral in fact as well as in name . . . [and] impartial in thought as well as in action," President Roosevelt declared in 1939, "This nation will remain a neutral nation, but I cannot ask that every American remain neutral in thought as well. Even a neutral has a right to take account of facts. Even a neutral cannot be asked to close his mind or his conscience."[12]

During the next two years, Roosevelt's outspokenly pro-Allied utterances and "aid short of war" policies would nearly always command strong congressional and public approval. It is true that after 1939 polls by the Gallup and Roper organizations showed majorities opposed to intervention in the new war right up to Pearl Harbor, but those same polls consistently showed majority support for aid to the British and later the Soviets and for policies that plainly drew the nation ever closer to the conflict. This turn of the tide of popular opinion has not gotten the attention it deserves from scholars, and I think it points to a mixed legacy of the previous war in public memory.

During the three and a half years the United States fought in what *Time* magazine lastingly labeled "World War II," lessons to be learned from its predecessor continued to occupy a central place in policymaking and in political and popular discourse. At the highest levels, thinking departed from Wilson's circumspection about war aims and avoidance of triumphalism. Franklin Roosevelt took leaves from his kinsman's playbook in proclaiming all-out common cause with the Allies and seeking nothing less than total victory. The need to allay suspicions among the wary Soviets provided the main diplomatic rationale for "unconditional surrender," but also at work was determination to avoid perceived "mistakes" of the preceding generation. Ironically, what FDR and Winston Churchill were rejecting was not Wilson's idealism or supposed utopianism but his sense of limitation and realism.

At the popular level, the lesson learning ran in the opposite direction. Wilson's posthumous reputation had sunk to abysmal depths in the mid-1930s, but now he enjoyed an apotheosis that included books, magazine articles, and the biggest-budgeted movie yet made in Hollywood: Darryl F. Zanuck's *Wilson* would be more expensive than *Gone with the Wind*. The widespread conviction that Wilson had been an unheeded prophet undergirded support for both the founding of the United Nations and a resolve never again to retreat from international commitments and leadership.

Gratifying as it was to Wilson's admirers, this retrospective glorification came at a price. It had the unfortunate side effect of reinforcing images of him as a gentle, professorial dreamer and utopian idealist. Such notions set his war leadership and peace program up for a "realist" counterattack. Even during the heyday of the wartime Wilson revival, Walter Lippmann criticized him for not having entered the war earlier and for not justifying intervention on the correct grounds—namely, maintenance of the balance of power in general and the beneficial influence of Britain's sea power in particular. Instead, in Lippmann's view, Wilson had indulged in wrongheaded idealism and had failed to pursue limited, realistic war aims. Lippmann neglected to mention that he had not thought along those lines himself between 1914 and 1917 and that almost no one, including himself, had any inkling that when the United States intervened the Allies were on the verge of losing the war.[13]

During World War II others also sought to draw present-day lessons from what they saw as earlier leaders' mistakes. The most penetrating and constructive of these efforts was the historian Thomas A. Bailey's two-volume examination of peacemaking abroad and at home, *Woodrow Wilson and the Lost Peace* (1944) and *Woodrow Wilson and the Great Betrayal* (1945). Bailey had begun work on this project a decade earlier, well before the outbreak of World War II, and he had been able to interview some participants in the domestic debate; most notably Senators Borah and Johnson. The timing of the publication of his books allowed him to give a current twist to his interpretations. He ended each volume with two lists: one of Wilson's mistakes and the other of ways to do things right this time. The items on all four lists numbered fourteen.[14]

The "realist" critique of World War I policies and actions continued into the early years of the Cold War. Several writers, most notably George F. Kennan and Hans J. Morgenthau, took earlier policymakers, particularly Wilson, to task along the same lines as Lippmann, deploring excessive "legalism" and "moralism." Kennan differed from Lippmann, however, when he argued in his hugely popular *American Diplomacy, 1900–1950* (1951) that Imperial Germany was not such a bad regime and its victory in the war would not have been too bad for the United States or the world—the same view more recently espoused with variations by Niall Ferguson and others.[15] Whether that would have been so remains a hot topic for debate, and the kind of peace imposed on Russia at Brest-Litovsk raises doubts about the benignity of Wilhelmine Germany.

As for the paucity of "realism," these critics are themselves open to the charge of utopianism. They ignore the near total absence of realism in American political rhetoric during and after World War I. On a personal note, it surprised me to discover in my research on the League fight how no one, not even the harshest critics of the treaty and the League, espoused anything resembling European-style *raison d'etat*. To the contrary, many of Wilson's opponents accused him of having sold out to Old World imperialism and bought into a dressed-up version of the preceding century's monarchical Holy Alliance.[16] The best response to the "realist" critics came in 1953, not from a Wilson defender, but from a University of Chicago colleague of Morgenthau's, Robert E. Osgood. In his magisterial *Ideals and Self-Interest in America's Foreign Relations: The Great Twentieth-Century Transformation* (1953), much of which concentrates on the World War I period, Osgood exposed the shortcomings of trying to rely on one approach if divorced from the other. Coincidentally, Osgood's book appeared in the year that marked the end of the presidency of the only combat veteran of World War I, Harry S Truman.

Thereafter, this war has aroused only sporadic interest outside academia. Barbara Tuchman's best-selling *The Guns of August* (1962) came out two years before the fiftieth anniversary of the war's outbreak, and reading her book supposedly inspired John Kennedy to be circumspect and restrained during the Cuban Missile Crisis. The centennial of the war's outbreak spawned a rush of books by British authors about the war's origins and outbreak, most notably Margaret MacMillan's *The War That Ended Peace: How Europe Abandoned Peace for the First World War* and Christopher Clark's *The Sleepwalkers: How Europe Went to War in 1914*. The 2015 centennial of the sinking of the *Lusitania* has witnessed the publication of Erik Larson's best-selling book about that event, *Dark Wake*. Otherwise, this conflict has receded into the "forgotten wars" corner of American memory.

The year 2015 has also witnessed two particularly egregious examples of such forgetfulness. When forty-seven Republican senators issued a public letter opposing negotiations over Iran's nuclear capabilities, the avalanche of criticism that fell upon them featured claims by a number of well-educated people that such a move was unprecedented. Those making that claim included Secretary of State John Kerry, who studied at Yale with the great historian of twentieth-century American politics John Morton Blum, as well as a number of other public officials and spokespersons who likewise attended estimable colleges and universities. Television commentators, who were presumably leaning on their mostly young and uncertainly educated research staffs, resorted to snide remarks about the Logan Act of the 1790s, while the *New York Times* published an op-ed contribution by an academic historian about freelance forays into foreign policy in those early days of the Republic. Forgotten in all this flurry of outrage was the "round robin" of March 1919, which came less than four months after the end of World War I and was signed by almost as many Republican senators, who were rejecting Wilson's Draft Covenant of the League of Nations while the president was still negotiating at the Paris peace conference. Another precedent from the end of World War I went equally forgotten at the same time. Amid the furor following House Republicans' bringing Israeli Prime Minister Benjamin Netanyahu to the Capitol to blast the Obama administration's overtures toward Iran before a joint session of Congress, no one seemed to remember that in November and December 1918, just after the Armistice, TR and his friend Senate Republican leader Henry Cabot Lodge had repeatedly contacted British and French leaders in an effort to undermine Wilson's position at the upcoming peace conference.[17]

Such evidence of amnesia shows that we Americans have little appetite for learning from the experiences of World War I. Moreover, the 2017 centennial of American intervention in that war hints that it is unlikely that it will find itself in company with Britons in debating again whether American ancestors should have entered this war.[18] This is a great loss because that question is still worth asking. After all, the person who took the United States country into the war felt a heavy burden of doubt about his decision. As he was making up his mind whether or not to intervene, Wilson bared his conscience to the journalist Frank Cobb of the New York *World*. Abroad, if the United States went in, he feared "a dictated peace, a victorious peace, ... an attempt to reconstruct a peacetime civilization with war standards." At home, it would be even worse: "Once lead this people into war and they'll forget there ever was such a thing as tolerance. To fight, you must be brutal and ruthless, and spirit of ruthless brutality will enter into the very fibre of our national life."[19] Even after he made up his mind to go to war, Wilson studded his finely wrought address to Congress with expressions of sadness and doubt, and he closed with the haunting wish, not the certainty, that his country was doing the right thing, paraphrasing Martin Luther to say, "God helping her, she can do no other."[20]

As promised, let me end by referring to those "Augustinian accents" in explicating what Wilson thought. In 2006, I gave a talk in Washington in which I said, "Woodrow Wilson did not take the United States into World War I because he believed God was telling him to do it." I was well aware of where I was and the time when I said that. I paused and then added, "I do not mean that as an implied criticism of the way a certain Republican president took us into war." I paused again and then said, "I do not mean that as an implied criticism of the way President McKinley took us into war in 1898."[21]

In fact, Wilson made himself clear on this matter. In May 1915, just after the sinking of the *Lusitania*, a correspondent implored him to declare war in the name of God. "War is not declared in God's name," the president remarked to his stenographer. "It is a human affair altogether."[22] Of course Wilson drew on his deep religious faith in making the decision to go to war in 1917, but not in a spirit of certainty or zeal. Several times in print I have interpreted that last sentence of his war address, which transparently echoes Martin Luther's declaration to the Diet of Worms, "God helping me, I can do no other." I believe that Wilson was casting the United States in the same role as Luther's individual Christian in a sinful world. As limited, fallible creatures, none of us can presume to know God's will, nor can we avoid sin. We can only pray and consult Scripture, and then, humbly and imperfectly seeking to do God's will, we must do what Luther admonished us to do: "Sin boldly."[23] Wilson knew he was committing a terrible sin and asking millions of others to join him in committing that sin. The question remains, did that sin lead to greater good? By whatever name we call it, were we right to enter this war?

NOTES

1. *New York Herald Tribune*, May 1, 1937; Millis, *The Road to War*; Millis, "1939 Is Not 1914," 69 ff.

2. Wilson speech to Congress, April 2, 1917, in Link, *The Papers of Woodrow Wilson*, vol. 41, 525.

3. On Wilson's circumspection in the Fourteen Points, see Throntveit, "The Fable of the Fourteen Points."

4. Wilson's remarks to foreign journalists, April 8, 1918, in Link, *The Papers of Woodrow Wilson*, vol. 47, 268.

5. Kennedy, *Over Here*, 92.

6. On the dissenters, see Kazin, *The War against War*.

7. On Nye and his committee, see Cole, *Senator Gerald P. Nye and American Foreign Relations*, and on the "revisionists" of the 1930s, see Cohen, *American Revisionists*.

8. On the Neutrality Acts, see Divine, *The Illusion of Neutrality*.

9. Franklin D. Roosevelt speech, August 14, 1936, in Rosenman, *The Public Papers and Addresses of Franklin D. Roosevelt*, vol. 5, 288. Appropriately, FDR was speaking at Chautauqua, New York, which was closely associated with the previous generation's peace promoter and opponent of intervention in World War I, William Jennings Bryan.

10. *The Nation*, vol. 149, 234 (September 2, 1939).

11. Ibid., 283–284.

12. Wilson statement, August 18, 1914, in Link, *The Papers of Woodrow Wilson*, vol. 30, 394; Roosevelt statement, September 1939, in Rosenman, *The Public Papers and Addresses of Franklin D. Roosevelt*, vol. 8, 463.

13. Lippmann, *U. S. Foreign Policy*; Lippmann, *U. S. War Aims*.

14. On Bailey's work and the historiography of the debate over the peace treaty, may I immodestly suggest my essay, "The League Fight."

15. See Ferguson, *The Pity of War*.

16. See Cooper, *Breaking the Heart of the World*. On Wilson's strongest senatorial opponents, see also Stone, *The Irreconcilables and the Fight against the League of Nations*.

17. On the 1919 round robin, see Cooper, *Breaking the Heart of the World*, 55–71, and on efforts by TR, Lodge, and other Republicans to undermine Wilson with Allied leaders see ibid., 38–43. The essay on early foreign policy ventures is Duval, "We Have a President for a Reason."

18. One small exception has already occurred, an exchange between Michael Kazin and myself in the *New Republic* in July 2014 about whether we should have entered the war.

19. Heaton, *Cobb of "The World,"* 268–270. There has been an academic dispute about whether Wilson really said these things to Cobb. On that dispute, see Cooper, *Breaking the Heart of the World*, 642n51. One thing I did not point out in that note is that the book containing Cobb's recollection was published while Wilson was still living and presumably in a position to repudiate it if it was inaccurate.

20. Wilson speech, April 2, 1917, in Link, *The Papers of Woodrow Wilson*, vol. 41, 527.

21. A published version of that talk, which does not include the comment about Republican presidents, is "Making a Case for Wilson," in Cooper, *Reconsidering Woodrow Wilson*, 9–23.

22. Entry, May 10, 1915, Diary of Charles L. Swem, in Link, *The Papers of Woodrow Wilson*, vol. 33, 138.

23. I develop this line of thinking most recently in Cooper, *Breaking the Heart of the World*, 387–388.

PART 2

The United States

A Society Intervenes

4

Blinking Eyes Began to Open

Legacies from America's Road to the Great War,
1914–1917

Michael S. Neiberg

Two artifacts recently on display at the New-York Historical Society highlight the importance of the issue of ethnicity and assimilation in a time of war. One, a photograph taken in the days following the September 11, 2001, attacks, showed a sign that read "Arab-Americans Are Fellow Americans." The other, in a temporary exhibit on the Chinese-American experience, highlighted the mid-1950s comic book *Yellow Claw* in which a Chinese-American FBI agent named Jimmy Woo helps to uncover a plot by Chinese communists to invade Taiwan and the United States. Together these exhibits highlighted the nature of shared identity in a pluralistic society, especially in times of war and heightened international tensions.[1] These pressures, of course, are nothing new. America's road to the First World War offers a lens through which to see the tensions and ambiguities of a nation of diverse people with transnational linkages to the theaters of war.

American notions of ethnicity and the First World War all too often center on silliness like dachshunds being renamed "liberty puppies" and sauerkraut being called "liberty cabbage." Such simple images obscure the fascinating and complex relationship between the American people, their government, and the war in Europe prior to American entry.[2] Because of these links, the American people could not remain impartial to what was happening across the Atlantic. Despite President Wilson's call on August 19, 1914, for his countrymen to remain "neutral in fact, as well as in name," Americans had a definite sense of why they thought the war had begun.[3] From the very first days, the American people saw the war as a direct product of the autocratic and undemocratic nature of the imperial German state. Americans did not want to see their nation enter what they still saw as a European war; many in the Irish and German communities harbored serious doubts about the Allies as well. As a nation, however, Americans pointed the finger of blame for this great catastrophe squarely at Kaiser Wilhelm and his regime. As the popular war correspondent Frederick Palmer wrote in the war's early weeks, the blame for the war fell on the "goose-stepping, alert sprout of German militarism," which had animated the German people since unification in 1871.

Palmer and his fellow Americans drew sharp distinctions between the Prussians and the remainder of Germany. The Prussians had put "the spirit of the Middle Ages in [German] hearts," while the efficiency of Prussian methods meant that the new German militarism could be "organized for victory by every modern method."[4] Americans also understood the difference between Germans (or Prussians) in Europe and German-Americans. The Harvard historian William Roscoe Thayer, who wrote increasingly vicious screeds against the German government in 1914 and 1915, took great pains to separate Germans in Europe from those Americans of German ancestry living in the United States. "When the show-down comes," he wrote in a book published in March 1916, "there will be a tragic surprise for those who have been banking on the disloyalty of any large number of persons in the United States."[5]

German-Americans, of course, formed one of the largest ethnic groups in the country. They proved the success of the American model of assimilation. Nevertheless, Americans, including those of German descent, had ambivalent attitudes toward Germany in 1914. On the one hand, the American people admired German education, culture, and industry. On the other hand, they despised the autocratic and militaristic foundations of the Hohenzollern dynasty. In the years before the war, the *New York Evening Post*'s Oswald Villard, himself born in Wiesbaden, had helped to popularize the idea of the Two Germanys: one, the "imperial and military" Prussian state, ruled with a mailed fist over the other, a humanistic and democratic German nation. "America has much in common with the great German nation," Villard wrote in September 1914, "but has little in common with the military caste and the imperial attitude" of the martial state.[6] A year and a half later, Thayer described non-Prussian Germans as "not a race of fighters, but thinkers, scholars, visionaries, fed on pig meat and beer, docile peasants and masterful musicians. . . . Not until the Prussian will energized them did the non-Prussians loom up as Moloch worshipers, thirsting for world empire."[7]

Just a few months before the outbreak of the war, a stormy political crisis in the Alsatian garrison town of Zabern (Saverne) highlighted the perception of two Germanys in conflict with each other. An aristocratic nineteen-year-old

Prussian lieutenant had publicly insulted both the Alsatians and the French in the town, and had then promised his soldiers ten marks for each local they shot should disturbances result from his remarks. Instead of punishing the lieutenant for his adolescent stupidity, the German army fully supported him, leading to a major political crisis inside Germany over the source of ultimate authority in modern Germany. "The Zabern affair" resulted in the only vote of no confidence in the history of the Second Reich when socialists and delegates from the non-Prussian states allied in the Reichstag to support the civil government in Alsace and the rights guaranteed to it under the German constitution. Eventually, the Kaiser himself stepped in, transferring the offending garrison out of Zabern, but giving out only minor punishments to the officials who had so badly mismanaged the crisis.[8]

American newspapers followed the crisis carefully and offered devastating critiques of the German system. They saw the Zabern incident as an example of the militarist and absolutist nature of the Kaiser's regime that placed Germany in the same reactionary family as Austria-Hungary, Japan, and Russia. Americans hoped that the Zabern incident might lead to the development of real representative government so that Germany might one day join Britain, France, and the United States in the camp of modern democracies. Only then would the German people have the liberty to develop their full, peaceful qualities for the greater good of world civilization.

Most importantly for the war that began shortly after, the Zabern incident helped to condition American attitudes about the two Germanys. Americans saw the essentially good and decent German people as victims of their own government, and the excessive militarism of the regime as a product of its backward system of autocracy.[9] Even many German immigrants to the United States, especially Catholics and socialists, shared this viewpoint. The problem Americans saw in Germany had nothing to do with the German people, but with the "blood and iron tonic" that their leaders fed them in lieu of giving them a democratic system of governance.[10]

Whatever their president later said, Americans did not respond to the start of the war in Europe with entirely neutral eyes. Wilson, of course, shared many of these same views. Americans from Pennsylvania Avenue to Main Street tended to see France and Britain as the defenders (flawed though they may themselves have been) of a democratic order, and Belgium as the completely innocent victim of naked German aggression of the worst kind. *Life* magazine noted in late August 1914 that "the English, French, and Russians are fighting in this war in [sic] behalf of the liberties of the world," while "Germany and Austria are seeking to impose on the world a despotic authority to which it would be ruinous to yield."[11] As Newton Baker, the future American secretary

of war, wrote about the spirit of his country in 1914, Americans had "a very definite conception of the German theory of life and generally disapproved of it."[12]

These prewar attitudes conditioned American responses to the outbreak of
the war itself. We should be careful about attributing too much of the American
response to the war's outbreak to British propaganda and the lurid tales coming out of Belgium. Although there is no way to gauge with any accuracy
how Americans read the news coming from Europe, the evidence suggests
that most Americans expressed a healthy cynicism about atrocity stories. *Life*
magazine simply did not report them. The celebrity journalist Irvin Cobb, who
reported from Europe on a number of German violations of the rules of war,
nevertheless told his readers that "a dozen seasoned journalists, both English
and American," agreed with him that no proof existed to sustain the most sensational charges leveled against the Germans, such as the murder of priests,
the killing of children, and the systematic rape of Belgian women. "We need
not look for individual atrocities," he told his readers. "Belgium herself is the
capsheaf atrocity of this war."[13] Similarly, the famous mystery writer turned war
correspondent Mary Roberts Rinehart reported in great detail about the horrors
of war in Belgium, but she, too, told her readers not to believe the atrocity tales
then swirling in the American media. The Germans, she wrote, in a reflection
of the Two Germanys concept, were "not butchers or fiends, but victims of a
system against which some day they would rise and rebel."[14]

Germany's behavior in the war's opening months led Americans to sym-
pathize further with Britain, France, and Belgium, the states they saw as
standing up to German militarism. Cobb, Rinehart, Palmer, and other war
correspondents warned against lurid propaganda in part to keep the focus on
the German atrocities that reporters could confirm. Enough evidence existed
of real crimes committed by the Germans in Belgium to lead even the mili-
tantly neutral William Jennings Bryan to call German behavior in Antwerp
"an outrage against humanity." From London, Ambassador Walter Hines Page
wrote to President Wilson to tell him that "the horror of the thing outruns all
imagination."[15] Cobb, Rinehart, and Richard Harding Davis, all well known to
American newspaper readers, quickly abandoned their neutrality and became
vocally pro-Allied in response to what they saw in Europe.

Lacking scientific opinion polls, we cannot know for sure what percentage
of Americans shared their views, but the anecdotal evidence powerfully suggests a pro-Allied bias from the start. From Washington, British Ambassador Sir
Cecil Spring-Rice wrote to a friend in November 1914 that "the larger part of the
American people are with us or rather against our enemies, not from our merits but owing to the demerits of the antagonist. Their deeds are mightier than
their words." In another letter written at the same time, Spring-Rice estimated

that 90 percent of America's English speakers and even 50 percent of its Irish population were pro-Allied and that German propaganda had backfired in America because of the outrage Americans felt toward German activities in the war to date.[16] One survey of 350 American newspapers done in November 1914 showed that 46 percent expressed pro-Allied sentiments, while just 5 percent (most of them German-language) sympathized with the Germans. The rest remained neutral, although they often expressed their concern for the victims of war in France and Belgium.[17] Even one of Germany's most eloquent defenders, the Danzig-born Harvard professor Hugo Münsterberg, bemoaned "the almost universal hope in America that Germany will be thoroughly chastised for her ruler's monstrous crimes against the peace of the world."[18]

Nevertheless, Americans did not press for their nation to become directly involved in the war. The muckraking journalist Ray Stannard Baker, a man with deep suspicions about what he called Germany's "momentous conception of the totalitarian state," later noted with some amazement that in 1914 "we went on being happy."[19] For the first few months of the war, American leaders counted on the Atlantic Ocean and President Wilson's statement of neutrality to safeguard their nation's interests. They hoped to pursue a benevolent neutrality that could both allow the United States to serve as an arbiter of good faith between the warring powers, and allow the United States to trade freely—or, less euphemistically, to make money from the war. After a period of economic crisis in the summer when European trade suddenly stopped, the American economy rebounded on the strength of war orders for everything from steel and copper to beef and cotton.

Both circumstance and sympathy led American neutrality to, in the words of the time, speak with a British accent. The differences in the British surface and German submarine blockades are well known, but they do not represent the entire story. Simply put, the United States needed the acquiescence of the British Empire. The American merchant fleet in 1914 carried less than 10 percent of American overseas trade. Efforts to solve the problem in the years before the war had foundered on partisan differences in Congress. As a result, American firms relied on British shipping to deliver more than half of their overseas trade. Thus, although the United States had disagreements with British blockade policy, especially the items the British put on their contraband lists, both sides had a shared interest in keeping the trade between them open.[20] The United States needed Great Britain to maintain the global commons of the open seas even if British contraband policy created occasional conflicts with America's stated policy of neutrality.[21]

The sinking of the *Lusitania* in May 1915 clearly showed the limits of American policy and opened a new phase of American interaction with the

AMERICAN VICTIM OF "LUSITANIA"

FIGURE 4.1 The German sinking of the *Lusitania* stunned Americans of all backgrounds. It also forced Americans to begin to address the thorny question of how the nation should respond. Library of Congress, LC-USZ62-84435.

expanding World War (Figure 4.1). The *Lusitania* incident demonstrated that neither the nation's own self-proclaimed, and self-interested, neutrality nor distance could keep the United States from the direct effects of the war. As Nelson Lloyd noted in 1919, because of the *Lusitania*, "blinking eyes began to open."[22] Ray Stannard Baker wrote that after the *Lusitania* the war began to threaten "everything I had been interested in," and future Secretary of War Newton Baker noted that the sinking "plumbed our national conscience with the first realization that the World War might be our war."[23]

Americans from all ethnicities were outraged by the *Lusitania*. Former president Theodore Roosevelt led a group that called for war. Few wanted to go that far. At the other end of the spectrum from Roosevelt, Secretary of State William Jennings Bryan resigned over what he saw as the harsh tone of President Wilson's notes to Germany and even the relatively slim risk of war that the notes might produce. The vast majority of Americans found themselves somewhere between the two. The *Lusitania* undoubtedly made Americans angrier at the Germans. Charitable contributions to Germany, already far lower than those to the Allies, dropped significantly and Americans previously professing neutrality turned anti-German. Shortly after the incident, Robert Lansing, who replaced Bryan as secretary of state, wrote in a memorandum to himself,

I have come to the conclusion that the German Government is utterly
hostile to all nations with democratic institutions because those who
compose it see in democracy a menace to absolutism and the defeat
of the German ambition for world domination. Everywhere German
agents are plotting and intriguing to accomplish the supreme
purpose of their government. . . . [D]emocracy throughout the world
is threatened.[24]

Not all Americans went as far as Lansing did, but attitudes toward Germany
had clearly changed.

The sinking of the *Lusitania* did not make Americans want to become
directly involved in the war; it did, however, awaken them to the need to take
more concrete steps either to protect their interests short of war or prepare
themselves for a war against either Germany or Mexico, where events seemed
just as unstable. The recent opening of the Panama Canal increased American
anxiety and fear, as the canal suddenly seemed vulnerable to hostile action.
The United States sent troops to Nicaragua and Haiti in part to quell pro-
German sentiment in those countries, and Wilson considered sending troops
to Colombia as well.

Secretary of the Interior Franklin Lane, whose tone had been neutral
before the *Lusitania*, wrote to a friend in July 1915 that he had grown tired of the
"damned goose-stepping Army officers in Germany" who would "spit upon the
American flag." The United States had, he noted, "talked Princetonian English
to a water front bully," a reference to Wilson's diplomatic notes. That approach
had failed, leading Lane to support a drastic change in policy. "We must all
learn," he wrote, "that sacrifices are necessary if we are to have a country."[25]

The country had come to agree with Lane, and Americans began a lengthy
debate after the sinking of the *Lusitania* about the best ways to prepare for those
sacrifices. As it turned out, that debate lasted two years, revealing much about
American society in the process. Most famously, Theodore Roosevelt, Gen.
Leonard Wood, and others supported a movement to train young men in the
basics of officership at voluntary summer camps. The first so-called Plattsburg
camps opened in the summer of 1915, just after the uneasy diplomatic resolution of the *Lusitania* crisis. Roosevelt and his allies, most of them native-
born Americans from the eastern elite, saw the camps as a necessary response
of private citizens to fill a need that the government had shown insufficient
interest in filling itself. More moderate voices saw the movement as a pathway
between the Scylla of mass conscription and the Charybdis of a head-in-the-
sand neutrality.

The Wilson administration reacted coolly to the Plattsburg camps, but the president did take steps of his own. He announced in late 1915 that he intended to seek major increases in both the navy and the army. The enormous navy bill he supported called for the construction of ten battleships, ten heavy cruisers, fifty destroyers, and the recruitment of the sailors to man them.[26] On land, Secretary of War Lindley Garrison backed a plan to introduce Universal Military Training (UMT) and vastly increase the size of the national army to 140,000 men on active duty and another 400,000 more in a federal reserve. UMT remained a controversial and generally unpopular idea. So, too, did the idea of increasing the national army at the expense of the state National Guard units. Governors and those suspicious of increasing the authority of the federal government argued for increasing the size of the National Guard instead. Professional soldiers bristled at that idea because the National Guard did not answer to the president but to forty-eight individual governors. It also had a reputation for political infighting and generally lower quality.

In the end, Garrison's Continental Army Plan proved too much for Wilson to support, even though Garrison himself bemoaned how much he had watered it down for political reasons. Instead Wilson signed the 1916 National Defense Act that kept power centered in the National Guard.[27] The act authorized the National Guard to grow from 100,000 men to a theoretical maximum of 400,000 men, although few people expected it to get anywhere near that number. The Guard also received precious federal defense dollars to standardize its training and equipment. In exchange, it became subject to federalization in the case of a national emergency.

The act marked a victory for local officials over the desires of the army. Garrison and Assistant Secretary of War Henry Breckenridge both resigned when they heard about Wilson's decision to support it instead of their plan. They saw the National Guard model as vastly inadequate, and both had grown "unable to stomach Presidential pacifism" in the face of the growing national crisis.[28] Wilson chose as Garrison's replacement the reformist mayor of Cleveland and opponent of UMT, Newton D. Baker. The choice appalled professionals who saw Baker as a "pacifist of the capital P group."[29] Baker himself had come to the conclusion that peace, while precious, was not in and of itself a means. Peace, he had determined by 1916, needed to be backed up by military might as the only way to keep America out of a horrid war.[30]

Baker, like most of his fellow Americans, continued to advocate neutrality in 1916 but they saw how much more precarious that neutrality became with each passing month. Wilson himself told Secretary of Navy Josephus Daniels, another self-described pacifist, that "I can't keep the country out of war. . . . Any little German lieutenant can put us into the war at any time by some calculated outrage."³¹ If one did, American senior officials understood all too well, the nation stood in no position to defend its interests or itself.

Increasing uncertainty in Mexico added fuel to the fire. Intelligence, unsubstantiated but growing in volume, suggested that German agents in Mexico were trying to stir up trouble for the United States. Maud Hawkes, an American living in Mexico whom Pancho Villa had kidnapped then released, told reporters that Villa had bragged about the support he had received from both Germany and Japan. Secretary of State Robert Lansing and American Ambassador to Germany James Gerard both believed in the existence of an anti-American plot between Villa and the German government.³²

Fears of a growing Japan added to this environment of concern, if not quite paranoia. Just before Villa's infamous raid on Columbus, New Mexico, *Chicago Tribune* reporter Floyd Gibbons wrote about Japanese interests in building a naval base on Cedros Island off the coast of Baja California. Gibbons chartered a fishing boat to see the island for himself and reported having seen evidence of Japanese efforts to fortify it, although he saw no Japanese personnel there.³³ With Germany, Mexico, and Japan all becoming a problem, Americans had begun to worry about a tripartite alliance aimed at encircling them. *Life*'s cover for February 10, 1916, featured a new map of the United States: California, Oregon, and Washington appeared as "Japonica"; Florida as "Turconia"; a rump New Mexico as the "American Reservation"; and the rest of the country as "New Prussia," complete with renamed places such as New Berlin (Washington), Hindenburg (Cincinnati), and the Von Tirpitz (Atlantic) Ocean. To the north, the map labeled Canada "Barbarians," a reference not to the Canadians themselves, but to the Germans who might seize it (as well as Britain's Caribbean possessions) as spoils of war.

With a small military in no position to take the lead in defending the nation from such global plots, the United States government took nonmilitary steps to secure the nation's interests. The State Department, concerned about the safety of the Panama Canal, revived a scheme to purchase the Danish West Indies. American officials had grown concerned that Germany might invade Denmark and take the islands or demand their cession as the price of not invading. From there, the State Department feared, the Germans could build a naval base that might threaten the canal from the Caribbean side while the Japanese threatened it from the Pacific side. The Danes had resisted American offers in the past, but in 1916 they grew anxious to remove a potential source of trouble with the German government. In August, therefore, the Danish West Indies became the US Virgin Islands. William Jennings Bryan also floated a plan to buy Canada, but he received a notably frostier reception from the British than Lansing had from the Danes.³⁴

In October 1916, as European armies engaged in the frustrating battles of Verdun and the Somme, President Wilson confided to a friend that the era of American neutrality had ended.[35] America, he now fully believed, had to take a more active role to enforce peace among the belligerents of a war that seemed to have no end and no purpose. Wilson also argued that the nation had to begin to make preparations to defend itself. He spoke in favor of the Navy Bill and preparedness more generally at lectures nationwide. The Navy Bill faced far less controversy than Garrison's army plan had because the administration could more easily defend a naval bill as defensive in nature and a naval bill of the size Wilson supported would mean thousands of jobs in dozens of congressional districts. Much to the surprise of observers of past congressional parsimony, Congress voted $313,000,000 to build modern destroyers and battleships. Around the same time, Wilson kicked off his reelection campaign at, notably enough, a Preparedness parade. Clearly, the national mood had changed.

Even amid this new mania for greater Preparedness, few Americans sought war. Neither Wilson nor his Republican challenger in the 1916 election, Charles Evans Hughes, campaigned on a platform of direct involvement in the war. Wilson, of course, famously used the slogan "He Kept Us Out of War," and his campaign often tried to frighten Americans by hinting that the bellicose Theodore Roosevelt would gain a position of prominence in a Hughes administration, perhaps as secretary of state or war.

Tensions rose significantly in the wake of another sinking, that of the *Sussex*, an English Channel ferry, in March 1916. Of the eighty Americans on board, four sustained injuries. Some Americans demanded war or at least a breaking of diplomatic relations. The *Sussex* sinking seemed to show Americans both that the Germans had embarked on a new policy of submarine warfare and that the time for diplomacy had ended. Secretary of the Interior Lane wrote to Frank Cobb of the New York *World*, "The situation here is tense.... I am getting tired of having the Kaiser and [Mexican President] Carranza vent their impudence at our expense, because they know we do not want to go to war and because they want to keep their own people in line."[36] Even Senator William Borah of Idaho, a noted isolationist, wrote after the sinking of the *Sussex*, "I am not afraid of war if it is necessary to protect American rights."[37]

By the end of 1916, moreover, Catholic and Jewish Americans had come to see the war in terms that looked more like those of Protestant Americans than had been the case two years prior. Historians have focused on the nasty and vituperative "anti-hyphen" and "100% Americanism" campaigns that both Republicans and Democrats used to besmirch the loyalty of America's ethnic minorities. One Yale graduate and self-described social Darwinist, for example, decried "the people of mixed blood" for undermining the sacred principles of "historic America" built on the "best of England, and freshened by the soul of France."[38]

Such Nativist campaigns, however, were both misinformed and unnecessary. By late 1916, Catholic and Jewish Americans had developed their own reasons for coming to support the Allied cause independent of the 100% Americanism campaigns.[39] The war thus catalyzed the processes of assimilation; in each case and for distinct reasons, part of that process of accelerated assimilation involved an increased identification with the Allied cause. External pressures to show "Americanism" by supporting the Allies surely existed, but internal pressures from the communities themselves exerted a greater force than historians have heretofore recognized. A brief sketch of three large groups will illustrate the pattern.

Italian-Americans reacted to the war with indifference in 1914. That indifference changed, however, when Italy joined the war on the Allied side in the spring of 1915. Thereafter, Italian-Americans had relatives fighting on the Allied side; more than 65,000 Italians living in the United States returned to Italy to fight for the country of their birth. Because immigration from Italy to the United States slowed to a trickle during the war, Italian immigrant aid societies redefined their mission. From 1915 to 1917 they stopped performing their original mission of helping new arrivals adjust to the United States. Instead they helped Italians in the United States get back home to fight for their motherland.[40] Thus by the start of 1917 Italian-Americans, indifferent to the war in 1914, may have been even more pro-Allied than most of their fellow Americans.

American Jews (with the exception of some socialists) hoped in 1914 for a German victory in order to destroy the notoriously anti-Semitic Russian regime. By 1917, however, the British and French governments had both issued public statements of support for Zionism, and life for Jews under German rule seemed only marginally better than life under the Russians.[41] By the time of American entry into the war, Jews had undergone a complete transformation. The Tsarist regime they so despised lay in tatters, and American Jews (now including the socialists) hoped that Alexander Kerensky's provisional government would lead to equality of treatment for those Jews still in Russia.

Irish-Americans present the most complex case, but the pattern is broadly similar. Intensely anti-English, and therefore mostly anti-Allied, in 1914, Irish-Americans, with the exception of the most radical Irish Republicans, also came to support the Allied cause by 1917. German wartime treatment of Catholic Belgium and Poland made the German model look no better, and quite possibly much worse, than the proposed English Home Rule model. More important, the outbreak of the Easter Rising in Dublin in 1916 made most Irish-Americans

FIGURE 4.2 A political cartoon alleging German involvement in the Easter Rising in Dublin. Irish-Americans were sensitive to charges that the behavior of rebels in Ireland itself put their loyalty to the United States under scrutiny. Library of Congress, LC-USZ62-84113.

sensitive to accusations that much of the money and planning for the Rising had come from Irishmen in America (see Figure 4.2). Mainstream Irish-American leaders rushed to pledge their loyalty not just to America, but to the democratic ideals for which the British and French had pledged to fight. Tens of thousands of Irishmen were, of course, among those British soldiers fighting and dying ostensibly for those same ideals.[42]

These transformations occurred as the international picture grew more menacing for Americans. In the first few weeks of 1917, American officials became increasingly alarmed at the rumors and hard news coming from Germany. The Germans, no longer as sure of their final victory, were contemplating a harsher line, even at the risk of war with the Americans. In early February, rumors began to spread around the Washington diplomatic corps that the German embassy had in its possession a declaration of German intention to resume unrestricted submarine warfare (USW). If true, the rumor not only proved to American officials the insincerity of the *Sussex* pledge on which the United States had staked German-American relations, but also confirmed the base dishonesty of the German government.

The rumors contributed greatly to the growing sense of unease in Washington. If the Germans did resume USW, the United States would have no choice but to cut diplomatic ties with Germany at the very least and probably declare war. To do otherwise, Newton Baker believed, would give "Germany a license to kill all Americans in the future."[43] The news especially surprised American leaders because the German ambassador had promised Wilson just ten days earlier that his government envisioned no resumption of USW.[44]

Thereafter, events happened at a rapid pace. Congress took up debate on a bill to arm merchant ships, a step that the German government announced it would treat as an act of war. The publication of the Zimmermann Telegram on March 1 rekindled fears of a German, Mexican, and Japanese alliance aimed at encircling the United States and taking some of its territory. Although most officials had already decided on war by the time of the telegram's publication, it confirmed in their minds the wisdom of their choice. It also stirred up the anger of the American people, especially in the south and west where sentiment had been more isolationist.

Three important legacies emerge from these events for American foreign policy and America more generally. First, we can see the birth of the distinctly American conception of declaring war upon governments, not people. Wilson made this point crystal clear in his declaration of war address to Congress.[45] The modern origins of this idea lie in the Two Germanys concept that Villard and many others posited. That concept had the additional virtue of separating the vile actions of the German government from the millions of ethnic Germans living in the United States itself. Living freely under American democracy, not imperial German autocracy, they would see the world largely as their fellow Americans did—or so the theory posited—and thus the vast majority of German-Americans would pose no threat. In part because they so deeply admired the contributions of German-Americans, the American people sought to fight the German government, not the German people. This war would have the effect of liberating the decent German people from their own tyrannical government and return Germany to its rightful place among the nations of the world. Thus, according to Otto Kahn, a German-American banker, Germany could return to "the ideals of Luther, Goethe, Schiller, Kant, and a host of others who had made the name of Germany great and beloved until fanatical Prussianism, run amok, came to make its deeds a byword and a hissing."[46] Born out of the circumstances of 1914–1917, the ideal of war against government not peoples has had a long legacy, as witnessed most recently in the rhetoric of American leaders about the goals of the wars in Iraq and Afghanistan.

Second, the long, two-year period of debate about preparedness that occurred between the sinking of the *Lusitania* and American belligerence led Americans to become involved in foreign and military policy in ways they had never done previously. From 1915 to 1917 the American people debated, voted, and discussed. They were not reacting to a single, sharp event as in 1898 or 2001; they were instead watching their nation enter the global arena in unprecedented ways before their very eyes.

Lastly, for reasons having little to do with coercion or propaganda, the goals of most Catholic and Jewish Americans came to overlap with those of Protestant Americans. Like the person holding the "Arab-Americans Are Fellow Americans" sign and comic book hero Jimmy Woo, Americans of diverse backgrounds from 1914 to 1917 identified with the United States and placed the interests and needs of America first. This process furthered both the development of what Kevin Schultz has called a "tri-faith America" and a rough American consensus on foreign policy that broadly held until the 1960s.[47] The former had enormous implications for American society more generally; the latter did not erase disagreements on foreign policy, but it did mean that those disagreements would no longer be based in ethnicity or religion.

As we approach the centenary of American entry into the First World War, we need new research into the entire period from 1914 to 1917. Only then can we understand the journey of Americans like Mississippi Senator John Sharp Williams, a self-proclaimed "peace fanatic" who had opposed war until February 1917. He had concluded by then, however, that "there are some things in this world that men must fight for. War is idiocy when it is not insanity." Nevertheless he accepted the need for it in 1917 in order to prevent "widowing the women, orphaning the children, destroying the churches and the universities, making to crumble in one short year the accumulations of mankind for a hundred years."[48] His journey mirrored that of many of his countrymen. It is time to replace the simple answers with more nuanced and sophisticated ones that will give us better clarity on American entry into what Williams called the War to Stop War.

NOTES

The views expressed herein are those of the author, not those of the US Army War College, the United States Army, or the Department of Defense. My forthcoming book will deal with these issues in much greater detail than space permits here.

1. New-York Historical Society, "Chinese-American: Inclusion/Exclusion" exhibit, seen March 11, 2015.

2. These changes in nomenclature have as little to do with the history of the First World War as french fries being renamed freedom fries has to do with the history of the war in Iraq.

3. http://wwi.lib.byu.edu/index.php/President_Wilson's_Declaration_of_Neutrality.

4. Palmer, *My Year of the Great War*, 87, 90.

5. Thayer, *Germany vs. Civilization*, 192.

6. *Review of Reviews*, vol. L, no. 3 (September 1914), 265.

7. Thayer, *Germany vs. Civilization*, 21–22.

8. The lieutenant himself got off with a slap on the wrist. He died on the Eastern Front in 1915.

9. Michael Neiberg, "L'Affaire de Savern vue des États-Unis," presented at L'Affaire de Saverne Conference, Saverne, France, February 5–7, 2014.

10. *Life*, August 20, 1914, 300.

11. *Life*, August 27, 1914, 344.

12. Baker, *Why We Went to War*, 20. In 1920, German Ambassador to the United States Johann von Bernstorff noted that negative American attitudes toward the German imperial system doomed efforts by German propagandists to present the German side of the story.

13. Cobb, *Paths of Glory*, 375.

14. Rinehart, *My Story*, 161.

15. Doenecke, *Nothing Less Than War*, 28, 32.

16. Baker, *Why We Went to War*, 34, 36.

17. Doenecke, *Nothing Less Than War*, 20.

18. Münsterberg, *The War and America*, 110.

19. Baker, *American Chronicle*, 298.

20. Floyd, *Abandoning Neutrality*, 19.

21. See Lambert, *Planning Armageddon*.

22. Lloyd, *How We Went to War*, 5.

23. Baker, *American Chronicle*, 298; Palmer, *Newton D. Baker*, 41.

24. Lansing, *War Memoirs of Robert Lansing*, 19.

25. Lane and Wall, *The Letters of Franklin K. Lane*, 175–176.

26. Moore, *America and the World War*, 46.

27. The National Defense Act lifted the legal limit of 102,000 soldiers, authorizing the army to grow to as many as 175,000, but it did not provide the resources for recruiting or training them.

28. Palmer, *Newton D. Baker*, 6.

29. Palmer, *Bliss, Peacemaker*, 111.

30. Cramer, *Newton D. Baker*, 86.

31. Ibid., 88.

32. Boghardt, "Chasing Ghosts in Mexico," 11–15.

33. Gibbons and Gibbons, *Floyd Gibbons, Your Headline Hunter*, 59.

34. Lansing, *War Memoirs of Robert Lansing*, 20.

35. Paxson, *American Democracy and the World War*, 261.

36. Lane and Wall, *The Letters of Franklin K. Lane*, 207.

37. Johnson, *Borah of Idaho*, 199.

38. Gleason, *Our Part in the Great War*, 6–8.

39. Space unfortunately forbids a discussion of the German-American story. I also apologize for painting these large, diverse communities with such broad brushstrokes.

40. Bencivenni, *Italian Immigrant Radical Culture*, 83; Iorizzo and Mondello, *The Italian-Americans*, 132.

41. Laskin, *The Long Way Home*, 91.

42. See Campbell, *Ireland's New Worlds*; Cuddy, "Irish-Americans and the 1916 Election," 228–243.

43. Baker, *Why We Went to War*, 93.

44. Lane and Wall, *The Letters of Franklin K. Lane*, 233.

45. http://wwi.lib.byu.edu/index.php/Wilson's_War_Message_to_Congress.

46. Kahn, "Americans of German Origin and the War," 7.

47. Schultz, *Tri-Faith America*. My thanks to Andrew Preston for his discussion with me about this book. If my argument here is correct, then the process Schultz identified must have powerful antecedents in the 1914–1917 period.

48. Williams, "War to Stop War."

5

Ambivalent Ally

*American Military Intervention
and the Legacy of World War I*

Michael Adas

The year 1917 was very bad for the unwieldy coalition of nation-empires that had somehow managed to fight the powerful military forces of the German Empire to a stalemate for three and a half years. The February Revolution and the fall of the Tsarist regime in the east were followed in April and May by the failure of the much-heralded Nivelle offensive on the Western Front. The disarray of the French armies was soon overshadowed by the disintegration of Russian allied forces following the Austro-German rout of the hastily assembled units sent into battle by Kerensky's Provisional Government in the summer of 1917. Led by Richthofen's "flying circus," the Germans had also regained air superiority on the Western Front and launched Gotha bombing raids against London in the months before the British plunged in mid-summer into the Third Battle of Ypres. By late October the ill-fated operation had bogged down in the rain and mud of Flanders. Months later it finally ground to a halt, but only after hundreds of thousands of additional casualties had been added to the Allied toll. French and British reverses were soon compounded by yet another botched operation by the Italians on the Isonzo front. The Bolshevik seizure of power in Petrograd in October effectively finished Russia as a major combatant and soon made it possible for the Germans to redeploy over a million troops to the Western Front (Figure 5.1).

Despite these demoralizing reverses, there were systemic and strategic shifts in 1917 that made it possible for the leaders of a disarmingly reduced Allied coalition to keep alive hopes for ultimate victory.

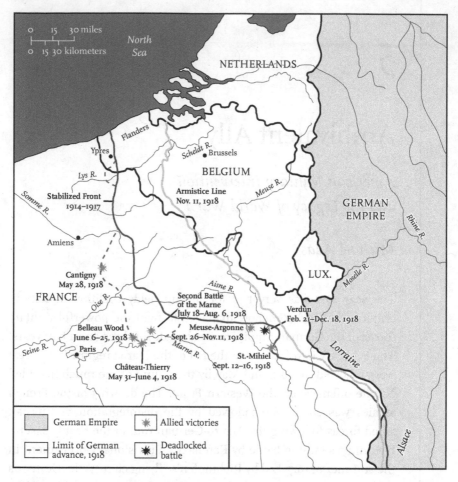

FIGURE 5.1 The Western Front: US participation, 1918.

In Georges Clemenceau and David Lloyd George, the French and British had finally found steady, determined prime ministers willing to check their generals' lethal excesses and able to oversee wartime economies that were actually accelerating munitions production while managing to maintain broad support on the home front for the war. In terms of weaponry, the success of the massed tanks deployed at Cambrai amid the mounting losses of the ill-conceived Ypres offensives in November, marked a significant shift in the war. Not only had the Allies achieved a major advance in offensive weaponry, but the Germans, who were already stretched almost to the limit just manufacturing enough shells, machine guns, and airplanes due to the very effective British blockade, could not begin to match Allied production of the new weapon. The stressed industrial sector was symptomatic of the German economy as a whole, which was riddled with food shortages, strikes, and growing mass protests on the part of a half-starved civilian population.¹ These internal disorders, as well as the stalemated conflict, provided the impetus for the German General Staff—dominated by Field Marshal Paul von Hindenburg and Erich Ludendorff—to effectively shut down what was left of civilian government and concentrate all power in a handful of military advisers favored by Kaiser Wilhelm II.

Ludendorff's growing influence within this closed circle meant that German diplomacy and military decision making were entrusted to an increasingly unstable Quarter-Master General who had no use for negotiations and possessed little aptitude for strategic thinking. These deficiencies were evident in his obsession with "break[ing] the power of mighty England"² at any cost and his utter failure to comprehend the ways in which drawing the United States into the conflict would alter fundamentally the balance among the powers engaged in the war and ultimately undo all of the gains Germany had made in 1917.³ Ludendorff, of course, was not alone in targeting the British and in disregarding American responses to the German decision at the end of January 1917 to resume unrestricted attacks on US ships and those of other neutral nations trading with Britain and France. Despite political divisions over the issue, the majority view among both military and civilian leaders with regard to the possibility that unrestricted submarine warfare might bring America into the war was perhaps best summarized by the Vice Admiral Eduard von Capelle, who declared during the Reichstag deliberations on the eve of the fateful decision that the effects of American entry into the war would have "zero" impact on the outcome of the conflict.⁴

The reasons for the seemingly foolhardy indifference on the part of German policymakers to American entry into the war were diverse and in some cases long-standing. A half century earlier, Prussian officers were among the contingent of European observers who were decidedly unimpressed with the performance of American soldiers and officers on both sides of the Civil War. Just before the outbreak of the Great War, German reporters and officers made similar assessments of the mobilization and conduct of American soldiers soon to be committed to a punitive expedition in Mexico.⁵ Most German leaders and very likely a clear majority of the German citizenry also felt that—given the prodigious support the United States had given the Reich's adversaries in terms of loans, food, raw materials, and manufactured goods—America was already in the war on the side of the Entente Allies. The German leadership was nearly unanimous in decrying Woodrow Wilson's claims of neutrality in view of his bellicose responses to German submarine warfare in contrast to his refusal to condemn the intrusive, even draconian, blockade the British had imposed on much of continental Europe from the first days of the conflict. Perhaps most critical in German calculations concerning American responses was the fact that the republic's standing army was minuscule compared to those of the major European powers. Hence, most informed German observers, and certainly Ludendorff and the General Staff, believed that the United States could not recruit, drill, and deliver significant armed forces before the war in Europe was decided—with Germany presumed to be the victor.

In the essay that follows I focus on four dimensions—each involving a different phase of the war—of the legacy of the German decisions that brought the United States into the stalemated conflict. The first is centered on the boost in morale America's entry into the war gave to the beleaguered Allies, first in the spring and then again in the summer of 1917. The second phase began a year later when US land and air forces—initially integrated into Allied divisions—became major combatants in operations first to turn back furious German offensives and by mid-summer in the counteroffensives that brought an end to the war in November 1918. My overview of the varying and increasingly contentious assessments of the effectiveness of the strategies and tactics adopted for American combat operations in the last year of the war owes much to the fine revisionist scholarship that has appeared in the past couple of decades. Strands of the third main theme are woven throughout the essay in dealing with issues that relate to the extent to which the overall support of the United States for the Allied cause—both in terms of military interventions and the provision of war materials—affected the outcomes of the war. Finally, I suggest ways in which discordant views of the offensives of the American Expeditionary Forces (AEF) informed postwar debates regarding organizational, logistical, and strategic approaches to future conflicts. I also argue that the long predominant perceptions of US interventions in the war as overwhelmingly successful reinforced assumptions of United States exceptionalism that were often linked to notions of Americans' superior aptitudes for technological innovation.

Although the decision to renew unrestricted submarine attacks on neutral shipping left Woodrow Wilson with little choice but to bring America into the conflict on the side of the Allies, Britain—not the United States—was the focus of German strategic thinking. Frustrated by the continuing stalemate on the Western Front, Ludendorff and most of the high command had been won over to the commercial warfare option by the detailed statistics generated by the *Admiralstab*. The estimates of past tonnage and carriers lost in the Atlantic crossing indicated that if the submarines were unleashed, they could force Great Britain out of the war within five or six months. In the spring and summer of 1917, the toll on merchant shipping to the British Isles soared alarmingly—reaching nearly three million tons lost by the end of August. By late summer, British government projections indicated that if the trend continued, the supply of some staple foods and essential materials for the war industries would run out within several weeks.[6] The navy's previous failure to come up with an effective deterrent to U-boat attacks on Atlantic shipping fed a growing sense that the war might be lost at sea, which had been Britain's mainstay for well over a century.

As the crisis deepened, Prime Minister David Lloyd George and other prominent political leaders as well as several courageous junior naval officers openly challenged the Commander in Chief of the Grand Fleet, Sir John Jellicoe, over his staunch opposition to the adoption of a convoy system to reduce the effectiveness of German submarine operations. The American entry into the war soon bolstered the efforts of those favoring the convoy solution to the sub-marine menace. Rear Admiral William Sims, who had been appointed the main naval envoy to Great Britain even before the United States was officially at war with Germany, had initially been skeptical about the efficacy of the convoy system. But he had begun to change his mind by the time he met with Jellicoe, who was an old friend, in London on April 10, 1917. Surprised by Jellicoe's pes-simism regarding a solution to the submarine menace and his fear that con-tinued shipping losses could drive Britain from the war, Sims became a strong advocate of the convoy option. Within days of his encounter with Jellicoe, Sims sent an urgent cable requesting the Secretary of the Navy to provide as soon as possible the "maximum number of destroyers [and] other anti-submarine craft" as were ready to join the British fleet.[7] By May a small flotilla of American destroyers was stationed in the British Isles. In the following months the con-voy system steadily reduced Allied shipping losses and increased the flow of vital foodstuffs and war materials, and more gradually troops, to Britain and the war zones in Belgium and northern France. By November, shipping losses were down by two-thirds of the 881,000 tons sunk in April, and by the last month of the war a year later they had been reduced to 1 percent of the total supplies crossing the Atlantic.[8]

Within months it was clear that Ludendorff's gamble that America's entry into the war would have little impact on the outcome of the conflict had back-fired. Not only had the German leadership as a whole underestimated the strength and reach of the American navy, they had completely failed to take into account its readiness to enter into combat. The timely arrival of America's destroyers, which along with large and small sub-chasers numbered over four hundred by the end of the war, proved critical to the success of the convoy system and the defeat of the submarine offensive.[9] Though often neglected or simply left out of narratives of American military participation in the war, the navy's operations were arguably one of the most decisive US contributions to Allied victory. They established the convoy system as the most potent antidote to submarine warfare, so much so that it would be adopted in a second global conflict two decades later without serious consideration of other options that new technologies made feasible.

In contrast to the rather immediate impact of the American engagement in the sea war, the potential for the United States to significantly affect the military stalemate on the Western Front remained marginal until well into the second year after its entry into the conflict. Although major reforms, including the much belated installation of a general staff and steps toward the integration of state militias into regular military units,[10] had been accomplished in the decade before April 1917, the American army was too small and poorly trained to engage the massive, modern armies of the European powers. Although "little wars" had been fought on the western frontier and in the Philippines, the Caribbean, and Mexico, American forces were mainly deployed for coastal defense or engaged in cavalry operations that had been rendered obsolete by the mechanized trench warfare in Flanders and northern France. The passage of the National Defense Act in June 1916 made it possible to double the size of the regular army to 250,000, but just over half of this increase had been accomplished by April 1917. Any assessment of America's mobilization, the capabilities of its officers, and the combat effectiveness of the soldiers and equipment sent to the Western Front must take into account the sheer magnitude of this undertaking. A rapidly augmented bureaucracy and military hierarchy had overseen the recruitment, training, and safe transport of nearly two million soldiers to European battlefields by the Armistice in November 1918—and another two million had been inducted.[11] But in the early summer of 1917 formidable challenges of coordinating newly created administrative departments, turning raw recruits into disciplined combatants, and providing logistical support for forces initially dispersed across the Western Front meant that the capacity to support the allies with significant numbers of battle-ready units was many months in the future (see Figure 5.2).

As both American and allied leaders realized, in the short term the major impact of the US entry into the land war would be psychological. The cheering crowds that greeted the arrival in Paris of the American Commander in Chief John Pershing and his substantial entourage of staff officers in June certainly confirmed that expectation. Perhaps no contemporary witness captured the impact on Allied morale that the arrival of American soldiers on the Western Front had as vividly as Vera Brittain, a British nurse serving in the hospitals behind the front lines in Flanders during the first German offensive on the Somme in March and April 1918. She recalled being unable to identify a passing troop of soldiers, who "looked larger than ordinary men; their tall straight figures ... in vivid contrast to the undersized armies of pale recruits to which we had grown accustomed." Learning from the shouts of the crowd that they

PUNCH, OR THE LONDON CHARIVARI.—April 10, 1918.

AMERICA TO THE FRONT.

[In view of the present needs of the Allies, America has not waited to complete the independent organisation of her Army, but
has sent her troops forward to be brigaded with British and French units.]

FIGURE 5.2 "America to the Front," *Punch*, April 10, 1918.

were Americans, she exulted: "So these were our deliverers at last, marching
up the road to Camiers in the spring sunshine! There seemed to be hundreds
of them, and in the fearless swagger of their proud strength they looked a formidable bulwark against the peril looming from Amiens."[12]

The enthusiasm displayed by French and British politicians and generals
in welcoming Pershing was tempered by their realization that he represented
the commitment of American troops still at the training stage rather than soldiers who could soon move into the trenches beside the beleaguered forces
of the Allied coalition. From the time of his arrival, disagreements between
French and British commanders and staff officers, on one hand, and Pershing
and his subordinates, on the other, with regard to the deployment of American

units proved a source of division and often acrimony within the newly con-
figured alliance. Pershing's determination personally to command separate
US forces once they went into battle was at odds with the urgent need for
reinforcements to replace British and French losses, which had soared in the
failed offensives of 1917. Pershing's personal inclinations were buttressed by
the explicit order of his superiors in the War Department that American forces
remain an independent force.[13] He assumed that this imperative was backed by
Woodrow Wilson in anticipation of the leverage the American army's decisive
contributions to Allied victory would give the president in shaping the postwar
settlement.[14] In view of the past performance of French and British commanders, particularly Sir Douglas Haig who doggedly persisted in launching failed
offensives in a war of attrition that had resulted in appalling levels of casualties
for little or no gain, Pershing had good reason to be wary of conceding control
over any of the soldiers under his command. But in the early months of 1918,
it was soon clear that if he did not relent, the war might be lost before most of
the American reinforcements could be deployed.

Having failed to force Britain out of the war through the resumption of
unrestricted submarine assaults, and having thereby brought America into
the conflict, it was apparent to Ludendorff, Hindenburg, and the German
General Staff as a whole that time was on the side of the Allies. Opportunities
for military stalemate and a negotiated peace, which could well have worked
to Germany's advantage, had been squandered. With America's abundant
resources and seemingly limitless reservoir of manpower thrown into the balance, going on the defensive behind the daunting fortifications the Germans
had built from Belgium across occupied northern France would lead to the
loss of the momentum gained in 1917 and likely result in eventual surrender.
Ludendorff's response to this predicament was to return to his obsession with
breaking Britain's power and forcing it from the war, but this time through
all-out offensives by Germany's more formidable armies. German commanders were confident that innovative tactics—including silent registration of
artillery and short bombardments followed by storm-trooper assaults on
select enemy positions, which had been first encountered in the offensives
led by General Alexei Brusilov on the Russian front in 1916 and improved
upon thereafter by Georg Bruchmüller and Oskar von Hutier—could break
the trench deadlock. Gambling yet again on an assault that would bring victory, German forces set out to destroy the British Third and Fifth armies
in late March 1918. When that massive assault failed despite unprecedented
early advances, Ludendorff's strategic shortcomings were again on display in
a series of costly offensives that finally petered out on August 8th, the "Black
Day" for the German army.[15]

During the months of crisis brought on by the German offensives, Pershing reluctantly agreed to attach American units to French and British divisions. From the Allies' perspective his resistance to what they perceived as an essential concession was frustrating at the very least in view of the fact that most of the US soldiers who arrived in France had received further training, specifically in trench warfare, directed by French and British officers. Pershing's insistence on an independent command and operations for American units also seemed perverse since US forces were dependent on British and French armaments—including airplanes, transport vehicles, tanks, and especially artillery, which had proved to be the most lethal weapon deployed in the conflict. It was also clear that the Americans did not have sufficient numbers of officers with enough training in mechanized trench warfare to effectively lead the units that Pershing balked at amalgamating with Allied forces.[16]

This perspective on Pershing's often-acclaimed resolve regarding the positioning of American forces on the Western Front underscores the importance of recent scholarship on the nature and impact of the United States' military interventions in the war. Until the last two or three decades or so, American historians mainly lionized Pershing and focused accounts of the conflict on what they depicted as highly successful offensives by courageous doughboys against the St.-Mihiel salient and German defenses in the Meuse-Argonne region in the last months of the war. But research in hitherto little-used archival sources has raised serious objections to these semimythic narratives. Not coincidentally they tend to mirror Pershing's uniformly upbeat, anodyne assessment of US operations in his report to the Secretary of War, delivered just a week after the Armistice was signed on November 11, 1918.[17] Detailed exploration of neglected contemporary sources, both those authored by European commanders and works by Pershing's subordinates, also foreground some of the enduring lessons learned by combat and line officers who later sought to apply them in the interwar decades and the Second World War.

With regard to Pershing's leadership and strategic vision, the rather different perspectives provided by sources beyond those that had long been standard suggest that US units that had *not yet* been brought into a unified American army under his command may well have made some of the most decisive contributions to the Allied victory in 1918. In the early battles in the spring and early summer of 1918, American units were led and fought best, judging by comparing casualties against the damage inflicted on the enemy, when they were integrated into larger contingents of British and Australian divisions. Although the objectives of the combat operations in which US forces were first deployed in late May were too limited to draw broader conclusions, the well-trained soldiers of the 28th Infantry advanced over relatively open terrain and captured Cantigny, the town at the center of the Allied assault, and held it against German counteroffensives. The Allies' spirits were lifted by the fact that the American forces were at last engaged in battle, and Pershing was of the opinion that the success of the attack confirmed his faith in his strategy of "open warfare." Upon reflection, however, American line officers—and Allied commanders—raised concerns regarding the heavy losses inflicted by the German machine guns and artillery on forces advancing over open ground. Those questions would be amplified by the aggressive and "successful" but highly lethal defense of key positions at Château-Thierry in June by American divisions facing renewed German offensives and the subsequent and the even more causality-laden capture of Belleau Wood.[18]

Perhaps the most successful Allied operation in which American forces played a significant role came in early July when they had the good fortune to join with Australian divisions under the command of Lieutenant-General John Monash in an offensive centered on the village of Le Hamel in the vicinity of Amiens near the Somme River. Though Monash had only assumed command of the Australian Army Corps in May, he had built a reputation as an able leader who was deeply committed to meticulous planning, thorough training, and optimizing the chances of survival of the soldiers under his command. He and his Canadian counterparts, and the soldiers from the British dominions that served under them, accounted in large measure for the ability of the British armies to both mount and survive the failed Allied offensives of 1916 and 1917 and the German onslaught in the spring of 1918. Of all of the generals who grappled with the complexities of highly mechanized warfare, Monash best understood the murderous futility of sending infantry "to expend itself upon heroic physical effort ... to wither away under merciless machine gun fire ... [and] tear itself to pieces in hostile entanglements."[19] In the counteroffensive on July 4th centered on Le Hamel, he directed an operation that melded together the artillery, machine guns, tanks, and air cover that he insisted must support the infantry in modern warfare. Provided with a leader of his caliber, the four American companies in his charge acquitted themselves valiantly. The combined US and Australian forces accomplished all of the objectives of the assault with remarkable speed. The battle was over in an hour and a half, and significantly the units deployed did not try to extend their advance beyond the positions targeted in planning the carefully coordinated assault.

In late September, the 27th and 30th divisions of the American II Corps, who were effectively on permanent loan to the British, had the distinction of being chosen to relieve the exhausted Australian Corps, who under Monash had spearheaded the breakthroughs in the Hindenburg line at the St. Quentin Canal. Although Monash readily accepted the offer of American troops, whose earlier exploits under his command he deemed "eminently satisfactory," the 27th and 30th had not yet been in battle and were to lead the assault on some of the most formidable of the German trench fortifications. Stiffer German resistance than expected, persisting fog, and ineffective tank support foiled the attempted breakthrough and led to higher casualty rates than in Monash's earlier operations. Nonetheless, the overall offensive put Allied forces across the Canal and through the German defenses.[20] Though not as well executed as the Le Hamel attack, Monash again demonstrated in the St. Quentin offensives that he had a good deal to teach the inexperienced American commanders, including Pershing (as well as the British and French), about overcoming the advantages of well-entrenched forces that had been demonstrated repeatedly on all fronts throughout the Great War. But Pershing had strategic plans and his own ideas about tactics, and he remained determined to command an independent force. As later AEF offensives were to demonstrate, US field officers actually directing combat divisions may have mastered Monash's superior approaches to offensive operations more ably than any of the allied generals or staff officers on the Western Front.

Yet another major German offensive—the last in the war—in mid-July against Rheims and that city's railway link to Paris forced Pershing once again to put his pursuit of a separate front on hold. After a second five-day Battle of the Marne stymied the German advance, the Allies counterattacked with six American divisions coordinating operations with the French Fourth and Fifth Armies. The soldiers of the 1st and 2nd divisions (many of whom were marines and well trained) fought ably in their opening counteroffensives south of Soissons, but they suffered heavy casualties in continuing head-on charges against experienced and well-entrenched German machine gunners. Pershing and many of his subordinate officers attributed the exceptionally high American losses to the indifference of the mercurial General Mangin and other French commanders, who refused to abandon the cult of the offensive and readily deployed American units to spearhead them. These suspicions, of course, redoubled the American commander's resolve to form and lead an army independent of other Allied forces.[21] Nonetheless, the combined counteroffensives that drove the Germans back from the Marne and forced Ludendorff to give up on another planned offensive against the British in Flanders were seen by most Allied leaders as a decisive turning point in the war. In his August 7th Order of the Day, Marshall Foch acknowledged the importance of the increasing military role of American forces in reversing the momentum of the struggle for dominance on the Western Front. He declared, "Yesterday I said to you: Obstinacy, Patience, your American comrades are coming. To-day I say to you: Tenacity, Boldness, and Victory must be yours."[22]

The credibility of Foch's prophecy was enhanced by the arrival of well over 300,000 American soldiers each month with more than a million more in training across the Atlantic. Finally, even Ludendorff had to concede that the race against time had been lost, that Germany could not win the war.

Once the Allied counteroffensives had driven the Germans back across the Marne and begun to penetrate their defensive systems, Pershing renewed his lobbying for the consolidation of American forces on a separate sector of the front. The Allied Command gave in to his demands on July 24th. He and his staff were now empowered to carry out the strategy of "open war" that Pershing was convinced would force the Germans to retreat from France and Belgium and allow American forces to win the war by taking Berlin in 1919. Informed in large part by the Plains Wars on the US frontier and Pershing-led cavalry operations in northern Mexico, the very designation of "open war" suggested expansive space and potential for maneuver that was at odds with the trench-configured, combat conditions on the Western Front. Time pressures, and the US War Department and government bureaucracies more generally, shared responsibility for the substantial glitches in the training, arming, and logistical support for American troops. But the overly ambitious military agenda pursued by Pershing and his staff also contributed significantly to these short-comings, and most especially to what recent scholarship has demonstrated were excessive casualties on the American front in Lorraine. To begin with, the obstacle-laden terrain where US forces would concentrate their offensives was of Pershing's choosing. The Meuse-Argonne region was covered with dense forests punctuated by bluffs and rugged outcroppings. Both proved ideal for the formidable defenses in depth, replete with machine-gun nests and heavily fortified ridges dotted with observation posts that coordinated with artillery units, which the Germans had been building since their invasion of northern France in 1914. It was no wonder then that the region had been considered a "quiet front" until Pershing's armies arrived in the last months of the war.

The rush to get troops into battle contributed in major ways to the logistical foul-ups, faulty planning, and the often ill-advised *élan* of American staff officers that account for the high casualty rates documented for US offensive operations. These losses were particularly egregious during the assaults in the St.-Mihiel salient against what were presumed to be demoralized German defenders. But Pershing's ambitious military and political agenda as well as planning based on his flawed vision of open war also go far to explain these lethal excesses.[23] His insistence that American officers and regular soldiers be trained to fight his kind of war was at cross-purposes with the instruction in trench tactics they had received from French and British officers at the front. Ignoring the all-too-obvious lessons of the first three years of the war, Pershing and his staff oversaw successive, overly ambitious offensives that may well have diverted scarce German resources from the fronts to the west where the British and French were advancing, but only at the often profligate loss of young American lives in the pursuit of dubious objectives. Pershing's emphasis on an aggressive spirit, which recalled the platitudes of French generals in the prewar decades, had been rendered foolhardy by three years of trench slaughter.[24] His continued confidence in the efficacy of infantry offensives with rifles and bayonets was reminiscent of Douglas Haig's refusal to abandon massed infantry assaults over open ground on enemy entrenchments despite a succession of disastrous defeats and mounting statistics suggesting that less than 1 percent of combatant casualties were inflicted by bayonet wounds. Perversely, the human cost of Pershing's approach to battle was so high that even Haig felt empowered to conclude that the AEF "had suffered a great deal on account of its ignorance of modern warfare."[25]

Whether Pershing was oblivious to the lessons that Monash and some of the European commanders—especially the Germans—had to offer or he consciously dismissed them, we cannot know because he was not a man given to acknowledging the advice of others.[26] But some of his field officers, perhaps most notably Charles Summerall and Conrad Lanza,[27] did learn a good deal during their months on the Western Front when new weapons and tactics had begun to transform a war of stalemate and attrition into a conflict in which maneuver, tactical proficiency, and the restoration of offensives garnered reasonable gains with significantly fewer casualties. The alternative approaches that they employed—often in implicit defiance of orders from AEF headquarters at Chaumont—proved to be some of the most significant legacies of America's engagement in the Great War. Their battle plans contravened in varying degrees Pershing's insistence that tanks, artillery, and airpower were to serve as auxiliary support for infantry units, which he considered basically "self-reliant" and the critical component of successful offensives. Aerial surveillance of enemy positions, extensive planning, and careful preparation and coordination of units to be deployed were stressed. Brief but potent artillery bombardments of enemy positions were seen as essential preludes, and tanks and planes were massed to support the advancing infantry. Stress was placed on limited objectives and avoiding prolonged assaults. Some of Pershing's field officers also contested directives from headquarters to push weary troops to continue offensives that had gained their initial objectives. Learning from earlier operations at Soissons, Château-Thierry, and the St.-Mihiel salient that artillery units could not effectively cover further advances, line officers were reluctant to push their soldiers into additional assaults similar to those that had made for appalling losses in earlier engagements.

Pershing's self-discipline, his confident demeanor, and the respect and support these qualities garnered from most of his subordinate officers as well as Allied commanders contributed in significant ways to building an expeditionary force that made a difference in the final months of combat on the Western Front and helped secure the ultimate victory of the Entente Allies. Though it owed a great deal to the skills of key members of the Washington bureaucracy and Pershing's staff and field officers in France, his success in surmounting the challenges of starting virtually from scratch and in a little over a year overseeing the mobilization, training, and deployment of a massive armed force in battle was a remarkable achievement. His decisions—despite President Wilson's admonitions and misgivings of many of his subordinates—to allow his combat-ready units to be attached to British and French armies struggling to withstand the German offensive onslaught in the spring and early summer of 1918 proved to be a major factor in the Allies' ability to stabilize a imperiled front and soon after launch counteroffensives. The AEF's steadily expanding role in driving German forces from Belgium and France in the following months made it clear to all who were engaged in the war that America had become—not just as an economic colossus but as military adversary—the equal of the nation-empires of Europe and potentially superior to any of them. Thus, in the years after the end of the conflict numerous French and British observers of international trends dolefully counted the many ways in which the Great War had advanced the emergence of the United States as the dominant global power of the twentieth century.

Yet the once-hyperbolic estimate of Pershing's leadership has been contested and found wanting in major ways. Recent research has faulted the dubious choice of fronts on which he chose to deploy his often-inexperienced soldiers, and his decisions in the final stages of the war to order units made up of poorly trained draftees to take key, heavily fortified enemy positions manned by hardened German veterans.[28] It is also essential in assessing his legacy to take into account the very high casualty rates of AEF units under his command that resulted from his refusal to concede the limits of massed infantry assaults and his resistance to the well-documented need for strong artillery support for *all* offensive operations. Any measure of Pershing's impact as a strategist and military thinker ought also extend to his failure to make full and effective use of tanks and airpower, despite his growing recognition that they were essential for offensive operations. These and other fundamental misjudgments, which attest to the limits of his understanding of modern, mechanized warfare and the nature of the battlefields on the Western Front, lead one to wonder how he and his armies would have fared had they faced the far better-trained, armed, and committed forces the Germans fielded earlier in the conflict. The resemblances between his attitudes toward infantry offen-sives over open ground against entrenched defenders make it very likely that Pershing would have been at least as controversial a commander as Sir Douglas Haig was during and immediately after the war and has been throughout the century that followed.

In addition to his willingness to cooperate with often difficult Allied lead-ers, Pershing's most enduring legacy may well have been due to his ability to recognize and reward the talents and prescience of several of his subordi-nate commanders. As we have seen, he was willing to give his more able field officers considerable latitude in terms of modifications in tactics their forces employed in combat. Even more impressive was the extent to which he actively supported three brilliant, visionary subordinates—William (Billy) Mitchell, George S. Patton, and especially George C. Marshall, Jr.—whose innovations in AEF operations not only contributed significantly to Allied successes in the final months of fighting on the Western Front, but also made it possible for them to become influential advocates of major reforms in American armed forces in the interwar decades. Although their postwar pursuits were often hamstrung by major reductions in the size of US forces and appropriations for defense that had been standard procedure in the aftermath of the nation's pre-vious wars, they pushed for weapons and tactical advances and organizational overhauls that better prepared the United States for the second and even more devastating global war, in which two of the three would serve with distinction. The three future commanders were from the same generational cohort that came of age in the fin-de-siècle decades when the United States was emerg-ing as a leading industrial society and joining in the imperial expansionism of the European powers by building a modest colonial empire in the Caribbean and the Pacific. All three had ancestors or close family members who had dis-tinguished themselves in military service, attended private schools, and were drawn to military careers early in their lives and advanced rapidly in the army hierarchy.

Of the trio of Pershing's subordinate officers who continued long after the end of World War I to shape in major ways US military policy and bolster the nation's preparedness, Billy Mitchell was the least beholden to the AEF com-mander. Mitchell was also the most contentious and outspoken of the three with a tendency to publicize his contempt for those in the military who refused to back his determination to build an independent air force superior to any of America's potential rivals.[29] In his early years of service in the Army Signal Corps in Cuba, the Philippines, and Alaska, Mitchell had shown little inter-est in the wartime potential of airplanes, which were in their infancy and dis-missed by most military analysts as little more than flying kites. By the time he arrived in Paris in March 1917, however, Mitchell had renewed contacts with George Squier who had been appointed chief of the army's Aviation Section in the spring of 1916. When serving as the US military attaché in London in the first years of the war, Squier had issued a stream of reports on the uses of airplanes for reconnaissance and increasingly in combat by the adversary European powers. His reports kindled Mitchell's interest in airpower to the point where he had himself paid for civilian flying lessons when the army would not. As America's entry into the war approached in early 1917, Squier chose Mitchell as an aeronautical observer on the Western Front. Once in France several months ahead of Pershing and his small entourage, Mitchell made good use of the spoken French that he had acquired in early childhood to contact and learn from French aviation specialists. Some months later he also worked with the British air chief, General Hugh Trenchard, to create an AEF component capable of joining Allied air forces in the counteroffensives in the summer and fall of 1918.

Even though Mitchell and Pershing often disagreed about the potential uses of airplanes in AEF operations, Pershing promoted Mitchell several times and eventually made him chief aviation officer of the First Army. When Mitchell was able to muster a fleet of nearly 1,500 planes in support of AEF offensives in the St.-Mihiel salient and equivalent forces later for operations in the Meuse-Argonne, Pershing conceded the importance of air surveillance of enemy positions and cover for advancing infantry. Thus, Mitchell, as an influential advocate of airpower in industrial warfare, had his career peak in the final months of World War I. Subsequently, his often-abrasive, postwar advocacy of an independent American air force, well-publicized criticisms of those in command of both the army and navy, and highly controversial demonstrations of the vulnerability of battleships to air assaults alienated many potential supporters of the radical changes that he sought. But his legendary determination, ability to publicize the case for military reform, and the fame generated by both his provocative crusade and the court-martial that resulted ultimately advanced the development of American airpower to levels unmatched by any Allied or adversary nation in the last half of the twentieth century. Fortunately, the changes Mitchell had tirelessly advocated came in time for the US services to surmount the challenges of a massive multiple front war in Europe and the Pacific, but not soon enough to avert the devastating Japanese attack on Pearl Harbor, which he had characteristically anticipated and warned against.[30]

Although he worked more closely and on more amiable terms with Pershing than Mitchell, Lieutenant-Colonel George Patton strongly disagreed with the American commander in chief's view that tanks could have only a very limited role on the battlefield. In the summer after his arrival in France,

Patton had dismissed tanks as "not worth a damn."[31] Some months later, bored by his noncombatant duties as a staff officer at AEF headquarters at Chaumont and having been persuaded that tank corps were in the process of replacing the cavalry, the service branch in which Patton had risen in the ranks, he lobbied Pershing to assign him to the newly formed tank force. Sharing Mitchell's facility with French, Patton soon became absorbed in being schooled by French and British counterparts, including J. F. C. Fuller, in the technical and operational potential of the new weapon. In the spring of 1918, he was promoted to lieutenant colonel and placed in charge of organizing, training, and leading into battle the US light tank battalion. But he was frustrated by Pershing's battle plans that included tanks only peripherally and failed to coordinate tanks and infantry effectively. In the assault on Varennes in late September, Patton, who had become the combat leader of the tank corps, convinced infantry units to join his assault force, which he characteristically personally led into combat. Soon after the joint operation succeeded in capturing the pivotal town, Patton was wounded and carried off the battlefield. Though his wounds sidelined him for the weeks remaining in the war, afterward he became a leading and forceful promoter of tanks as the key weapon in land warfare. Patton and Mitchell pursued their quests for military innovation on separate tracks, but together they had forged the coordination of airpower and mechanized land weaponry that would prove to be decisive components of ground combat in the Second World War. Patton went on to serve as one of the more effective, but also highly controversial, leaders of the mobile, mechanized forces that spearheaded allied campaigns against the Nazi empire in North Africa, Italy, and Western Europe.

The lessons of the infamous traffic pile-ups that delayed the delivery of ammunition and critical supplies to American units engaged in the St.-Mihiel salient and later the Meuse-Argonne were not lost on Lieutenant-Colonel George Marshall, the operations officer for the American 1st Division. Despite nightmarish conditions, Marshall successfully managed what seemed at the outset an impossible logistical assignment. He orchestrated the evacuation of hundreds of thousands of French troops from the salient and their replacement by even greater numbers of US forces, along with thousands of artillery pieces and hundreds of thousands of tons of ammunition and supplies—in miserable weather and over mud-clogged, often unpaved roads.[32] Having won the full confidence of Pershing and the respect of British and French commanders, Marshall went on to a truly remarkable interwar career that eventually earned him the distinction of being one of Franklin Roosevelt's most trusted advisors and the obvious choice for chief of staff of the US Army in World War II.[33]

Marshall's logistical wizardry across more than half a century exemplified another legacy of global significance resulting initially from his success as a staff officer in World War I. The prodigious quantities of food and manufactured goods the United States supplied the Entente Allies beginning in the early months of the conflict, which had made in the German view a mockery of American claims of neutrality before April 1917, also transformed the American "way of war" and provided key precedents for the use of "soft power" in US diplomacy. Marshall realized that America's industrial and financial predominance made feasible massive increases in the size and complexity of logistical support systems for not only its own military but also those of its allies and adversaries. The importance of material assistance through the lend-lease programs extended to Britain, the Soviet Union, and China—in which Marshall was predictably, extensively involved—in securing the defeat of the Axis Powers in the Second World War cannot be overestimated.[34] Along with Herbert Hoover's efforts in supplying food and raw material for war-torn Belgium throughout the First World War, and postwar Allied efforts to prevent widespread starvation in Germany, relief for those afflicted by the war's devastation established the principle of humanitarian aid on an international basis. Building on these precedents after World War II, as secretary of state in the postwar Truman administration, Marshall finished his remarkable career by overseeing the US-assisted reconstruction of Western Europe in the 1950s, a process that has since served as a model for postwar settlements that have a strong likelihood of deterring subsequent conflicts.

Pershing's widely disseminated and soon quasi-official, inflated assessment of America's military contributions to Allied victory and his tendency to play down the tribulations of the soldiers who fought under his command go far to explain why the great majority of the nation's citizenry and most historians have long regarded the Great War as a "good" war. Despite a brief postwar slump, the conflict—both before and after April 1917—greatly enhanced the power, prosperity, and influence of the United States. Because America became a significant combatant just as maneuver and battles had again become decisive, and within a year emerged as one of the three major victorious allies at the cost of far fewer casualties than any of the other main adversary powers, it was perhaps inevitable that triumphalism would prove pervasive in the nation's collective memory of the war. But the nation's triumphalist narrative obscured the unprecedented devastation and dehumanization that had been unleashed by a mechanized war of attrition between industrialized nations. In contrast to leading European intellectuals and the emerging leaders of the colonized peoples, including Mohandas Gandhi and Léopold Sédar Senghor who challenged the long-prevalent assumption that science and technology were necessarily progressive,[35] Americans embraced a new wave of innovation and machine-driven social transformations. Rapid economic growth and America's emergence as the world's financial center and engine of commercial expansion were seen to confirm long-standing convictions of United States exceptionalism at a time when Europeans were increasingly ambivalent, if not profoundly skeptical, of their mission to civilize.[36] Further affirmation of the United States as a "redeemer nation" with reference to comparable outcomes (albeit at far greater costs) in a second global war redoubled these certitudes and intensified the determination of US leaders, buoyed by the backing of a vocal majority of the citizenry to impose America's historical trajectory—by force if necessary—on the peoples and emerging nations of the postcolonial world.[37]

The extent to which America's military interventions in the final stages of World War I proved decisive for what proved to be a pyrrhic victory for the European allies remains highly contested. But the sequence of German responses and setbacks that the US entry into the conflict set in motion has been brought into clearer focus by recent research in neglected sources and new perspectives on the endgame of the conflict. The failure of unrestricted submarine warfare to drive Great Britain from the war meant that Ludendorff and the German leadership had foreclosed the option of meaningful peace negotiations and a compromise settlement that would likely have favored Germany and significantly altered the course of twentieth-century history. The need for a clear German victory on the battlefield, before the full force of American industrial productivity and potential military might could be brought to bear, pushed Ludendorff into a second great gamble—an all-out offensive in the spring of 1918 to destroy the British land forces and compel the Allies to surrender. Once the offensives stalled, and confronted by the hundreds of thousands of US soldiers arriving monthly by the spring of 1918 and a home front in Germany descending into civil strife and nascent revolution, the German high command had run out of viable options.

Ludendorff and Hindenburg contemplated falling back to and fighting a holding action along the Rhine that might still have resulted in a settlement of the nonpunitive sort that Wilson had proposed in the spring of 1917. But neither the British nor the French, nor even Wilson, were willing to consider that possibility. The German surrender that followed left the newly installed Catholic Center and Socialist leadership with virtually no bargaining power—or even the right to participate in the treaty deliberations that followed. Thus, the future of Germany depended on the Allied agreement to abide by Woodrow Wilson's vision of a democratic, capitalist global future that was imperiled by Bolshevism and of little interest to America's revenge-minded allies. Because Clemenceau and Lloyd George rebuffed US efforts to claim credit for the defeat of Germany— though the adoring crowds of Paris that greeted Wilson in early 1919 might have given them pause—the president proved unable to fashion the sort of progressive settlement at Versailles that he desired.[38] Congressional rejection of Wilson's scheme for an international organization that he hoped might eventually correct the injustices of a vindictive settlement sealed the continuing and accelerating demise of the Western-dominated world system and opened the way for decades of violent contestation both within Europe and worldwide that would determine the nature of the global order that would replace it.

NOTES

My thanks to Joseph Gilch, graduate student and current coauthor, for his able research assistance for this essay.

1. Davis, *Home Fires Burning*; Chickering, *Imperial Germany and the Great War*.

2. This objective was given top priority in December 1916 by the German Chief of Naval Staff, Adolf von Trotha. Quoted in Hough, *The Great War at Sea 1914–1918*, 301.

3. See Ritter's magisterial *The Sword and the Scepter*, vols. 3 and 4. I have also consulted the memoirs of Ludendorff and Hindenburg.

4. Ritter, *The Sword and the Scepter*, vol. 3, 334.

5. Luvaas, *The Military Legacy of the Civil War*; Coffman, *The War to End All Wars*, 11. See also the comments of Admiral Capelle quoted in Trask, *The AEF and Coalition Warmaking, 1917–1918*, 11.

6. Bennet, *Naval Battles of the First World War*, 257–267.

7. Sims quoted by Coffman in *The War to End All Wars*, 94 (quoted phrasing) and chapter 4.

8. Coffman, *The War to End All Wars*, 97.

9. Weigley, *The American Way of War*, 194.

10. Nenninger, "The Army Enters the Twentieth Century, 1904–1917"; Coffman, *The War to End All Wars*, 123.

11. Coffman, *The War to End All Wars*, 17; Braim, *The Test of Battle*, 144–145.

12. Brittain, *Testament of Youth*, 420–421.

13. Coffman, *War to End War*, 48–49; Weigley, *The American Way of War*, 200–202.

14. Rainy, "The Questionable Training of the AEF in World War I."

15. Two of the most engaging accounts of this phase of the war are Terraine's *To Win a War*, especially 51–82; and for all of the last year Hubert Essame's *The Battle for Europe, 1918*.

16. Millet, "Over Where?" 242, 246; Braim, *The Test of Battle*, 38–39, 76–77, 113, 120.

17. Subsequently published as *General Pershing's Story of the American Army in France*.

18. Millet, "Cantigny, 28–31 May 1918," especially 180–185; Grotelueschen, *The AEF Way of War*, 200–227; Braim, *The Test of Battle*, 67–68.

19. Monash, *The Australian Victories in France in 1918*, 96.

20. Terraine, *To Win a War*, 142–150; Yockelson, *Borrowed Soldiers*, chapters 16–20.

21. Grotelueschen, *The AEF Way of War*, 83–105; Millet, "Over Where?," 245.

22. Terraine, *To Win a War*, 72–82 (quoting Foch, 82).

23. In addition to the recent studies by Mark Grotelueschen on *The AEF Way of War* and *Doctrine under Trial*, the equally careful, revisionist scholarship of Timothy Nenninger, James Rainy, Allan Millet, and especially Paul Braim's detailed study of the St.-Mihiel and Meuse-Argonne offensives are essential sources for understanding the heavy losses suffered by American forces in the late-1918 offensives.

24. Grotelueschen, *The AEF Way of War*, 143–144.

25. Quoted by Rainy, "The Questionable Training of the AEF in World War I," 101. See also Terraine, *To Win a War*, 165–166.

26. Monash, for example, is not even mentioned in his two-volume memoir, *My Experiences in the World War*.

27. Grotelueschen, *Doctrine under Trial*, especially 51–52, 115–125, 142–145.

28. See especially Braim, *The Test of Battle*, 96–98, 101–103, 108.

29. Mitchell's blueprint for the air force as a separate branch of the US military was set out in considerable detail in numerous addresses that often devolved into political diatribes, especially in his best-selling book *Winged Defense*.

30. Cooke, *Billy Mitchell*. An earlier, somewhat less critical assessment can be found in Hurley, *Billy Mitchell*.

31. Quoted in D'Este, *Patton*, 205.

32. Terraine, *To Win a War*, 135, 204; Millet, "Over Where?," 247; Braim, *The Test of Battle*, 111; Shaffer, *America in the Great War*, 155; Marshall, *Memoirs of My Services in the World War 1917–1918*, chapters 10 and 11.

33. For Marshall's broader feats in World War I, see the first volume of Pogue's *George C. Marshall*. For his subsequent achievements, see Stoler, *George C. Marshall*; and Jeffers and Axelrod, *Marshall*.

34. Overy, *Why the Allies Won*, chapters 6 and 7; Adas, *Dominance by Design*, 219–227.

35. Scheub, "Soukeina and Isabelle"; Gandhi, *Young India*, October 7, 1926, and December 8, 1927; Adas, "Contested Hegemony."

36. See Orwell's essay "Shooting an Elephant," in *Inside the Whale*. For Europe thinkers more broadly, see Adas, *Machines as the Measure of Men*, chapter 6; and for America in the 1920s, Adas, *Dominance by Design*, chapter 4.

37. Gilman, *Mandarins of the Future*; Latham, *Modernization as Ideology*.

38. For the motives and maneuvers of the big three that shaped the ill-fated Settlement of Versailles, see Gardner, *Safe for Democracy*; Mayer, *Politics and Diplomacy of Peacemaking*; MacMillan, *Paris 1919*.

6

Legacies for Citizenship

Pinpointing Americans during and after World War I

Christopher Capozzola

During World War I, people everywhere clamored for maps. They pored over atlases, tore maps out of newspaper supplements (see Figure 6.1), and even gathered around kiosks in town squares. They were looking for the war, of course, curious to find Sarajevo and Gallipoli, Verdun and Versailles, hopeful that tracing the shifts of battlefronts could make sense of the conflict's human devastation and political significance. But, perhaps without even knowing it, they were also looking for themselves and their own place in the war. For Americans, the impulse to locate oneself was both a reflection and a cause of changing mappings of citizenship during and after World War I. And it was not without consequences. By war's end, Americans increasingly found themselves—culturally, legally, and geopolitically—in only one place on the world's maps, as the war transferred a web of cultural sentiments and formal political attachments into single pinpoints.[1]

World War I marked a fundamental transformation in the political structures and cultural meanings of US citizenship that shaped the American polity for two generations and indeed continue to resonate a century later. From day to day, the changes that Americans experienced were varied and unpredictable—lurching expansions and contractions of citizenship that can be difficult to categorize collectively in retrospect. But by 1924, ideas and rules of citizenship had become increasingly uniform, focused around a single allegiance, articulated in paperwork, and managed by a federal government that had greater power to regulate the borders of citizenship and alienage after—and because of—World War I.

FIGURE 6.1 Published immediately after the outbreak of the First World War, this issue of the *Seattle Star* urged readers to "cut out this map and follow moves from European war." War forced many Americans to seek out unfamiliar sites of conflict in Europe. As they did so, they began to reconsider their own place in American and world politics. *The Seattle Star* (Seattle, WA), August 4, 1914. *Chronicling America: Historic American Newspapers*. Library of Congress.

This chapter draws on recent work in the history of political culture that sees citizenship not only as a formal legal category but also as a set of cultural and discursive practices. While it is centrally concerned with the institutional history of US citizenship, it also considers how law structured social dynamics outside of the state. It links diplomatic, immigration, and social histories, viewing nonstate actors as historical agents who remade US foreign relations by enlisting, migrating, marrying, and gossiping. While states wielded decisive power over citizens during and after World War I, individuals played crucial roles in shaping the course of events at home and abroad.[2]

The wartime pinpointing of citizenship was a global phenomenon, but it had specific dynamics in the United States, where the political equality promised by the Constitution's Fourteenth Amendment—ratified in 1868 but unevenly applied in the generations that followed—struggled toward redefinition in an era of mass migration and social upheaval. This chapter tells this history in three parts. First, it tracks the legal and political history of citizenship during wartime, focusing in particular on immigration and naturalization policy in the years between the war's outbreak in August 1914 and the adoption of the Immigration Act of 1924 a decade later. Second, it explores the ways that World War I militarized US citizenship. Honorable service could yield political rewards and occasionally even disrupt the logics of racial discrimination that structured formal and informal political inclusion. Paths to inclusion, though, increasingly depended on one's willingness—even if solely in theory—to serve the nation's war aims. At the same time, those who refused or were excluded from service found it more difficult than ever to access US citizenship, and all noncitizens fell under the gaze of surveillance and policing that emerged from wartime practices. Third, the chapter stresses that expansions of citizenship were not always victories for equality. Some proponents of a single allegiance embodied in a uniform citizenship law trumpeted the triumph of Americanism over the other—the alien, the radical, the melting pot. This was inclusive without being particularly egalitarian. Nor were incorporations always welcome, as will be shown by the Indian Citizenship Act of 1924, one of the more paradoxical cases of the expansion of US citizenship after World War I. Pinpointing did not eliminate hierarchies within the national polity.

During World War I, the terms of American citizenship—like the terrain of the Western Front itself—were uneven, often muddy, and, when crossed, sometimes deadly. But taken collectively, citizenship reflected the war's impact through increased federal power, heavier reliance on official documentation, and the privileging of a single allegiance mediated through Uncle Sam's wartime authority. Immigration from Europe dropped; migration from the

Western Hemisphere and mobility within the United States increased. The state regulated more closely the movements of aliens and clarified the status of groups—among them women, colonial subjects, and dual citizens—that had stood in ambiguous relation to US nationality law.

Perhaps the first and most significant transformation in the membership of the American polity came when the war's outbreak brought a sudden end to the era of transatlantic mass migration. Wartime mobilization among the European powers demanded the registration and military service of young men across Europe, many of whom would otherwise have been among the millions of migrants who came to the United States in search of work in the decades before the war. Industrial and agricultural mobilization created jobs in Europe that made the ocean journey economically less imperative, and submarine warfare certainly made the Atlantic passage less appealing. European migration dropped from a peak of 1.06 million in 1914 to just 198,000 in 1915; after April 1917, Ellis Island sat nearly empty. Overall rates of immigrant entry to the United States would not return to pre–World War I levels until the 1990s—and, adjusted for the base population of the United States, they have never matched those of the 1910s.[3]

The drastic downturn in European migration both generated and accommodated new migratory streams. Revolution and civil war in Mexico between 1910 and the 1920s prompted more than one hundred thousand Mexican nationals to flee across the border as political refugees. Even more entered the United States as economic migrants, seeking to fill new jobs that opened at the same time that European migrants disappeared from northern and midwestern cities. These were not only spontaneous choices in dynamic labor markets, but reflections of public policy, including the importation of Mexican migrant labor that began with the formal recruitment of seventy thousand Mexican workers during World War I and would continue until the 1950s. New political configurations followed in turn, as Mexican Americans articulated claims to political equality in US-based organizations, some of which would later coalesce as the League of United Latin American Citizens, founded in Corpus Christi, Texas, in 1929.[4]

It was likewise the war and its economic impacts that ignited the twentieth century's mass migration of nearly nine million white and black Americans from the rural South to urban regions of the North and West. Migration was under way before 1914, and for African-Americans in particular was prompted by a complex mix of political and economic pressures and attractions. But the war and its disruption of the southern agricultural economy—particularly the labor shortages wrought by conscription, the recruitment of labor by northern enterprises, and the infusion of dollars into a cash-poor southern economy—generated migrations on such a large scale. By relocating, African-American southerners remapped the terms of political belonging in the century to come.[5]

The mass mobilization of nationals of the warring states required clear documentation of the political status of people, especially draft-age men in countries that raised armies by conscription. While the systematic documentation of identity was already under way by 1914, those technologies were uneven in their quality and patchy in their coverage. By 1918, the terms of citizenship increasingly required a clearly authorized identity, most notably in provisions of the Selective Service Act of 1917 that required all male citizens between eighteen and forty-five to register for the draft and carry on their persons at all times their draft registration cards—the first mass, state-issued identity documents in US history. Much could ride on documentation: Selective Service practice assumed that draft-age men were liable for service unless they could prove they were not. Little surprise, then, that some two hundred thousand noncitizens ended up entering the army, sometimes simply because they were unable to document to local draft boards that they were nationals of other states. Paperwork increasingly defined border crossing as well. In July 1917, the US State and Labor departments issued new rules requiring passports and visas for all aliens entering the United States; Congress turned the order into a law in May 1918 and in August of that year the State Department established a visa office. Identities were more rigorously documented, and that rigor was imposed primarily by the federal government.[6]

As important as it was for states to find their citizens so that they could draft them, it was also important for governments to identify aliens—to pinpoint them on the map—so that they could keep an eye on them. Days after the US declaration of war in April 1917, President Woodrow Wilson invoked the Alien Enemies Act of 1798—a forgotten relic of the xenophobic moment of the Quasi-War with France—to impose obligations on German citizens that required them to register and restricted their movements and employment. By war's end, some six thousand had been interned as enemy aliens. US policies were hardly unique. The laws of war, as codified at the turn of the twentieth century, subjected enemy aliens around the world to registration and internment. But wartime innovations also reflected prewar concerns about the influence of noncitizens on American politics and society. A system that had accommodated multiple allegiances with relative ease now came to view dual citizenship with skepticism. In the United States, attention focused in particular on a 1913 provision of German nationality law that extended German citizenship to Germans abroad, even when—like second-generation Americans born after the ratification of the Fourteenth Amendment—they were also citizens by birth of another country. After 1917,

German-Americans' dual status made them vulnerable to discrimination and even assault. The war's anti-alien mood also accelerated the closer coupling of citizenship and voting rights. In the nineteenth century, not all voters were citizens (nor, of course, were all citizens voters) and political machines such as New York's Tammany Hall relied on immigrants' easy access to the ballot. But with only a handful of exceptions, the last remaining state and local alien suffrage provisions were repealed during or immediately after the war.[7]

The war also shook up debates about citizenship and political participation in policy areas that had stagnated or hardened into partisan battles. Dramatic changes in women's suffrage, US colonial policy, and immigration restriction would have the greatest impact on the terms of belonging for American citizenship, and in each case they led to the adoption of a more uniform standard of inclusion, managed by the federal government. The century-long struggle for women's suffrage came to a head during and because of the war. In the 1910s, the movement appeared bogged down in a slow state-by-state strategy that placed little hope in the possibility of a constitutional amendment. But new political configurations during the war and a new dynamism for federal power in Washington changed this outlook dramatically. The millions of women active in the mainstream National American Woman Suffrage Association (NAWSA), and the thousands who picketed with the more radical National Woman's Party, tapped into wartime politics to stake claims for suffrage. In September 1918, President Woodrow Wilson publicly endorsed the suffrage amendment, which was ratified in August 1920. Whether the Nineteenth Amendment made American women into equal citizens, or merely extended the voting rights of elite women, women's suffrage marked an expansion of citizenship that was inclusive without being egalitarian.[8]

Making US citizenship more uniform also required clarifying the status of transnational marriages. Wartime efforts to amend the Marital Expatriation Act of 1907—under which an American woman who married a foreign man lost her US citizenship—came to naught, even as advocates pointed to cases of American-born women forced to register as enemy aliens because they had married German citizens. On Capitol Hill, one representative defended the 1907 law as "a good lesson to our American girls to marry American boys." But peace and suffrage finally changed the political dynamic, and the 1922 Cable Act eliminated derivative citizenship provisions except for American women who married Asian men, who continued to be barred from naturalization. Legal provisions and military policies aimed at facilitating the migration of over five thousand war brides also reflected the war's effects on citizenship and marriage law.[9]

In the two decades after the wars of 1898—in which the United States defeated the Spanish Empire, seized its colonies in the Caribbean and Pacific, and suppressed indigenous independence movements—US colonial policy had been a thicket of partisan controversy. The terms of colonial belonging were marked by a complex web of inclusions and exclusions, articulated by the US Supreme Court in a series of rulings known as the Insular Cases, which affirmed Congress's claim that Puerto Ricans and Filipinos were neither citizens nor aliens, but American "nationals," who nonetheless owed allegiance to the United States. The wartime push toward a uniform single national allegiance did not overturn the Insular Cases but it did disrupt their logic. America's colonial subjects seized on the war's rhetoric to make claims for national self-determination, particularly after the Jones Act of 1916 promised independence to the Philippines "as soon as a stable government can be established therein," a distressingly vague point in the distant future. The next year, the Jones Act of 1917 announced—without giving Puerto Rico any voice in the matter—that all Puerto Ricans were citizens of the United States, a status also accorded to residents of the US Virgin Islands, acquired from Denmark in 1916. America's colonial subjects could now be located more precisely, and citizenship and allegiance more closely matched territorial boundaries. But the Puerto Rican experience shows that inclusion in the US polity not only could come without equal rights, but could also happen without consent.[10]

Finally, much as it did with woman suffrage and colonial policy, the war broke a decades-long impasse on the question of immigration restriction, culminating in the passage of the Immigration Act of 1924. The shift on Capitol Hill began with the Immigration Act of 1917 (passed over Woodrow Wilson's veto), an omnibus bill that contained three key provisions: the institution of a literacy test, designed to make entry harder for poor and illiterate migrants from southern and eastern Europe; the establishment of an "Asiatic Barred Zone" that extended the restrictive provisions of the 1882 Chinese Exclusion Act to nearly all of Asia other than Japan and the Philippines; and a ban on entry by those deemed mentally ill, including men and women marked by "constitutional psychopathic inferiority," a clinical euphemism for homosexuality. While the 1917 act excluded relatively few compared to the systems that would be put in place in the 1920s, it launched a powerful drive toward restriction that silenced nearly all opposing voices.[11]

A year later, the Immigration Act of 1918 expanded the definition of anarchism—already an excludable category since 1903—to make it easier to bar entry to foreign anarchists or deport those already here. The Emergency Immigration Act of 1921 established quotas on migration from Europe as well as overall limits on European migration. Intended as a temporary measure to handle the threats posed (if only in legislators' imaginations) by postwar immigration and global radical movements, the act soon became a permanent feature of twentieth-century immigration law through the Immigration Act of 1924. Also known as the Johnson-Reed Act, the law as implemented limited overall immigration to 150,000 entrants per year, with a quota for each country of no more than 2 percent of the foreign-born of that nationality at the time of the 1890 Census. In practice, the law drastically reduced migration from southern and eastern Europe, and an additional clause barred almost all Japanese immigrants. Histories of the Immigration Act of 1924 have often situated the law's passage firmly in the cultural politics of the 1920s: a frothy mix of nativism, isolationism, eugenics, and a resurgent Ku Klux Klan. But the path to Johnson-Reed began during World War I.[12]

Pinpointing citizenship during wartime also firmly linked citizenship and military service. Revised laws of war demanded that all soldiers be citizens of the United States. A more significant shift came from the legal obligation and cultural expectation that all citizens were at least willing to be soldiers. And new regulations of citizenship would also be upheld by an increasingly militarized enforcement regime.

In the United States, as in almost all the warring powers, military mobilization required a clear path to citizenship for men serving in the ranks in order to regularize the terms of recruitment, protect noncitizen soldiers from punishment as mercenaries, and control the distribution of welfare provisions to veterans and their dependents. When the Selective Service Act—following the norms of international law—exempted nondeclarant aliens from conscription, a howl ensued, and Congress proposed drafting them regardless. "The country that is good enough to live in is good enough to fight for," one New York newspaper approvingly noted. The Military Naturalization Act of May 1918 made it easy for immigrant soldiers—who made up nearly 20 percent of the army—to naturalize, relieving them of residency requirements and paperwork burdens. Nearly two hundred thousand soldiers naturalized during the war, the majority of their oaths taken in military camps. Provost Marshal General Enoch Crowder boasted after the war that the policy "resulted in the conversion of the 'Foreign Legion' of the Army into a host of loyal American citizen-soldiers."[13]

Cultural pressures toward military conformity and 100% Americanism could also generate protest: after the army initially handed over care of soldiers' leisure to the aggressively Protestant Young Men's Christian Association (YMCA), Catholic and Jewish soldiers complained and the Knights of Columbus and Jewish Welfare Board joined the YMCA in service. And there were limits to the inclusiveness of military policies. Many Asian immigrant soldiers—barred from citizenship by provisions of the Naturalization Act of 1870 that restricted naturalization to "white persons" and "persons of African nativity or African descent"—hoped that the Military Naturalization Act would open the terms of citizenship to them. For some it did, until a series of appeals in the post-war period culminated in *Toyota v. U.S.* (1925), in which the Supreme Court ruled that a Japanese-American veteran's naturalization certificate was "illegally obtained." Openness proved temporary in other respects as well: in 1920, Congress restored its ban on military enlistment by new immigrants, and the War Department set down a rule requiring that all officers be US citizens.[14]

The wartime citizenship regime also made it more difficult for those who refused military service to claim citizenship. Bureaucracy reflected changed mindsets: the requirement that naturalized citizens "support and defend the Constitution and laws of the United States against all enemies, foreign and domestic," had been part of US citizenship law since the Naturalization Act of 1906, but only after 1922 was adherence explicitly asked on US naturalization forms. Several high-profile cases made headlines in the interwar period, most notably *U.S. v. Schwimmer* (1929), which denied pacifist Rosika Schwimmer's naturalization petition on the grounds that she refused to agree to "take up arms in defense of country" (setting aside the relevance of the fact that as a fifty-one-year-old woman, Schwimmer would not have been allowed in the army had she sought to enlist). The Court similarly refused the naturalization petitions of Douglas McIntosh and Marie Bland, the latter a Canadian-born woman who had actually spent nine months working as a nurse along the Western Front during the war. But far more significant than these high-profile cases was the systematic exclusion from naturalization of immigrant men who had claimed exemption from the draft during the war, either as conscientious objectors or as nondeclarant aliens. Some tens of thousands of men were denied citizenship for claiming rights that were legally theirs.[15]

Conscription's linkage of citizenship and military service also shaped citizenship for those outside its reach. During the war, American women remade the meanings of political belonging through their wartime participation as volunteers. Under the leadership of Carrie Chapman Catt, NAWSA endorsed US entry into war and insisted that its members "stand ready to serve our country with zeal." But when pacifist women criticized the war, or when radicals in the National Woman's Party insisted that "we will not bargain with our country for our services," they found themselves subject to prosecution, imprisonment, and even diagnosis of mental illness. Most remarkably, a decade after the war, the US Supreme Court extended the logic of conscription to extreme ends when it used its ruling in *Arver v. U.S.* (1918)—which had upheld the constitutionality of the Selective Service Act—to justify the forcible sterilization of a young Virginia woman in *Buck v. Bell* (1927).[16]

Citizenship was not only more militarized in its principles and its con-notations, but also in its enforcement, as a wide array of federal agencies took up the task of securing the borders, keeping watch over aliens, and exclud-ing them in greater numbers. In 1918, Attorney General Thomas W. Gregory offered no understatement when he boasted that "it is safe to say that never in its history has this country been so thoroughly policed." Civilian agencies, including the Justice Department's Bureau of Investigation, which grew dra-matically between 1917 and 1920, wielded wartime emergency powers such as those found in the Espionage and Sedition Acts of April 1917 and May 1918, and they increased authority to deport aliens and denaturalize recent immigrants. The US Army's Military Intelligence Division kept tabs on radicals and paid particularly close attention to transnational movements, from Bolshevism to the syndicalism of the Industrial Workers of the World to the anticolonialism that motivated members of the Garvey movement, South Asians in the Ghadar Party, Japanese pan-Asianists in territorial Hawai'i, and Irish nationalists in New York. Ratification of the Eighteenth Amendment and implementation of Prohibition in the Volstead Act ramped up federal policing power, particularly along the US-Canadian border, in south Florida, and the Caribbean. The link-age of citizenship with military service—and its increasingly rigid surveillance and enforcement—empowered the federal government. While federal officials never worked alone, Washington increasingly set the terms.[17]

Citizens could also be created without their consent, as was the experience of Native Americans during and after World War I. Wartime political circum-stances accelerated ongoing trends, broke through seemingly intractable politi-cal impasses, and in the end generated a uniform system of citizenship with a single allegiance authorized by the federal government and linked to military service. Taking Native sovereignty and citizenship seriously, though, challenges assumptions about the relationship between citizenship and military service in this era. The standard story that white Americans told themselves about Indian participation in World War I embraced Native people's declarations of willingness to serve, documented their high rates of military volunteerism, and praised the voluntary sacrifice of money and land to the war effort, all of which justified Indians' quest for US citizenship, which was duly granted, quid pro quo, in the Indian Citizenship Act of 1924. Nonetheless, every aspect of this narrative is wrong.[18]

Several Indian nations declared war on Germany during World War I, but their motivations were more complex than suggested by accounts that sometimes reduced expressions of national sovereignty to humorous anec-dotes. Arthur Parker, a leading member of the Seneca Nation and president of the Society of American Indians, drafted the Onondaga declaration of war in July 1918. Senecas asserted sovereignty guaranteed by a 1783 treaty and justified their declaration as a response to the mistreatment of members of the Onondaga Nation who had been displayed in circus sideshows in Germany in the 1910s. Later, Parker pressed the Senecas to declare war, too. Doing so would "establish your independent right to act as a Nation and not as a ward-bound tribe that had no powers of a Nation. The Senecas have lost none of their sovereignty since 1812 and a war declaration would serve to emphasize our status."[19]

Postwar tributes to Native American loyalty made much of their military service. Indeed some twelve thousand Native Americans bore arms during the war, most in the army. While African-Americans served in segregated units, the army refused calls for distinct Indian regiments. Cato Sells, the Commissioner of Indian Affairs, defended the army's policy on the deliberately assimilationist grounds that "the military segregation of the Indian ... does not afford the associational contact he needs and is unfavorable to his preparation for citizenship." About 40 percent of America's 350,000 Native people were noncitizens, mostly those who lived on reservations or had not, in the eyes of the US government, "adopted the habits of civilized life." As noncitizens, they were thus exempt from the draft. Provost Marshal General Crowder, noting that the "ratio of Indians claiming deferment was negligible," saw evidence of Native American patriotism, but Indians' own experiences were quite different. Because the Selective Service Act required all men in the territorial United States between eighteen and forty-five—even noncitizens—to register, many Native men found themselves drafted against their will or without knowledge of their rights.[20]

Of course, many Native Americans served eagerly and took pride in their enlistment. "The Indian is not a slacker, and I didn't mean to be one," wrote William Leon Wolfe, an Ojibwe student at the Carlisle Indian School. Sam Thundercloud, a Winnebago man from Wisconsin, was more skeptical: "I am fighting for the rights of a country that had not done right by my people." Others, either individually or collectively, asserted their rights to sovereignty and exemption. On June 5, 1917, the first day of registration for the new draft, Navajos in northwestern Arizona chased Selective Service agents off their lands; Utes in Colorado did the same and performed a war dance in opposition. That August, several hundred people in southeastern Oklahoma—including many from the Seminole and Muskogee-Creek Nations—joined the Green Corn Rebellion that hatched a plan to march on Washington and overturn the draft law. In early 1918, members of the Oneida Nation cited a 1769 treaty when they refused to register, and that February, rumors emerged from the tiny settlement of Ibapah, Nevada, where Goshute Indians had refused to register on the grounds that they had once made a treaty of peace with the Americans, "and now you come and want us to fight, but we won't do it." Federal officials disagreed about whether the Goshutes were being misled by German spies or Mormon troublemakers, but they wasted no time in sending troops from Fort Douglas, Utah, to crush the rebellion and register draft-aged men.[21]

Wartime accounts also praised the monetary sacrifices of Indian communities and the steps they took to increase acreage under agricultural cultivation. Such histories, though, overlook the fact that a June 1917 law empowered officials of the Bureau of Indian Affairs to invest Native Americans' funds in Liberty Loan war bonds—whether or not Native communities agreed. They omit the use of vagrancy laws against Native Americans who did not work for wages or in cultivation of cash crops and the pressures that Indians felt during a time of rising crop prices, labor shortages, and a scramble for arable land. Narratives of loyalty also obscure the ways that incorporating Native lands into US agricultural markets accelerated dispossession. "When a nation is at war," explained Commissioner Sells, "ordinary considerations do not govern." But for many observers of Indian affairs, it was business as usual.[22]

After the Armistice, some Indians and their allies clamored for full US citizenship for Native Americans, echoing a December 1918 editorial in the *Literary Digest* that asked, "If the Red Man Can Fight, Why Can't He Vote?" Red Fox Skiuhushu of the Northern Blackfoot told a Seattle audience that "we know not the hyphen.... We are 100 per cent Americans." Writing in the *American Indian Magazine*, Arthur Parker urged that "if we are consistent in our aim to bring democracy to all the people of the earth let us deal with the Indians in a democratic way." Native American veterans gained a clear path to citizenship: a November 1919 law granted citizenship to Indian men who served and attributed that nationality retroactively to the date of enlistment. The law's terms required that veterans seek out citizenship, but few did so. Some did not know of the option, but others rejected the idea of US citizenship. The campaign continued, as a rhetoric of service and reward framed the legislative debates surrounding the Indian Citizenship Act of 1924 (see Figure 6.2). The new law, which easily passed Congress and was signed on June 2—just a week after the Immigration Restriction Act—announced "that all noncitizen Indians born within the territorial limits of the United States [are] citizens of the United States."[23]

During and after World War I, Native American political culture reflected a vigorous attempt to articulate and defend an understanding of citizenship at odds with the one that was developing in Washington. It was also a spectacular failure: no one took Native sovereignty seriously; no one took their legitimate military exemption seriously; no one took their property rights seriously; and

FIGURE 6.2 President Calvin Coolidge meets at the White House with a delegation of Native leaders from the Pacific Northwest around the time of the passage of the Indian Citizenship Act in June 1924. Framed in public debate as a reward for Native American military service during the war, the law announced that all "Indians born within the territorial limits of the United States [are] citizens of the United States." Library of Congress, Prints and Photographs Division, Washington, DC, LC-H234- A-9417 [P&P].

no one took seriously the idea that many Native Americans did not want to be citizens of the United States. Instead, the Indian Citizenship Act is best seen as a coercive inclusion into the US polity that was a crucial aspect of this pinpointing moment in the history of citizenship: territorially inclusive without being egalitarian. When the logic of single allegiance got to the reservation, it did not merely place Native Americans at a single point on the map, but eliminated Indian Country from the maps altogether. For Native people after 1924, locating themselves on the map meant finding they belonged nowhere at all.

Indeed 1924 can be seen as the final year of a decade-long remaking of US citizenship. That year marked the adoption of the Johnson-Reed Act and its quota systems, the demographic consequences of which were the most enduring—if least immediately visible—legacies of World War I for American society. But it was not only that. The 1924 Immigration Act's ban on Japanese migrants completed four decades of agitation for Asian exclusion. The Indian Citizenship Act and the work of the Hawaiian Homes Commission reflected the coercive inclusion of all persons who lived under US sovereignty as citizens of the US state. And the formation of the US Border Patrol—rolled out on the Canadian and Mexican borders in the summer of 1924—reveals the power of the federal government to enforce its borders. This was, by 1924, a new nation, in terms of both legal definitions of citizenship and state structures to implement and enforce borders of belonging.

The legacies for citizenship that emerged from World War I were legal, cultural, and demographic. Pressed by government officials and supportive constituents, policymakers pushed American institutions and cultural practices toward a citizenship premised on a single allegiance to one state bounded by the territorial limits of the United States. This occurred despite the existence of millions of Americans whose political loyalties, cultural and linguistic affiliations, and labor practices spanned a single nation-state. From Ellis Island to the Texas border and from Puerto Rico to the Goshute reservation, the terms of US citizenship were remade, with consequences that would endure for generations. By 1924, persons in the United States—whether they were citizens or aliens—had mapped a new terrain of citizenship with clearer borders around the nation-state and a new landscape of boundaries within it. It was a story that few could have imagined as they gathered in the summer of 1914 and struggled to find Sarajevo on a world map.

NOTES

1. See, for instance, London Times, *The Times War Atlas*; Jeanneney, *Jours de Guerre, 1914–1918*, 402–403; "Cut Out This Map and Follow Moves from European War," *Seattle Star*, August 4, 1914, 1.

2. Gabaccia, *Foreign Relations*; Jacobson, *Barbarian Virtues*; Smith, *Civic Ideals*, 410–469; Welke, *Law and the Borders of Belonging*.

3. Zolberg, *A Nation by Design*, 238; Cannato, *American Passage*, 239–329. On conscription in Europe, see Chambers, *To Raise an Army*, 68–70. While submarine warfare was not a constant threat, it nevertheless was frequent enough to make the trip risky for civilian passengers at almost any time—and more expensive, as ticket prices rose to reflect both shipping risks and liners' preference for lucrative military contracts over passenger fares. Sondhaus, *The Great War at Sea*.

4. Ehrlich, Bilderback, and Ehrlich, *The Golden Door*, 153; Johnson, *Revolution in Texas*; Orozco, *No Mexicans, Women, or Dogs Allowed*, 50–57, 151–180; Ramirez, *To the Line of Fire!*; Zolberg, *A Nation by Design*, 241.

5. Gregory, *The Southern Diaspora*; Kirby, "The Southern Exodus, 1910–1960"; Wilkerson, *The Warmth of Other Suns*.

6. 40 Stat. 76 (1917); Capozzola, *Uncle Sam Wants You*, 27–28; Chambers, *To Raise an Army*, 228–229; Robertson, *The Passport in America*, 184–210; Zolberg, *A Nation by Design*, 240–241.

7. Aylsworth, "The Passing of Alien Suffrage"; Nathans, *The Politics of Citizenship in Germany*, 169–198; Office of the Judge Advocate General of the Army, *Compilation of the War Laws of the Various States and Insular Possessions*.

8. Capozzola, *Uncle Sam Wants You*, 103–114.

9. 39 Stat. 1228 (1907); 42 Stat. 1022 (1922); Bredbenner, *A Nationality of Her Own*, 70–74, 80–112 (quote on 74); Gardner, *The Qualities of a Citizen*; Kerber, *No Constitutional Right to Be Ladies*, 42–43; Zeiger, *Entangling Alliances*, 11–70.

10. 39 Stat. 545 (1916); 39 Stat. 951 (1917); Curbelo, "Puerto Rican Soldiers in the First World War"; Capozzola, "The U.S. Empire"; Chambers, *To Raise an Army*, 232; Burnett and Marshall, *Foreign in a Domestic Sense*; McPherson, "World War I and US Empire in the Americas"; Sparrow, *The Insular Cases and the Emergence of American Empire*.

11. 39 Stat. 874 (1917); Canaday, *The Straight State*, 19–54; Zolberg, *A Nation by Design*, 238–240.

12. 40 Stat. 1012 (1918); 42 Stat. 5 (1921); 43 Stat. 153 (1924); Hirobe, *Japanese Pride, American Prejudice*, 1–18; Ngai, *Impossible Subjects*, 21–55; Zolberg, *A Nation by Design*, 246–247.

13. 40 Stat. 542 (1918); Chambers, *To Raise an Army*, 227–228, 231; Crowder, *Second Report of the Provost Marshal General to the Secretary of War*, 101, 102; Ford, *Americans All!*; Jacobs and Hayes, "Aliens in the U.S. Armed Forces."

14. *Toyota v. U.S.*, 268 US 402 (1925); Chambers, *To Raise an Army*, 355n45; Lothyan, "A Question of Citizenship"; Salyer, "Baptism by Fire"; Sterba, *Good Americans*.

15. *U.S. v. Schwimmer*, 279 US 644 (1929); *U.S. v. McIntosh*, 283 US 605 (1931); *U.S. v. Bland*, 283 US 636 (1931); Capozzola, *Uncle Sam Wants You*, 81; Flowers, *To Defend the Constitution*, 27.

16. *Arver v. U.S.*, 245 US 366 (1918); *Buck v. Bell*, 274 US 200 (1927); Capozzola, *Uncle Sam Wants You*, 108–114.

17. 40 Stat. 217 (1917); 40 Stat. 553 (1918); 41 Stat. 305 (1919); Gregory, quoted in Peterson and Fite, *Opponents of War, 1917–1918*, 20; Cannato, *American Passage*, 343; Capozzola, *Uncle Sam Wants You*, 149–155; Hernández, *Migra!*; Jensen, *Army Surveillance in America, 1776–1980*, 160–177; Jung, "Seditious Subjects"; Sohi, *Echoes of Mutiny*; Weil, *The Sovereign Citizen*, 30–43.

18. For examples of the quid pro quo narrative, see Stein, "The Indian Citizenship Act of 1924," 264.

19. Foreman, *Indians Abroad, 1493–1938*, 211; Halsey, *The Literary Digest History of the World War*; Parker, quoted in Hertzberg, *The Search for an American Indian Identity*, 175. For an example of the interpretation of Native declarations as charming anecdotes, see "On the Warpath," *New York Times*, August 2, 1918, 10.

20. Britten, *American Indians in World War I*, 43; Chambers, *To Raise an Army*, 231–232; Crowder, *Second Report of the Provost Marshal General to the Secretary of War*, 198; Sells, quoted in Tate, "From Scout to Doughboy," 426.

21. Britten, "The Creek Draft Rebellion of 1918"; Crowder, *Second Report of the Provost Marshal General to the Secretary of War*, 212; Ellis, "'Indians at Ibapah in Revolt'," quote on 166; "Indians Refuse to Register," *New York Times*, June 6, 1917, 1; Krouse, *North American Indians in the Great War*, 20, 31; Tate, "From Scout to Doughboy," 429; Zissu, "Conscription, Sovereignty, and Land." On fears of German subversion, see Hertzberg, *The Search for an American Indian Identity*, 170.

22. "Daniels Urges Navy to Take Bonds," *New York Times*, June 12, 1917, 2; Tate, "From Scout to Doughboy," 433; Sells, quoted in Wood, "American Indian Farmland and the Great War," quote on 250.

23. 41 Stat. US 350 (1919); 43 US Stat. 253 (1924); Britten, *American Indians in World War I*, 159–181; Densmore, "The Songs of Indian Soldiers during the World War"; Densmore, "If the Red Man Can Fight, Why Can't He Vote?"; Krouse, *North American Indians in the Great War*, 159–161; Parker, "Making Democracy Safe for the Indian"; Stein, "The Indian Citizenship Act of 1924"; Tate, "From Scout to Doughboy," 435.

7

Taming Total War

Great War–Era American Humanitarianism
and Its Legacies

Julia Irwin

The First World War and its aftermath are often remembered—and rightfully so—as a period defined by violence, brutality, and inhumanity, an era that witnessed unprecedented suffering among soldiers and civilians alike. Yet at the same time, the years from 1914 through the early 1920s also gave rise to a seemingly more constructive historical legacy: the development and application of new approaches to wartime humanitarian relief. In an attempt to curb the conflict's staggering human toll, the governments and peoples of both belligerent and neutral nations took novel and concerted steps to aid the battlefield wounded and to care for those behind the lines. As total war raged, people throughout the world endeavored to minimize its calamitous social effects.

More than a century after the Great War commenced, these humanitarian legacies are worth remembering—and worth contemplating. By seeing the First World War era as not only a period of great suffering, but also a time in which millions of people joined in a movement to alleviate "the pain of others,"[1] historians of international relations stand to recover a profound history of transnational humanity and compassion. Simultaneously though, it is essential to analyze First World War–era relief efforts with a critical eye and to eschew the simple equation that if war is bad, humanitarianism must therefore represent an absolute good. The reality is far more complicated. For while altruistic intentions surely motivated many donors and relief workers, and while many soldiers and noncombatants certainly benefited from the provision of food, shelter, clothing, and medical care, a closer analysis of humanitarian relief reveals that it was never a purely beneficent undertaking. The ostensible goal of humanitarian aid may have been the betterment of international welfare, but it could—and did—serve other agendas. It functioned variously as a form of propaganda, a means of social control, and a tool of statecraft. Rather than acting as an antithesis to conflict, moreover, humanitarian aid arguably helped to validate war by softening its horrors. Even as we commemorate the impulse to treat wounded soldiers and to reduce the suffering of civilians, we must also come to terms with these less savory legacies of Great War–era humanitarianism.

Recently, a generation of historians has begun to do just this, advancing rich and nuanced interpretations about the history of humanitarian relief in the First World War and its aftermath. In this essay, I synthesize some of the key insights of this scholarship while providing new reflections on the history and mixed legacies of Great War–era humanitarianism.[2] Before moving into this discussion, however, a note on scope is in order. In this piece, I restrict my attention to aid that was organized and administered by US citizens and relief agencies. While some readers may take issue with the decision to concentrate on American assistance, there are at least two good reasons for limiting the discussion in this way. First, a study of American aid activities underscores the relevance of humanitarianism to US international history and foreign relations. Second, US aid efforts merit special attention because of the unparalleled and unprecedented role that Americans played in the relief effort. Groups such as the American Red Cross, the Commission for Relief in Belgium, the American Committee for Armenian and Syrian Relief, and the American Relief Administration, along with scores of other US voluntary and religious organizations, directed vast amounts of aid toward Europe and the Near East. Collectively, American relief agencies raised and distributed billions of dollars' worth of food, medical supplies, clothing, and other relief for American and European soldiers and for civilian men, women, and children in more than two dozen nations. This humanitarian undertaking had major implications for Europe and the Near East, as well as for the United States, both at the time and in the century that followed.

Analyzing the history of American relief during the Great War era provides valuable new perspectives on the histories of both US foreign affairs and international humanitarianism. To begin with, it encourages a reperiodization of US involvement in the war. Seen through the lens of humanitarianism, US participation in the conflict entailed more than a three-year window of US military intervention and postwar peace negotiations. It began not with the US declaration of war in April 1917, but rather in September 1914, when the American Red Cross first sent relief ships to Europe; it ended not with the Senate's rejection of the Treaty of Versailles in 1920, but instead when the last American Relief Administration workers departed Europe in 1923. By broadening the definition of "intervention" beyond the traditional spheres of militarism and diplomacy, the history of American humanitarianism extends the period of active US participation in the Great War to nearly a decade.

Likewise, the history of American wartime and postwar relief suggests the need to reframe the geography of US intervention in the conflict, and of the Great War more generally. US involvement was not limited to the Western Front, where the troops of the American Expeditionary Forces saw combat, nor to Versailles, where a small group of US policymakers carried out high-level diplomatic negotiations; it covered nearly the entire map of Europe and the Near East. During the Great War era, American donations, material supplies, and personnel reached dozens of countries. Before the United States entered the war in 1917, limited amounts of American aid flowed into both Central Powers and Allied nations. While American aid to Central Powers nations largely ceased once the United States became a belligerent, the nation's relief efforts expanded enormously elsewhere. During the remainder of the war and for several years after its conclusion, American assistance fanned out across Europe, from France to Italy to the Balkan States to Russia. In the Near East, too, American aid and aid workers reached scores of towns and cities, among them Jerusalem, Port Said, Aleppo, and Beirut. Together, these humanitarian efforts serve as an important reminder of the expansiveness of the US intervention and of the war's vast territorial reach.[3]

Studying American humanitarianism also offers alternative ways of thinking about US foreign relations during this era. For one, it brings novel actors into the history of the United States in the First World War. Tens of thousands of American women and men spent time in Europe and the Near East as relief workers, many serving in areas where US troops never deployed. In the United States, millions of other American adults and children supported those efforts by volunteering time and donating money to humanitarian organizations. These individuals played an important part in the American war effort and warrant inclusion in its history. Exploring the on-the-ground activities of American humanitarians, moreover, demonstrates a very personal side of the history of US foreign relations. While serving overseas, American relief workers forged tangible connections with millions of soldiers and civilians in Europe and the Near East. These humanitarians touched, soothed, fed, and bathed the men, women, and children of other nations. They surveyed refugee housing, inspected relief applicants, and instructed aid recipients to adopt different hygienic and sanitary behaviors. Together, these humanitarian activities call attention to the intimate nature of international exchange.

Finally, examining American humanitarianism in Great War–era Europe and the Near East is crucial in order to recognize the profound and lasting legacies that it left. The relief activities that the United States and its citizens carried out at this time had important implications for both US foreign relations and international humanitarianism, throughout the remainder of the twentieth century and into the present day. To demonstrate and expand upon these claims, this essay surveys and analyzes American aid efforts during the era of US neutrality, the period of US belligerency, and the postwar era, then concludes with a series of reflections on the legacies of these humanitarian interventions.

The Era of US Neutrality, 1914–1917

During the summer and fall of 1914, the empires of Europe and the Ottoman Empire plunged into the Great War. For the next two and a half years, the United States remained outside the fray militarily. This period of US neutrality, however, should not be mistaken for a time of American noninvolvement. From the start of the conflict, the United States intervened in the Great War in myriad ways: through diplomacy, through trade and commerce, and through humanitarian relief.[4]

This last form of participation—the provision of money, material supplies, and medical care to soldiers and noncombatants—constituted one of the most significant and far-reaching types of American involvement in Europe and the Near East at this time. From the earliest days of the war, US citizens organized and supported a major foreign relief undertaking. Thousands upon thousands gave money to aid organizations or volunteered their time collecting food, knitting socks and bandages, and raising funds. Scores of American men and women made an even greater commitment to the humanitarian effort by traveling to wartime Europe or the Near East to administer relief. Years before US troops ever set foot on European soil, American humanitarians arrived with aid. Coordinating their efforts was a dense network of relief organizations in both the United States and abroad. Significantly, assistance flowed into both Allied and Central Powers nations, enabling Americans to address health and welfare crises across the entire continent.

American humanitarians provided assistance to both soldiers and noncombatants (see Figure 7.1). Central to the US military relief effort was the American Red Cross (ARC), the organization designated by the Geneva Convention and congressional charters "to furnish volunteer aid to the sick and wounded of armies in time of war."[5] On September 12, 1914, just over a month

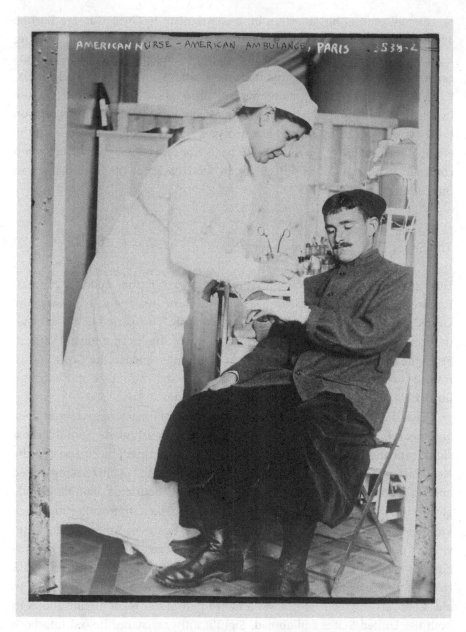

FIGURE 7.1 An American nurse with a patient in Paris, France, c. 1914 or 1915. Library of Congress, Prints and Photographs Division, LC-DIG-ggbain-19450.

after the war began, the ARC's leaders dispatched a relief ship to Europe. On board were 171 surgeons and nurses and tons of chloroform, stretchers, bandages, and other medical and hospital supplies. Upon arrival, these ARC supplies and personnel spread across the continent, reaching ill and wounded soldiers in England, Russia, France, Germany, Austria, Belgium, Serbia, and Bulgaria. Additional boatfuls of supplies and personnel followed this initial shipment.[6] Complementing the ARC's efforts, groups such as the American Fund for French Wounded and the American Ambulance Association, together with individuals such as the author Edith Wharton and the former ambassador to France Myron T. Herrick, organized additional forms of assistance for the armies of belligerent nations.[7] Other organizations targeted those on the home front. Groups such as the Commission for Relief in Belgium and the American Committee for Armenian and Syrian Relief, for example, provided vast amounts of food to avert starvation in the nations they had been organized to assist. The Rockefeller Foundation, a newly established philanthropy, also entered into the field of civilian relief. In late 1914, the foundation's leaders dispatched a War Relief Commission to study the conflict's effects on noncombatants. At the same time, they provided $145,000 to fund an antityphus commission in Serbia. Across Europe and the Near East, various other American individuals and organizations supplemented these efforts for noncombatants.[8]

From 1914 to 1917, Americans thus staged a far-reaching humanitarian intervention in Europe and the Near East. For a nation deeply divided over the question of US military involvement in the Great War, this form of American participation in the conflict generated relatively little controversy. As a type of foreign relations, foreign aid was appealing for several reasons. For one, it represented an incredibly inclusive means of international engagement. All Americans could take part, be they men, women, or children; members of the elite or the working class; in support of the Central Powers, the Entente, or of continued nonintervention. Regardless of their position on the war, Americans could cast participation in relief activities positively. Rather than fighting on the front lines, they would direct their energies toward combating hunger, homelessness, and ill health. Humanitarianism also appeared compatible with—even complementary to—the preservation of US neutrality. In working to alleviate foreign suffering, American citizens acted in a manner that was consistent with Wilson's promise to treat Europe "not as a partisan, but as a friend."[9] The US relief effort was not without critics. Some American socialists, for instance, argued that humanitarianism only promoted and prolonged war by returning soldiers to the front lines and placating noncombatants. Other US citizens feared that any kind of involvement, armed or otherwise, risked dragging the United States into the conflict. By and large, however, large proportions of Americans saw the humanitarian intervention as an impartial, apolitical, and beneficent undertaking, a positive alternative to entering the war.

Bolstering this belief in the inherent neutrality of humanitarian assistance was the fact that the US aid effort (as the foregoing examples attest) was organized and funded by private citizens and relief organizations, not by the state. It is important to note, however, that the US government greatly facilitated this work. Secretaries of State William Jennings Bryan and Robert Lansing communicated frequently with the American Red Cross, the Commission for Relief in Belgium, and other aid organizations. They also engaged in extensive negotiations with belligerent nations to allow for the safe passage of American aid. Throughout Europe and the Near East, US ambassadors and consuls worked closely with humanitarian agencies to distribute relief supplies. Back in the United States, politicians at the federal, state, and local levels served as spokesmen for relief campaigns. Recognizing the potential for aid to diminish social and political unrest and to demonstrate America's neutral commitment to the people of Europe and the Near East, government officials gave private humanitarian organizations their strong and active support.

If the US government's involvement in American humanitarian activities belies the idea that aid was apolitical, so do the actual patterns of relief distribution. Although American aid during the period of US neutrality reached belligerent nations on both sides of the conflict, the preferences of donors and aid organizations ensured that far larger proportions of American aid went to Allied nations. In late 1915, moreover, the British government began limiting what items were allowed through the Allied blockade, eventually prohibiting relief as a "contraband of war."[10] When US diplomatic officials failed to persuade the British to reverse this decision, American aid largely ceased to reach Germany, the Ottoman Empire, and other Central Powers nations.[11] Even before the United States entered the conflict, American humanitarian aid had proven neither impartial nor apolitical. This fact would only become clearer after the United States entered the war in April 1917.

The Era of US Belligerency, 1917–1918

Americans constructed a broad network of humanitarian assistance during the period of US neutrality, but after US entry into the conflict, in April 1917, the nation's humanitarian intervention in Europe and the Near East swelled to enormous proportions. During the nineteen remaining months of the war, millions of Americans donated money to, and labored for, humanitarian causes in the United States. Tens of thousands of American nurses, physicians, and lay volunteers traveled throughout Europe and the Near East to administer relief. While the largest number of Americans worked in France, relief workers could be found as far afield as Belgium, England, Greece, Italy, Lebanon, Palestine, Russia, and Syria. US diplomatic and military officials, already willing promoters of American humanitarianism before 1917, strengthened their support for US aid projects further still; while much relief continued to flow through private channels, the US government also expanded its own role in American humanitarianism considerably. Enjoying broad private and state support, humanitarian engagement served as a vital complement to the US armed intervention.

This intensified enthusiasm for humanitarian causes after April 1917 can be attributed to several factors. Most obviously, with the US military now at war, many American citizens and policymakers supported relief efforts in order to help the nation's doughboys.[12] Yet the new impulse to aid US troops fails to fully explain the sudden burst of humanitarian fervor, as American relief efforts for Allied soldiers and noncombatants also expanded tremendously. The increased attention to these populations stemmed, in part, from a genuine desire among Americans to alleviate foreign suffering and to make a positive contribution to the war effort. More than this though, it reflected an understanding that humanitarian assistance was suddenly of real strategic importance to the United States. Improving the welfare of Allied troops and civilians was no longer just for the benefit of those aid recipients; now, it bolstered the shared war effort. Through the provision of medical care, food, shelter, and other aid, US humanitarians could help keep friendly soldiers fit for fighting while reducing social and political unrest on the Allied home front. Such aid also served as invaluable propaganda, visibly demonstrating the US commitment to the cause. As soon as the United States entered the war, in short, aiding the Allies became a crucial weapon in the US war arsenal and, as such, garnered increased support. This transformation in the strategic nature of humanitarian assistance, however, carried a significant consequence: as US citizens and policymakers focused their attention on bettering the conditions of the Allies and winning the war, they largely abandoned their earlier willingness to aid all belligerents. Though the ARC would continue to provide aid to wounded enemy soldiers and to prisoners of war, other avenues of relief for Central Powers nations ceased. With the United States at war, American humanitarianism fully relinquished its earlier claims to neutrality.[13]

If the nature of American aid changed following US entry into the conflict, so did the channels through which assistance flowed. In 1917 and 1918, numerous nongovernmental agencies—including the YMCA, the American Friends Service Committee, the Knights of Columbus, and the Salvation Army, among others—raised funds, mobilized volunteers, and organized aid operations abroad (see Figure 7.2). But in these years, one organization—the American Red Cross—dominated the humanitarian field, serving as the nation's unrivaled leader in both civilian and military relief. By the signing of the Armistice

FIGURE 7.2 Poster urging Americans to volunteer as drivers for the American Field Service, 1917. Library of Congress, Prints and Photographs Division, LC-DIG-ppmsca-34350.

in November 1918, 22,000,000 adults and 11,000,000 children (roughly one-third of the US population) had become donating members of the ARC. Such support allowed the organization to amass a war fund of over $400,000,000, an astronomical sum. These finances, in turn, enabled the ARC and its personnel to orchestrate a mammoth humanitarian intervention in Europe and the Near East.[14] When combined with the relief activities of the scores of other American relief organizations operating in Europe and the Near East, the scale of the US aid enterprise amounted to a truly colossal undertaking.[15]

US government officials, recognizing the importance of aid to the war effort, did much to facilitate the work of American voluntary relief organizations. Most notably, Woodrow Wilson took several steps to define the ARC as a quasi-official arm of the wartime state. Soon after the United States entered the war, Wilson appointed a War Council to lead the ARC for the duration of the conflict. Over the next year and a half, he also played an active role in promoting the ARC, publicly identifying the organization as the recognized aid association of the United States. Although the ARC remained privately funded and (other than the War Council) privately staffed, the US government exerted unprecedented sway over its operations. US government officials assisted the efforts of the ARC, and of other humanitarian agencies, in additional ways as well. The wartime Committee on Public Information, for example, publicized fundraising campaigns in the United States, while State Department, consular, and military officials all helped aid organizations to orchestrate relief activities abroad, both on the battlefields and on the home front. Acutely aware of the benefits of partnering with private humanitarian agencies and promoting their work, officials within the wartime state acted as willing and eager collaborators.[16]

In the field of military relief, the US government itself became a much more active participant in humanitarianism. With the US mobilization for war, the Army Medical Department assumed responsibility for the health care of millions of US draftees and enlisted men. The Medical Department also recruited American medical professionals and militarized many hospitals, ambulance units, and medical personnel in Europe. In so doing, the military extended its reach over the work of many aid workers and over the bodies of US and Allied soldiers.[17] The state's authority over military relief, though, was by no means exclusive or absolute. In 1917 and 1918, as in the era of US neutrality, privately funded and staffed organizations remained critically important. Insufficiently prepared for the war, the Army Medical Department relied on the ARC and other voluntary organizations to provide many of its supplies, equipment, and base hospitals. It also depended on outside agencies to enlist and train many of its nurses, physicians, surgeons, ambulance drivers, and other personnel.[18] The task of organizing activities for the welfare and morale of troops behind the lines, moreover, fell largely to nongovernmental agencies and their volunteers. Thousands of American civilians—many of them women—staffed canteens and rest houses, organized recreation and entertainment, and prepared coffee and donuts for soldiers.[19] Thus even as the US government, through its Army Medical Department, greatly expanded its involvement in humanitarian affairs, voluntary organizations remained at the heart of the American military relief enterprise.

In the sphere of civilian relief, the Wilson administration relied almost exclusively on privately staffed and funded agencies to administer aid on behalf of the United States. These voluntary organizations did not disappoint. From April 1917 through November 1918, US aid workers carried out a veritable humanitarian occupation of Allied Europe and the Near East. American physicians, nurses, missionaries, and lay volunteers traversed the continent, many working in areas where US troops never set foot. Behaving as representatives of the United States, American relief workers constructed a wide-ranging and comprehensive humanitarian program for Allied noncombatants. Many of their projects focused on ameliorating pressing health and welfare problems, including hunger, homelessness, and illness. American volunteers established and staffed thousands of feeding stations, hospitals, and clinics; they distributed clothing, created employment opportunities, and assisted refugees and orphans in finding new homes. But while emergency relief took priority, American humanitarians attempted to achieve more long-range and complex social welfare goals as well.[20] Assuming a role as missionaries of American medicine, aid workers established nursing schools for women and fresh air camps for children. They organized nationwide antituberculosis and antityphus campaigns. They constructed model health exhibits and launched a vast array of hygienic and sanitary reform initiatives. Going well beyond the quest to reduce wartime suffering, American humanitarians transformed civilian relief into a broader project of social engineering.[21]

Taken together, the dense web of military and civilian relief efforts that American aid workers organized in Europe and the Near East during 1917 and 1918 constituted a fundamental part of the US intervention in the Great War. On the front lines, while US doughboys fought alongside Allied militaries, American humanitarians battled to improve the health, welfare, and morale of US troops and Allied soldiers. In the cities and villages of Allied Europe and the Near East, meanwhile, US aid workers formed personal and intimate relationships with the men, women, and children they assisted. Through their aid, they attempted not only to alleviate the immediate suffering that war had produced, but also to fundamentally and permanently transform health, welfare, and civil society in Europe and the Near East. These relief activities, far from peripheral, represented one of the principal avenues through which the United States and its citizens engaged with Europe and the Near East during the nineteen months of US belligerency.

The Postwar Era, 1918–1923

With the signing of the Armistice on November 11, 1918, the US humanitarian intervention in Europe and the Near East again underwent a profound transformation. Yet just as the conclusion of the war did not arrest American diplomatic involvement in the region's affairs, nor did it suddenly bring American aid efforts to a halt. At the end of the Great War, Europe and the Near East faced a profound humanitarian crisis. More than four years of conflict had left millions hungry, homeless, widowed, and orphaned. Rates of typhus and tuberculosis surged, as did a new, virulent epidemic of influenza. Refugees awaited resettlement, prisoners of war awaited release and repatriation, and soldiers—many wounded physically and psychologically—awaited reintegration into society. Complicating matters, agriculture and food supplies had been greatly disrupted, as had institutions of health and social welfare. So had railroads, telegraph lines, and other forms of transportation and communication.[22] Resolving this complex social catastrophe presented one of the greatest challenges of the postwar era.

In late 1918 and early 1919, many US policymakers and citizens assumed a responsibility to continue aiding Europe and the Near East. For these proponents of postwar relief, the grim state of these societies constituted not merely a humanitarian problem, but a political one as well. These Americans lamented the tragic burden that starvation, illness, and upheaval had placed on individual lives, and they felt obliged to alleviate that suffering. Yet just as important, they feared that such conditions would breed political and social unrest, undermining any hope of forging a lasting peace. They also warned that hunger and material deprivations, if left unchecked, would drive civilians in these regions to embrace Bolshevism, anarchism, and other radical ideas. Foreign aid, according to its American advocates, stood to rebuild shattered lives while securing a stronger, more stable postwar Europe and the Near East.

During the early months after the Armistice, this mixture of compassion and strategic interest motivated many US government officials, voluntary organizations, and private citizens to support a major postwar humanitarian intervention in Europe and the Near East. While American relief workers continued many of their aid efforts within Allied nations, they once again began to deliver assistance to areas formerly controlled by the Central Powers, including

Armenia, Austria, the Baltic states, Bulgaria, Constantinople, Czechoslovakia, Germany, Hungary, Persia, Poland, and Soviet Russia. In all of these sites, ARC, the Young Men's and Women's Christian Associations, the Jewish Joint Distribution Committee, Near East Relief, and other agencies began transitioning out of war work and into new relief projects. These ranged from resettling refugees to treating influenza patients to rebuilding crumbled infrastructures.[23] The leaders of these various agencies, however, harbored serious reservations about their ability to resolve one colossal problem: providing the populations of these regions with sufficient food.

It was at this juncture that US government officials increased the state's involvement in foreign assistance tremendously. Taking on an unprecedented role in civilian relief, the US government organized a comprehensive program to feed Europe. In late February 1919, Woodrow Wilson issued an Executive Order to create the American Relief Administration (ARA), an organization charged with acquiring, transporting, and distributing foodstuffs to European civilians, and he appointed Herbert Hoover to run it. Congress, in turn, gave a $100,000,000 appropriation to fund the ARA's operations through June 30, 1919.[24] In creating and financing this new state-sponsored aid organization, US government officials had broken with their traditional reliance on voluntary organizations to administer the nation's civilian assistance. Convinced of the diplomatic and moral importance of averting European famine, US policymakers embraced a novel role for the state in humanitarian relief.

The ARA quickly came to be regarded as the principal postwar US foreign aid agency—and for good reason. Over the next several months, ARA personnel purchased and distributed hundreds of millions of dollars in food and other assistance, reaching millions of civilians in more than twenty nations, primarily in eastern Europe. Over the objections of many US policymakers and much of the US public, ARA aid even reached Germany and Bolshevik Russia. At the same time, the ARC and other privately led and financed relief agencies continued to organize their own relief activities. However, the medical, sanitary, and reconstruction work of these organizations tended to complement—rather than compete with—governmental feeding efforts. Together, the ARA and American voluntary aid organizations administered a significant and far-reaching program of post-Armistice relief.

Ultimately, however, the grand scope of this peacetime aid program proved short-lived. By mid-1919, even though millions of people in Europe and the Near East continued to face hunger, homelessness, and other challenges, American public and political willingness to back a major postwar foreign assistance program began to wane. It would only continue to decline as the Great War faded further into the past. Private donations dropped off sharply; Congress chose not to provide further funds to the ARA. Mirroring the mounting popular reaction against Wilsonian internationalism, and amid growing calls to "Return to Normalcy" and to put "America First," US humanitarianism lost much of the support that it had so recently enjoyed.

Yet even as American interest in the ongoing postwar crisis in Europe and the Near East flagged, some US citizens were not prepared to abandon the humanitarian intervention. For these individuals, providing food and other forms of assistance remained a moral obligation and a strategic imperative— now, perhaps, all the more so. In an era of growing resistance to US political involvement abroad, relief represented a way to exert continued influence over Europe and the Near East while simultaneously winning the hearts and minds of civilians in those regions. Propelled by this logic, and despite dwindling finances and diminished attention to their efforts, many American aid organizations continued to manage relief activities in Europe and the Near East for several more years, albeit on a much more limited scale. After the ARA's federal mandate expired, Hoover reorganized it as a nongovernmental relief organization. In this new permutation, the ARA remained a central player in the relief field. Its personnel continued to distribute food in Europe until 1922 and in Soviet Russia until 1923.[25] The ARC also stayed involved in postwar aid efforts, particularly in the field of child health, overseeing various assistance projects until the summer of 1922.[26] Near East Relief, now operating under a congressional charter (which it received in 1919), provided millions of dollars' worth of food, clothing, shelter, and other aid to assist orphans and refugees in the former Ottoman Empire.[27] Other major American relief organizations, likewise, continued to raise money and awareness for postwar relief and to organize a wide-ranging set of relief activities in Europe and the Near East.

This US postwar aid program, even as it decreased in size, represented a complicated and controversial postwar political issue. US policymakers and private citizens engaged in fierce debates, for example, over whether to aid Germany, other Central Powers countries, and the Soviet Union. While aid organizations continued to enjoy some support from political officials and civilians, moreover, they faced significantly more scrutiny and criticism than they had during the war years. In the United States, aid organizations weathered critiques over the state of their finances and the scope of their activities. In Europe and the Near East, while many welcomed American assistance, others began to voice strong resistance to continued relief. Opponents objected to aid that often smacked of blatant American propaganda. They also resented some US aid workers, particularly those who seemed more eager to Americanize or control Europe and the Near East than to assist these places. In the postwar era, just as it had in the past, foreign relief proved neither neutral nor apolitical.

From the signing of the Armistice in 1918 until the last ARA personnel departed Russia in 1923, the US government and US citizens thus executed a prolonged postwar humanitarian intervention of Europe and the Near East. Although the colossal scale of these efforts quickly diminished, this endeavor nonetheless constituted a principal form of American involvement in postwar foreign affairs. American aid workers and their assistance directly affected the lives of millions of civilians in Europe and the Near East. At the same time, the subject of humanitarianism informed contemporary political and cultural discourses on US international involvement. Such facts encourage a reframing of the traditional narrative of postwar US foreign relations. In 1920, the Senate rejected a seat for the United States at the League of Nations, while voters issued a stinging rebuke to Wilsonian internationalism at the ballot boxes. Through humanitarian assistance, however, the American intervention in the global Great War persisted long after the United States had "returned to normalcy."

The Legacies of Great War–Era American Humanitarianism

American aid workers may have departed Europe and the Near East by 1923, but the legacies of their Great War–era humanitarian intervention endured, reverberating throughout the years that followed. One important legacy is that during the First World War and its aftermath, the US federal government greatly expanded its reach into the field of foreign relief, sparking a trend that would escalate dramatically in coming decades. Private citizens and aid organizations may have funded and administered most aid efforts during the First World War, but as US diplomatic and military officials came to recognize the strategic importance of aid, they facilitated these voluntary efforts in myriad ways. In addition, the US government, through its Army Medical Department and the ARA, expanded its own humanitarian role enormously. This increasing state involvement in the relief field prefigured the US government's later embrace of aid and development as tools of Cold War–era statecraft.[28] Yet significantly, even when American policymakers extended their control over foreign assistance during the latter half of the twentieth century, they continued to cooperate closely with nonstate organizations, just as they had in the past. As these various precedents and continuities indicate, American humanitarianism in the Great War era represents a crucial early chapter in the history of US foreign assistance, a prelude to the humanitarianism of the American Century.

A second legacy of Great War–era American humanitarianism can be found in its implications for civilians in wartime. Not until 1949 did the

Fourth Geneva Convention formally establish provisions for the "Protection of Civilian Persons in Time of War."[29] More than three decades prior to this, however, American relief workers took part in a crusade to safeguard the health and welfare of noncombatants. From the beginning of the war in 1914, and for several years after the 1918 Armistice, American humanitarians provided food, shelter, clothing, and medical care to refugees and other civilians across Europe and the Near East. Admittedly, these relief efforts had limits. They sometimes bred resistance and resentment, and they did little to prevent future wartime atrocities. Nonetheless, these early twentieth-century attempts to protect civilians invite a reconceptualization of the Great War and its consequences. Even as it generated unprecedented human suffering, the conflict simultaneously gave rise to new humanitarian sensibilities. The role that Americans played in mitigating the war's human effects, moreover, highlights the centrality of the United States and its citizens to the broader history of international humanitarianism.

A third and final legacy, somewhat more philosophical in nature, concerns the ethical questions that the history of Great War–era humanitarianism raises. As this essay has argued, the relief activities that Americans organized from 1914 to 1923 were never purely altruistic, neutral, or apolitical, nor could they be. Foreign aid certainly helped to mitigate suffering, but it simultaneously served diplomatic and military agendas. Although many welcomed and benefited from US assistance, others found legitimate reasons for objecting to it, seeing it as a propaganda tactic or a form of cultural imperialism. Humanitarianism, in short, was complicated and contested terrain in the First World War era; a century later, it continues to be. Rather than blithely celebrating its virtues, it is essential for scholars to interrogate the critiques, the hypocrisies, the paradoxes, and the power struggles that lie at the heart of the history of foreign assistance. Even when we do, we will invariably be left with unresolved moral dilemmas. For instance, while most would probably agree that reducing human distress is a positive good, how do we reconcile this belief with the notion that humanitarianism actually makes war more palatable by mitigating its atrocities? We must also come to terms with the fact that the emergence and development of modern humanitarianism coincided with surging nationalism, brutal imperialism, and the mechanization of modern warfare—and that these historical trends were, in fact, intimately intertwined.[30] Raising these points is not meant to dismiss the idealism inherent in the quest to make the world a more humane place, nor to deride the noble intentions and tireless labors of many relief workers. It is simply to encourage a more balanced, more reflective, and more nuanced commemoration of Great War–era humanitarianism and its profound and enduring legacies.

NOTES

1. Sontag, *Regarding the Pain of Others*.

2. My evidence in this essay draws especially from the following books, articles, and dissertations: Cullather, "The Foreign Policy of the Calorie"; Proctor, *Civilians in a World at War*; Barnett, *Empire of Humanity*, chapter 4; Irwin, *Making the World Safe*; Moranian, "The Armenian Genocide and American Missionary Relief Efforts"; Veit, *Modern Food, Moral Food*; Gillett, *The Army Medical Department, 1917–1941*, chapters 1–13; Clements, *The Life of Herbert Hoover*, chapters 1, 5, and 9; Adams, "Herbert Hoover and the Organization of the American Relief Effort in Poland, 1919–1923"; Watenpaugh, "'A Pious Wish Devoid of All Practicability'"; Patenaude, *The Big Show in Bololand*; Cabanes, *The Great War and the Origins of Humanitarianism, 1918–1924*; Watenpaugh, *Bread from Stones*; Watenpaugh, "Humanitarianism in the Era of the First World War"; Little, "Band of Crusaders"; McGuire, "An Ephemeral Relationship"; Polk, "Constructive Efforts"; Tanielian, "The War of Famine"; Westerman, "Relief."

3. This echoes a historiographical point made by the essays in Gerwath and Manela, *Empires at War*.

4. For the former two forms of intervention, readers are urged to consult the other essays in this volume.

5. American National Red Cross Congressional Charter, 1905 (33 Stat. 599–602).

6. Irwin, *Making the World Safe*, chapter 2.

7. Hansen, *Gentlemen Volunteers*; Price, "Edith Wharton at War with the American Red Cross."

8. See Little, "Band of Crusaders"; McGuire, "An Ephemeral Relationship"; Tanielian, "The War of Famine"; Westerman, "Rough and Ready Relief"; Moranian, "Armenian Genocide and American Missionary Relief Efforts."

9. Wilson, Message to Congress, 63rd Cong., 2nd sess., August 19, 1914.

10. *Papers Relating to the Foreign Relations of the United States, 1916. Supplement, the World War* (Washington, DC: US Government Printing Office, 1916), 941–959.

11. Irwin, *Making the World Safe*, chapter 2.

12. For a discussion of this wartime fervor, see Capozzola, *Uncle Sam Wants You*.

13. Veit, *Modern Food, Moral Food*, chapter 3; Irwin, *Making the World Safe*, chapter 4.

14. Davison, *The American Red Cross*, chapters 1–11; Bicknell, *With the Red Cross in Europe, 1917–1922*.

15. Granick, "Waging Relief"; Proctor, "An American Enterprise?"; Little, "Band of Crusaders"; McGuire, "An Ephemeral Relationship"; Polk, "Constructive Efforts"; Tanielian, "The War of Famine"; Westerman, "Rough and Ready Relief."

16. Irwin, *Making the World Safe*, chapter 3; Little, "Band of Crusaders," chapter 3.

17. Gillett, *The Army Medical Department, 1917–1941*, chapters 1–13.

18. Hansen, *Gentlemen Volunteers*.

19. Bristow, *Making Men Moral*.

20. Cullather, "Foreign Policy of the Calorie."

21. Irwin, *Making the World Safe*, chapter 4.

22. For details on these conditions, see Surface and Bland, *American Food in the World War and Reconstruction Period*. See also Cabanes, *The Great War and the Origins of Humanitarianism*; Watenpaugh, *Bread from Stones*.

23. Irwin, *Making the World Safe*, chapter 5; McGuire, "An Ephemeral Relationship"; Polk, "Constructive Efforts."

24. Clements, *The Life of Herbert Hoover*, chapters 1, 5, and 9; Adams, "Herbert Hoover"; Patenaude, *The Big Show in Bololand*; Cabanes, *The Great War and the Origins of Humanitarianism*, chapter 4; Little, "Band of Crusaders," chapter 6.

25. Clements, *The Life of Herbert Hoover*, chapters 5 and 9; Little, "Band of Crusaders," chapter 6.

26. Rodogno, "The American Red Cross and the International Committee of the Red Cross' Humanitarian Politics and Policies in Asia Minor and Greece (1922–1923)."

27. Watenpaugh, *Bread from Stones*.

28. For a good synthesis, see Latham, *The Right Kind of Revolution*.

29. For the text of this document, see https://www.icrc.org/ihl/INTRO/380.

30. For stimulating discussions of these moral issues, see Barnett, *Humanitarianism in Question*; Fassin, *Humanitarian Reason*; and Fassin and Pandolfi, *Contemporary States of Emergency*.

8

To Make the World Saved

American Religion and the Great War

Andrew Preston

In 1915, New Year's Day was hardly an occasion for celebration. The Great War in Europe had not only lasted past Christmas, it was threatening to devour much of Western civilization. To Americans, many of whom still had direct personal ties to Europe, it seemed as if the continent was on the edge of an abyss. To American Christians, it seemed as if their religion was in the throes of the most brutal civil war, and they called for the madness to stop. One such Christian was the industrialist Andrew Carnegie, a man of loosely defined but devout personal faith. "Is this, the most terrible, most destructive and most uncalled for of wars to be the last between civilized nations?" he asked in a New Year's message. The answer seemed to be yes no matter what happened: either the Allies and the Central Powers would completely destroy each other, with the victor inheriting a fundamentally broken continent, or they would pull back from the apocalypse and agree to reorder their international affairs so as to prevent such a calamity from ever happening again. Carnegie was hopeful that this second outcome would prevail. "Surely," he wrote, "after an armistice is established between the nations now unfortunately at war, the majority of enlightened people in all civilized lands will realize that permanent world peace would be the Earth's greatest blessing." How would the great powers realize such a noble vision? It would be "entirely practicable through a union of a very few powerful nations pledged to maintain it," Carnegie argued. "The Brotherhood of Man would then have arrived, and life on this Earth flash forth glimpses of Heaven."[1]

Carnegie may not have been the most theological man, and his atten-
dance at church was not all that regular, but he was committed to bringing
about God's glory through peace on earth. A year before, Carnegie donated
two million dollars to endow Church Peace Union, a New York–based nongovernmental organization dedicated to fostering peace through arbitration and
international organization. Designed to supplement the efforts of the Carnegie
Endowment for International Peace, established only four years before, Church
Peace Union had close ties to liberal Protestantism's missionary and ecumenical movements. Reflecting Carnegie's hope that religious tolerance would
provide a basis for peace, Church Peace Union closely collaborated with prominent Catholics and Jews, with the Young Men's and Young Women's Christian
Association (YMCA and YWCA), and especially with the Federal Council of
Churches (FCC), the largest church organization in the United States that had
been founded in 1908 to further the spread of the Social Gospel.[2] These "mainline" Protestants were liberal in their outlook, both politically and theologically.
They were optimists, who believed that nations, chastened by the harsh lessons
of war, would learn from their experience and seek measures to end war as a
practice of human behavior. Inspired by relatively new theories of biblical criticism, they believed the Bible was metaphorical, not the literal word of God. In
the parlance of the time, they were modernists.

Yet while liberal Protestants represented the core of the American establishment, they were by no means the only Protestants with strong views on
the Great War. At precisely the same time Carnegie and organizations such as
the FCC and the YMCA were trying to define Christian America's approach
to the world, legions of conservative Protestants were offering their own alternative vision, darker and more pessimistic and thoroughly at odds with the
optimism and progressivism of the liberal churches. By coincidence, the era
of World War I was also the era in which Protestant fundamentalism was
born.[3] Unlike their mainline, liberal rivals, self-described fundamentalists
did not believe that progress was in motion; as biblical literalists, they found
little cause for optimism in scripture. They did not believe in the perfectibil-
ity of humanity, and the war in Europe provided them with ample justification of their outlook. "We see in this great European upheaval a vindication
of the Word of God concerning the present age," warned Reverend Arno
C. Gaebelein, one of the early architects of fundamentalism, shortly after
the outbreak of war in 1914. "How the Higher Critics have sneered at Bible
Prophecy and ridiculed those who have stood up for it!" The apocalypse would
precede the millennium, Gaebelein believed, and events in Europe seemed to
be proving him right.[4]

Modernist and fundamentalist reactions to the catastrophe in Europe were emblematic of larger trends in the United States. Rather than serving only as an era of science, technology, and industry, the Progressive era was also an age of metaphysics and spirituality in which people strove for meaning.[5] The Great War punctuated this spiritual quest. For four years, at a time of bewildering social and political change and in the midst of an inexplicably awful war propelled by modern science and technology, Americans interpreted the war's social, cultural, and political implications in highly spiritual and theological terms.[6] In the process, religion provided Americans with a moral framework for comprehending the war and its broader meaning. This was not simply because the United States was a very religious nation. American security was not under threat from Germany in 1917–1918. In the absence of the need for immediate self-defense, highly idealistic justifications for war predominated, most of which were infused with either a moralistic indignation and righteousness grounded in Christian culture or theories about salvation and redemption inherent to Christian thought. At crucial moments in the years between 1914 and 1919, and for decades afterward, religious Americans put forth compelling interpretations of the war's significance. Religion helped give shape not only to Americans' view of their place in the world, but also to the war's place in the American imaginary.[7]

For Protestants, modernist and fundamentalist alike, as well as Catholics and Jews, World War I was a transformative event even if they never set foot on a muddy battlefield in France or Belgium. For American religion, the war, before and after April 1917, provided a forum in which religious identities became sharply defined. The war's high moral and political stakes forced religious Americans to claim theological and political positions that in short order formed the core of their very identities, many of which have endured in the century since.[8]

The Great War is often remembered as a threshold of modernity, when religion and romanticism gave way to science and secularism. It is assumed, at the time and ever since, that the disillusionment that accompanied the ebbing of intensely patriotic wartime fervor stimulated a newly secular America and what Robert T. Handy famously labeled a "religious depression." As the theologian Walter Horton lamented in 1929, looking back on a hedonistic decade of high modernism, World War I brought forth a wave of "religious skepticism, widespread and devastating."[9] Intensely devout and dedicated missionary organizations, such as the Student Volunteer Movement (SVM), lost their fervor and momentum; by the 1930s, the SVM, once one of the major nongovernmental organizations in the United States, had declined to the point of insignificance.[10] And in 1932, at the behest of an anxious consortium of mainline

Protestant denominations, Harvard's William Hocking authored the so-called Laymen's Report, a wide-ranging and thoughtful but unflinching investigation into whether overseas Christian missions mattered in the modern age.[11] In the wake of the war, cultural hegemony began to pass from religious (namely, Protestant) orthodoxy to secular modernist media exemplified by cars, movies, jazz, and a new generation of disaffected writers.[12]

Yet the passing of hegemony was never complete, and while the war wrought profound changes in American society the decline of religion was not one of them. The reality was more complex, as religion in fact flourished in the age of pragmatism, scientism, and empiricism. The war, and the profound disillusionment it caused, did indeed hasten the rise of secularism and materialism. But that is only part of the story: the war also provoked a demand for spirituality and faith, and it stimulated countless quests for deeper meaning. The United States is, perhaps uniquely, both one of the world's most secular societies and one of its most religious. Secularization in America has not meant the decline of religion, as it has in much of western Europe and Canada, but the privatization of religion and the partial desacralization of the public sphere. In this sense, the Great War marked the birth of a modern America in which religious adherence continued to flourish despite the rise of secularism. Within a few decades of World War I, neither religion nor secularism prevailed in America. Instead, they formed an uneasy, sometimes unstable, and often unwilling partnership that shared cultural and social power. This dual nation, somewhat secular yet only partially under God, has endured ever since.[13]

While accurate in some respects, then, Handy's notion of a "religious depression" can also be deeply misleading, for it implies that American religion overall went into a period of decline. Handy's primary subject, liberal Protestantism, certainly fits this model, but many other religious groups thrived in the decades after World War I—not only Roman Catholics and Jews, but conservative Protestants who identified with the fundamentalist and holiness movements. As Matthew Avery Sutton has conclusively demonstrated in a brilliant recent book, the growth of American evangelicalism and fundamentalism did not stall in the interwar years only to reemerge in revolt against the social and cultural changes of the 1960s. Conservative Protestants were never apolitical, and they never separated themselves from American society to retreat into their own subculture. The formative experience was instead World War I, which marked a point of departure and an enduring influence on a mass movement of evangelicalism that was to have enormous consequences for American culture, politics, and society.[14]

In fact, as with so many other social and cultural changes in the United States, from industrial development to women's rights, World War I acted as a catalyst for the transformation of American religion. Developments that stretched back into the nineteenth century were radicalized and accelerated under the pressure of modern war.[15] Religion was no different. Protestant modernists and fundamentalists had been waging internecine warfare since the 1890s. Modernists, represented by most of the Protestant elite, had made peace with science and the new empiricism. Alarmed by the erosion of the traditional bases of Christian faith, fundamentalists responded by asserting what they believed were the nonnegotiable tenets of religion; they saw the Bible as the literal, inerrant word of God, miracles included. The differences between modernists and fundamentalists—ancestors to the religious liberals and conservatives of more recent culture wars—went beyond theological interpretation, however, because their clashing theologies underpinned completely different worldviews and political ideologies. Modernists were postmillennialists who believed that life on earth must be perfected first before Christ would return in the Second Coming, and they promoted the Social Gospel as an agenda for Progressive reform and the amelioration of social conditions in the here and now. Fundamentalists, on the other hand, were premillennialists who believed that Christ would return to earth only when conditions had deteriorated to such an extent that presaged the rise of Satan's rule. The world would have to get much worse before it would get better, they believed, and they opposed the Social Gospel and other reform initiatives as a result. These fault lines were already visible before the war. Throughout the Progressive era, advocates of the Social Gospel pushed the boundaries of acceptable religion by attempting to broaden Christianity to include elements of science, Darwinism, Freudian psychology, and even Marxism. In response, between 1910 and 1915 conservative Protestant leaders authored ninety pamphlets, known collectively as *The Fundamentals*, in an attempt to establish a baseline for true faith.[16]

Trends may already have been in place, but it took the Great War to crystallize them. This was not a fringe development; it unfolded in the nation's largest centers and attracted widespread attention. Contrary to popular views of a Southern and rural Bible Belt, fundamentalism was initially a Northern and urban phenomenon. New York, Philadelphia, Boston, and Los Angeles all hosted increasingly bitter theological contests. Chicago, home to both the leading liberal and conservative centers of religious learning (respectively, the University of Chicago Divinity School and the Moody Bible Institute), was in particular on the front line of this religious war.[17] Both sides in the struggle for American Protestantism used the war in Europe as a site of contestation and legitimation. Modernists charged fundamentalists with being isolationist. But modernists, who represented Protestantism's established elite, proved to be more vulnerable on the most important issue of the day: loyalty.

Fundamentalists attacked their liberal counterparts for subscribing to German ideas of empiricism and biblical criticism, which could easily be linked to the ideas undergirding autocratic statism. Given that many scholars in the nation's leading theological seminaries and divinity schools had been trained in Germany and received doctorates from German universities, this was not an abstract accusation. Fundamentalists also attacked the pacifism embraced by many modernists; although several self-described fundamentalists had also been pacifists, in the decades before World War I the mainline churches had been heavily invested in the peace crusade, and several of their most prominent representatives—among them Jane Addams, Frederick Libby, Kirby Page, Walter Rauschenbusch, and a young Norman Thomas—refused to support American entry into the war even after April 1917.[18] This made modernists easy targets for fundamentalist charges of betrayal. Given their reflexive antistatism, fundamentalists were in theory open to similar accusations, but after April 1917 they compensated with shrill and unquestioning support for America's cause. It could be said, then, that the conservative dichotomy of loving America but hating the US government was born in the sectarian strife of 1917–1918.

Catholics and Jews did not use the war as a way to define their theology; instead, they used the war as a means to define the legitimacy of their citizenship. By supporting America's war after 1917, even when they had doubts about the war's justice or necessity, Catholics and Jews staked a claim to a "true" American identity. The war thus created a platform for assimilation into the mainstream. To be sure, assimilation was fraught with conflict, as the era of World War I also marked the beginning of serious immigration restriction in the United States. After the heady days of full-throated patriotism and expressions of national unity, the war ushered in a decade of reactionary nativism, anti-Semitism, and racism.[19] From US entry into the war through the Red Scare of 1919 through the rise of the Second Ku Klux Klan in the 1920s, large numbers of Protestants, particularly the new legions of self-described fundamentalists, distrusted Jews and Catholics. Jews were widely suspected of sympathizing with Bolshevism, anarchism, pacifism, and other forms of leftist radicalism, while cultural and religious anti-Catholicism, which had deep roots in American culture, intensified after the war as Prohibition and government funding for education became political flashpoints.[20]

Nonetheless, large numbers of Catholics and Jews overcompensated for their own wartime reservations and for Protestant suspicions by fervently supporting America's war effort. That many Catholics, among them large numbers of Irish and German immigrants who had no love for Britain, unhesitatingly endorsed America's cause in 1917–1918 made this process all the more powerful and effective. The American Jewish League formed its own battalion for military service and the National Council of Jewish Women, the Jewish Welfare Board, the Knights of Columbus, the National Council of Catholic Women, and the National Catholic War Council—renamed the National Catholic Welfare Conference shortly after the war and eventually reconstituted in 2001 as the United States Conference of Catholic Bishops—all volunteered their services, complementing a wide array of Protestant organizations involved in the war effort.[21] The war is usually seen as bringing an end to Progressivism, but left-liberal Catholics used it as a springboard to launch their own role, previously marginalized, within national movements for government reform.[22] With a critical mass of Protestants willing to accept this Jewish and Catholic support at face value, the war marked an important if incomplete transitional phase in the forging what would later come to be called, in the 1930s and 1940s, "tri-faith" and "Judeo-Christian" America.[23]

The war, then, was a crucial moment of transition in American religious history; it profoundly shaped the body and soul of American faith communities. But the reverse was also true: for many Americans, probably most, religion gave shape to the meaning of the war.

For liberal Protestants at the time, whose churches formed the backbone of the American establishment, American entry into the war made it, in Richard Gamble's apt phrase, "a war for righteousness."[24] John R. Mott (Figure 8.1), possibly the most respected religious figure in the nation and a recipient of the Nobel Peace Prize, typified the mainline churches' response to American belligerency. Before 1917, Mott had lent his enormous prestige and vast network of political and religious contacts to the cause of peace. He spent the last four months of 1914 touring Britain, France, and Germany, and he witnessed scenes of carnage firsthand. He returned to urge his close friend, President Wilson, to keep America neutral and free from Europe's "indescribably awful" suffering. With assistance from Quaker friends in London, he founded the American Fellowship of Reconciliation, a pacifist organization that would prove to be instrumental in later antiwar crusades as well as the civil rights movement. But when Wilson and the nation began the rapid turn toward war in early 1917, Mott turned as well. On the day Congress declared war against Germany, Mott cabled Wilson to offer the services of the YMCA to the US military. For the next eighteen months, the Y would minister to the pastoral needs of millions of young Americans shipped to the battlefields of France and Belgium. Mott was deeply involved in US foreign policy—he had rebuffed Wilson's attempts to name him the US ambassador to China and embarked, under the leadership of Elihu Root, on a presidential fact-finding mission to revolutionary Russia in 1917—and so it is not surprising that he came out strongly in support of Wilsonianism after the war, particularly the League of Nations. For Mott as for

FIGURE 8.1 John R. Mott. Yale University Divinity School Library.

Wilson, as for millions of other American Protestants, sacrifice in war would redeem the world. "For the world it is a new birth, a great day of God such as comes once in 100 or 1,000 years," Mott declared after Wilson pronounced the Fourteen Points. War, a demonstrable evil, would nonetheless make the world saved—for peace, prosperity, security, and democracy.[25]

The mainline churches' support for Wilsonianism flowed naturally from liberal Protestant theology and practice. Modernist churches had been heavily involved in two intimately related enterprises—the ecumenical and missionary movements—that were ideologically akin to Wilson's vision. Protestant ecumenism emerged from a desire to quell bickering between denominations and facilitate cooperation to further the advance of the Social Gospel.

The underlying premise was utterly Wilsonian: interdenominational cooperation, and thus religious peace, would occur only when the denominations were
brought together in a common cause under a common institutional umbrella.
For the Protestant churches, the causes were social justice at home and the
abolition of war abroad; the institutional umbrella was the Federal Council
of Churches, along with several partner organizations such as Church Peace
Union, the YMCA/YWCA (see Figure 8.2), the Student Volunteer Movement,
and the World Alliance for the Promotion of International Friendship through
the Churches. Unlike many other Americans, however, their passionate support for a war for righteousness burned just as brightly for a Wilsonian peace.
American Protestants had long championed ecumenical solutions to the problems of world order, but their efforts reached a peak in the first half of the
twentieth century. They were not the only architects of international organization and collective security, but they were certainly among the most fervent and
unwavering. As David Hollinger has pointed out, being ecumenical was the
defining trait of modernist, liberal Protestants and shaped their worldview.[26]

A YMCA IN FRANCE.

FIGURE 8.2 Soldiers at the entrance to a YMCA hut in France. Kautz Family YMCA
Archives, University of Minnesota Libraries.

Woodrow Wilson himself was the ecumenist-in-chief. His intensely religious upbringing and knowledge of church politics and doctrine have long been recognized, but it is only recently that historians have tried to link Wilson's religious views to the formation of his international thought and foreign policy.[27] Following the example of John Mulder, who argues that Wilson's religious background was the foundation on which his politics was built, several historians have illustrated the ways in which religious ideas informed Wilsonianism. Mulder pays particular attention to Wilson's Southern Presbyterianism and its emphasis on covenant theology derived from the radicalism of the Scottish Reformation. According to this idea, God struck a covenant with his people: in return for grace, they promised obedience. The notion that both ruler and ruled had reciprocal rights and responsibilities bound by a formal contract had strong appeal in a nation with such powerful strains of constitutionalism and federalism.[28] Since Mulder, Malcolm Magee has deftly and convincingly shown how Calvinist covenant theology, and other theological principles such as antinomy, shaped Wilson's thinking on neutrality, belligerency, and the League of Nations.[29] Mark Benbow has done similar work on a more specific case study, Wilson's intervention in Mexico.[30] Cara Burnidge's examination of Wilson's faith offers what is probably the most detailed and comprehensive analysis yet of the links between religion, social reform, and Wilsonianism.[31]

Even after the ebbing of Wilsonianism, liberal Protestants continued to champion ecumenical solutions to the problems of world order with an ardor that remained undimmed in the supposedly isolationist interwar era.[32] But many of them also felt chastened by the Great War, and by the failure of the Social Gospel to alleviate industrial conditions, and in response forged a more hard-headed approach, Christian realism, that nonetheless maintained a modernist, ecumenical sensibility.[33] The efforts of ecumenists and realists culminated, both geopolitically and theologically, in the founding of the United Nations in 1945 and the World Council of Churches in 1948; in between, Mott collected his Nobel Peace Prize, in 1946, for his efforts to create "a peace-promoting religious brotherhood across national boundaries."[34] During World War II, John Foster Dulles chaired the FCC's Commission on a Just and Durable Peace, one of the most influential of the several wartime NGOs focusing on planning for postwar world order, which represented perhaps the clearest and most direct application of ecumenical principles to international relations. Dulles participated as a member of the official US delegation at the San Francisco conference that established the UN.[35] In San Francisco, Dulles was joined by Frederick Nolde of the Joint Committee on Religious Liberty. Nolde was not part of the US delegation, but he was instrumental in steering much of the UN's mission toward the promotion of individual human rights.[36]

American Catholics and Jews also lent their support to a Wilsonian peace, albeit for different reasons. They also supported the president's global ambitions, but they also perceived the benefits of Wilsonianism as more direct. National self-determination, about which Wilson himself was more ambivalent than his supporters realized, was particularly appealing.[37] Underlying the support for Wilsonianism by American Catholics and Jews was the shared experience of immigration and the lingering ties to communities in their homelands. For Irish Catholics, Wilsonianism offered the hope of home rule for Ireland and the permanent expulsion of the British. For eastern European Catholics, it offered the hope of independence for countries, such as Poland, that had long been under the yoke of more powerful neighbors. For Jews, similarly, it offered the prospect of an independent Jewish state in Palestine, especially after the British government issued the Balfour Declaration in 1917. For German Catholics, meanwhile, who had suffered the ignominy of hailing originally from America's enemy, Wilsonianism represented the only viable way to end the war without imposing a harsh peace settlement on their mother country.[38]

While virtually all ecumenical Protestants, and many Catholics and Jews, supported a Wilsonian peace grounded first and foremost in the League of Nations and the principle of national self-determination, a significant number of conservative Protestants did not. Initially, before 1917, many if not most fundamentalists had opposed US entry into an unholy civil war of Christendom, brought on by the apostasy and backsliding of the nations involved, that had been foretold in scripture as a prophetic sign that the end times were approaching. But as with many other groups in American society, religious or not, the first four months of 1917 changed perceptions dramatically, and by the time Wilson called for a declaration of war Christian conservatives were squarely behind the president. In fact, while emotions in the mainline churches' crusade for redemption were strong, nobody could match the patriotic fervor of the fundamentalists. Partly this was out of pure and simple patriotism, which ran high in conservative circles and was heightened by the nation going to war. Partly it was in order to counteract liberal, modernist charges that fundamentalists were unpatriotic. But whatever the reason, from April 1917 on fundamentalist support for the war was intense.[39]

By contrast, conservative Protestant ardor for a Wilsonian peace was decidedly tepid. It may seem counterintuitive today, given the intimate relationship between conservative religion and Republican Party politics in recent decades, but evangelicals and fundamentalists had traditionally been the strictest defenders of the First Amendment's separation of church and state. Indeed, until the 1960s, the further right a Protestant denomination was on the theological spectrum, the stricter its defense of church-state separation was likely to be. The reason was simple: separation worked only one way, keeping the state free from the church but allowing the church—that is, Protestant churches— virtually unlimited opportunities to embed itself within the state.[40] The notion of a hard and high wall of separation may have originated with Thomas Jefferson, but its implementation actually dates back only to the decades following World War II, when Jews, Catholics, Jehovah's Witnesses, and others began to resist the nation's de facto Protestant establishment.[41] Before the 1945–1965 period, then, this separationism nurtured a passionate hostility to the state within conservative Protestantism. With their religion more or less untouched, and their freedom to shape politics and culture unimpeded, conservative Protestants' antistatism flourished in part due to its theological roots. Christian conservatives flinched when confronted with the growth of government in the Progressive and New Deal eras, but their antistatism reached a fever pitch with Wilson's League of Nations. Fundamentalists perceived the League as the apogee of the state—a prototype for world government—that would override American sovereignty and open up pathways for the regulation of social life, including the practice of religion.[42] Moreover, an international organization such as the League would have to recognize the inviolable sovereignty and therefore legal equality of all nations—including those that were Catholic, Islamic, Hindu, Buddhist, or even atheistic communist. "How can God bless these nations who continue in idolatries, who defy His laws?" Gaebelein demanded in a pamphlet entitled *The League of Nations in the Light of the Bible.* "Can He bless professing Christian nations, banded together in pact with heathen nations?"[43] In an era when nativism and anticommunism were at a fever pitch, these were heresies to be resisted at all costs.

Other faith communities objected to all aspects of the war. Just as America's first major overseas war confronted US foreign policy and military mobilization with a new set of challenges, conscientious objectors tested the American way of warfare in completely new and difficult ways. All previous American wars had attracted antiwar protest, of course, but war objectors had usually been opposed to the specific aims of a specific war at that particular time; they were not necessarily opposed to all wars for all time on grounds of pacifist principle. At a time when the United States itself was not about to be invaded, intervention in the Great War raised awkward questions about the obligations of citizenship for both conscientious objectors and the US government. Moreover, in previous foreign wars conscientious objectors who were opposed to all wars as a matter of principle had been able to take shelter in the anonymity offered by relative isolation and obscurity. But in 1917, as Christopher Capozzola has shown, national mobilization for total war made anonymity impossible for faith-based conscientious objectors, as communities of sects in sparsely populated areas in the Midwest and Southwest discovered. Historic peace churches, such as the Society of Friends and the Mennonites, received official recognition as conscientious objectors and were protected from the federal government. This new status was eventually extended to other pacifist denominations, such as the Seventh Day Adventists and Jehovah's Witnesses, though not without friction, controversy, and repression.[44]

Yet faith-based conscientious objectors were a tiny minority. For millions of ordinary soldiers, sailors, medical personnel, and relief workers who waged America's first major overseas war, religious faith provided definition of the war and its larger meaning. The war, observes Jonathan Ebel in his careful and compelling study, marked "a moment in America's religious history when cultural and religious currents, fueled by concerns about the nation's future, gave rise to a military impulse suffused with, and framed by, Christianity. Following this impulse, Americans served and fought and died."[45] Theirs was a fight for American righteousness and global redemption no less than it was for Wilson and the clerical elite of the Federal Council of Churches.

Overall, religion was crucial to how people experienced the Great War, whether it be in the trenches near Belleau Wood or the pews of a church in Chicago. Americans turned to religion when they interpreted the war, and they sanctified the war as a spiritual crusade. In turn, how people interpreted the war transformed religions at home, notably Protestantism but also Catholicism and Judaism too. Though different faiths responded to the war in different ways, it was for virtually all of them a religious struggle.

The legacies of American religion's encounter with the Great War were enduring and important. By intensifying the modernist-fundamentalist schism, it helped trigger America's first culture war. By rallying nearly all Protestants to a righteous banner of peace-through-strength and redemptive violence, and by offering Catholics and Jews a platform for assimilation, the war infused politics with religion and embedded patriotism and citizenship with the prerequisite of faith. And by drawing on religious values to justify a war in which US security concerns were peripheral and indirect, American Christians set a lasting standard of perceiving war as a normative, moralistic crusade to right the wrongs in other lands. More than anything else, the war launched America's errand to the world. In ways religious as well as secular, then, the shadow of the Great War continues to linger over the United States.

NOTES

1. Carnegie, "With New Year's Greetings: War Abolished—Peace Enthroned," January 1, 1915, John R. Mott papers, Box 14, Folder 255, Yale Divinity School Archives, New Haven.

2. Wall, *Andrew Carnegie.*

3. For overviews, see Marsden, *Fundamentalism and American Culture;* and, most important, Sutton, *American Apocalypse.*

4. Quoted in Sutton, *American Apocalypse,* chapter 2.

5. Lears, *No Place of Grace.*

6. For similar reasons, Americans also turned increasingly to "irrational psychologies," such as Freudian psychoanalysis, that acknowledged humanity's predilection for primitive behavior. See Ross, *The Origins of American Social Science,* 319–326.

7. Piper, *The American Churches in World War I.* Americans were by no means unique in turning to religion for interpretations of the war. For a broad international overview, see Jenkins, *The Great and Holy War.*

8. For general overviews, see Marty, *Modern American Religion;* and Handy, *Undermined Establishment.*

9. Handy, "The American Religious Depression, 1925–1935," Horton quoted on 6.

10. Showalter, *The End of a Crusade.*

11. Laymen's Foreign Missions Inquiry, Commission of Appraisal, *Re-Thinking Missions.* On Hocking and the Laymen's Report, see Hutchison, *Errand to the World,* 158–175.

12. On World War I as the crucible of modernity, see Eksteins, *Rites of Spring.* On the shift in cultural hegemony, see Douglas, *Terrible Honesty;* and Kemeny, "Power, Ridicule, and the Destruction of Religious Moral Reform Politics in the 1920s."

13. Hollinger, "The 'Secularization' Question and the United States in the Twentieth Century."

14. Sutton, *American Apocalypse.* For the most influential interpretation that stresses the reemergence of evangelicalism in the Cold War after a period of self-induced separation, see Carpenter, *Revive Us Again.*

15. On the war as a catalyst but not necessarily a cause of wider social and cultural change, see Dumenil, *The Modern Temper;* and Goldberg, *Discontented America.*

16. Marsden, *The Fundamentals.*

17. Marsden, *Fundamentalism and American Culture.*

18. Chatfield, *For Peace and Justice,* 13–87; Kosek, *Acts of Conscience,* 16–48.

19. Gerstle, *American Crucible,* 81–122.

20. MacLean, *Behind the Mask of Chivalry,* 91–97; Morone, *Hellfire Nation,* 318–344.

21. Piper, *The American Churches in World War I,* 21–30; Capozzola, *Uncle Sam Wants You,* 31–32, 92–93.

22. McShane, *"Sufficiently Radical."*

23. Schultz, *Tri-Faith America,* 26–29. This was not the first instance in which American wars had facilitated the process of assimilation and cultural acceptance: both the Civil War and the Spanish-American War received ardent backing from Catholics and Jews (and, indeed, Mormons) as a means to demonstrate their bona fide American patriotism. This use of war as a legitimation of citizenship unfolded despite the fact that Irish Catholics protested against one of the Civil War's main objectives, black emancipation, in the notorious draft riots of 1863, or that in 1898

most of the Catholic hierarchy privately felt it was wrong to fight a Catholic power, Spain, over the fate of a Catholic colony, Cuba. And the process would not be complete until World War II and, especially, the early Cold War. But, along the way, World War I marked a crucial threshold. See Preston, *Sword of the Spirit, Shield of Faith*, 172–174, 216–218, 268–274.

24. Gamble, *The War for Righteousness*.

25. Hopkins, *John R. Mott, 1865–1955*, 398–400, 476–597; Preston, *Sword of the Spirit, Shield of Faith*, 242–243, 261, 265–267, Mott quoted on 243, 275.

26. Hollinger, *After Cloven Tongues of Fire*, 21.

27. Some of Wilson's most perceptive and authoritative biographers have acknowledged the importance of Wilson's religion but argued that it had little relevance to his politics and foreign policy. See, for example, Thompson, *Woodrow Wilson*, 18–20; and Cooper, *Woodrow Wilson*, 4–5. An authoritative exception that affords religion a great deal of causal weight is Link, *The Higher Realism of Woodrow Wilson*, 3–20.

28. Mulder, *Woodrow Wilson*.

29. Magee, *What the World Should Be*.

30. Benbow, *Leading Them to the Promised Land*.

31. Burnidge, "The Business of Church and State"; Burnidge, *A Peaceful Conquest*.

32. Gorman, *The Emergence of International Society in the 1920s*, 213–258.

33. Edwards, *The Right of the Protestant Left*.

34. Mott's Nobel citation quoted in "John R. Mott-Facts," Nobel Media, http://www.nobelprize.org/nobel_prizes/peace/laureates/1946/mott-facts.html (accessed May 7, 2014).

35. On Dulles and the commission, see Pruessen, *John Foster Dulles*, 178–217; Toulouse, *The Transformation of John Foster Dulles*, 61–86; Hollinger, "The Realist-Pacifist Summit Meeting of March 1942"; and Preston, *Sword of the Spirit, Shield of Faith*, 384–409.

36. Nurser, *For All Peoples and All Nations*.

37. On the ambivalence of this aspect of Wilson's worldview, see Manela, *The Wilsonian Moment*.

38. Preston, *Sword of the Spirit, Shield of Faith*, 285–287.

39. Sutton, *American Apocalypse*, 47–78.

40. Sehat, *The Myth of American Religious Freedom*.

41. Hamburger, *Separation of Church and State*.

42. Fundamentalist opposition to the League has received its fullest treatment in Ruotsila, *The Origins of Christian Anti-Internationalism*. But see also Marsden, *Fundamentalism and American Culture*, 154–156; Preston, *Sword of the Spirit, Shield of Faith*, 287–290; and Sutton, *American Apocalypse*, chapter 2. For more on the dynamic of conservative separationism and its applications to foreign relations, especially international organization, see Preston, "Universal Nationalism."

43. Quoted in Ruotsila, *The Origins of Christian Anti-Internationalism*, 38.

44. Capozzola, *Uncle Sam Wants You*, 55–82. See also Chatfield, *For Peace and Justice*, 55–58, 68–87; Chambers, *To Raise an Army*, 173–175, 205–237; and Kosek, *Acts of Conscience*, 37–41.

45. Ebel, *Faith in the Fight*, 1.

PART 3

America in the World

Empire, Revolution, and Power

9

The Geopolitics of Revolution

Lloyd C. Gardner

An apparition with countenance different from any yet seen on
earth stood in the place of the old Ally. We saw a state without a
nation, an army without a country, a religion without a God.
— Winston S. Churchill, *The World Crisis,*
1918–1928

Two weeks after the United States entered the Great War in April 1917,
Walter Lippmann wrote in the *New Republic*, "We are living and shall
live all our lives now in a revolutionary world. This means among
other things a world of restless experiment." All this activity could
lead to chaos unless our minds were disciplined "by some great central idea." The war had erased *all* boundaries, moreover, including
those between domestic affairs and foreign policy. So reshuffling the
"Great Game" the industrial powers had played over previous decades
would not be enough. The "great central idea" is best known today to
historians as the "New Diplomacy," and the struggle to understand its
implications and how it could be used is often personified as "Wilson
vs. Lenin."[1]

Lippmann was certainly right about one thing: ideas were in the
saddle now and they would drive governments to seek better solutions to questions of war and peace—and social justice—than the
complex treaty systems that led to "the Great War."[2]

When the war began President Woodrow Wilson asked the nation
to be neutral in thought and deed. Early on, however, he sought a role
as the arbiter of peace terms. Indeed, on the very brink of the war
in 1914, his envoy, Col. Edward M. House, had urged the German
government to abandon its self-absorbed militarist posturing and
recognize the need for the industrial powers to join in developing
the "waste places" of the earth to minimize or eliminate dangerous

competition among the metropolitan nations. Neither Wilson nor House (or anyone else) could foresee the war lasting so long, however, or cutting Europe's material and moral reserves down to the bone.[3]

Nearly two years later House reiterated the point in much darker terms. Talking with German Chancellor Theobald von Bethmann-Hollweg, House minced no words: "I told him Western Civilization had broken down, and there was not a market-place or a mosque in the East where the West of to-day was not derided."[4]

The war in Europe soon became known as the Great War or, later, World War I, because of the almost immeasurable numbers of the dead, and the geographical scope of the conflict extending into every continent. But geography alone is only the most superficial of understandings of what a "World War" was that had roots in colonial rivalries and challenges to the existing order and that continued in religious ideological fervor. It was not uncommon, for example, for political war leaders to say, on the one hand, that the war was fought on God's order to save the "whole" world from a militaristic and atavistic Germany; or for the other to appeal to Germany's right to defend itself, and the whole world, against "Asiatic barbarism" that threatened in the wake of a Russian advance.[5] That particular metaphor, of course, later became a rallying cry against the Bolshevik Revolution.

The war began with the scramble for Africa among the European colonial powers in geographical terms all but over, and with envious eyes looking to stake or solidify claims on Chinese territory as the fall of the Manchu dynasty seemed to open up opportunities for exploitation of resources and markets for Russia and for newcomer Japan. Americans had always imagined a special role for themselves in China's development, politically and economically. It is worth going back a moment to that time when the partition of China was under way at the turn of the twentieth century and the American reactions, for it provides a guide to World War I policy toward revolutions. During the Boxer Rebellion in China at the turn of the century, President William McKinley's cabinet debated the wisdom of sending a contingent of American Marines from the Philippines to join the "allied" relief forces to rescue the besieged legations. Secretary of State John Hay warned the American minister in China that there must be only a minimum involvement with the other powers. "We have no policy in China except to protect with energy American interests and especially American citizens.... There must be no alliances."[6] After the powers crushed the antiforeign rebellion, they demanded the Chinese government pay an indemnity for damages to foreign property. The American diplomat W. W. Rockhill felt trapped in the European alliance system as a result of participation in the military expedition: "I trust it may be a long time before the United

States gets into another muddle of this description."[7] In a small gesture to set the United States apart from the Europeans, President Theodore Roosevelt thought it would be a good idea to use some of the indemnity money China was forced to pay the powers for scholarships to educate Chinese students in American universities. The gesture was a typical example of American methods and its claim to be the "exceptional" empire of liberty.

In 1913, as one of his first acts in foreign policy, Woodrow Wilson took the United States out of an international banking consortium that he believed desired special privileges that would impinge on China's sovereignty as it attempted to emerge from the years of special concessions and extraterritorial humiliations. When it became clear in World War I that a new consortium might be the only way to preempt independent actions of the powers and Japan, he reversed himself! In Mexico, meanwhile, a nationalist president had emerged out of the turmoil following a long dictatorship and the short ineffectual presidency of Francisco Madero. Venustiano Carranza wanted to write a new constitution, however, that threatened the oil and mineral concessions that Porfirio Diaz had handed out in an attempt to balance the interests and rivalries of the new imperialist era dominated by engineers instead of conquistadores. Wilson addressed Mexican newspaper editors with a promise that American entry into the war meant that the peace that would be written would ensure fair dealing and would allow Mexico to feel it could open the country to new foreign investment. "So soon as you can admit your own capital and the capital of the world to the free use of the resources of Mexico, it will be one of the most wonderfully rich and prosperous countries in the world."[8]

Surely international fair dealing was a better way to protect Mexico's natural resources than socialist-style nationalizing of Carranza's proposed constitution. American policymakers thus agreed that Germany's would-be interference in the Mexican Revolution was a reason for going to war—to turn back a dual challenge of reaction and revolution with a third way, reformed nations acting like America's fair-dealing Uncle Sam. Cries for self-determination had started the war. In the Balkans, where it all began, the area around Sarajevo was a boiling cauldron of Serbian nationalism. When Gavrilo Princip rushed out of the crowd to shoot Austrian Archduke Franz Ferdinand, he said it was because as sovereign he would pursue a reformist program that would drain away the ardor for true Serbian independence.[9]

In all these places—and others including the stirrings in French Indochina—young nationalists argued among themselves about what kind of revolution their country needed, just as the European powers and the United States struggled to understand the challenges they faced. They were, in a sense, wrestling with the question the Russian radical and Marxist theoretician

V. I. Lenin had put in a 1901 pamphlet, "What Is to Be Done?" Lenin had called for a political party, not just protests for improving the conditions of labor-ers. The rise of a "leftist-nationalist" political consciousness, in which debates over what kind of agenda suited the traditions and needs of the previously "excluded" classes, took shape in both the industrial metropolis and the periph-eral dependencies and colonies. And these were not the concerns simply of the disenfranchised. Intellectuals and some political leaders in the metropolitan countries envisioned a form of "socialism" at home, and capitalism abroad—in order to prevail in the international struggle for existence.[10]

In the case of the United States, for example, Theodore Roosevelt's "Square Deal" program fit well alongside his determination to play a leading role in international affairs, both as imperialist and "disinterested" arbiter of disputes among the other powers, as in the Russo-Japanese War, lest their over-reaching folly bring the delicately balanced imperial system crashing down around their ears—letting loose all sorts and varieties of nationalist movements in the dark alleys behind the broad, palm-lined streets that fronted on the harbors where Western-built trains brought rice and rubber, cocoa and cotton for export. Woodrow Wilson would go beyond TR in his thinking about what caused revo-lutionary fevers, in his determination to replace the old imperial system with a League of Nations, whose members would not only enforce peace, but also fol-low an American example in fair dealing with the countries that hosted invest-ments in extractive oil and mining enterprises. One could say that he was the most revolutionary leader, pre–World War I, in the sense of disturber-in-chief of the old order, whether the scene was China, Mexico, or Europe.[11]

Of course, that did not mean that Wilson dreamed up America's role in world affairs as the leader in forming a new world order. As Walter LaFeber points out in *The American Search for Opportunity, 1865–1913*, the growth of the presidency and presidential initiatives in foreign policy had been the prod-uct, both in substance and chronology, of the work of decades. Thus Wilson's keen sense of right and wrong in all political matters came from America's history as well as his personality and enabled him to make distinctions among the nations locked in terrible mortal combat on the stalemated battlefields of France. Frustrated by his administration's inability to make headway in per-suading the warring sides to understand the real stakes of the conflict, Wilson sometimes complained he could see no real differences in the war aims of either side. He shocked Walter Hines Page, his ambassador to Great Britain, for example, by saying the war centered on "economic rivalries": "England's having the earth and Germany wanting it."[12]

Wilson also, like other American political leaders, feared the war would divide the United States along ethnic lines and would promote radical thinking about the social order. The assassination of William McKinley in 1901, almost an afterthought in present-minded histories, was, in fact, part of a pattern of terrorist acts by anarchists in European countries that signaled danger to the old order.[13] Hence the double meaning of his famous phrase "The world must be made safe for democracy."[14] Wilson and House held views similar to the English thinker John A. Hobson's contention that imperialism was a *choice* of capitalist nations, and not, as the Marxist-Leninist analysis would claim, an *inevitable outcome* of capitalism.[15] Such an analysis fueled Wilson's belief in self-determination—as Americans defined the term. Like his predecessors, he believed in America's special mission to the world, and that domestic democracy could be—had to be—projected abroad.

Lippmann's colleague at the *New Republic*, Walter Weyl, wrote about American entry into the war, "We can no longer stand aside and do nothing, for that is the worst and most dangerous of policies. We must either plunge into national competitive imperialism, with all its profits and dangers . . . or must seek out some method by which the economic needs and desires of rival industrial nations . . . may be compromised and appeased . . . and capital develop backward lands without the interested nations flying at each other's throat." Then came the critical answer to how this was to be done, which then became the American response to the Bolshevik Revolution: "It is out of the frontier mind," he added, "that we have evolved our present American notion of war and foreign policy." American economic development had been accomplished by railroads—the connecting links between eastern capital, the frontiersmen, and economic prosperity for the nation. The development of the American West showed that peace was natural, said Weyl, war just so much foolishness.[16]

This formula for preserving peace and countering revolutions, as will be seen below, became highly useful to American policymakers as they wrestled with what to do about revolutionary Russia. But it applied also to other cases, not just Russia driven by Lenin's band of Marxist all-or-nothings. It extended (and extends) from the American reaction to the Boxer Rebellion, through Lyndon Johnson's dream of countering Ho Chi Minh's appeal with dams on the Mekong River to provide electricity to and economic development for the entire area that included Vietnam and its neighbors, down to American hopes for the "Arab Spring" after the disappointments of the Bush phase of the war on terror. It is sometimes called modernization theory, and it is not a legacy of World War I but was given a powerful stimulus by the war and ideas for reconstruction. The theory included prompting revolutionary Russia—after the "temporary" Bolshevik regime imposed by force alone fell before the onslaught of reason and American "help"—to see the light.

But in the specific instance of the Great War, how was one to find a difference between the alliances to justify the risks of American intervention and
to launch the new world order? After the sinking of the *Lusitania* in May 1915,
Wilson exclaimed, "Shall we ever get out of the labyrinth made for us all by
this German 'frightfulness'"?[17] Unrestricted submarine warfare made it possible for Wilson to satisfy his conscience and to draw distinctions between the
combatants—but he most certainly did not want to go to war for a "specific"
cause without having established a "peace" plan that would address and blunt
the arguments of war critics, right and left, such as Eugene Debs (Figure 9.1),
the Socialist candidate for president in 1912 who garnered a million votes.

FIGURE 9.1 Eugene Debs. Library of Congress, LC-USZ62-54841.

Each time Wilson approached the brink, he stepped back. As he confided to House, "We are the only one of the great white nations that is free from war to-day, and it would be a crime against civilization for us to go in." Germany's resumption of unrestricted submarine warfare in early 1917 did not block out his fears. He told his hawkish secretary of state, Robert Lansing, he was "more and more impressed with the idea that 'white civilization' and its domination in the world rested largely on our ability to keep this country intact, as we would have to build up the nations ravaged by the war."[18]

On January 22, 1917, he made a remarkable final appeal for a peace without victory:

> The question upon which the whole future peace and policy of the world depends is this: Is the present war a struggle for a just and secure peace, or only for a new balance of power?
>
> Victory would mean peace forced upon the loser, a victor's terms imposed upon the vanquished. . . . Only a peace between equals can last.

In a letter to an editor, he added that he was not addressing the Senate or foreign powers, but "the *people* of the countries now at war." If he could create enough pressure their regimes would be forced to seek peace.[19]

Two nearly simultaneous events finally convinced the president to ask Congress to declare war: the intercepted Zimmerman Telegram from Berlin to Mexico City in late January offering the Mexicans a military alliance, and the overthrow of the Russian Tsar Nicholas II weeks later. Both incidents provided him with a foundation to argue that he was acting to protect revolutionary governments from German intrigues (and from their own follies) by entering the war and taking charge of the peace. Under the war strain Tsarist Russia had cracked wide open and competing forces tried in vain to rally a shattered military and exhausted population for one more military offensive or, its opposite, an effort to lead an international conference to find a peace formula. Wilson's war message to Congress in early April contained this paragraph:

> Does not every American feel that assurance has been added to
> our hope for the future peace of the world by the wonderful and
> heartening things that have been happening within the last few
> weeks in Russia? Russia was known by those who knew it best to
> have been always in fact democratic at heart, in all the vital habits
> of her thought, in all the intimate relationships of her people that
> spoke their natural instinct, their habitual attitude towards life. The
> autocracy that crowned the summit of her political structure, long as
> it had stood and terrible as was the reality of its power, was not in fact

Russian in origin, character, or purpose; and now it has been shaken off. . . . Here is a fit partner for a league of honour.

Saving the new Russia had thus become a rationale for American intervention. Only this way, moreover, could imperial Germany be controlled and changed internally. If the new government failed in Russia, and it left the war, Berlin's position would become—both militarily and ideologically—impossible to overcome. Revolution had become the vital X factor in calculating the future. "We are at the beginning of an age in which it will be insisted that the same standards of conduct and of responsibility for wrongdoing shall be observed among nations and their governments that are observed among the individual citizens of civilized states."

Thus, when Wilson asked Congress to declare war in 1917, it was as an "associated" power without commitments to integrate its army into a unified command or tie itself to the tail of the Allies' specific war aims. The Allies welcomed American entrance into the war, even if they viewed traditional American doctrines such as the Open Door and the Monroe Doctrine as pretentious rhetorical covers for the United States' own economic ambitions, feared American interference with what they hoped to gain out of a war that had cost so much sacrifice—that they somehow had to justify to their own peoples—and resented American assumptions of moral superiority.[20]

But American policymakers had always believed they were different (even exceptional among nations) and, moreover, in a perfect position geographically and ideologically to bring the new world to the old world's rescue—thereby fulfilling Lord Canning's famous boast about the Monroe Doctrine: "I called the New World into existence to redress the balance of the old."

In 1917, excitement about the "new" Russia freed from both German—and Allied—domination was mixed with fear about a separate peace. Wilson was quite upset about "the movement among the Socialists to confer about international affairs. They are likely to make a deal of mischief, especially in connection with affairs in Russia." The mischief these "Socialists" were up to included the so-called Petrograd Formula put forward by the All-Russian Congress of Soviets for a peace settlement based on national self-determination, no annexations, and no indemnities. The Reichstag gave the proposal a thumbs-up vote by a decisive majority, but President Wilson saw in the proposal nothing but a German effort to "lead the people of Russia astray" into a separate peace that would leave Germany in control of Eastern Europe.

At first there was some heartening news from Russia. The Provisional Government was cheered by American entrance into the war. Only the radicals led by the recently returned exile, V. I. Lenin, opposed the war. Lenin said the so-called revolution had actually been a plot of the British and French, who believed the Tsar was no longer able to control the people.²¹ In a response of sorts to Lenin's charge, Wilson delivered a speech on Flag Day, June 14, 1917, that was the polar opposite of his Peace Without Victory speech in January. There had always been a German plot, he now argued, a "plan which compassed Europe and Asia from Berlin to Bagdad." The president also introduced in this speech the agent theory of revolution that would become a staple of American Century policymakers puzzled by untoward events abroad—and domestic dissent. Wilson stated, "The sinister intrigue is being no less actively conducted in this country than in Russia and in every country of Europe into which the agents and dupes of the Imperial German Government can get access." If one is to speak of World War I legacies, the Flag Day speech and the enactment of the 1917 Espionage Act certainly qualify as examples of a legislative effort to get around the constitutional guarantees of free speech and freedom from unwarranted searches, beginning with the imprisonment of the Socialist leader and war critic Eugene Debs, and continuing down to the use of the Act to indict whistleblowers/leakers in the post-9/11 era.

Wilson's chief ideological rival, Lenin, countered with a similar appeal to the "masses" and would seize on Wilson's self-determination credo to protect the Bolshevik government against intervention when it came to power. Wilsonian hopes for the postwar world now focused on the "Eastern Military Front," along with the fears that Bolshevism might infect other countries from the Eastern *Political* Front (and even colonies) and make them ungovernable. In fact, Russia had always been near the center of American hopes and concerns about the war's outcome.

It is necessary to backtrack here to fill in the background to the particular American plan for "intervention" in the Russian Revolution and its ultimate legacy in the Cold War and post–Cold War years. Only a few weeks into the conflict, Foreign Minister Sergei D. Sazonov had alerted American diplomats to the opportunity to replace Germany's commercial role in Russia.

"You know from the many serious talks I have had with you recently," he told Charles Wilson, "that my hobby is having America take the place here that Germany has occupied in our commercial life." Sazonov always stressed, however, that Russia needed cash advances to fight the Germans. In other words, the United States would have to buy its way into the Russian market with government loans. At this point the United States had not decided whether loans were neutral or not. Secretary of State William Jennings Bryan was sure they were not. Wilson had not yet spoken out definitively. Sazonov was quoted in the *Washington Times*, meanwhile, as observing, "for Americans especially does Russia open opportunity for an industrial outlet such as hardly can be over-stated."[22]

While it is too much to say the change in American policy was a response to such overtures, Bryan's successor, Robert Lansing, pushed trade negotiations with Russia as a high priority. He would play a key role later in opposing any dealings with the Lenin government. Meanwhile, Wilson removed the bar blocking war loans even in the midst of the *Lusitania* crisis, writing his new secretary of state, "My opinion in this matter, compendiously stated, is that we should say that 'Parties would take no action either for or against such a transaction,' but that this should be orally conveyed, so far as we are concerned, and not put in writing."[23]

But nothing happened about Russia for months. Then on January 14, 1916, Lansing received an urgent message from Willard Straight, who represented American bankers interested in breaking an Anglo-French monopoly and who would use the 1916 Paris Economic Conference of the Allies as a warning to Washington that the peace could be lost before America entered the war. An old Asian hand, Straight was part of a new effort to mobilize banking resources for loans to Russia. Negotiations were under way, wrote Straight, but the bankers worried about "persistent reports" that the Allies were planning special tariff understandings between them. Therefore, would it not be wise to tie the proposed loans to assurances about fair treatment for American commerce after the war?

Yes, he was working on that very problem, Lansing replied. So was the new ambassador to Russia, David Francis, a man determined to make sure the Allies did not close out American bankers from participating in the postwar development of an anticipated vast market. In June 1916 the Allies held a meeting in Paris to counter what they saw as Germany's determination to seal off Central Europe—or *Mitteleuropa*—after the war for an unlimited time, until in fact it had the ability to force Russia into its combine permanently. The Paris Economic Conference called for extensive revisions in trade relations with those outside the alliance—neutrals—as well as the Central Powers.

The conference had been called to devise means to make sure Germany did not steal a march on economic recovery after the war, but with Allied war debts to the United States piling up, its proposals were also interpreted in Washington as preventives against an American forward movement in postwar Russia. Good news came from the American ambassador in Paris: the Russians were not really happy with the results of the Paris Economic Conference. Francis had indeed set out to detach Russia from Anglo-French schemes about the war-after-the-war through a comprehensive trade agreement, and he succeeded in negotiating a loan six months later—the first step, he hoped, in larger financial transactions to come.[24]

Francis soon reported another happy development: the American loan had already led to the purchase of 350,000 tons of rails from the US Steel Corporation, "the largest order perhaps ever given at one time." These transactions would offset the "well designed plan of England, and perhaps France also, to capture the trade of Russia after the war through the operation of the resolutions passed at the Economic Conference of the Allies."[25]

When the February Revolution began, Francis saw great opportunities ahead. Financing the Provisional Government would be the "master stroke" to cement the American position in the new Russia. It would require a huge loan—$500 million—and "not through British intervention as heretofore." From London came another suggestion that the best way to help the Russians would be a railroad mission to reorganize the Trans-Siberian Railway. "It has been suggested to me by a man who knows Russia that American management would greatly help the Russian military situation and prove to be also an invaluable key after the war to industrial development."[26]

The president then decided to send two commissions to Russia: one to counter malicious "socialist" propaganda, headed by former Secretary of State Elihu Root, and a second mission headed by "Col." John F. Stevens, accompanied by more than two hundred railroad experts. The latter took on the Herculean task of using American methods and materials to modernize the Trans-Siberian Railway. A key artery both in keeping the Russian war spirit alive and helping its economy recover, the Trans-Siberian was nearly six thousand miles long. Its connecting lines, the Chinese Eastern Railway and the South Manchurian Railway, had long been coveted by Western interests and recently by Japanese developers as well. Before the war the railroad had facilitated the settlement of nearly four hundred thousand new "Siberians" every year—the promise of Russia's future development—and a process most like the American "Western" experience.[27]

The end point of the Trans-Siberian was Vladivostok, and through that portal the door opened to the Russian Far East (or America's imagined new West), a route that would push aside the "sinister" designs of the Germans and Japanese. Stevens had solved big engineering problems on the American transcontinental system, and Secretary of Commerce William Redfield was sure he would succeed in Russia, too. The prospects for Siberia once the railroads got properly organized, he believed, were stupendous. "Before the war settlers from European Russia were coming to Western Siberia at the rate of 300,000 yearly. The cities are increasing in population with astonishing rapidity. Railroads, cold-storage plants, electric lights and street car systems, the lumber industry, shipbuilding, mining, and the cultivation of the fertile southern section are held up as opportunities both for the sale of goods and for the investment of

capital." The United States had developed its frontier West with such a combination in the past century; now it was ready to apply the same capital and
management skills to the new frontier Siberia offered.[28]

In the short life of the Provisional Government, the American engineer
made great progress in modernizing the Trans-Siberian with American materials and know-how. When the Bolsheviks seized power in November, however,
it all seemed to come apart. "I can not stand Russian winter," Stevens wrote
to the State Department. "Will shortly leave for the United States." Officials
in Washington ordered him to stay near for he would have a role to play as
developments played out.[29] Consequently, he did not leave the area, instead taking his two hundred engineers to Nagasaki, Japan, to await orders that would
eventually bring him back to Vladivostok once again to act as the historian Leo
Bacino aptly describes his mission as "a minister plenipotentiary for Russia's
railroads."[30]

Stevens actually was eager to block Japanese efforts to take advantage of the
turmoil to increase their grip on Northeast Asia. With Russian-German peace
negotiations looming, and Allied military landings in other parts of Russia at
Archangel and Murmansk, it appeared that the Bolshevik Revolution had let
loose a partition mania like that which had occurred in China only decades
earlier. "We should all go back shortly with man-of-war and 5,000 troops," an
aroused Stevens cabled Lansing. "Time is coming to put fear of God into these
people."[31]

It was not entirely clear who "these people" were—the Japanese or the
Bolsheviks. Top officials in Washington did not believe the Bolshevik period
would last, but the interlude before "reason" (in the form of a strong man) took
over again could be a disaster for the outcome of the war and, in Wilson's word,
poisonous for the world. The Allies pressed Wilson to join them in intervening
ostensibly to reopen the Eastern Front as Russo-German peace negotiations
began. A massive shift of German forces from the East back to France was a
genuine fear as American intervention in the war had yet to be calculated, but
Allied motives were hardly so clear to Washington when British and French
troops landed in great numbers on Russian soil in places far distant from
scenes of combat. Soon high commissioners were appointed for these areas,
the British in the north and the French in the south; and in occupied areas military authorities issued special currencies. The British even requested that the
United States show its intentions to maintain its position in Siberia by appoint-
ing a high commissioner there. To Washington all this looked exactly like the
sort of scramble for "spheres of influence in China" two decades earlier—and
exactly the opposite of what Wilson meant by self-determination.

But now Secretary of State Robert Lansing argued there must be no direct dealings with the Bolsheviks, the "dangerous idealists." He had expected they would fail at once, because of their inherent contradiction of human nature. "Up to the present, however, the logic of events has failed." Their goal was a "'social revolution,' which will sweep away national boundaries, social distinctions and modern political, religious and social institutions, and make the ignorant mass of humanity dominant in the earth. They indeed plan to destroy civilization by mob violence."[32]

Russia, the military Eastern Front, was not as dangerous—by far—as the political Eastern Front. Lenin understood that and hoped to make use of such fears; he had denounced the Allies' peace terms as mere rhetoric and sheer hypocrisy. "Are they willing," he said, "on their part to give the right of self-determination to the people of Ireland, Egypt, India, Madagascar, Indo-China, etc, as the Russian Revolution has given this right to the peoples of Finland, Ukraine, . . . etc." To demand self-determination for peoples in enemy states and their colonies, while refusing those in their own colonies "would mean the defense of the most naked, the most cynical imperialism."[33]

Fearing the president would be so disgusted by Allied actions that he would consider dealing with the Bolsheviks, Lansing urged Wilson to issue a statement refusing diplomatic recognition to the new government. Since Russia was by definition "overwhelmingly democratic in spirit and purpose," the secretary of state reminded Wilson of his own words, "it cannot be that the Bolshevik leaders represent the Russian people or express their will." The president proved reluctant to commit himself publicly on support or nonsupport for the allies. But he authorized financial assistance to anti-Bolshevik forces organizing in southern Russia, and later ordered American troops to Siberia ostensibly to guard the Trans-Siberian Railway.[34]

Complicating the scene, the Bolshevik "foreign minister" Leon Trotsky had delivered a speech explaining why the United States had entered the war (see Figure 9.2). It almost seemed he had been reading State Department correspondence about great opportunities in postwar, post-Bolshevik Russia. Trotsky readily agreed with Wilson's frequent statements that the United States desired no territory. Instead, it sought ascendancy in the capitalist world order. Since that was so, it could tolerate a Soviet-organized Russia, because with the decline of the other capitalist coalitions, "America is interested in investing her capital in Russia." Wilson read the speech to his cabinet and dismissed it as opéra bouffe, but he understood the consequences of an "armistice with Germany when a child would know Germany would control and dominate and destroy any chance for the democracy they desire."[35]

FIGURE 9.2 Vladimir Lenin speaking at a meeting in Sverdlov Square in Moscow on May 5, 1920, with Trotsky on the side of the platform. Photo by Grigori Goldstein, public domain.

Somehow the United States had to find an answer or a platform now that Russia was effectively under a new "alien" regime. He did not consider the alternative of attempting a modus vivendi. Instead, Wilson and House listened to advice from Boris Bakhmeteff (Figure 9.3), the ambassador whom the Provisional Government had sent to Washington. He urged the president to refrain from an explicit denunciation of the Bolsheviks—something that would only alienate the Russian people and "aid the Maximalists [Bolsheviks] to go to extremes." The president should restate his war aims, adding words of friendly encouragement to Russia with promises of substantial help in their quest. These consultations—and those with other advisers—produced the Fourteen Points speech in January 1918. Point VI promised Russia help in obtaining "an unhampered and unembarrassed opportunity for the independent determination of her own political development and national policy." And he added, "Whether their present leaders believe it or not, it is our heartfelt desire and hope that some way may be opened whereby we may be privileged to assist the people of Russia to attain their utmost hope of liberty and ordered peace."[36]

The speech actually encoded Wilson's conviction the Bolsheviks would not last and that he was ready to help when a new government came to power—one

FIGURE 9.3 Boris Bakhmeteff (center), July 1917. Library of Congress, Prints and
Photographs Division, LC-DIG-ggbain-24849.

that would promise "real" self-determination. Therefore, he funded the continued existence of the Bakhmeteff embassy as the only recognized government
of Russia out of contingency funds in the president's budget—even though the
embassy's authority ended at its front door in Washington, DC. He did more
than that, allowing money to be laundered through the British and French to
"un-organized movements" still fighting the Germans, even though he had
"no power to lend money direct" to the various would-be leaders of a future
redeemer Russian government.[37]

A few weeks later, Lansing authorized John F. Stevens (Figure 9.4) to
return to Siberia to take up once again the work on Siberian railroads. This

FIGURE 9.4 John F. Stevens. Library of Congress, LC-USZ62-124261.

time it was part of an "intervention" that included Japanese and American troops. Wilson's hand had been forced by the Japanese determination to have a role in Far Eastern questions. Francis had reason to believe, however, that Trotsky would not openly oppose an American railroad mission, especially if it were done to block Japanese ambitions. The Stevens mission soon became simply more than reorganization of railroads, however, or watching over Japanese moves. With reports coming into Washington that local "self-governing" groups were springing up in Russia's Far Eastern provinces, Wilson wrote Lansing, "It would afford me a great deal of satisfaction to get behind those the most nearly representative of them if it can indeed draw leadership and control to itself."[38]

Stevens had given a press interview at the time of the Fourteen Points speech that expressed somewhat similar hopes. "Siberia is not so much disturbed as Russia," he said, "and it is the people's desire to support any government appearing to be stable." Here, apparently, was that elusive democratic spirit that Wilson had once talked about in his war message. Germany would not succeed in getting a separate peace, Stevens went on, if America managed the diplomacy of the Trans-Siberian. But he seemed to disagree with the policy of excluding the Bolsheviks from American aid. "The Maximalists now in control," he said, are much stronger than is generally credited. "In any future reorganization or attempts at a stable government the Maximalists must be considered and handled rightly."[39]

Holding off a cease-fire on the Eastern Front proved impossible, but it can hardly be said that alone had remained Wilson's major concern—as he looked to preserve a Siberian alternative to the Bolsheviks. The Treaty of Brest-Litovsk surrendered to Germany "about one-third of its prewar population, one-third of its agricultural land, 54 percent of its heavy industry, 33 percent of its railway system, 73 percent of its iron ore output, and 89 percent of its coal mines." If the Bolsheviks were not actually German agents, some charged, the results could hardly have been different—at least in the immediate sense.[40]

The standard "geopolitical" argument about the American role in the Allied military intervention holds that fear that Germany would dominate all Eastern Europe explains the American decision to send troops to Siberia. But suppose the Bolshevik Revolution had occurred some months later, after American aid and soldiers had turned the tide in the West, and the Kaiser had abdicated? Would Lansing's fear that the Bolsheviks would overturn civilization be any the less? Would Wilson have acted differently?[41]

Wilson remained as adamant against exploring any hints that Bolshevik leaders were open to discussions about aid in exchange for a truce in their ideological warfare against the West. "I don't think you need fear any consequences of our dealing with the Bolsheviks," Wilson wrote to Senator James Hamilton Lewis, who had expressed a concern, "because we are not going to deal with them."[42] He had been "sweating blood" about what was right and possible to do, he wrote House. "It goes to pieces like quicksilver under my touch, but I hope I see and can report some progress presently, along the double line of economic assistance and aid to the Czecho-Slovenes."[43]

The complicated story of the Czech involvement in the Russian Civil War cannot be retold here.[44] It must suffice that the American troops Wilson sent to guard the Trans-Siberian inevitably became enmeshed in the conflicts between those freed prisoners of war traveling to Vladivostok to reach the Western Front and pro-Bolshevik armies. One can take Wilson's words to mean that he intended only to support Russians who were making efforts at self-determination, or that he fully understood the objective was to over-throw the Bolsheviks. Either way the Czech forces represented a kind of American "Foreign Legion." It is equally impossible here to go into all the hopes and disappointments of the American intervention in the Bolshevik Revolution and the civil war that followed. The course Wilson pursued led to dealings with pretenders who had little or no interest in anything remotely like what Americans imagined. There was Alexey Kaledin, Georgi Semenov, and Alexander Kolchak, plus other minor figures.

As Wilson was reaching his final decision, he received a letter from a nota-ble liberal and supporter, Lincoln Colcord, warning against entering into the civil war against the Bolsheviks. Such action, said Colcord, would split world liberalism and the "general design" (another way of putting Walter Lippmann's "great central idea") would never be realized, because the reactionaries would have triumphed before the peace conference. "When you need them, the peo-ples of the world will not know how to look you up. They will not heed your appeals. There will be no world liberalism left to lead."[45]

Colcord's warning was not unwarranted. And Wilson needed support to counter objections to his League of Nations, which now appeared to both liberals and conservatives as intended only to uphold a dubious agreement at Paris that the Allies had dictated. Theodore Roosevelt, in almost his dying words, had denounced Wilson's peace program. "Let civilized Europe and Asia introduce some kind of police system in the weak and disorderly coun-tries at their thresholds," he wrote, and the United States would take care of the Western Hemisphere. Wilson knew that would not suffice as an answer to the radical challenge, even though Col. House had proposed just such a plan on the eve of war, and though he, himself, had voiced almost similar comments about the dangers to "white" dominance—before the Russian Revolution.[46]

Lenin had aimed his arrows at the soft spot in Wilson's self-determination credo: its differentiation between the alliances based on submarine warfare, which led the president at the Paris Peace Conference to agree to the stripping of Germany's colonies, and the partition of the defeated Ottoman Empire as League of Nations "mandates," which in reality simply transferred the flags flying over forts, as well as the war-guilt clause of the Versailles Treaty blaming Germany for the war. It became—out of necessity, not preference—Wilson's answer to Lenin's condemnation of the combatants as equal oppressors of the world's masses. Resolving future issues in a more just way simply had to be postponed, he now told himself, until the League of Nations could get to work.[47]

Even the effort to prevent Japan from establishing itself in Siberia seemed to Secretary of War Newton D. Baker to be having the opposite effect. In other words, intervention encouraged geopolitical rivalries. Thus Baker wrote to Wilson at the time of the Armistice, the longer American troops stayed, the longer the Japanese would stay. "I do not know that I rightly understand Bolshevism," he concluded. "So much of it as I do understand, I don't like, but I have a feeling that if the Russians do like it, they are entitled to have it and that it does not lie with us to say that only ten percent of the Russian people are Bolsheviks and that therefore we will assist the other ninety percent in resisting it."[48]

Not surprisingly, Robert Lansing put the argument for staying. No matter how the war ended, the Siberian operation was part of a larger problem. The world would see a great growth of Bolshevism. The problem had become to keep it from moving west, into Germany and beyond behind the doctrine that the poor should take what they need from the rich, "and vent their anger upon those who have dared to accumulate property."[49]

Returning to the United States with the peace treaty signed, Wilson undertook a cross-country tour stressing Senate action to approve the treaty and membership in the League of Nations. Several times on the tour he spoke about Russia and the dangers of Bolshevism in an unsettled world. "Do you honestly think, my fellow citizens," he said in Des Moines, Iowa, "that none of the poison has got into the veins of this free people? Do you know that the world is all now one simple whispering gallery? These antenna of the wireless telegraph are symbols of our age."[50]

Wilson returned to the White House a stricken man in body and spirit, his hopes for the treaty barely alive. Lansing wrote a long memorandum Wilson may never have read, appealing for a last-ditch effort in Siberia—a $25 million shipment of military and nonmilitary supplies for Russians resisting the Bolsheviks. The Bolsheviks were bound to fail, he insisted, but "we must create a situation favorable to the rapid movement of events." And then this parting thought:

> It is an appealing thought that we, who have seen our own far-
> flung democracy grow strong with the development of railway
> communication, should help the Russians to bind together in the same
> way the exterior regions which it may be expected will one day form
> parts of a great democratic nation. It is for these reasons possibly that
> the Siberian route seems the channel of future interchange between
> Russia and America. We should feel that if this channel were stopped
> by the disintegrating forces of political instability and social unrest, the
> widest door to Russia would be closed.[51]

The results of this policy extended far beyond the Wilson administration and into attitudes about later revolutions as simply wrought by the agents of the Soviet Union. In the immediate situation, the United States was left as a disgruntled sideline watcher as Europeans probed possibilities. The only essential thing was to stand apart from any Anglo-French ideas of restoring the old regime or dividing Russia into spheres of influence. This stance led to some strange conclusions, as when Wilson refused to recognize the independence of the new Baltic countries, out of fear that it would discourage Russians from fighting the Bolsheviks and thus deprive Russia of true self-determination! Assuming responsibility for Russia's future, he believed he was protecting the new states from a German-Bolshevik menace, which was more dangerous than Russian plans would be under a "legitimate" government. Actually, by this time Wilson was less than fully alert, and his spokesperson, the new secretary of state, Bainbridge Colby, using logic squeezed thin as spaghetti, expressed opposition to a European conference in 1920 to negotiate with Moscow on a variety of pressing questions needing settlement. The United States, he informed the Italian ambassador, opposed a general conference that would deal with parts of the "former Russian Empire" on the grounds it could not condone dismemberment. "We are unwilling that while it is in the grip of a non-representative government, whose only sanction is brutal force. Russia shall be weakened still further by a policy of dismemberment, conceived in other than Russian interests."[52]

Here was another legacy like the World War I Espionage Act that would set precedents about recognizing revolutionary governments in a variety of situations, or voiding the results of elections that one did not like or feared—as in John Foster Dulles's refusal to countenance the possibility of a "legitimate" all-Vietnamese election that would return Ho Chi Minh as president—should one be held after the 1954 Geneva Conference that ended the first Vietnam War.

Whether a different policy would have made a difference remains a question that historians continue to debate. Interestingly, the diplomat-historian George F. Kennan, writing at the height of the Cold War, ended his detailed "realist" study of Soviet-American relations on an uncertain note. Whether anything could have been achieved by taking up the challenge another way instead of sending troops "is a matter of conjecture." But the military involvement of several thousand troops "lost what rationale it might once have had and which could not ... have been more confused, more futile, or more mistaken." It sacrificed the slender thread of communication with the new government in Russia, even as some possibility of achievement could not be ruled out, "if only because this is a changing world, where people influence others and are influenced by them in unexpected ways, and where things are constantly moving on, creating new opportunities as older ones lose their reality."[53]

When the Great War began, American policymakers believed the metropolitan powers had to put an end to rivalries in the colonial world that undid their claims to rule over "others" as a natural order of things. If they instead came out of the war with hardened blocs of super-imperialism perpetually vying with one another for the slightest of advantages, future conflicts were certain. The United States had entered the war not only to fight German autocracy, but to prevent a resumption of the Great Power struggles of the prewar era, only to find itself enmeshed in the struggle to control the revolutionary forces the war had let loose in the world. Washington held out from "recognizing" the Soviet Union—the last nation to do so—until 1933. This was indeed the "first" Cold War.

NOTES

I explored these issues in *Safe for Democracy: The Anglo-American Response to Revolution, 1913–1923*. The present essay derives from research for that book and later works, and it attempts to synthesize those new insights.

1. Walter Lippmann, "A Clue." The classic statement about the new politics and new diplomacy remains Mayer, *Wilson vs. Lenin*.

2. When America entered the war, Col. Edward M. House organized the "Inquiry," an aptly named Wilsonian effort with Lippmann as its secretary. House thought he was a perfect choice with "ties to the left liberals, yet 'realistic' in accommodating his idealism to political necessity." Steel, *Walter Lippmann and the American Century*, 128.

3. Adas, *Machines as the Measure of Men*, 370–372.

4. House to Woodrow Wilson, February 3, 1916, *The Papers of Woodrow Wilson*.

5. See Jenkins, *The Great and Holy War*.

6. "Anti-imperialists agreed that America should never emulate the colonial practices or join in corrupting alliances that would bind the nation to the monarchical excesses of Old Europe." Nichols, *Promise and Peril*, 73. See also Young, *The Rhetoric of Empire*, 149.

7. The marines, of course, had recently been sent to the Philippines to "pacify" the former Spanish colony, the first counterinsurgency conflict of the new century. McCormick, *China Market*, 177.

8. Gardner, *Safe for Democracy*, 204.

9. Clark, *The Sleepwalkers*, 50–51.

10. On this point, see Semmel, *Imperialism and Social Reform*.

11. For Wilson's "interventions," see LaFeber, *The American Search for Opportunity, 1865–1913*.

12. Doenecke, *Nothing Less Than War*, 187.

13. See MacMillan, *The War That Ended Peace*, 258–260.

14. On this point, see Nichols, *Promise and Peril*; and Freeberg, *Democracy's Prisoner*.

15. The classic statements of these views remain Hobson, *Imperialism*; and Lenin, *Imperialism*.

16. Weyl, *American World Policies*, 71.

17. Wilson to Col. Edward M. House, September 7, 1915, *The Papers of Ray Stannard Baker*, Library of Congress, Washington, DC.

18. House, Diary Entry, January 4, 1917, in Seymour, *The Intimate Papers of Colonel House*, II, 412; Lansing, "Memorandum on the Severance of Diplomatic Relations with Germany," February 4, 1917, in Link, *The Papers of Woodrow Wilson*, vol. 41, 118–123.

19. Doenecke, *Nothing Less Than War*, 243.

20. The list of books touching on this theme is almost endless, but see Smith, *American Empire*, especially 118–125. Other important recent studies include Immerman, *Empire for Liberty*; Hodgson, *The Myth of American Exceptionalism*; and Norton, *Leo Strauss and the Politics of the American Empire*.

21. Cable to the *New York Times*, "Socialists Back Cabinet," April 14, 1917.

22. Charles Wilson to Secretary of State, September 15, 1914, General Records of the Department of State, National Archives, Washington, DC, 661.003/50 (hereafter NA followed by file number); Consular Bureau to Wilbur Carr, September 24, 1914, NA 125.0061/37.

23. Wilson to Lansing, August 26, 1915, US Department of State, *Foreign Relations, The Lansing Papers*, I, 144.

24. Wilson to Lansing, August 26, 1915.

25. Sharp to Secretary of State, June 30, 1916, NA 600.001/24; Francis to Secretary of State, July 5, 1916, NA 600.001/26; Francis to Lansing, August 14, 1916, *Foreign Relations, Lansing Papers*, II, 318–319.

26. Francis to Secretary of State, March 21, 1917, NA 861.51/130; Francis to Secretary of State, April 6, 1917, NA 861.51/133; Page to Secretary of State, March 31, 1917, NA 861.77/45.

27. The Stevens mission is examined in several books, but see first Ekbladh, "'Wise as a Serpent and Harmless as a Dove'."

28. Redfield to Lansing, April 11, 1917, NA 125.006/40.

29. Stevens to Secretary of State, November 26, 1917; Secretary of State to Stevens, November 27, 1917, *Foreign Relations, 1918, Russia*, III, 209–210.

30. Bacino, *Reconstructing Russia*, chapter 2, for an introduction to Stevens's role.

31. Stevens to Secretary of State, December 20, 1917, *Foreign Relations, 1918, Russia*, III, 213–214.

32. Lansing, *War Memoirs of Robert Lansing*, 339–343.

33. Francis to Secretary of State, encl. speech, December 31, 1917, NA 763.72119/1059.

34. Foglesong, *America's Secret War against Bolshevism*, 62–64.

35. Francis to Secretary of State, November 24, 1917, encl. Trotsky Speech, NA 763.72119/957; Cronon, *The Cabinet Diaries of Josephus Daniels*, 243.

36. Cronon, *The Cabinet Diaries of Josephus Daniels*, 65.

37. Davis and Trani, *The First Cold War*, 98–99.

38. Francis to Secretary of State, March 10, 1918, NA 861.00/1262; Wilson to Lansing, April 18, 1918, *Foreign Relations: Lansing Papers*, II, 360.

39. *Commercial and Financial Chronicle*, January 5, 1918.

40. Kennedy, *The Will to Believe*, 135–136.

41. See Bacino, *Reconstructing Russia*; and Richard, *When the United States Invaded Russia*, as studies of America's intertwined objectives in opposing dealings with the Bolsheviks.

42. Wilson to Lewis, July 24, 1918, *Wilson Papers*.

43. Wilson to House, July 8, 1918, *House Papers*.

44. Ekbladh, "'Wise as a Serpent and Harmless as a Dove'," is an excellent account of the Stevens mission and its complications.

45. Colcord to Wilson, July 13, 1918, *Wilson Papers*.

46. Quoted in Knock, *To End All Wars*, 229.

47. In the middle of the peace conference, Wilson returned from Paris ostensibly to attend to business connected with the end of the congressional session. He was anxious as well to test the political ground since the 1918 midterm elections had deprived him of a reliable majority in the Senate. A dinner that House had proposed with members of the Senate to convince them that American ideas for a just peace centered in the plan for a League of Nations did not go well at all. The experience hardened the president's conviction that he must go another step in separating out the good nations from the bad, not only to satisfy American emotions about what the war had cost, but also to put forward a liberal response to Bolshevism. Hodgson, *Woodrow Wilson's Right Hand*, 233–234.

48. Baker to Wilson, November 27, 1918, *Ray Stannard Baker Papers*.

49. Lansing, "Memorandum on Post-Bellum Conditions and Bolshevism," October 28, 1918, *Lansing Papers*.

50. Quoted in Acting Secretary of State to Consul at Vladivostock, September 9, 1919, *Foreign Relations, 1919, Russia*, 119–120.

51. Lansing to Wilson, December 4, 1919, *Wilson Papers*.

52. Gardner, *Safe for Democracy*, 326.

53. Kennan, *Soviet-American Relations, 1917–1920*, 470–471.

10

From Sideshow to Center Stage

Legacies of the Great War (and Peace?) in the Middle East

Matthew Jacobs

Our general tendency is to think of the Ottoman Empire and the area that we have come to call the Middle East as little more than a sideshow of World War I. Moreover, that sideshow has been defined in particular by two seemingly made-for-theater events: Gallipoli and the Arab Uprising, and especially the latter event's *dramatis personae*, Lawrence of Arabia. Indeed, even Lawrence himself referred to the Arab Revolt of 1916 as "a sideshow of a sideshow."[1]

I would suggest that such a rendering of the Great War in fact does a disservice, both to our understanding of the war itself and to this area of the world. One could make a reasonable case that World War I had as great an—if not a greater—impact on the Ottoman Empire and Middle East as it had on Europe. This theater of the war was enormous, extending from Gallipoli in the west through Eastern Anatolia almost to Central Asia in the east, and in the south from the Sinai across Palestine and Mesopotamia into Persia. Moreover, European involvement in the region before and during the war was also extensive: much of the Ottoman economy had been mortgaged to the British and French by the late nineteenth century; the Germans were invested in early efforts to build a railway that was intended to grant them access to the Persian Gulf; the British used their control of Egypt and a military base at Suez as a massive staging area for soldiers and supplies deployed across the entire region; the Russians fought Germany and its allies on a front that ran along the northern half of the theater; and the British and French worked to devise a scheme through which they would reap the postwar rewards by dividing much of the region between themselves.[2]

Moreover, while I do not wish to dwell on the horrors of war, it is worth noting that the death and destruction that defined Europe were equally, if not more, pronounced in the Ottoman and Middle Eastern theaters. Precise numbers are difficult to come by, but estimates of total deaths in the Ottoman Empire range from a low of approximately three million to a high of perhaps five million people. The overall death toll in Europe was, of course, far greater, but of the primary European participants in the war—Britain, France, Belgium, Austria-Hungary, Germany, and Russia—only the latter two suffered similar total losses. Roughly 775,000 of the Ottoman dead occurred within the military, with the remainder coming among civilians. Many of these civilian deaths occurred as part of the massacre of Armenians, Assyrians, Chaldeans, Kurds, and others—either the result of an unfortunate "accident" of the war as the Turkish government has consistently claimed or the direct product of policies implemented by the ruling Committee of Union and Progress (the Young Turks), which believed the war presented an opportunity to implement specific population control measures. All told, with a wartime population of approximately twenty-one to twenty-two million, one of between every five and seven Ottomans perished during the conflict. Persia underwent a similar demographic collapse, with perhaps as much as 25 percent of the population dying, mostly due to famine in the latter years of the war. In Europe, only Serbia suffered a similar demographic fate. Most other European participants lost approximately 10 percent or less of their populations.[3]

To be sure, these losses were horrific, but the war exacted another human toll—this one on the survivors—through economic, political, and social upheaval on both the individual and collective levels. It is common to hear or see in public discourse considerations of the social implications of World War I and its impact on everyday life in Europe, yet despite the excellent work of several scholars who have tackled the issue, we hear little public discussion of these topics with respect to the former Ottoman Empire and wider Middle East. The historian Leila Fawaz, in particular, has documented the fundamental alterations in day-to-day living that World War I left as an enduring legacy for the Middle East, ranging from changes in the production and distribution of food resources such as bread among the poor, to the emergence of war profiteers among the upper classes, and to changes in local affiliations and politics that became necessities of survival in truly chaotic times and environments. At the same time, she has made a strong case for not only why, but how, we might take more seriously the collective memory of the war and ways of remembering it in the region.[4]

Yet as important as the horrors of World War I and their social implications are—and they are very important—I wish to evaluate the legacies of the war on a different plane. In the pages that follow, I examine some of the broader transformations that the war either directly initiated or accelerated with respect to the former Ottoman Empire and the broader Middle Eastern region and the legacies those transformations left behind. In particular, I focus on four main transformations: (1) increased international involvement in the region, (2) the creation of the modern Middle Eastern state system, (3) the accelerated development of nationalist movements in the region, and (4) the emergence of the international oil industry with the Middle East at its center. And rather than examine these transformations independently, I think it most valuable to view them as fundamentally interconnected. These transformations left behind a legacy of chronic instability, foreign intervention, and social upheaval that continues to define many of the central challenges with which we still wrestle today. In this way, then, we should view the Middle East as less of a sideshow and more as occupying center stage both in our conceptions of World War I itself and in the international political legacies that endure a century after its start.

Any inhabitant or interested observer of the Ottoman Empire and the Middle East in the summer of 1914 would have been hard-pressed to imagine how very different the region would appear just a few years later. To be sure, regional dynamics had been in flux for decades, as Ottoman power gradually weakened in the face of growing European involvement and emerging nationalist movements, and as US and Western European policymakers became convinced of the region's geopolitical and strategic value. Nonetheless, within a decade after the start of the war, foreign control over much of the Middle East had been formalized through the League of Nations mandate system, the political boundaries and broader political system of the region had completely changed, the internal political dynamics were moving toward an explicitly more nationalist phase, and the Middle East would assume an increasingly significant role in a rapidly expanding international oil industry.

Expanding foreign involvement in regional affairs and growing internal unrest had been a central feature of cultural, economic, and political life for several decades preceding the onset of World War I. Britain had taken formal control of Egypt in the early 1880s, while Britain and France gained greater access to and control over the Ottoman economy and finances. British prospectors also had the first major petroleum strike in the region in Persia in 1908, creating an even greater economic impetus for further engagement in regional affairs. Internally, Sultan Abdul Hamid II sought to stem the tide of decline by asserting greater central authority across the empire through the construction of railroads, new economic policies, and the implementation of a vast spy network. Overall, these policies did open up some new economic opportunities and tie the empire more closely together, but at the expense of greater social, political, and economic instability overall and some instances of extreme ethnic violence, such as widespread assaults against Armenians and others in the 1890s. The internal unrest culminated in the Young Turk Revolution of 1908, in which a group of Turkish-speaking Muslim military officers known formally as the Committee of Union and Progress overthrew the Sultan.[5]

There were many areas and issues in which external forces of decline and instability overlapped with internal unrest, and it was often missionaries from the United States in particular but also Britain and France who tried to navigate between them. The American missionaries specifically had become more visible in the latter half of the nineteenth century by constructing educational and other philanthropic institutions in the region, but they had become especially prominent in the 1890s and later by providing relief to Armenians and other distressed populations.[6]

The American missionary presence in the Ottoman Empire also presented a challenge for President Woodrow Wilson and US policymakers. As an evangelical Presbyterian, Wilson was very much supportive of the missionary presence in the Ottoman Empire. Moreover, the family of one of his closest friends and biggest financial supporters—Cleveland Dodge of the Phelps Dodge mining company—was heavily involved in missionary activities. Protecting the American missionaries and their property became a central concern as the likelihood of a US entry into the war against Germany and its allies increased. Wilson addressed this problem by specifically excluding the Ottoman Empire from his 1917 request for a congressional declaration of war in order to protect the American missionary community and to allow it to keep working in the region.[7]

As World War I progressed, it seemed less and less likely that the Ottoman Empire—the "sick man of Europe" in Western European discourse—would survive, and in that context we might read well-known wartime initiatives as European efforts to define the post-Ottoman future. In this light, the Hussein-McMahon correspondence appears quite differently than a British act of wartime expediency designed to bring Arabs into the war against their Ottoman rulers and the Central Powers more broadly. Instead, the discussions seem a much more concerted, though still expedient, effort on the part of the British to formalize a collaborative relationship with certain Arab leaders and to gain legitimacy in Arab eyes for British interests in the region, to the complete exclusion of Arab recognition of any other outside interests. Similarly, we may read the Sykes-Picot agreement, which attempted to divide up much of the declining Ottoman Empire and its environs between the British and French with a limited nod to Arab desires for independence, as a reversion to traditional European imperial behavior. Much the same can be said for Russia's wartime desires and negotiations with the British regarding taking control of Constantinople and the Bosphorus Straits.

European powers may have utilized more traditional imperial tactics during the war, but it was actually new postwar institutions—the League of Nations, the mandate system it authorized, and the range of international agreements through which it was implemented—that formalized and brought international recognition to European control over large portions of the former Ottoman Empire. Negotiators at Versailles designed the League of Nations and the basic principles of a three-tiered mandate system in which territories would be classified by how ready for independence the League of Nations believed them to be, ranging from Class A mandates that might be nearly ready for independence to Class C mandates that should be directly administered under the laws of the mandatory power and for whom independence was considered to be at best a distant possibility. The League designated former Ottoman territories as Class A mandates under British or French guidance. It was then up to either mandatory power to provide administrative assistance and advice until it or the League of Nations deemed each mandated area ready for complete independence. The actual division of the territory took place through meetings held in London and San Remo, and it was ultimately finalized in the Treaty of Sèvres in August 1920. Britain took control of Transjordan (currently Israel, the West Bank, and Jordan) and Mesopotamia (currently Iraq and Kuwait), while France assumed responsibility for the area that would become Syria and Lebanon. With the exception of Iraq, which acquired its independence in 1932, it would be World War II or later before any of these mandates became independent countries.

That mandate system not only formalized foreign intervention and control in much of the region for the next quarter century, but also proved critical in the second significant transformation that World War I brought about: drawing the geopolitical boundaries that would guide the emergence of and define the Middle Eastern state system. Negotiations between Britain and France about the geographical extent of their mandates fixed the boundaries of future independent states. Nowhere was this point made more directly than in the area that became northern Iraq, where the French transferred control over territory north of Mosul to the British in exchange for payments from future oil profits.

These same European leaders also recognized the independence of much of the Arabian Peninsula, which 'Abd al-'Aziz Ibn Saud was in the process of unifying under his control, and defined the northern border of what would become Saudi Arabia. Finally, the British declaration of support for the creation of a "national home" for Jews in Palestine and US acquiescence to that statement conferred some measure of international legitimacy to the movement of growing numbers of European and American Jews into the region. The accelerated movement of peoples that took place from the end of World War I into the 1940s, of course, provided the foundation for the post–World War II division of the British mandate in Transjordan into two states, Jordan and Israel, with the majority of indigenous Palestinians left to struggle to survive as stateless refugees for decades to come.[8]

While Europeans and other outsiders proved influential in defining the new Middle Eastern state system that emerged from World War I and used violence ruthlessly in the immediate postwar years to implement and enforce it, indigenous actors also utilized the wartime and postwar environments to pursue their own geopolitical agendas. This was particularly the case in Turkey, which emerged as the successor state to the former Ottoman Empire. Mustafa Kemal had been one of the most effective Ottoman military officials during the war, demonstrated in part by his leadership of Ottoman forces at Gallipoli. Following the war, he and other Turkish leaders rejected the Treaty of Sèvres in part because of the large amount of Ottoman territory it ceded to European control, and then undertook a two-year campaign against occupying French, Greek, and Italian forces across Anatolia to solidify Turkish control over that disputed territory. Kemal built upon his successes by implementing a new constitution in 1922, and he ultimately agreed to terms in July 1923 in the Treaty of Lausanne formally to end the war between the Ottomans and the various Allied powers in exchange for international recognition of Turkish sovereignty inside newly defined borders (see Figure 10.1). Kemal then declared an independent Republic of Turkey, with Ankara as its capital, in October 1923. Though it would still be decades before much of the Middle East would be truly independent, the implementation of the mandate system, the negotiation of the borders that accompanied it, and finally the creation of Saudi Arabia and Turkey established a completely new political structure for much of the region and finally put to rest most debates and discussions about how to handle the slow demise of the Ottoman Empire.[9]

The combination of Ottoman decline, more formalized external involvement, and the creation of a new state system assisted with the third significant transformation that World War I helped to bring about: the development of a range of nationalist sentiments that would slowly build over several decades

FIGURE 10.1 The delegation of Turks sent to the Conference of Lausanne. The Treaty of Lausanne in 1923 ended World War I between the Allies and the Ottoman Empire, and it paved the way for an independent Republic of Turkey under Mustafa Kemal to replace the declining Ottoman regime. Library of Congress, Print and Photographs Division, LC-USZ62-102035.

and ultimately reach a crescendo in the 1950s and 1960s. Some of these nationalist movements—Turkish, Arab, Armenian, and Kurdish in particular—had existed before the war but were given new energy during the conflict. These emerging nationalist sentiments were at least partly responsible for Ottoman attacks on Armenians and others in the 1890s, then again came into play in the wartime massacres due to the heightened sensitivities of the war. Consequently, and not surprisingly, a parallel counternationalism, fundamentally anti-Turkish and anti-Ottoman in nature, took root among those who had been the target of those attacks. Meanwhile, other subjects of the Ottoman Empire had themselves been staking greater claims to a distinctly Arab nationalism as they pressed for greater autonomy, and they willingly bought into British professions of support for the creation of an independent Arab state once the war concluded.[10]

In some instances, however, new nationalist sentiments had to be created out of whole cloth. No inherent allegiance existed within the populations of many of the new Middle Eastern states to ruling regimes or states that existed within borders defined by outside powers. The internal leadership of these new states therefore had to find ways to build a new national identity. Too often, however, the sense of nationalism that emerged over time did so in opposition to conservative regimes whose power originated from and rested on collaboration with European powers. Moreover, these efforts to construct new nationalist identities frequently bumped up against a more deeply felt sense of pan-Arab nationalism that had emerged during the late Ottoman period and drew strength from opposition to the European intervention and control that sprung from World War I. Over time, these anticolonial pan-Arab sentiments developed into a combustible mix that exploded in the nationalist revolutions and upheavals of the 1950s and 1960s.[11]

While the tension between a nascent pan-Arab nationalism and conservative and collaborationist state-building efforts drove post–World War I nationalist politics in the new Arab states, in Turkey Mustafa Kemal used the institutions of the state to enforce a new nationalist identity that explicitly sought to sever the new state from its Ottoman roots. The seeds of this new Turkish nationalism had in fact been sown in the last decades of the Ottoman period, were given sustenance through the ethnic conflict that occurred in the 1890s, through the Young Turk Revolution in 1908, and then again through the much more brutal round of ethnic violence during the war. The postwar fight to define borders and to cleanse the new state from outside, particularly Greek, forces helped harden these new sentiments. Once in charge of the new Turkish Republic, Kemal moved the capital from the ethnically mixed Constantinople to the much more homogeneous Turkish city of Ankara. He then began the process of separating Turkey from its Muslim Ottoman past and promoting a new secular nationalism by implementing a wide range of reforms, including abolishing the institution of the Caliphate, prohibiting or discouraging the wearing of any traditional religious attire, banning the use of Arabic and traditional Ottoman script in public forums and education and replacing them with an entirely new script based on the Latin alphabet, and putting in place an entirely new European-based system of civil, commercial, and penal laws. The overall impact of these reforms was that, by roughly 1930, Turkey had completely replaced the Ottoman Empire, both in the literal sense of being the successor state to the now defunct empire and in the more figurative sense of ridding itself and its people of as many remnants of Ottomanism as it possibly could.

Yet, as important as the Arab and Turkish cases were, developments in Palestine were perhaps the most revealing of the highly nationalist post–World War I atmosphere in the region. Zionism offered a potent combination of religious identity and nationalist sentiment, and beginning around the turn of the century it drove increasingly large numbers of Jews to move to Palestine. Over time, the movement to create a Jewish state in Palestine grew increasingly well funded and well organized. By 1917, it had established enough of a foothold in the area to convince the war-weary British to weigh in on the issue. Even though the British had already pledged support for postwar Arab independence in 1915 in the Hussein-McMahon correspondence and tried to divide the hoped-for postwar spoils in the region with France in 1916 in the Sykes-Picot agreement, they sought to strengthen their position in the region by currying favor with Jews—in Europe, in America, and globally. The British did so by issuing the Balfour Declaration, which pledged support for the creation of a "national home for the Jewish people" in Palestine. With international recognition, even support, for the cause now in hand, Jews began migrating to Palestine in even larger numbers. That flow of people only increased from the late 1920s through the 1930s as anti-Jewish sentiments and policies gained strength in Europe, especially in Germany, in part as a response to the economic consequences of World War I.[12]

Much like the American missionary presence created challenges for President Wilson and the United States, so, too, did the Balfour Declaration and the drive to create a Jewish state in Palestine. Wilson's religious beliefs and personal relationships, especially with Louis Brandeis, a Supreme Court justice and head of the Zionist Organization of America, suggested support for the Zionist cause. Yet Wilson hesitated to express support publicly for several reasons. Publicly supporting the creation of a Jewish state in Palestine, which was then under Ottoman control, potentially endangered the missionary communities, and it also contradicted to some extent Wilson's efforts to avoid declaring war on the Ottoman Empire. The British had notified the Wilson administration of their intentions at least by early September 1917, but it was mid-October before Wilson noted that he agreed with the British plan in a memo to his closest advisor, Colonel Edward House. The more enduring problem for Wilson and the United States, however, was the contradiction between his support for the Balfour Declaration and its imposition of external control over a piece of the Ottoman Empire on the one hand and Wilson's increasing reliance on the concept of self-determination on the other. Supporting either policy necessarily meant renouncing the other. Wilson's two positions were therefore irreconcilable, and the tension between them has remained a defining feature of US involvement in the Middle East ever since.[13]

Palestinians themselves, and Arabs more generally, had multiple responses to the growing Jewish presence. The challenge to Palestinian land ownership, labor, and political power inspired the growth of a vibrant Palestinian nationalism in its own right that clashed—both peacefully and violently—with Zionism. At the same time, some Palestinians as well as Arabs more generally viewed the pursuit of Zionism as another form of postwar European intervention and control, and it therefore added fuel to a more generalized anticolonial nationalism that would spread across the region from the 1920s through the 1950s and 1960s. Still others, such as the Muslim Brotherhood, combined the religious with the nationalist to form a powerful political force that would grow dramatically from the late 1920s into the late 1940s and beyond. The Brotherhood itself emerged in 1928 in opposition to British involvement in Egypt, but branches of the group or other similar groups took root in countries all around the region and used opposition to the Jewish presence in Palestine to mobilize support for a resurgent religious nationalism.[14]

The fourth area in which World War I had a dramatic impact in both the short and long terms on the Middle East was in the development of the Middle Eastern oil industry. As with each of the other areas of transformation, the process actually began before the war, as British prospectors first struck oil in Persia in 1908. The war itself, and particularly its last two years, demonstrated the value of petroleum in mechanized warfare at the same time an emerging automobile-based consumer culture was emerging in the United States and Europe. In combination, these heightened demands meant that oil, and the places that possessed it, acquired newfound significance in international economics and politics. The Middle East was at the center of this contest for oil, as beginning in the 1920s prospectors and geologists representing a broad range of companies and countries began crisscrossing the region searching for evidence of subterranean riches.

The growing demand for oil and the widely held belief that the Middle East possessed large amounts of it therefore featured dramatically in postwar negotiations and interactions. Negotiators agreed at San Remo in 1920 to switch control over what would become northern Iraq from the French to British in exchange for a percentage of future profits from oil drawn from the region. Those same negotiators also agreed to try to shut the United States out of the development of regional oil resources, thereby challenging the principles of former Secretary of State John Hay's Open Door Notes, which had been issued two decades earlier to promote open international economic competition in China. The San Remo agreement sparked a mini-crisis in Anglo-French-American relations, leading the US Congress to pass a law prohibiting any country that denied US interests access to markets under that country's control from doing business in the United States. Within less than a year, both the British and French relented to the pressure and welcomed the United States into the contest for Middle Eastern oil.

The ways in which the United States would engage in that contest also had dramatic implications for both the United States and the Middle East. Just a decade earlier new antitrust laws had led to the forced breakup of Standard Oil, the world's largest oil company, on the basis that the Supreme Court found that it held a monopoly. In the postwar battle for Middle Eastern oil, however, the State Department lobbied to overturn those antitrust provisions to allow for the creation of a consortium—known as the Near East Development Corporation (NEDC)—consisting of just five US companies that would be granted sole American rights to participate in negotiations for Middle Eastern oil concessions. State Department wishes were granted, and in the Red Line Agreement of 1928 the NEDC was granted equal shares (23.75 percent each) as British, French, and Dutch participants in a larger holding company that was to be in charge of the development of regional oil resources. The agreement did not work in practice, as other US and international companies began negotiating directly with specific countries, such as Saudi Arabia, and curried favor by offering large up-front payments leveraged against future profits to win concessions. In principle, however, from the signing of the San Remo agreement forward, the US government displayed its willingness to exercise its power in support of Hay's Open Door Notes and US companies abroad in general, even when doing so was in direct conflict with domestic laws and established policies.[15]

There were two other consequences that the development of the Middle Eastern oil industry had on the region in the years following World War I. First, more than any other issue discussed here, the evolution of the oil industry highlighted the Middle East's growing integration into the broader global economic and political system and, by extension, the conflicts that would define that system over the coming decades. It would be World War II and beyond before the full impact of this integration took effect, but the outlines of what was to come were visible quite early after World War I. The second impact connects back to the earlier discussions of increasing foreign control and the growth of nationalism. Given that outsiders controlled the Middle Eastern oil industry for the first several decades of its existence, it fit all too easily into a broader narrative of a region dominated by foreigners and thus contributed to the growing nationalist sentiments that defined many aspects of regional politics moving forward. These tensions were most visible in the Anglo-Iranian crisis of the late 1940s and early 1950s, but could also be detected in the development of the Saudi oil industry in the 1930s and 1940s.

So how might we assess these four fundamental transformations that World War I either initiated or cemented within the Middle East and thereby identify and characterize a larger legacy of the Great War for the Middle East? I would suggest that World War I and its aftermath represented a clash between the old and the new in the Middle East. In some ways, the prosecution of the war and the "peace" that followed were outdated efforts by Europeans and Americans to formalize in the Middle East a distribution of power and territory and a pursuit of resources somewhat akin to what had been worked out for Africa in the 1880s and for parts of Asia around the turn of the century. Yet new forces and changing dynamics—the assertion of indigenous nationalist and political forces; the impact of imported nationalist economic and political forces; the demand and scramble for petroleum; an ascendant even if occasionally hesitant United States; and declining French and British power, among other things—meant that the stability that outsiders believed they were bringing to the Middle East in the wake of World War I was to be temporary at best.

Indeed, through the remainder of the twentieth century and into the twenty-first, the mix of foreign involvement, the nature of the post–World War I state system, competing nationalist visions, and the enduring consequences of having or not having oil resources left a combustible legacy. Populations across the region bristled against collaborationist conservative monarchies in numerous states, then also suffered under authoritarian secular leaders who cloaked themselves in pan-Arab nationalism to obscure their failures to live up to their own revolutionary promises. At the same time, leaders of countries with oil used it to curry favor with external powers and used the profits from its sale either to buy off internal opposition or to purchase high-grade military hardware that was used against domestic enemies as much or more as foreign ones. It might be unreasonable to lay all the blame for a century of political upheaval, social instability, poor leadership, and a host of other problems at the feet of regional and international decision makers during World War I and immediately after, but it is also undeniable that the consequences remain with us.

In no situation is this point more visible than in the emergence of ISIS (the Islamic State of Iraq and al-Sham) since 2012. ISIS is very much a product of the 2003 US war in Iraq and the Syrian civil war that has raged since 2011, but there can be no doubt that both its emergence and its objectives are in part defined by World War I and its aftermath. Most obviously, the leader of ISIS, Abu Bakr al-Baghdadi, has sought to restore the Caliphate and thus issues a direct challenge to the political leadership and the geographic boundaries of the Middle Eastern state system. Moreover, ISIS's emphasis on shari'a law at the community level and religious purity at the individual level is clearly an effort to overcome the social and cultural instability that has dominated daily life across much of the Middle East ever since World War I. It remains to be seen how the situation will play out, but it seems increasingly likely that the combination of the 2003 Iraq War, the Syrian civil war, and the emergence of

ISIS may in combination fundamentally alter the Middle East state system in particular. It is difficult to imagine how either Iraq or Syria remain fully unified states within their post–World War I boundaries and ruled directly from Baghdad and Damascus, respectively. The follow-on effects of the potential collapse of those two states and the redefinition of their borders would be enormous. The Kurds, who have long sought a unified independent state formed from territory taken from Turkey, Syria, Iraq, and Iran, might be the most immediate beneficiaries of such an outcome, but it would also present the possibility of redefining sectarian relationships across the region.

Overall, then, the greatest legacy of the Great War in the Middle East is undoubtedly turmoil. The war seemed finally to sound the death knell for the "sick man of Europe," but the postwar "peace" and the Middle Eastern state system that replaced the Ottoman Empire appear to have been not much healthier over the long term. The stability that Europeans and Americans believed they had imposed on the Middle East through the League of Nations mandate system and other agreements proved illusory. Instead, World War I initiated or cemented four great transformations in the Middle East that proved in many instances to be more problematic the more entrenched they became. And with that we return to the horrors of war for those who died and those who lived. Unfortunately for the Middle East and its people, there has been far too much of both in the century since the start of World War I. In that regard and others, it should be clear that the Middle East was never a sideshow, and that it was, and remains, at the center of the stage of World War I and its legacies.

NOTES

1. There are, of course, numerous works—scholarly, fictional, and film—on Gallipoli and perhaps even more of each on T. E. Lawrence. For the quotation, see Anderson, *Lawrence in Arabia*, 4, the most recent work on Lawrence. For a demonstration of the broader point about the marginalization of the Ottoman and Middle Eastern theaters in our conceptions of World War I, see Lyons, *World War I* and, more importantly, Keegan, *The First World War*, generally considered one of the best overall histories of the war. Lyons's work includes twenty-one chapters, one of which focuses exclusively on Gallipoli, and one of which (only twelve pages) covers "The War Outside of Europe." Keegan's work includes a single chapter out of ten that covers "The War beyond the Western Front."

2. Information on the broader interactions between Europe and the Middle East in the early twentieth century can be found in any basic survey of the region, including Gelvin, *The Modern Middle East*; and Ochsenwald and Fisher, *The Middle East*.

3. See Clodfelter, *Warfare and Armed Conflicts*, 479–483, for estimates of World War I casualty figures. For a second take on Ottoman military casualties, see Erickson, *Ordered to Die*, especially 237–243. For more general comparisons, as well as information on Persian losses, see Gelvin, *Modern Middle East*, 171–172.

4. Fawaz, *A Land of Aching Hearts*.

5. Again, these events and issues are covered in Gelvin, *Modern Middle East*, and Ochsenwald and Fisher, *The Middle East*.

6. See Jacobs, *Imagining the Middle East*, 13–21, for an overview of the missionary presence in the Ottoman Empire.

7. On Wilson's interest in American missionaries in the Ottoman Empire and his relationship with Cleveland Dodge in this regard, see Christison, *Perceptions of Palestine*, 26–30; and Davidson, *America's Palestine*, 15–18. Woodrow Wilson, "Address to a Joint Session of Congress Requesting a Declaration of War against Germany," April 2, 1917, available at http://www.presidency.ucsb.edu/ws/?pid=65366 (last accessed April 28, 2015).

8. In addition to Anderson, *Lawrence in Arabia*, and Jacobs, *Imagining the Middle East*, see Fromkin, *A Peace to End All Peace*, on the European role in creating the Middle Eastern state system.

9. See Jacobs, *Imagining the Middle East*, 58–63, for a lengthier discussion of the emergence of Turkey in the postwar years.

10. See Gelvin, *Modern Middle East*, 197–205, for a general discussion of the rise of nationalism in the Ottoman Empire.

11. Jankowski and Gershoni, *Rethinking Nationalism in the Arab Middle East*; Mufti, *Sovereign Creations*.

12. For a broader discussion of the Balfour Declaration, including the specific quotation, see Jacobs, *Imagining the Middle East*, 190–193.

13. Wilson's views on Zionism and the Balfour Declaration, along with the contradiction they present with the concept of self-determination, are discussed at length in Christison, *Perceptions of Palestine*, 26–34, and Davidson, *America's Palestine*, 14–21.

14. On Palestinian nationalism, see Khalidi, *The Iron Cage*; and Khalidi, *Palestinian Identity*. For a brief overview of the Muslim Brotherhood, see Jacobs, *Imagining the Middle East*, 65–68.

15. There is a large body of literature on the Middle Eastern oil industry and the US role there. The most exhaustive work overall is Yergin, *The Prize*, but more brief overviews can be found in Jacobs, *Imagining the Middle East*, 142–149, and Little, *American Orientalism*, 43–76. For a more focused case study, see Vitalis, *America's Kingdom*.

11

The Great War as a Global War

Imperial Conflict and the Reconfiguration of World Order, 1911–1923

Robert Gerwarth and Erez Manela

Toward a Global History of the First World War

When the First World War formally ended in late 1918 with an Allied victory, three vast and centuries-old land empires—the Ottoman, Habsburg, and Romanov empires—vanished from the map. A fourth—the Hohenzollern Empire, which had become a major land empire in the last year of the war when it occupied enormous territories in East-Central Europe—was significantly reduced in size, stripped of its overseas colonies, and transformed into a parliamentary democracy with what Germans across the political spectrum referred to as a "bleeding frontier" toward the east. The victorious Western European empires were not unaffected by the cataclysm of war either: Ireland gained independence after a bloody guerrilla war against regular and irregular British forces. Further afield, in Egypt, India, Iraq, Afghanistan, and Burma, Britain responded to unrest with considerable force. France fought back resistance to its imperial ambitions in Algeria, Syria, Indochina, and Morocco, and, even further from the main theaters of the Great War, Japan did the same in Korea. The United States, having been catapulted into a position of unprecedented prominence and influence in world affairs, was struggling to define its role in the world and reconcile its republican traditions with its growing power and expanding imperial domain.

Benito Mussolini famously commented on the disintegration of the great European land empires and the new challenges confronting the blue-water empires with a surprisingly nervous reference: neither the fall of ancient Rome nor the defeat of Napoleon, he insisted in an article for *Il Popolo d'Italia*, could compare in its impact on history to the current reshuffling of Europe's political map. "The whole earth trembles. All continents are riven by the same crisis. There is not a single part of the planet . . . which is not shaken by the cyclone. In old Europe, men disappear, systems break, institutions collapse."[1] What would come to replace the fallen old order, he did not say. But he had a point. For centuries, the history of the world had been a history of empires, both within the European continent and beyond it, marked by maritime exploration, expansion, and conquest of overseas territories. Indeed, the decades that preceded the war arguably saw an unprecedented expansion of the imperial world order, as new entrants such as the United States, Japan, and Germany sought to carve out their own spheres of colonial domination. On the eve of the Great War much of the landmass of the inhabited world was divided into formal empires or economically dependent territories. That world unraveled dramatically in the twentieth century, beginning with the cataclysm of the First World War.

The First World War is hardly a neglected subject of historical research. Yet—understandably perhaps, given the impact of the fighting on Western Europe—a great deal of the literature produced over the past ninety years has focused on the events on the Western Front and their impact on metropolitan Britain, France, and Germany. Most of these histories are framed within two "classic" assumptions: first, that the war began with the sounding of the "guns of August" in 1914 and ended with the Armistice of November 11, 1918, and, second, that the war was primarily one fought in Europe between European nation-states. Meanwhile, ethnic minorities, imperial troops, and Eastern European or non-European theaters of fighting, conscription, and upheaval have remained at best sideshows in general history accounts of war and peace on the Western Front.[2]

These assumptions have dominated and defined the Western historiography of the Great War for decades. And while the literature based on them has produced many valuable insights into the causes and consequences of that conflict, this essay argues that the history of the Great War must be drawn on a wider canvas, one perched on two premises that diverge from the usual assumptions. The first premise is that we must examine the war within a frame that is both longer (temporally) and wider (spatially) than the usual one. This move will allow us to see more clearly that the paroxysm of 1914–1918 was the epicenter of a cycle of armed imperial conflict that began in 1911 with the Italian invasion of Libya and intensified the following year with the Balkan wars that reduced Ottoman power to a toe-hold in Europe.[3] Moreover, the massive violence triggered by the conflict continued unabated until 1923, when the Treaty of Lausanne defined the territory of the new Turkish Republic and ended Greek territorial ambitions in Asia Minor with the largest forced population exchange in history until the Second World War.[4] The end of the Irish Civil War in the same year, the restoration of a measure of equilibrium in Germany after the end of the Franco-Belgian occupation of the Ruhr, the decisive victory of the Bolshevik regime in Russia in a bloody civil war, and the reconfiguration of power relations in East Asia at the Washington Conference were all further signs that the cycle of violence, for the time being, had run its course.

The second contention of this essay is that we should see the First World War not simply as a war between European nation-states but also, and perhaps primarily, as a war among global empires. If we take the conflict seriously as a *world* war, we must, a century after the fact, do justice more fully to the millions of imperial subjects called upon to defend their imperial governments' interest, to theaters of war that lay far beyond Europe including in Asia and Africa, and, more generally, to the wartime roles and experiences of innumerable peoples from outside the European continent. In so doing, this essay builds on a growing literature on the experiences of the Indian *sepoy*, Chinese laborers, African *askaris*, the French Armée d'Afrique, and African-American soldiers to offer both a synthetic analysis of empires during World War I and an agenda for future research.[5] We can now also draw on scholarship that has explored the effects of the war on regions outside of Western Europe, including Asia, the Middle East, Africa, and also Eastern Europe, a region that has long and quite rightly been called "the forgotten front" and that recent scholarship is now bringing back into focus as the region in which the Great War originated and played out in a most violent way.[6]

The mobilization of millions of imperial subjects proved essential for nearly all of the combatant states, from Germany to the Ottoman, Habsburg, and Romanov empires and, of course, the Entente powers. Indian, African, Canadian, and Australian soldiers (see Figure 11.1) among others all served on the Western Front, as well as in a range of ancillary theaters, and hundreds of thousands of them died. Noncombatant laborers—notably from China—also proved vital to the conduct of the war, as did the involvement of the Japanese Empire (see Figure 11.2), which used the war as an opportunity not only to try to penetrate further into China but also to stage an extensive occupation of Siberia that lasted until 1922. Fighting also took place in many locations outside the European theater of war—from Siberia and East Asia to the Middle East, from the South Pacific to the protracted campaigns in East Africa. The impact of the war was profoundly felt by hundreds of millions living across the imperial world, as the war brought conscription, occupation, inflation, and economic

FIGURE 11.1 The pull of home: An Australian soldier in Egypt sustains his bond to the nation while fighting for the empire. Australian War Memorial Collection CO2588.

FIGURE 11.2 "Qingdao." Cover of *Tōkyō Puck*, October 1, 1914. This cover of the monthly Japanese graphic journal, *Tōkyō Puck*, anticipates a quick Japanese victory at Qingdao and a celebratory drink of Japanese sake out of a German helmet. Courtesy of Shimizu Isao.

dislocation, while also in many instances kindling new opportunities, ideas, plans, and hopes.

Mobilization in a colonial context was a delicate and difficult task. After all, a war fought on both sides with native auxiliaries was likely to undermine the very principle of which colonialism rested: the notion of white racial superiority. As early as 1902, influential commentators such as J. A. Hobson cautioned that the use of nonwhite troops in a European war would lead to the "degradation of Western States and a possible debacle of Western civilization."[7] If a "colored" man was trained to kill white men, what guarantee was there that he would not one day attack his own colonial masters?

In many of the colonies, there was a political calculation on the part of those who chose to enlist or those who encouraged others to do so. Leaders of the Indian National Congress or many "Home Rulers" in Ireland supported the war in the hope of greater political autonomy, perhaps even national independence. Mahatma Gandhi, who returned to India from his long sojourn in South Africa in 1915, famously campaigned to recruit his fellow Indians to fight for the empire. This puzzled observers at the time and since who have wondered how this campaign squared with his already long-professed principles of nonviolence. But Gandhi, like many other Indian nationalists, hoped that Indian participation in the imperial war effort would place India within the imperial structure on par with the white dominions and qualify them for home rule. London encouraged this line of thinking, making wartime promises for the greater participation of Indians in their own government.[8] This imperial strategy was applied elsewhere as well, most famously perhaps in the incompatible wartime promises made to Arabs and Jews over the disposition of Ottoman Palestine.[9] In this respect, the war proved a great disappointment for a great many who had hoped to parlay support for the Allied war effort into advances in claims for self-government, setting the tone for decades of conflict to come.

One of the supreme ironies of the war, of course, was that a war fought for the protection and expansion of empire in fact led to the dissolution of empires. Its most immediate victims were the vast, multiethnic empires of Austria-Hungary, Russia, and the Ottomans and also the newer, aspiring German Empire. But the war also delivered a severe body blow to the empires on the winning side, generating new forms of upheaval, disorder, and resistance that presented unprecedented challenges, both practical and ideological, to imperial managers. In the immediate aftermath of the war, the victorious empires, the British and French in particular, saw significant territorial expansion in the Middle East, Africa, and elsewhere. But this expansion came at a heavy price, overextending the resources of imperial control even as they faced new and more intense forms of resistance as well as the novel duties and constraints imposed by the League of Nations mandate system.[10] The war thus hastened a process of imperial decline that would eventually lead to the collapse of a global order based on territorial empires and replace it by one predicated on the nation-state as the only internationally legitimate form of political organization.

Viewing the war as a war of empires also helps us see how the violence that came before August 1914 and after November 1918 was in fact part of the same process of the realignment of global patterns of power and legitimacy. Large-scale violent conflict continued for years after 1918 as the Great War destroyed the dynastic empires of Russia, Austria-Hungary, and Ottoman Turkey and created a heavily contested border in Germany's east, thereby leaving what some have called "shatter zones," or large tracts of territory where the disappearance of frontiers created spaces without order or clear state authority.[11] Revolutionary regimes came to power and then fell in quick succession as massive waves of violence engulfed the East and Central European shatter zones of the defunct dynastic land empires. The massive carnage of the Russian Civil War only intensified after the Armistice, as did a number of major but hitherto little studied relief projects, not least the American Relief Administration led by Herbert Hoover, which delivered more than four million tons of relief supplies between 1919 and 1923.[12] And, of course, civil war accompanied by large-scale massacres and population transfer of unprecedented scope raged in Anatolia. The massive violence did not come to an end until the Treaty of Lausanne in 1923, which stabilized, at least temporarily, the postimperial conflict in Southeastern Europe and Asia Minor.

It was not only the losers who suffered; the conflict dealt a substantial blow even to those empires that emerged victorious. The period that followed the Armistice, after all, saw a series of major upheavals across the colonial world and there is much truth in John Gallagher's argument that the British Empire faced its most severe crisis to date in the period 1919–1922. As early as the spring of 1919 Britain was facing major civil unrest in Egypt and the Punjab. By May, British forces were engaged in the opening stages of the Third Afghan War and Ireland was beginning its descent into an extended period of insurgency. From January 1919 onward, British regular and irregular troops were engaged in a prolonged and ultimately unsuccessful guerrilla war with the Irish Republican Army that would lead to the establishment of the Irish Free State. The British Empire deployed extreme and widespread violence, including civilian massacres and aerial bombardment to quell revolts in Ireland, India, Iraq, and elsewhere and they were not alone in doing so. The French fought viciously to beat back fierce resistance to their expanding rule in the Levant and Indochina; the Japanese struggled to contain challenges to their empire on the Korean Peninsula even as they sought to expand their influence deep into Siberia, a move that in turn helped prompt the Western Allies, including the United States, to send forces to intervene there. Indeed, the entire edifice of the imperial world order was convulsing violently in the aftermath of the Armistice even as it reached its greatest territorial extent. The organized mass violence of the war had not ended; it had only shifted its modes and focal points.

In short, thinking about the Great War as a conflict of nation-states is a case of reading history backward. The world before 1914 was at least as much a world of empires as it was a world of nations even within Europe, not to mention in vast expanses of Asia and Africa. Clearly, nationalist myths, propaganda, and popular sentiments were vigorously mobilized to recruit manpower and build support for the war effort. But the war itself was fought as much—indeed, arguably more—for the defense and expansion of empire as for the nation. In almost all cases it was, in fact, empires rather than nations that were mobilized for the war. This essay therefore sets out to lay out the different trajectories of the major world empires in the era of the First World War, exploring how different imperial societies mobilized for total war and how the conflict changed the relationship between the colonizer and the colonized.

Dismantling Empires, Expanding Empires

The announcement of the Armistice on November 11, 1918, augured a new world of sharp contradictions. Empires both disintegrated and expanded, and while violence ended on the Western Front and in some other theaters, it continued unabated and sometimes even intensified elsewhere. In much of the former territories of the Habsburgs, the Romanovs, and the Ottomans, the blood continued to flow freely for years after. For many others, too, the war did not end with the Armistice. For two weeks after the guns fell silent on the Western Front, German commander Paul von Lettow-Vorbeck carried on his campaign in East Africa (Figure 11.3), and large-scale violence persisted in places such as Egypt, India, Korea, and Indochina. In Europe, Chinese laborers started clearing up the battlefields and French African troops were stationed in the Ruhr region. For those black African soldiers who returned home in 1918–1919, demobilization proved to be a slow and difficult process full of disappointments.

In Europe itself, the Armistice of November 11, 1918, brought anything but peace. In fact, the cessation of hostilities on the Western Front was atypical for interwar Europe as violent upheavals, pogroms, and civil wars remained

FIGURE 11.3 November 25, 1918: two weeks after his empire was defeated in Europe, General Paul Lettow-Vorbeck's undefeated East African force surrenders to the British at Abercorn on the edge of Northern Rhodesia (present day Mbala, Zambia). National Museum of Zambia.

a characteristic feature of life in postwar Europe. Violence was particularly intense in the vast territories of the defeated dynastic land empires—the Habsburg, Romanov, and Ottoman empires—whose disappearance from the map provided the space for the emergence of new and often nervously aggressive nation-states.[13] Those who fought in the name of these new nation-states sought to determine or defend their real or imagined borders through force and strove to create ethnically or religiously homogeneous communities. The birth of these new nation-states in East-Central Europe and the Baltic region was generally most violent in those regions where national and social revolutions overlapped. For herein lay one of the peculiarities of the "wars after the war":[14] in the collision in Eastern and Central Europe of two currents of global revolution, the revolutions of national self-determination and the social revolutions for the redistribution of power, land, and wealth along class lines.

Despite regional variations in the intensity of violence and its causes, hardly any territories east of the river Elbe remained unaffected. An extensive arc of postwar violence stretched from Finland and the Baltic states through Russia and Ukraine, Poland, Austria, Hungary, Germany, all the way through the Balkans into Anatolia, the Caucasus, and the Middle East, with newly founded Czechoslovakia under President Tomas Masaryk remaining an exceptional island of peace.[15] In the absence of functioning states, militias of

various political persuasions assumed the role of the national army for themselves (often against armed opposition from other groups that harbored similar
ambitions) while the lines between friends and foes, combatants and civilians,
were far less clearly demarked than they had been during the Great War. Not
since the Thirty Years' War had a series of interconnected civil wars been as
messy and deadly as now, as civil wars overlapped with revolutions, counter-
revolutions, and border conflicts between states without clearly defined frontiers or internationally recognized governments. German freebooters fought
with (and against) Latvian and Estonian nationalists, and Russian whites and
reds clashed throughout the region while Polish, Ukrainian, and Lithuanian
armed bands fought over ill-defined borders. The death toll of the short period
between the Great War's official end in 1918 and the Treaty of Lausanne in 1923
was extraordinary: including those killed in the Russian Civil War, well over
four million people, not counting the millions of expellees and refugees, lost
their lives as a result of civil wars or interethnic struggles.[16]

The abrupt breakup of Europe's land empires and the inability of the successor states to agree on borders with their neighbors certainly played a prominent role in triggering postwar violence. All national movements in the former
land empires took inspiration from US President Woodrow Wilson's promise,
manifested most famously in the Fourteen Points speech of January 1918, that
the nations of East-Central Europe should have an opportunity for "autonomous
development" as well as from the Bolsheviks' insistent advocacy of the principle
of "national self-determination."[17] But while the slogan of "self-determination"
provided a powerful rallying cry for the mobilization of anti-imperial emotions
and personnel both within and outside Europe, the nascent national movements of Eastern Europe quickly encountered opposition from various camps.
In Estonia and Latvia, where national movements seized the opportunity of the
Bolshevik coup to declare their independence, the legitimacy of the new national
assemblies was swiftly called into question.[18] The situation became more confus-
ing in the spring when a German offensive led to the occupation of all of Latvia,
Estonia, Belorussia, and Ukraine, only to be reversed when the German war
effort collapsed in November that year and was followed by a Red Army advance
toward Minsk and Vilnius.[19] In Poland, too, the attempt to restore a powerful
nation-state in the heart of Europe encountered severe problems: by the spring
of 1919, Josef Pilsudki's reorganized Polish armed forces were engaged on four
fronts: in Upper Silesia against strong German volunteer forces, in Teschen/
Teshyn against the Czechs, in Galicia against Ukrainian forces, and against the
Soviets threatening to invade from the west.[20]

The fate of territorial dismemberment also affected another defeated
state: the Ottoman Empire, which lost all of its Arab possessions and was

threatened in Western Anatolia by an initially successful Greek advance into Asia Minor shortly after the Ottoman defeat in October 1918 as well as an Armenian insurgency and a Kurdish independence movement in the east.[21] What the Young Turks and nationalist historians in Turkey to this day refer to as the "War of Liberation" (İstiklâl Harbi, 1919–1923) was in essence a form of violent nation-state formation that combined mass killing, expulsion, and suppression and that represented a continuation of wartime ethnic unmixing and exclusion of Ottoman Greeks and Armenians from Anatolia—a process that began long before the proclamation of a Turkish nation-state on October 29, 1923.[22] Here, as elsewhere, the nation-building process came at a high price, paid in particular by the minorities of the country. When Smyrna was reconquered by Turkish troops in 1922, some thirty thousand Greek residents were massacred and many more expelled in what became the largest population transfer in European history before the Second World War. All in all, some seventy thousand people died violent deaths in Turkey during the decade after the war's end, while approximately nine hundred thousand Ottoman Christians and four hundred thousand Greek Muslims were forcibly resettled in a "homeland" most of them had never visited before.[23]

In imperial domains beyond Europe, postwar violence, while not nearly as massive as it was on the continent, was nevertheless widespread; even where there was little violence the imperial edifice was often knocked off balance. Indeed, by the time of the Paris Peace Conference, the relationship between the white dominions and the British Empire had fundamentally changed. The dominions claimed a place at the conference in their own right and fought for their own interests. Australian Prime Minister "Billy" Hughes was a particularly disruptive force, driving US President Woodrow Wilson (who referred to Hughes as a "pestiferous varmint") to exasperation, antagonizing the Japanese delegation with his fierce opposition to the inclusion of a "racial equality clause" in the League of Nations covenant, and irritating everyone with his incessant demands that Australia be granted mandated territorial control over the former German New Guinea.[24] Nonetheless the form of postwar nationalism in the settler dominions varied. For Canada and South Africa the pressing problem of appeasing large, disgruntled non-British ethnic communities, further embittered by the war, drove the mobilization of nationalist sentiment as the ideological glue to keep these fragile polities together in the immediate postwar years. In both these dominions nationalism was articulated around moving away from the empire—more republican, self-sufficient, and grounded in a sense of cultural difference from the British.[25] In Australia and New Zealand, however, postwar nationalism was equally strong but in contrast oriented around the twin themes of national maturity and empire loyalty. Far from nationalism being the antithesis of empire, as in other settler dominions, in Australia and New Zealand, nation and empire were inextricably linked.[26] The bloodshed of Anzac troops at Gallipoli in particular maintains its central position in Australian and New Zealand collective memory as the violent passage to nationhood, but it also proves the bond between "Anglo-Saxon" settlers and the imperial motherland.[27]

If the crisis of empire had a rather mixed impact in the white dominions, its effects across nonwhite territories was far more consistent in its destabilizing effect on imperial legitimacy and authority. Indeed, the years immediately after the war saw widespread upheaval across much of the Middle East and Asia. In Egypt, the 1919 Revolution that erupted in the spring following the Armistice included mass street protests in the cities and widespread acts of sabotage in rural areas, targeting telegraph lines and other symbols of imperial authority. Egyptian nationalists, who saw the peace conference as an opportunity to be rid of British meddling, established a political party—the Wafd, or "delegation," whose express purpose was to present the case for Egyptian independence in Paris—and grew increasingly frustrated as their hopes for a hearing evaporated; they then mobilized forcefully against the British presence. Though London managed to stave off the internationalization of the Egyptian question, the continuing instability eventually led it to give Egypt its independence unilaterally in 1922 while keeping for itself the "core interests" of defense and the Suez Canal. But Egyptian nationalists, who grew increasingly assertive in the postwar years, remained recalcitrant. The tense relationship persisted for decades until 1956 despite London's efforts to retain a decisive influence over Egyptian politics with the time-tested method of divide and rule, pitting the royal court against the elected, Wafd-controlled government.[28]

In India, too, the spring of 1919 saw widespread disturbances, as Gandhi and others had mobilized Indians against Westminster's so-called Black Acts, the Rowlatt Acts that extended wartime emergency measures into peacetime; it was an imperial effort to stem resistance that begat greater resistance still. The killing of hundreds of unarmed protesters who broke curfew in the Panjabi city of Amritsar became a rallying cry and a focal point of nationalist resistance. As in Egypt but more successfully, the British authorities continued to play on the divisions among Indians to retain their influence for a while longer, but they struggled in vain to restore the atmosphere of imperial harmony and legitimacy that had surrounded the Delhi Durbar of 1911, held to mark the coronation of George V as the sovereign of India. When the mainstream Indian National Congress adopted "complete independence" (purna swaraj), the complete severance of the imperial connection, as its goal in 1930, it brought into the heart of the independence movement a position that, until 1914, had been articulated only on the far margins of Indian political discourse.[29]

As Britain's imperial managers strained to restore order and contain cascading crises across their old domains, they also struggled to shape and control the new territories they acquired as a result of the war, especially those detached from the defunct Ottoman Empire and awarded to the British Empire under the novel arrangement of the League of Nations mandate. The question of Palestine seemed—at least for the time being—relatively manageable. But efforts to reconcile the wartime commitments made to London's French and Arab allies and the concurrent need to find an instrument of control for the newly acquired, oil-rich mandate territory of Iraq led to the idea of installing an ally, the Hijazi prince Faisal bin Hussein, recently run out of his homeland by the rival House of Sa'ud and shortly thereafter out of Syria by the French, as monarch over Mesopotamia. That move, along with the brutal application of newly developed British airpower to suppress restive tribal revolts, managed to stabilize the situation in the mandate by the early 1920s, at least for a time.[30]

The French mandates proved even more troublesome in the interwar period, as did other parts of the French Empire: serious uprisings against French colonial rule in the interwar period included the Rif War (1925–1926), the Syrian revolt (1925–1930), the Kongo Wara in French Equatorial Africa (1928–1931), and the Yên Bái mutiny in Indochina (1930–1931).[31] It is clear that the encounter of colonial workers and *troupes* with Europe's competing political, social, and economic ideologies (socialism, syndicalism, and communism among them) began to have an effect in many French colonies. Wilson's call for self-determination famously inspired Ho Chi Minh to inquire about the concept's applicability to colonial possessions outside Europe. In Africa, meanwhile, prominent political figures like Blaise Diagne exploited the rhetoric and ideals of French universalism and egalitarianism to carve out an enhanced role for nonwhite people within the French Empire, while in restive North Africa, Messali Hadj's nationalist North African Star organization in the later 1920s challenged the legitimacy of the colonial state and cultivated links with international anticolonialism through the Ligue contre l'Impérialisme et l'Oppression Coloniale, formed in 1927.

To be sure, the vast majority of African veterans did not rise against their colonial masters. As Gregory Mann has shown in the case of ex-*tirailleurs* in Mali after both world wars, veterans often suffered frustration when the full promise of their service was not realized (in the form of preferential treatment, employment, pensions, and even citizenship). Yet they often framed their demands to colonial authorities in a language of reciprocity that did not necessarily call into question the colonial order. In fact, even if sometimes "unruly clients" of the French state, veterans could be rather conservative, since they themselves had invested so much in that order and thereby hoped to gain from it.[32] If *troupes indigènes* did not provide a constituency for the organization of anticolonial violence, as some contemporary observers might have expected and feared, it was not because these men were satisfied in the happy enjoyment of increasing rights and acceptance under a progressive and humanitarian French republican colonialism. First of all, there were practical obstacles to paramilitary mobilization. Once demobilized and thrust back into colonial societies, these men resumed their places in a social and political hierarchy that was profoundly more racist and rigid than that of the metropole or the army, and where the mechanisms of social and political control were more or less well developed and deployed by vigilant and suspicious colonial governments assiduous in the use of racial and legal controls to uphold white "prestige."[33]

Where rebellions did occur, they invariably met a ruthless response. The French army and colonial authorities deployed overwhelming force against the four major rebellions of the interwar period, making use, like the British, of the latest military technology, such as airpower, gas, and tanks, as well as superior numbers, firepower, communications, and logistics. Even a thoroughly humiliated and much weaker France made clear at least its short-term advantages in these areas right after the Second World War, killing tens of thousands by putting down uprisings in eastern Algeria (Sétif and Guelma, 1945) and Madagascar (the MDRM uprising, 1947). In this context, it is perhaps not surprising that veterans of the Great War in the colonies failed to translate their war experience into anticolonial unrest.

It is often forgotten that the British and French were not the only ones struggling to consolidate territorial gains and revive the legitimacy of imperial rule in the immediate postwar years. Japan's leaders fought mightily and successfully in Paris to retain their wartime gains of territory and other concessions in China, obtaining the recognition of the other Allied powers of their takeover of former German territories in Shandong Province. At the same time they brutally suppressed the widespread resistance associated with the March First Movement in their colony of Korea, a movement that erupted in the spring of 1919 inspired in part by the Wilsonian rhetoric of self-determination. Despite the hopes that such rhetoric raised among Koreans, Washington adopted a studied posture of neutrality on the question of Korea, whose status as a colony it considered a settled matter.[34]

Indeed, though the United States possessed several colonies during this period, territorial legacies of its victory in the Spanish-American War of 1898, these colonies played a relatively minor role in the structure of US power in the postwar period and an ever smaller one in the order that US leaders sought to construct in the immediate postwar period. Having already moved much further in allowing native self-government than other colonial powers,

Washington experienced little resistance in its formal colonial possessions, including the Philippines and Puerto Rico, though US Marines occupied Haiti in 1915 and the Dominican Republic the following year and carried on sporadic but brutal campaigns to suppress resistance there over the next five years even as Washington consolidated quasi-protectorates in Cuba, Nicaragua, and elsewhere in the circum-Caribbean region.

Still, US leaders, Wilson most conspicuously but also his Republican successors, led by Charles Evans Hughes and Herbert Hoover, were already imagining and beginning to work toward an imperium of a kind very different from the vast, multiethnic, hierarchical territorial empires, whether land- or sea-based, that undergirded and defined global power in the prewar era. Instead, Wilson and his successor imagined a global imperium of nation-states, interlocked within a system of international organization and governed by the principles of free trade, an imperium in which US economic (and later, military) preponderance would sustain Washington's hegemony globally, patterned to no small degree on the hegemony it had already achieved, or imagined itself to have achieved, in the Western Hemisphere under the Monroe Doctrine. The pursuit of this vision in the interwar years was, of course, haphazard, held hostage to domestic resistance of various stripes made at least temporarily ascendant by the ravages of the Great Depression. But it is within this framework that we must view the US pursuit of a stable and congenial order in East Asia, a goal at least temporarily achieved with the Washington Conference of 1922, which sought to stabilize the postwar order in the "Far East" in much the same way that Lausanne would do in the "Near East" the following year.

One of the great historical ironies of the Great War is that a war of empires, fought primarily by empires and for the survival or expansion of empire, delivered a debilitating blow to dynastic empires, which were for centuries the preeminent type of state organization and to imperial expansion and acquisition as the main logic of relations between states in world affairs. None of the four dynastic empires on the side of the Central Powers survived the war in their prewar form, and all of them (and their constituent parts, at least within Europe) were reorganized after the war into one republican form or another even while (sometimes) preserving the territorial forms and (usually) some form of the oppressive practices of their imperial predecessors in new guises. The empires on the Allied side—with the notable and significant exception of Russia—managed to survive and even expand their imperial territories, but a war fought for the "rights of small nations" could not but undermine severely the legitimacy of imperial formations and strained the relations of imperial centers with even the most enthusiastic of imperial peripheries, namely the British crown's "white dominions."

It was not simply that equality in sacrifice implied equality in status and rights—after all, "peripheral" populations had been fighting for empires for millennia without expecting, or receiving, such a reward. It was that the logic of popular rule, which argued that political legitimacy derived not from divine sanction but from the people, had finally, after a long and arduous process, achieved near universal recognition. The argument from civilization—the imperial scoundrel's last redoubt—largely drowned in the ocean of blood that flowed in the battlefields even—especially—in the empires' most "civilized" European provinces.

The postwar violence that wracked the territories of most of the participants, both winners and losers, was in part a struggle over the remnants of fallen empires. But it also reflected, at least in part, the crisis of imperial legitimacy ignited by the war and its aftermath. The spectacular appearance of President Wilson on the international stage, with his talk of self-determination and the rights of small nations, and the yet uncertain but growing specter of revolution in Russia and elsewhere in east and central Europe made for a volatile mix of ideas, examples, and potential sources of support for the enemies of empire everywhere. The global movement of information and ideas, its pace quickened by the war and recent technological and institutional development, meant that the anti-imperial contagion spread quickly.

By 1923, even as the United States retreated off the global stage for the moment, networks of communist organizers, emboldened by the support of the now-consolidated regime in Moscow, set about establishing the organizational structure for revolution against empire across the colonial world. Meanwhile, the former European territories of the Habsburgs, in an often bloody and generally chaotic process whose general direction was nevertheless quite clear, were established as nation-states. Across the world, the imperial state as a form of territorial governance was under attack and in retreat, while the nation-state was on the rise. And while it took another several decades and an even more murderous war between 1939 and 1945 to usher the process of imperial dissolution toward completion, the Greater War of 1911–1923 remains a global watershed in that process.

NOTES

This essay draws significantly from the work the authors have done on a coedited volume, *Empires at War, 1911–1923*. We would like to express special gratitude to the contributors to that volume, from whose work we have learned a great deal. We also want to thank the participants and organizers of the Conference on the Legacies of the Great War held at Williams College in Williamstown, Massachusetts, in April 2014, where we had an opportunity to present and refine the ideas presented in this essay.

1. Mussolini as quoted in Bosworth, *Mussolini*, 121.

2. Despite recent attempts to write transnational histories of the Great War, the global history of its immediate aftermath is yet to be tackled. The most recent attempts at transnational histories of the Great War include Kramer, *Dynamics of Destruction*. On the global ramifications of the Paris Peace Treaties, see Manela, *The Wilsonian Moment*.

3. Hall, *The Balkan Wars, 1912–1913*; Bloxham and Gerwarth, *Political Violence in Twentieth-Century Europe*, 1–10.

4. Gingeras, *Sorrowful Shores*.

5. Echenberg, *Colonial Conscripts*; Omissi, *The Sepoy and the Raj*; Smith, *Jamaican Volunteers in the First World War*; Lunn, *Memoirs of the Maelstrom*; Koller, "Von Wilden aller Rassen niedergemetzelt"; Fogarty, *Race and War in France*; Liebau et al., *The World in World Wars*. For the African-American contribution, see, e.g., Barbeau and Henri, *The Unknown Soldiers*.

6. Gross, *Die vergessene Front*.

7. Hobson, *Imperialism*.

8. See Ryland, "Edwin Montagu in India, 1917–1918."

9. See, e.g., Fromkin, *A Peace to End All Peace*.

10. Pedersen, "The Meaning of the Mandates System."

11. The term "shatter zone" was first used in the interwar years, but it was in the 1960s that the term became an analytical tool. In its modern sense, it was first used in East, "The Concept and Political Status of the Shatter Zone," before being further developed in Bloxham, *The Final Solution*, 81. For an overview of the ethnic violence attendant on the collapse of the multiethnic empires, see Roshwald, *Ethnic Nationalism and the Fall of Empires*; Bartov and Weitz, *Shatterzone of Empire*.

12. Fisher, *The Famine in Soviet Russia, 1919–1923*; Irwin, *Making the World Safe*.

13. Reynolds, *Shattering Empires*; Prusin, *The Lands Between*, 72–97; Wróbel, "The Seeds of Violence."

14. Gatrell, "Wars after the War."

15. Recent literature on some of these conflicts include Yekelchyk, *Ukraine*; Reynolds, *Shattering Empires*; Reynolds, "Native Sons"; Newman, "Post-imperial and Post-war Violence in the South Slav Lands, 1917–1923"; Eichenberg, "The Dark Side of Independence"; Gingeras, *Sorrowful Shores*; and Wilson, *Frontiers of Violence*.

16. Gerwarth and Horne, *War in Peace*.

17. To what extent the late European empires were indeed "people's prisons" remains a controversial question to this day—recent scholarship has emphasized the Habsburg Empire in particular as an evolving civil society rather than as a decrepit polity doomed to dissolution by the forces of centrifugal nationalism. See Kwan, "Nationalism and All That."

18. Prusin, *Lands Between*, 74f.; Roshwald, *Ethnic Nationalism and the Fall of Empires*.

19. On the German occupation of "Ober-Ost," see Liulevicius, *War Land on the Eastern Front*.

20. Eichenberg, "Soldiers to Civilians, Civilians to Soldiers: Poland and Ireland after the First World War."

21. Keegan, *The First World War*, 415; Zürcher, "The Ottoman Empire and the Armistice of Moudros."

22. Zürcher, *The Unionist Factor*; Dumont, "The Origins of Kemalist Ideology"; Akural, "Ziya Gökalp"; Hanioğlu, "Garbcilar."

23. There are no reliable statistics on the postwar Kurdish massacres, but the approximate numbers are 5,000 deaths in 1921, 15,000 deaths in 1925, 10,000 deaths in 1930, and 40,000 deaths in 1938. See Gerwarth and Üngör, "Imperial Apocalypse."

24. See Fitzhardinge, "William Morris Hughes."

25. Careless, *Canada*, 339–346.

26. See, for example, Garton, *The Cost of War*; Damousi, *The Labour of Loss*; Larrson, *Shattered Anzacs*.

27. Garton, "Demobilization and Empire."

28. Botman, "The Liberal Age, 1923–1952."

29. Low, *Congress and the Raj*.

30. Satia, "The Defense of Inhumanity."

31. See Thomas, *The French Empire between the Wars*, 211–244.

32. Mann, *Native Sons*.

33. Saada, "The Empire of Law." See also her *Empire's Children*.

34. Manela, *The Wilsonian Moment*, 197–214.

12

The Great War, Wilsonianism, and the Challenges to US Empire

Emily S. Rosenberg

In 1918, even as the military phase of the Great War was ending, the political and rhetorical struggle over the shape of the postwar world had already begun. For years, former president Theodore Roosevelt had faced off against now-president Woodrow Wilson over foreign policy issues. Roosevelt had bitterly denounced Wilson for trying to remain neutral during 1915 and 1916 rather than rallying the nation to fight. Now with peace in view, he again took to the hustings with a refreshed critique.

This time, in an editorial that circulated in newspapers around the country, he excoriated Wilson's "glittering words" about internationalism, self-determination, and the League of Nations. "Our continuing action in Santo Domingo and Haiti makes it hypocritical for us to lay down any universal rules about self-determination for all nations.... We have with armed force invaded, made war upon, and conquered the two small republics, have upset their governments, have denied them the right of self-determination, and have made democracy within their limits not merely unsafe but nonexistent." It was not possible to judge whether these two US military occupations were "right or wrong," Roosevelt argued, because of Wilson's "inveterate predilection for secret and furtive diplomacy." He concluded that Wilson's idealistic "phrase-mongering" on behalf of open diplomacy, self-determination, and a League of Nations not only bred impractical policies but also made the country look blatantly hypocritical.[1]

Roosevelt was hardly alone in noting the irony that the Wilson who talked of spreading democracy and self-determination was also the Wilson sustaining two draconian military occupations and domination over several colonies and dependencies. People whose countries were subjugated by what they considered to be US imperial power also felt those contradictions every day.

Wilson's lofty rhetoric, mixed together with his vigorous exercise of control over US colonies and dependencies, raised major questions: Would the postwar negotiations push the world away from the Great Power imperialism that had marked the era before 1914? What would be the legacies of Wilsonian proposals about self-determination and a League of Nations as they rippled through a world still carved into imperial spheres—including the one controlled by the United States?

European historians have long debated the impact of the Great War on early twentieth-century empires. World War I can be considered as marking the twilight of empire, as German colonies were stripped away and what Erez Manela has called the "Wilsonian moment" spread the rhetoric of self-determination that helped spark opposition to colonial regimes in many parts of the world. But the war can also be viewed as a minimal break with the imperial past, as League "mandates" remained in subdominant, quasi-colonial arrangements and the major empires—Britain and France—in many cases redoubled their efforts at maintaining control over their realms. In European history, this ambiguous nexus between the Great War and empire has long been a theme.[2]

No comparable body of scholarship exploring the connection between World War I and the early twentieth-century colonies and dependencies of the United States, however, has developed. Perhaps it may not seem too surprising that historians of European empires have ignored the question of the war's impact on US Empire. Scholarship on comparative empires has long had a European orientation in which US processes of domination, if they figure at all, mostly emerge as a story of settler colonialism on the North American continent.[3] Much more surprising is the relative invisibility of the topic of World War I and empire in research by historians of the United States. US histories have expended a prodigious amount of ink on explaining why and how the United States acquired an overseas empire around the turn of the century. Indeed, the reasons for this US imperial expansion constitute one of the most studied and taught topics in US history. US historians, however, have devoted far less attention to the aftermath of America's prewar imperial seizures or to how a war supposedly fought to advance democracy highlighted the contradictions that Roosevelt and an array of anti-imperialists at home and in dependencies pointed out. In most narratives of US history, the "imperial debate" over whether or not the United States should hold colonies and dependencies occupies a central place in framing the pre–World War I era, but both US empire and the debate over it appear to evaporate with the Great War.

At the centennial of World War I, though, it should be worth asking questions about the impact of the war on US empire: How did the "Wilsonian moment," which popularized the concept of self-determination and brought greater visibility and voice to anti-imperialism around the world, resonate in Wilson's own imperial backyard? How did the war to "save the world for democracy" and Wilson's championing of self-determination intersect with the structures and justifications that supported America's own imperial sphere? What follows does not pretend to even approach a comprehensive examination of these issues, but it is a plea for giving more attention to the historical legacies of World War I in the US Empire.

US Empire, 1898–1918

It is important to make clear that this essay is not addressing what historians have called "informal empire"—an economic and/or cultural and/or threat presence that is so overwhelming that it circumscribes sovereignty. The United States was certainly building an "informal empire" in various places during and after the war, but this essay is concerned with formal empire in the old-fashioned sense—that is, the control and governance over territories that were not slated for incorporation into the United States on an equal basis. What constituted the formal US Empire during the period of World War I?

In 1898, the United States had fought a war with Spain and, in its aftermath, took over the Spanish colonies of the Philippines and Puerto Rico. Other territories also became part of the American Empire in this period or before: Samoa, Guam, and Hawaï'i, long an object of imperial eyes. After that war, in 1903, the United States forced protectorate status onto both Cuba and Panama—arrangements that allowed these countries to keep their flag and semblance of a national government but sharply proscribed their sovereign powers and provided the United States with Guantanamo Naval Base and the Panama Canal Zone.

When the Wilson administration entered office in 1913, it did not repudiate this US empire. Instead, Wilson expanded its scope and style, becoming, by many measures, one of America's most interventionist presidents. His administration maintained colonial presences in the Philippines, the territory of Hawaï'i, Samoa, and Guam. It invaded Mexico, seizing the country's major port of Veracruz and sending an army into the north. Even during World War I, US officials retained control over Mexican customs houses at Veracruz—at a time

when customs revenue was the Mexican government's main source of revenue. It consolidated US domination over the Caribbean and Central America—
expanding stricter controls (sometimes enforced by US Marines) over the
protectorates of Cuba and Panama, purchasing the Virgin Islands, and creating
dependencies in Nicaragua, Dominican Republic, and Haiti, all of which were
held through ever-tightening regimes of economic control and, in the case of
the latter two, by US military governments and armies of occupation. Nicaragua
was also occupied by US Marines on a partial and intermittent basis.

Wilson did not view this US sphere as an empire. Leaders in imperial centers almost always justify their actions in terms of spreading enlightenment,
civilization, and freedom. But others certainly labeled the processes of US domination with the words "empire" and "imperialism." This American empire
appeared about to play a dominant role in the Pacific as a gateway to China
and to control all transoceanic shipping across the Isthmus of Panama (in an
age before airpower). Far from being insignificant, this empire announced
the United States had become a major two-ocean power. It held strategic and
economic importance in the geopolitics of the age, and it incorporated some
fifteen million people (at a time when the total US population was around one
hundred million). This empire was neither nonexistent (as many Americans
imagine) nor was it small or unimportant.[4]

Because World War I coincided with an enlargement and a tightening of
controls over the US empire of colonies, protectorates, and dependencies in the
Caribbean and the Pacific, it is hardly surprising that President Wilson's rhetoric about self-determination and democracy sparked a "Wilsonian moment"
in the American Empire itself—one directed at Wilson's own administration.
As Erez Manela has pointed out, Wilson's message stood independently of the
man, and it could be used without regard, sometimes in conscious disregard, of
his intent.[5] The survey that follows suggests that, in this "Wilsonian moment,"
anti-imperialist leaders in America's sphere not only stepped up their advocacy
for self-determination but also participated in the broader transnational currents that were energizing anticolonial movements everywhere.

Challenging the Military Occupation of the Dominican Republic and Haiti

Roosevelt's attack on Wilson's policies in late 1918, which centered on the ongoing military occupations of the Dominican Republic and Haiti, provided an
introduction to a renewed, broader postwar debate over US imperialism. At
first Roosevelt's bombast might seem disingenuous. After all, Roosevelt was

the president who used military force to coerce Cubans into accepting their status as a protectorate of the United States and granting US rights to a naval base at Guantanamo Bay. He was the president who orchestrated the creation of Panama and bragged that he had seized the canal while Congresses debated. And he was the president who established the basis for military occupation of the Dominican Republic by going around Congress and working with US private bankers to force on that country the loan conditionalities that converted it into a US dependency. Long a dedicated imperialist, Roosevelt deeply believed in an Anglo-American mission to enforce stability and progress for "backward" areas. Indeed, Wilson's policies in the circum-Caribbean might be seen as an extension and consolidation of Roosevelt's own vision to create an "American Lake" that would secure the growth of US economic and naval power in both Atlantic and Pacific arenas.

Was Roosevelt simply engaging in the same kind of hypocrisy and partisanship with which he charged Wilson? Roosevelt's argument with Wilson was, of course, political: partisan rivalry, dampened to some extent during the war, was reemerging, and Republicans were on the offensive against almost anything that Wilson and the Democrats advocated or did. It is hardly surprising to find consistency collapsing in the face of political expediency. But there is a deeper and more important layer to Roosevelt's critique against the military occupations in the Dominican Republic and Haiti. A close reading of Roosevelt's charges shows that his main complaint against Wilson concerned not so much the military occupations themselves, which he argued might well have been justified by the conditions on the ground, but the fact that Wilson's "secret diplomacy" had not laid out any such justification or provided any clear picture of the nature of the military campaigns currently being waged in each country. While Wilson rhetorically championed "open diplomacy," Roosevelt pointed out, Americans knew very little about the small wars being waged in their names and off their shores on the island of Hispaniola. The Wilson administration had made these wars nearly invisible by the secrecy and censorship of wartime controls in the United States and by the military governors' draconian suppression of dissent in those countries. If domination by a great power was needed to provide stability and uplift, in Roosevelt's view, then a leader should not be afraid to seize the bully pulpit and make the case. The justifications and practices in such interventions, he claimed, should be made known to the public, as had been his own actions during the Panamanian revolution. Empire-building in the shadows, especially by a leader gaining worldwide attention for championing open diplomacy, self-determination, and democracy, was duplicity of the tallest order. "Phrasemongering does not represent idealism," Roosevelt wrote. Roosevelt was, in effect, demanding not an end to policies of domination but a greater transparency about what he regarded as the inevitable and often necessary role of great powers. "Let us put our trust neither in rhetoric nor hypocrisy. . . . Let us be honest with ourselves." "Phrase making may win immense, though evanescent, applause . . . but may have a very mischievous effect."

Roosevelt was on to something important. As I have argued in *Financial Missionaries to the World*, US policy in this period had evolved into a pattern of "colonialism by contract." Roosevelt and Taft had first adapted the practice of working with private banks to extend conditional loans (then called "controlled loans") to countries that, in their view, needed to be subjected to US administration at a time when Congress would never have approved the overt seizure of colonies. (In charging Wilson with secrecy, Roosevelt conveniently ignored the fact that his administration, fearing European intervention to collect debts in the Dominican Republic, had begun the practice of hiding colonial-style administrative powers within the loan contracts extended by private US banks to avoid having to send a treaty stipulating administrative oversight through a reluctant Congress.) The Wilson administration enlarged and regularized the very practice that Roosevelt had introduced in the Dominican Republic. By the end of the war Wilson and his advisers had developed a broad vision for how to promote globally a US-administered sphere of influence enforced through the agency of private bank loans made to governments on condition of their acceptance of an economic supervisory regime appointed by the US executive branch. In these cases, US government influence was largely invisible except to those being governed under these loan arrangements: no treaties brought before Congress, no executive agreements, little public controversy.[6]

This loans-for-supervision formula made private bankers a "chosen instrument" for US state policy. It made dependency status disappear out of public process and into the "private" market governed by loan contracts. Controlling governments by forcing controlled loans on them (and the loans to the Dominican Republic and Haiti in this period *were* forced by US officials rather than requested by the receiving governments) was an early version of the process that Suzanne Mettler has, for a later period, called the "submerged state." The state exercised power by hiding it in the private sector, thus preserving the illusion of a liberal state while exercising the authority of an imperial power.[7]

The rub came when controlled loans brought not stability but greater debt and mounting resentment against both the US bankers and the US economic advisers and administrators. Controlled loans and a military occupation to enforce them ended up going hand in hand in both the Dominican Republic and Haiti during Wilson's administration. But the US military campaigns that swept the countrysides and suppressed political opposition to US administrators and their allies were largely overshadowed by the war in Europe. Wartime censorship, as Roosevelt correctly charged, made these occupations less visible and controversial than they might otherwise have become.

Toward the end of the Great War, attention turned to the increasingly dramatic reports about these two military occupations, which looked and acted like colonialism even though few Americans would have identified either the Dominican Republic or Haiti as a colony. Although Roosevelt's postwar opposition seemed concerned mainly with Wilson's secrecy and hypocrisy, political movements in the Dominican Republic and Haiti tried to use the end of the war to bring new visibility of their countries' plight under US economic and military rule. They seized on Wilson's rhetoric about democracy and self-determination secured through a League of Nations and made common cause with other anti-imperialist leaders from Asia and Africa.

In 1919, people with an array of objectives converged on Paris to participate, directly or indirectly, in the peacemaking that promised to put the world back together in a new way. The war victors had their agenda: keeping their colonies and making Germany pay for the war. Wilson had his agenda: trying to create ethnically homogeneous, self-determined states in Europe, turning German colonies into mandates, sustaining the infrastructure for open-door trade and investment policies, and enforcing the peace through a League of Nations. Japan had its agenda: trying to eclipse its second-class status by championing an antiracism resolution that would guarantee the proposition of equality among nations. And colonials from all parts of the world had their agendas that involved both national recognition and greater transnational solidarity among the colored peoples who had been targets of colonialism.[8] In postwar Paris, the global "Wilsonian moment," with all of the talk of self-determination, captured the imagination of many, including people in those once independent countries now living under US military rule.

The well-known Massachusetts-born intellectual W. E. B. DuBois, who had participated in a Pan-African Conference in London in 1900, was a primary organizer of a new Pan-African Conference that met at the Grand Hotel in Paris in February 1919. At the end of the war in November 1918, he had written Secretary of War Newton Baker that it would be "a calamity" for two hundred million people of color to be "without voice or representation at this great transformation of the world," and he hoped that the Pan-African Conference, coinciding with treaty negotiations that opened at Versailles in January 1919, would push back against this exclusion.[9] Although the fate of colonies in Africa held the Pan-African Conference's top priority, historians have tended to overlook that seven of the fifty-seven delegates who attended came from US-occupied Haiti and one from US-occupied Dominican Republic—that is, one-sixth of all delegates. DuBois would, throughout the 1920s, become an increasingly outspoken critic of US imperialism and US military interventions and occupations. He helped keep the African-American press especially focused on the occupation of Haiti.

One of Haiti's most illustrious intellectuals, writers, and diplomats, Dantès Bellegarde, emerged at Paris as a champion of Haitian independence and a major critic of the United States, especially of its twenty-year military occupation of the country (1915–1934). A member of Haiti's elite, whose family had held influential posts in government for over one hundred years since the Haitian Revolution, Bellegarde became acquainted with DuBois and was one of the officials at the Second Pan-African Congress held in Brussels in 1921. In 1920 Bellegarde had sought to bring the question of US occupation of his country before the first assembly held by the League, but other League members blocked the effort because they still hoped the United States would join the body and did not want to antagonize the US government. Throughout the 1920s, however, he continued to raise the specter of US empire, denouncing "the shadow of a dreadnought behind each Yankee dollar," and giving impassioned speeches before the League of Nations advocating an end to the US military rule of Haiti. In 1924 he gave a dramatic closing address to the International Federation of League of Nations Societies, which secured a unanimous resolution against the US occupation of Haiti, and in 1925 the League of Rights of Man, a powerful organization in France to which Bellegarde belonged, adopted a resolution that sought (unsuccessfully) to force the League of Nations to consider the issue of US military occupation. From its creation after World War I until its demise, the League of Rights of Man became his platform for highlighting a broad range of colonial outrages that he saw as linked to his country's own anti-imperial cause: He protested many colonial abuses throughout the world, and in 1930, he charged that US troops had massacred 3,500 Haitian peasants. Bellegarde persistently advocated, without success, for a "coloured" delegate to serve on the mandate committee of the League of Nations. For his anticolonial and antiracist stances after the war, DuBois called him the "international spokesman of 'black folk.'"[10]

Another figure, more important perhaps within the United States itself, was Francisco Henríquez y Carvajal, a medical doctor who had headed the government in the Dominican Republic that US military forces had ousted when they began the military occupation in 1916. Henríquez had refused to cooperate with the US military government, and throughout the war he denounced both the supervision mandated by the controlled loan contracts and the military censorship that blanketed the island. Together with Haiti's current president, Sudre Dartiguenave, in 1919 he appealed to the Versailles conference on behalf of their countries' self-determination, and he also appealed repeatedly to the Wilson administration itself. To understand the way that the war shaped the appeals of anti-imperial advocates in the US Empire, a closer look at one of his many memos to the US Department of State proves useful.

> At the very moment when the press of the civilized world published the admonition out by radio to all the nations from the Peace Conference . . . a spontaneous popular sentiment in favor of the Dominican people . . . culminated in Cuba in the foundation of pro–Santo Domingo committees. The number of these committees has spread from place to place and it is possible to foresee that they will soon extend over all Latin America. . . . The invitation issued by the Peace Congress to all the nations of the earth has made it easy for each one of them to present all the claims that they had to make concerning their legitimate rights and aspirations. No one of them is in a better position than the Dominican Republic to claim the restitution of her sovereignty as a state and nation, which she has lost neither by war nor by any international agreement, voluntary or otherwise. . . . Nations which appeared dead, supplanted for centuries by powerful neighboring states, have been recalled to life by the Peace Commission; why should the Dominican Republic, situated in a new continent, free and continually progressing, near the mightiest dominion of liberty and industry . . . remain, as at present she is, with her sovereignty sequestered and crippled?
>
> . . . Above the devastation and the heaped-up ruins which the Great War has left as the trace of its mad career, to the horror of humanity, there now passes a breath of liberty and regeneration which comforts the soul of nations and incites them to a common desire for peace and justice. Nations subjugated for long years are rising on all sides to claim their rights to self-determination. Old and new, all nations are coming together and agreeing on a convention of a League of Nations which will cement on solid foundations of international justice and the peace of the civilized world. . . . In this solemn hour of peace and concord, of justice and liberty, the people of the Dominican Republic, whose senti-ments the undersigned interprets, claims the rehabilitation of its own government, its right to self-determination, to accomplish its interna-tional obligations and to write itself in the list of the League of Nations.[11]

Henríquez's arguments were received politely but had little impact in the State Department. US officials took the position that the United States could not withdraw its troops of occupation until it had suppressed and pacified the insurgency in the countryside; Henríquez argued that the insurgency was the result of US occupation and would melt away if it ended. Making no headway

with the Wilson administration, he then joined with Wilson's political opponents in asking the US Congress to launch a postwar investigation of the ongoing military occupation of his country. Here he had a more receptive audience.

As the election year of 1920 approached, Republican presidential candidate
Warren G. Harding picked up the theme the ex-president Theodore Roosevelt
had been trumpeting, decrying the "unconstitutional" war in Haiti and Santo
Domingo. With newspaper censorship lifted at the end of the war, US abuses
in those countries turned into headlines. The *Washington Post* called for a "dis-
avowal" of "acts which begin to look like crimes," and it joined Republicans in
calling on Congress to "ventilate this scandal, as . . . public opinion will not tolerate a continuance of the misuse of the military force of the United States."[12]
After the presidential election brought Harding into the White House, the
Senate formed a Committee on the Occupation of Haiti and Santo Domingo,
and the occupations received their first highly public airing. Ex-President
Henríquez became a major figure at the hearings.[13]

The Senate committee, which solicited testimony collected by investigators
sent to both Haiti and the Dominican Republic and also heard from witnesses
who provided dramatic accounts, uncovered charges of torture, rape, and indis-
criminate killing. One of the most sensational charges involved the US military
government's use of corvée labor to build roads in Haiti, a system that looked
akin to a revival of slavery. The Republicans had wanted to discredit Wilson and
his Democratic regime through this committee, but these hearings became so
sensational and prompted such outrage that Harding's own secretary of state,
Charles Evans Hughes, quickly also felt the pressure. Demands increased for
an immediate end to military rule and for independence for the two countries.[14]

To the Republican senators' discomfort, the hearings galvanized a group of
domestic anti-imperialists who became highly vocal and visible. In US historiography until very recently, the US anti-imperialist movement has been generally located only in the very early twentieth century, well before World War I.
But the growth of US Empire under Wilson, which became suddenly much
more visible after the censorship from World War I was lifted and after the war
had given greater force to ideas of self-determination, ignited a new coalition of
people who opposed imperialism.

To get a sense of how the war seemed to legitimate opposition to US control, one might note, for example, one of the many letters sent to the Senate
committee—this one from the Patriotic Union of Haiti, a transnational group
founded in 1920 to demand independence for Haiti and withdrawal of US
armed forces:

> We make this demand in the name of justice, liberty, and the sacred
> right, upheld by the outcome of the World War to a separate existence

and complete freedom of every small nation and in accordance
with our historic American traditions . . . in direct violation of
the fourteenth peace point of the United States as enunciated by
President Woodrow Wilson.[15]

Upon seeing how these hearings were embarrassing the United States
and helping to fuel transnational connections among increasingly radical
anti-imperialists, Senator Medill McCormick, a Progressive Republican who
chaired the committee, suspended the investigation. The Harding administration made a few face-saving changes in the administrators of both countries,
and State Department officials began seeking a way out, although not until
1924 were troops withdrawn from the Dominican Republic and not until 1934
from Haiti, after which supervised loans and other economic connections continued to keep both countries closely within the US sphere of influence.

The pressure from anti-imperialists became an important force in US
politics in the postwar era. Some groups in this highly diverse anti-imperialist
coalition operated transnationally, taking up causes from segregation in the US
South, to workers' revolution in Mexico, to demands for US withdrawal from
Nicaragua and Liberia (also under the thumb of US controlled loans and a military guard), to self-determination in the colonies of the Philippines and Puerto
Rico and in the protectorates of Panama and Cuba. The military occupations
in Haiti and the Dominican Republic became one part of their much broader
agenda to challenge US empire globally. Not only did they continue to advocate
withdrawal of US troops, but they made it almost impossible to expand US
occupations or formal dependency contracts. In the late 1920s an insurgency
led by Augusto Sandino challenged the US economic supervision (accompanied by a small guard of marines), and the US government dispatched troops
to quell the uprising. The brief war in Nicaragua became highly controversial
domestically, however, and anti-imperialists in Congress led the effort to cut
off funds. President Calvin Coolidge·had no choice but to negotiate an exit
(although an American trained national guard there became the backbone of
the repressive regime subsequently led by the Somoza family, a situation that
foreshadowed future use of well-armed client-elites to maintain control).[16]

Challenging US Imperial Power in the Colonies
of the Philippines and Puerto Rico

Just as the end of the war brought visibility to the US military governments that
were administering Haiti and the Dominican Republic, postwar discussions
of colonialism prompted new questions regarding the US role in its colonies,

especially the Philippines. In the spring of 1919, a commission sent by the House of Representatives of the Philippines visited Washington to make the case for Philippine independence to President Wilson, the Congress, and the public. President Wilson's Democratic Party, of course, had aligned its rhetoric with anti-imperialism ever since Republican President McKinley had acquired the archipelago from Spain and suppressed Filipino independence fighters in the bloody Philippine War that followed. Democratic presidential candidates from the election of 1900 on had tried to use America's imperialism as an issue against the Republicans, had opposed the military tactics used in the Philippines, and had taken positions favoring independence for the colony. After Wilson became president, Congress passed the Jones Act in 1916 promising a process that would gradually lead to Philippine independence. In line with these policies, President Wilson promised in April 1919 that Philippine independence was "almost in sight," and Secretary Baker commented "I trust the day is very close at hand."

Such sentiments, expressed to the visiting Philippine commission, however, had by now become the standard position for US officials: The claim was that the United States had no self-interest in ruling the Philippines and only was executing its duty to provide tutelage in self-government, after which it would readily bow out. As the *New York Times* editorialized, "We are trustees for them, and must fulfill our trust."[17] Wilson had clearly never intended his talk of self-determination to be quickly or universally applied, especially to "races" he considered politically undeveloped. What "almost in sight" and "close," meant, then, was anything but clear.

The idea of a League of Nations, however, put a new twist on the issue of Philippine independence. Both Wilson and Filipino independence advocates seized on the idea that the League could provide an end to US colonial rule, but each party formulated this idea slightly differently. As Wilson stumped the country in 1919 trying to generate grassroots support in his political battle to secure US membership in the League, he argued that the League could solve America's "perplexing problem" about how to separate itself from the Philippines. The League, he suggested, would guarantee the independence and territorial integrity of a new country, thus safeguarding US interests there while allowing the United States to slip away from the taint of colonialism. In the event of external threats or internal "disorder," however, the League would be able to step in and place the Philippines into its mandate system, calling on the United States to again take control. This prospect could produce a kind of protectorate status for the Philippines that, although organized through the League, might be analogized to the US relationship with Cuba. A *New York Times* article explained Wilson's tactics in his battle to convince Americans to favor the League: By employing this logic, "the Philippines will be used to push along the League of Nations wagon."[18]

While Wilson used the example of the Philippines to try to attract support for the League, many Filipinos invoked the idea of the League to push for their country's self-determination and for a postcolonial order more generally. The *Revista Filipina*, edited by Gregorio Nieva—a member of the Philippines House of Representatives, a delegate on the Philippine Commission, and a businessman—championed not only Philippine independence but independence for Korea as well. Praising the Korean New Life movement, *Revista Filipina* articles argued that granting independence to the Philippines would put pressure on Japan to do likewise in Korea. "We hope the Allied conference will not fail to weigh the Korean contention, as well as all such other similar contentions, in their true merits, and thus remove all possible stumbling blocks on the road to a true and efficient League of Nations. There is no national opportunity for greatness as ample and as tremendous as that spelled by self-determination, for the full enjoyment and expansion of which the Allies have so happily and liberally dedicated the best of their efforts." In this formulation, the League might become that way to push along a broad agenda of national states emerging from colonial status.[19]

The future relationship between a new League and US imperial administrations, of course, could be seen in different ways. DuBois and Bellegarde, for example, took positions somewhat similar to Nieva's. They supported the League initially and, although coming to criticize it for not repudiating colonialism more strongly, continued to work toward the possibility that the League might still help leverage nations out of colonial status and help forge a postcolonial order. Discussion of self-determination and the League encouraged those advocating independence for America's dependencies to link their own positions to the aspirations of others—Koreans, Irish, Africans. And this linkage became a dominant characteristic of postwar anti-imperialist discourse both among US anti-imperialists and among those in US dependencies. The end of the war and the League, such anti-imperialists contended, pointed to ways in which new nations and nationalisms might flourish under the wing of postwar internationalism.[20] More radical anti-imperialists, some inspired by the socialist internationalism espoused by the Bolshevik movement in the new Soviet Union, however, came to reject the League as just another instrument by which colonial hegemony could be maintained. This group was also empowered after the war by the transnational currents that nurtured a broad critique of the racial and national assumptions that justified colonialism.

Puerto Rico, like other colonies in the world, produced nationalists of various persuasions in this postwar moment. Arturo Alfonso Schomburg, born in Puerto Rico but having moved to New York, embraced Pan-African solidarity and made the preservation of African diasporic heritage his lasting legacy. On the island of Puerto Rico itself, a new generation was coming of age. By 1920, Puerto Rico—like the Philippines—had already been a US colony for two decades, and the new generation, born around the time that US rule had begun, remembered little of Spanish rule and often defined their nationalism in opposition to US influence. As with anti-imperialists throughout the world, this generation was influenced by the Wilsonian discourse of self-determination, the anti-imperial ideas nurtured within the Pan-Africanist movement, and the transformative ideological commitments associated with the Mexican and Russian revolutions. The historians César J. Ayala and Rafael Bernabe write that in every school year between 1920 and 1922 in Puerto Rico conflicts erupted in which authorities tried to prevent students from displaying the Puerto Rican flag or adopting other symbols that criticized US rule.[21]

Within this atmosphere emerged the charismatic Puerto Rican nationalist Pedro Albizu Campos (Figure 12.1). After serving as a second lieutenant in a US army infantry regiment during World War I and excelling as a law student at Harvard University, Albizu Campos turned sharply against US influence. Having witnessed the racism in US life and influenced by the anticolonial legacies of World War I, he made Puerto Rican nationalism and independence his life's cause. Albizu Campos became a leader of and writer for Puerto Rico's Nationalist Party after 1924, and, like other anti-imperialists within the US Empire, situated his nationalism within the transnational struggle against both political and economic imperialism. Developing a unique brand of nationalist ideology that repudiated both Soviet socialist-internationalism and Wilsonian liberal-internationalism, he waged a half-century-long fight to advance Puerto Rican independence even as he also denounced repressions carried out anywhere in the world by great powers, including Britain, France, Italy, Germany, Japan, and the Soviet Union. After Puerto Rico became a self-governing "commonwealth" of the United States in 1952, Albizu Campos continued to fight for complete independence and eventually died in a US prison.[22]

These few examples provide a small window into a much larger history of anti-imperial, nationalist movements within the US Empire that were sparked or emboldened by World War I. As elsewhere in the world, advocates demanded rights for smaller nations and called attention to the mismatch between lofty wartime rhetoric and imperial realities. Forging transnational connections, anti-imperialists attacked the most visible dependent structures that imperial powers had created and helped turn the major powers away from formalized territorial colonialism. The United States did not stand apart from this larger global trend, and historians should accord the postwar anti-imperialists in its empire a stronger voice.

FIGURE 12.1 A top student at Harvard University who served in the US military during World War I, Pedro Albizu Campos, took up the cause of anti-imperialism after the war and devoted himself to the cause of Puerto Rican independence. New York World-Telegram and the Sun Newspaper Photograph Collection (Library of Congress), LC-USZ62-136400.

Silencing the Past

How might one explain the relative historical silence about the Great War's impact on anti-imperialist activism in the American Empire? In his 1997 book *Silencing the Past: Power and the Production of History*, Michel-Rolph Trouillot uses the Haitian Revolution as an example of how power shapes the recording of history to render some narratives highly visible and others silenced.[23] Trouillot's insights also apply to the story of the Great War and American empire. The nexus between World War I and imperial power has visibly structured—and troubled—European and Asian history for years, but the anti-imperialists in the US Empire during and after World War I have remained oddly silenced, leaving US history comfortably but erroneously within a zone of exceptionalism—seemingly unlike Europe, with no consequential imperial holdings and no important anti-imperialist movements.

Drawing on Trouillot but analyzing this particular case, it is possible to offer, if very briefly, some perspectives on the question of why historical memory has silenced the anti-imperialist "Wilsonian moment" in the US Empire and rendered nearly invisible the connection between the Great War and American empire. The issue of highly selective and situated historical memories is an ever-relevant one for historians. In this case, it is possible to postulate at least four different explanations for why this surge of anti-imperial thought was pushed into the shadows of historical memory.

First, history is often profoundly shaped by media from the era; journalism, it has been said, is the first rough draft of history. It is thus important to recognize that World War I pioneered very modern techniques of informational control and media censorship. Headed by George Creel, who was determined to employ all the new technologies of advertising, Wilson's Committee on Public Information (CPI) devised an extensive campaign of propaganda—augmented by the new medium of film and enforced by wartime controls over supplies of newsprint and film—to sell US participation in the Great War to a public that was generally opposed to US entry. The CPI constructed the war as a divinely inspired crusade to advance democracy, even as CPI rules censored out any reporting that might have tarnished the Wilson administration's benevolent image. In addition, the CPI stressed an identification between support for America's military effort and patriotism generally, leading many reporters and journalists to self-censor, screening out critical material lest they be assailed as unpatriotic.[24]

Second, US dependencies also experienced tight censorship of news and vigorous suppression of dissent against US policies. Indeed, the anti-imperialist movements in US dependencies often cited the lack of freedom of speech and press and the lack of processes of civilian justice as among their most important grievances, especially since these unfreedoms clashed so dramatically with the official rhetoric describing America's wartime aims. During the Great War, then, the lack of robust journalism kept imperial involvements in the shadows, as patriotic attention focused on the European theater—setting an agenda for future histories of the period.

During the postwar era, as censorship was lifted at home (though not in some dependencies), controversies surrounding America's military occupations of Haiti and the Dominican Republic, especially, became far more visible to the American public. Debate over whether or not the United States should dominate an overseas empire and dispatch marines within the hemisphere continued throughout the 1920s. Anti-imperialist positions filled the pages of most African-American–owned and –read newspapers. And many of the so-called Progressives in the Republican Party publicly denounced US military interventions that might expand American dependencies. Many of these anti-imperialist politicians became so determinedly anti-interventionist that they would go on to also oppose US preparations to enter what became World War II, and they would come to be derided as "isolationists." But during the 1920s, before the pejorative word "isolationist" had come into widespread use and before the threat of fascist Germany loomed large, this group considered them-selves "anti-imperialists" who opposed US military interventions and control over weaker states.

The fact that this group became later cast by historians as "isolationists," rather than "anti-imperialists," leads to a second major reason for the histori-cal forgetting: The shift in terminology nudged historical focus onto major European wars and away from the small imperial wars and occupations that had concerned this group in the period right after World War I.

Third, the United States did not significantly expand its formal empire after the World War I era. Indeed, largely because of the postwar opposition to US imperialism, US troops were withdrawn from the Dominican Republic in 1924; from Nicaragua later in the decade; and from Haiti in 1934. In 1946 the Philippines became a "commonwealth" and was promised independence in 1934, a promise that came about in 1946 at the end of World War II after the Japanese occupation of the islands had been terminated. Puerto Rico moved into commonwealth status after World War II, and Hawai'i moved toward state-hood. The United States continued to hold territories: It retained island pos-sessions such as the Virgin Islands, Samoa, and Guam, and it became a trustee over the Marianas in the Pacific after World War II. It oversaw an expanding arc of military bases throughout the world. And US governments of occupation prevailed temporarily in Germany, Austria, and Japan after World War II. Still, the days of extensive territorially based formal empires were fast waning—for the United States and for other colonial powers as well. Less formal means of influence prevailed, and the United States developed and deployed new sets of capacities: economic, cultural, and covert tools. With these trends, the World War I era of direct imperial power faded from memory—at least from the memories of Americans, if not from the memories of those in the dependent states that had been under formal US domination.

Finally, people and nations tend to remember and construct positive nar-ratives about themselves, erasing as unpatriotic what might seem negative.

World War II dramatically affected the ways that Americans constructed and understood their history. That "good war" was a great patriotic struggle, which held broad support from the American people and seemed to confirm that American power righted grievous wrongs in the world. After World War II, only small traces of the empire of previous days—and of the significant debate over it that had gone on throughout the 1920s—remained visible. The idea that Europe had an empire (which it still retained during World War II) but that the United States had always been anti-imperial became deeply ingrained in post–World War II histories and public memory. That idea has remained a dominant frame in public memory up to our day.

It seems time to unsettle historical formulations that isolate the United States from the anti-imperialist efforts that emerged during and after the Great War and to unsilence critics of the United States' imperial ventures during that era. This essay has argued that the Wilson administration, by tightening its grip on US dependencies in the Caribbean and the Pacific and by promoting Wilson's rhetoric about self-determination, helped to spark anti-imperialist movements within the US Empire. It has surveyed how advocates of national self-determination participated in broad transnational currents that, boosted by the legacy of World War I, were energizing anticolonialist movements everywhere. And it has also suggested why connections between the Great War and the early twentieth-century US Empire have tended to remain fairly invisible in historical accounts about America's role in the world. Histories that pay greater attention to anti-imperialists all across the US imperial realm better situate the United States within major themes in world history and, at the same time, challenge the exaggerated celebrations of US exceptionalism that have become prominent in our own day.

NOTES

1. "Roosevelt Flouts League of Nations," *Washington Post*, August 4, 1918. Roosevelt continued to denounce the League in these terms in other speeches and writings; see "Roosevelt Drafts League of Nations," *New York Times*, December 14, 1918.

2. Adas, "Contested Hegemony"; and Manela, *The Wilsonian Moment*, provide a good introduction to these issues.

3. Examples are a sampling of contents from the past decade of the *Journal of Colonialism and Colonial History*; Stoler, *Haunted by Empire*; and Burbank and Cooper, *Empires in World History*.

4. Go, *Patterns of Empire*, provides a survey.

5. Manela, *The Wilsonian Moment*, 34.

6. Rosenberg, *Financial Missionaries to the World*, details this process.

7. Mettler, *The Submerged State*.

8. Discussions of the emerging transnational anti-imperialist movement include Slate, *Colored Cosmopolitanism*; Gallicchio, *The African American Encounter with Japan and China*; Horne, *The End of Empires*; and Ballantyne and Burton, *Empires and the Reach of the Global, 1870–1945*.

9. See especially Rosenberg, *How Far the Promised Land?*, 15–74 (quote from DuBois letter is in note 4).

10. "Dante Bellegarde Dies in Haiti," *New York Times*, June 16, 1966; Sluga, *Internationalism in the Age of Nationalism*, 68–70; Appiah and Gates, *Africana*; "Haiti to Petition League Federation," *New York Times*, June 30, 1924; "Delegates of Haiti and America Clash on U.S. Occupation," *Washington Post*, July 3, 1924; "France May Assist Haiti," *Los Angeles Times*, March 23, 1925.

11. Memo from Doctor Henríquez y Carvajal to the Chief of the Division of Latin American Affairs of the Department of State (Stabler), April 19, 1919, *Papers Relating to the Foreign Relations of the United States (FRUS)*, 1919, 107–108.

12. "Haiti Seized by U.S. to Secure League Vote, Harding Charges," *Washington Post*, September 18, 1920; "The Haiti-Dominican Scandal," *Washington Post*, October 17, 1920 (quote).

13. United States Congress, Senate, Committee on Haiti and Santo Domingo, *Inquiry into the Occupation and Administration of Haiti and Santo Domingo, 1921–1922*.

14. For background on the occupations, see Calder, *The Impact of Intervention*; Schmidt, *The United States Occupation of Haiti, 1915–1934*; and Renda, *Taking Haiti*.

15. Union Patriotique d'Haiti, Statement for Committee, at http://historymatters. gmu.edu/d/4945/.

16. Rosenberg, *Financial Missionaries to the World*, 122–150; Johnson, *The Peace Progressives and American Foreign Relations*; Nichols, *Promise and Peril*, provide perspectives on interwar anti-imperialism.

17. "The Philippines," *New York Times*, April 7, 1919.

18. "League Will Solve Philippine Problem," *Washington Post*, September 7, 1919; "Peace League as Lever for Free Philippines," *New York Times*, April 13, 1919. Philippine independence would only come slowly, with the country assuming commonwealth status in 1934 and full independence in 1946.

19. "League Will Solve Philippine Problem"; "Peace League as Lever for Free Philippines."

20. See Sluga, *Internationalism in the Age of Nationalism*, for elaboration.

21. Ayala and Bernabe, *Puerto Rico in the American Century*, 74; Flores, *The History of Puerto Rico*, 89–94.

22. Flores, *The History of Puerto Rico*; Harmond, "Campos, Pedro Albizu," at http://www.anb.org/articles/11/11-01225.html, American National Biography Online, February 2000 (accessed May 21, 2014).

23. Trouillot, *Silencing the Past*.

24. I discuss this campaign more fully in my "War and the Health of the State."

13

War-Depression-War

The Fatal Sequence in a Global Perspective

Dietmar Rothermund

The First Industrial War

When the war began all participants believed that it would be a short one lasting for a few months only. This was not just optimism; it was based on an assessment of the structure of the integrated world economy that should make a longer conflict impossible. The German general Graf von Schlieffen, the author of a plan for the rapid conquest of France, had stated in a memorandum written years before the war that long wars among industrial nations are impossible in times when the existence of the nation is based on the uninterrupted progress of trade and industry. Defeating the enemy by a strategy of attrition is not feasible when the maintenance of millions requires the expenditure of billions.[1] Schlieffen's remarks seemed to be prophetic, but the actual course of the war proved that industrial nations could mobilize resources that would make the conduct of a long war possible. The progress of science and technology opened new avenues of production, which sustained the war effort.

The German synthesis of ammonia is a striking example of the impact of industrial progress on the conduct of the war. Germany had developed a giant chemical industry in the late nineteenth century. It had also spawned impressive institutes of higher technical education. The work of a German professor of chemistry, Fritz Haber, was breaking new ground in the synthesis of ammonia, which was important for the production of both nitrogen fertilizer and explosives for munitions. The use of nitrogen fertilizer enhanced agricultural productivity and helped to add billions to the world population. But during the war the production of explosives was more important. Haber performed the synthesis in his laboratory in 1909. It required high pressure at high temperatures and the availability of suitable catalysts. This was a problem to be solved by industrialists. Carl Bosch, a director of the leading chemical firm BASF, a mechanical engineer who had also studied chemistry, pioneered the industrial production of ammonia. The process of synthesis was named the Haber-Bosch process.[2] Both Haber and Bosch received the Nobel Prize in due course. Haber became a veritable scientific tsar during the war, commanding huge research facilities. He also sponsored the use of poisonous gas on the battlefield. His wife, also a chemist, was opposed to this use of poisonous gas and committed suicide when it was deployed by the German army.

Only a few months after the outbreak of the war, Germany faced a munitions crisis. The import of Chilean saltpeter for the production of gunpowder was stopped by the Allied blockade. At this point the ammonia produced by BASF solved the munitions crisis. Otherwise Germany would have had to sue for peace very early.[3] The resilience of industrial nations in the face of wartime challenges was demonstrated by this development. But the war also provided examples of enormous industrial futility. This was symbolized by the Battle of Jutland (Skagerrak), the largest sea battle in history, which ended inconclusive but witnessed a huge loss of ships and manpower—first of all by the British.

Before the war, the German Admiral von Tirpitz with the support of Kaiser Wilhelm II had launched an ambitious program of building a fleet that could challenge British sea power. The idea behind this plan was to create a potential that would discourage the British from joining a war against Germany.[4] The British took note of the challenge and invested an enormous amount in the production of "dreadnoughts"—super-battleships of great dimensions. It was an irony of fate that these huge fleets remained largely inactive during the war—except for the Battle of Jutland. In this battle the German navy performed very well and destroyed several great British ships. This was due to the superior firepower of the German ships and their more effective grenades. Most British grenades exploded after hitting the armor of the ship while the German grenades penetrated the armor and exploded inside the ship. The British used cordite, a new explosive, which was easier to handle than gunpowder. They stacked it carelessly in the turrets of the battleships, which then blew up when hit by German grenades. Several of the British ships were literally torn to pieces in this way and sank within minutes. These big ships were manned by more than a thousand sailors each, who drowned when their ships went down. After heavy losses the two navies disengaged and never joined battle again.[5] At the end of the war the frustrated German sailors played a decisive role in the revolution of 1918. They struck work and stopped their ships.

Instead of the battleships, the submarines played a decisive role in this war.[6] It was Germany's unrestricted use of submarine warfare that finally led to the entry of the United States into this industrial war. When the war began, Germany had just twenty-eight submarines, far outnumbered by those possessed by the Allied navies. But in the course of the war Germany produced more than three hundred submarines, half of which were destroyed in action.

Another decisive weapon in this war was the tank.[7] It finally served to defeat the Germans who had only a handful of tanks produced in the last years of the war. It is amazing that Germany missed the chance of using this modern weapon. It was due to the prejudices of the German generals who felt that tanks were useless on the battlefield.

The British, however, put hundreds of tanks to good use. They developed the so-called crawling advance, whereby columns of tanks progressed under the protection of well-aimed artillery fire. For this it was important to locate and eliminate the guns of the enemy. This was made possible by using microphones invented by William Tucker, a physicist-soldier who placed his new, very sensitive microphones in such a way that they could locate the enemy's guns with great precision.

In addition to the tanks, airplanes made their mark in this war. Most conspicuous were the fights between fighter pilots, but they were of little strategic significance. Airplanes were mostly used for reconnaissance. The British navy even had a small aircraft carrier, HMS *Engandine*, with four seaplanes on board, which had to be hoisted overboard. In the Battle of Jutland, these planes were used to spot the German fleet. The Germans used zeppelins, the huge airships of which eighty-eight were built during the war. They were mostly used for reconnaissance but could also throw bombs.[8]

The development of new types of small arms was also a feature of this industrial war. Hand grenades were first produced by the British in 1915, soon followed by the Germans. Altogether seventy-five millimeter hand grenades were produced in the course of the war. This war was first of all an artillery war. About two-thirds of the casualties were due to artillery fire rather than direct combat. New types of guns that had enormous firepower were introduced. They could even break fortresses that were supposed to be invincible. The strong Belgian forts were the first to be vanquished by "Dicke Bertha," a gun produced by Krupp in Germany just in time for this venture. This was a forty-two-centimeter-wide mortar that could fire grenades of more than eight hundred kilograms over a distance of nearly ten kilometers. At the other end of the spectrum of mortars there were small ones carried by one person, used with devastating effect in trench warfare.

The industrial production of armament was speeded up by all powers. A lack of skilled labor was felt by all of them. In some production lines standardized products were introduced, which could also be handled by unskilled labor.[9] It was one of the miracles of the war that the working class supported the war effort, although before the war trade unions and socialist parties had taken a strong stand against participation in an "imperialist" war.[10] The patriotic support for the war effort began to diminish as the war dragged on. The Russian Revolution of 1917 did not fail to make an impact on working classes elsewhere. By 1918 the resistance of workers to the war effort had spread.

The war took a decisive turn when the United States joined the Allies in April 1917. Even as a "neutral" country, the United States had greatly contributed to the Allied war effort.[11] It had supplied the Allies with many important goods, which were given on credit. The United States, which had earlier been a debtor, was fast becoming a major creditor even before entering the war. Whereas the participants in the war suffered increasingly from industrial fatigue, the United States enhanced its industrial potential very fast. The American economy profited immensely from participating in the war effort whereas the European economies experienced a severe setback. The German economy in particular could not regain its prewar dynamics for a long time.

The Long Shadow of the War

When the war was over, the nations that had participated in it were burdened by enormous war debts. They had financed their war expenditure to a large extent on credit. War bonds had been taken up by the people in addition to foreign loans, mostly from the United States. The United States provided $10.3 billion to the Allies, of which Great Britain received $4.1 billion. The debt service due on those credits was a crushing burden for the respective national budgets. The British had resorted to tax increases, particularly to a wealth tax, during the war, but they had also issued war bonds held by British citizens. Most of them were redeemed only after decades. The German government had trusted that it could pay for the war by imposing reparations on the vanquished—in the meantime it had resorted to printing money. The Germans had signed up for altogether nine issues of war bonds in the course of the war. They had a yield of 5 percent and were therefore very attractive. By the end of the war the German Reich was indebted to the tune of 156 billion Reichsmark.[12] By the end of the war the German Mark had depreciated by about 50 percent since 1914. Inflation was tolerated even after the war. This led to a brief postwar boom in Germany while other nations experienced a recession in 1920. However, Germany then experienced a hyperinflation in 1923, which has remained a memory haunting the nation ever since. The government could wipe out its internal war debt in this way,[13] but the social and political consequences were devastating. The people did not trust the government any longer. Many of them lost their savings of a lifetime. Only the owners of real estate and factories benefited from this radical cut. The ruin of a liberal or conservative middle class contributed to the rise of left-wing and right-wing parties, which challenged the political order of the Weimar Republic. The American Dawes Plan of 1924, which will be discussed later, restored the German economy briefly, but a decline could be noted already in 1926 even before the Great Depression affected Germany.[14] The need to pay reparations burdened the German economy, the more so as the victorious powers did not provide much of an opportunity for Germany to earn the money for such payments by means of the export of goods. This applied also to the French and British payments of war debts to the protectionist United States.

A peace conference, convened in Paris in January 1919, had resulted in the Treaty of Versailles, which imposed a heavy burden of reparations on Germany but also contained the Covenant of the League of Nations proposed by American President Woodrow Wilson. This League was supposed to be a kind of government of a peaceful world. It might have had some success if the United States had joined it. Since it did not do so, the League remained a toothless tiger, especially as its members often did not see eye to eye and obstructed joint endeavors. After the Treaty of Versailles had been signed, John Maynard Keynes published a devastating critique of it. He had worked in the British Treasury on wartime finance and had been sent to the Paris Peace Conference. In protest against the terms of the peace treaty he resigned from the Treasury and wrote his book *The Economic Consequences of the Peace*. It was published in London in 1919 and in New York in 1920 and attracted immediate attention. He pointed out that the burden imposed upon Germany would provoke a reaction, and he predicted that another war would break out after twenty years. This publication had unintended consequences. In the United States it provided arguments to those who saw to it that the Americans would not join the League of Nations. In Great Britain it was quoted by those who felt that Germany was justified in seeking a revision of the terms of the treaty and later on supported the policy of appeasement. The long shadow of the war would not disappear. It blighted the fate of Europe.

In the midst of the war Benjamin Strong, Governor of the Federal Reserve Bank of New York, had noted in his diary that "when the war stops—it should actually STOP."[15] Strong was an internationalist who had helped to finance the British and French war expenditures with American loans. He was afraid that the imposition of harsh conditions on Germany would lead to a renewal of the very conditions that had led to the war. His diary entry was prophetic, but neither he nor those who shared his views could change the course of events. It was an irony of fate that the Federal Reserve System (Fed) under the leadership of Strong adopted a policy in the 1920s that transformed the legacy of the war into a terrible liability. With the best of intentions Strong paved the way for the Great Depression, which he actually predicted before his untimely death in 1928. While the nations involved in the war had abandoned the gold standard in 1914, the United States had retained it and after the war Strong felt that it was his duty to assist the nations wishing to return to it. In doing this, he was caught on the horns of a dilemma. In its new role as the world's creditor, the United States experienced an enormous inflow of gold after the war. According to the doctrine of the gold standard this should have caused an inflation in the receiving country and a deflation in the countries losing gold. High prices due to inflation in one country and low prices caused by deflation in others would then lead to a return of the flow of gold. But the Fed was pledged to maintain domestic price stability. It could do this only by sterilizing gold, thus upsetting the automatism of the gold standard. While this solved the problem, it put increasing deflationary pressure on the countries losing gold. Strong wanted to relieve this pressure by providing ample credit to those nations. With an enormous treasure of hoarded gold, the Fed could create any amount of federal credit, which could be calibrated by its governors. With its inflationary monetary policy the Fed mimicked the effect that the inflow of gold should have had. There were two flaws in this procedure. First of all, the debt service of these generous credits would then lead to an additional flow of gold to the United States. Second, the policy of easy money followed by the Fed also fueled the exuberance of the American stock market. The United States could have got off the horns of this dilemma by canceling the war debts and/or permitting the free flow of gold, but these options were anathema to its political leaders. Strong was a tragic figure. He tried his best to restore the world order after the war with the means at his disposal, but in doing this, he just precipitated another crisis.

The international gold standard in whose contribution to world order Strong had firmly believed had never worked automatically in the past. It had been managed by the City of London, which supported the free flow of gold. It could do so because it was the hub of international finance and was well provided with capital. Before the war, Great Britain's annual capital export amounted to about GBP 170 million, which was mostly directed toward North and South America. India received at the most 10 percent. Dividends and interest received by Great Britain on this exported capital covered more than the annual outflow. Great Britain was truly affluent at that time. After the war this British capital export dwindled to about GBP 40 million per year.[16] Great Britain could no longer perform its prewar functions as a global financial hub. Nevertheless, the Governor of the Bank of England, Montagu Norman, strove to return to the gold standard at the prewar parity. He worked for this strenuously with the help of his friend Benjamin Strong and achieved this aim in 1925. In earlier times, the post of the Governor of the Bank of England had been filled at short intervals by elderly bankers. This bank, which performed all the functions of a central bank, was nevertheless a private bank owned by its shareholders. It was a bankers' bank and Norman was the very embodiment of its strength. It was a sign of turbulent times that, instead of serving the usual short term, Norman was confirmed in holding his post from 1920 to 1944. He was very active in organizing the cooperation of central banks throughout the world. However, he did not get along with his colleagues at the Bank of France. He struck up a close friendship with Hjalmar Schacht, the president of the German Reichsbank. The French knew about this and did not like it. Norman reached the zenith of his fame in 1929 when *Time* magazine lionized him, showing his picture on its front page. But then he had to admit that his achievement of 1925 had been a Pyrrhic victory, the British pound being "under the harrow" ever since. He had to defend the overvalued pound by following a severely deflationary monetary policy.[17]

When an international banking crisis loomed large on the horizon, Norman made a valiant attempt to stave it off by means of the international cooperation of central banks. It was due to his initiative that the Bank of International Settlements (BIS) was established in Basel, Switzerland, in 1930. The BIS had been mentioned in the Young Report, to be discussed later on. The leading American banker J. P. Morgan, Jr., was closely involved in this plan.[18] Ideally, the BIS would have been a kind of monetary League of Nations. But by the time it started functioning, it could no longer prevent the impending disaster. The brilliant French banker Pierre Quesnay, who was in charge of its operations, protected French political interests and was at loggerheads with Norman. Moreover, the BIS was starved of funds and could not even make an attempt at helping ailing financial giants such as the Austrian Creditanstalt, which collapsed in 1931, setting off an avalanche of bank failures throughout Europe. Instead of showing the power of central bank cooperation, the BIS demonstrated the banks' helplessness.[19]

The British finally cut the Gordian knot by abandoning the gold standard in September 1931. The pound was then allowed to float and it depreciated by about 30 percent. The text of the announcement with which the British government explained its momentous decision was drafted by the staff of J. P. Morgan Jr. in New York. Morgan was the greatest creditor of Great Britain at that time, and he endorsed this move at a press conference in London, expressing his faith in British creditworthiness. Norman was in the United States while all this happened and later on pretended that he did not know about this decision. But back in London he immediately took charge of Britain's new monetary policy by means of the Exchange Equalisation Account, which held both gold and foreign exchange reserves. He conducted vast open market operations that enabled him to calibrate the money supply as well as to adjust the exchange rate of the floating pound.[20]

Deflation had been the bane of the European economy. Due to it Europe caught the contagion of the Great Depression, which had its origin in the United States. The financial crisis that led to the collapse of many American banks soon also affected European banks. The crisis had a kind of self-reinforcing effect. As Ben Bernanke has shown in his studies of the Great Depression, such a crisis increases the cost of financial intermediation.[21] This then leads to a veritable credit famine. In the industrial countries this was accompanied by another counterproductive phenomenon: sticky nominal wages.[22] The econo-mist's textbook would prescribe that falling prices would be paralleled by fall-ing wages. According to orthodox views, the labor market is a market like any other and is therefore governed by the rules of market clearing. According to this view, unemployment should not really exist because every laborer would find employment at the right price (wage) for his work. Sticky nominal wages, which imply rising real wages when prices fall, should also not exist in a func-tioning labor market. Instead of this the credit famine was accompanied by a wage freeze. Employers would rather fire workers than try to reduce their nominal wages. This is sometimes explained by postulating that employers "hoard" skilled labor that they require if they have to expand production once more in better times.[23] But there may be an additional reason: unions normally defend the rights of the employed and not those of the unemployed. Thus the employer may find it easier to fire workers than to reduce wages. At any rate, there was growing unemployment during the Great Depression and no "clear-ing" of the labor market.

While these were problems faced by the industrial sector, the agricultural sector had a bitter fate of its own during the Depression. Peasants working in a subsistence economy would not have been touched by the Depression, but by the 1920s there were very few pockets of subsistence economy left at the periphery of the world market. Most peasants at the periphery depended on the market and on credit for their operations. In order to pay rent and/or land revenue and to service their debts the peasants had to sell part of their agri-cultural produce. These demands, which they had to meet, were very "sticky" and would not be readily adjusted once agricultural prices fell to an alarming extent. This fall was more dramatic than anything that happened in the industrial sector and it could also be traced to the fate of the gold standard.

Gold and Grain: The Avalanche of the Great Depression

The gold standard was the backbone of global commerce. It also supported the expansion of the worldwide trade in food grains, particularly wheat. As long as the gold standard prevailed, credit was freely available. This also helped to finance the storage of wheat. Stored wheat could be used as collateral to obtain further credit. The trade in wheat futures helped to stabilize prices internationally.[24] The 1920s had witnessed a rapid expansion of wheat production. In the United States large parts of the Great Plains had been reclaimed for wheat cultivation. In the 1930s these tracts turned into the "Dust Bowl," because the soil had dried up, due to large-scale farming, and the wind blew away land. This farming was facilitated by the spread of mechanization. Huge machines performed the work for which thousands of laborers were once required. Canada and Argentina had also extended their areas under wheat. In Argentina huge estates of cattle breeders were partly converted into land cultivated by itinerant tenants who lived in huts but owned modern combine harvesters.[25] In the period from 1924 to 1929 four countries dominated the wheat export market: Canada (38 percent), the United States (22 percent), Argentina (19 percent), and Australia (12 percent).[26] In 1925 these four nations produced altogether forty million tons of wheat of which they exported nineteen million tons. The previous year had been a bad one when world production amounted to a total of sixty-eight million tons, but 1927 and 1928 were good years. World production climbed to eighty-two and then ninety-two million tons and prices began to fall. Although 1929 was once more a bad year (seventy-seven million tons), prices did not recover. The storages were filled to the brim. In the meantime the Fed had raised the bank rate in order to control the exuberance of the stock market. But speculators deposited stocks with their banks, using them as collateral for buying more stocks. They did not mind a higher interest rate as they hoped to make more money from the stock market. But the higher interest rates hit those who stored wheat on credit. So far storage had provided the ratchet that prevented the decline of the wheat price. In 1929 the ratchet broke and an avalanche of wheat flooded the world market. Panic sales set in, because everybody wanted to get rid of his stored wheat before the prices declined even further. By 1931 the wheat price had fallen far below the prewar level (in 1913 it was $100, and in 1931 it was $62).[27] The stock-market crash in New York (1929) was not directly related to the causes of the wheat avalanche, but it contributed to the general recoil of the web of credit that had so far supported world trade.

Trade declined in terms of value, but not in volume. Supply and demand were fairly stable, but they no longer determined the price of commodities, which remained depressed for a long time.

The steep fall in wheat prices affected the peasants at the periphery of the world market. India is a case in point. Wheat prices declined even more precipitously in India than elsewhere. From 1929 to 1931 the wheat price fell by more than half. Cheap Australian wheat depressed the Indian price level and the government of India was forced to pass a Wheat Import Duty Act.[28] This was a move that did not at all agree with the free trade policy otherwise advocated by this government. But the Indian peasantry was in distress. Most of the peasants were indebted to money lenders and their debt service and revenue demands were not adjusted so as to make allowance for their loss in income.

Even more crushing than the fall of the wheat price that affected Western India was the sudden collapse of the rice price in January 1931, which hit Eastern India. This was totally unexpected, because rice was not overproduced and it was not stored in great quantities. It was mostly produced and consumed in Asia. Only a small percentage of it entered the world market. By 1933, the price of rice was lower than that of wheat. This had never happened before. It was a drastic case of contagion by credit contraction. In October 1930, there had been a good rice harvest in Japan. The Japanese price of rice then dropped by about 30 percent. This was also due to a deflationary monetary policy that had been pursued to keep Japan on the gold standard, which it had joined once more only one year earlier. Japan neither imported nor exported rice at that time, but in November 1930 the news from Japan affected the international rice market of Liverpool where the rice price was halved. This was communicated to Rangoon, the chief rice market of British India, where the price also fell by half when the winter harvest reached the market in January 1931.[29] A peasant rebellion in Myanmar followed, which was then violently crushed by the British. The impact of the Great Depression on the periphery of the world market could be noted in many other countries, too.[30]

The curious case of a delayed impact of the Great Depression was that of China, which had been on a silver standard. The price of silver fell steeply in parallel with that of all other commodities in 1930 and overseas Chinese living in gold-standard countries then bought silver and invested it in China. This gave rise to a short-lived boom at the very time when other countries were hit by the Depression. But the tide was soon reversed when the Silver Purchase Act was passed in the United States in 1934. This act obliged the US government to hold a quarter of its currency reserves in silver. Due to this the silver price doubled within a year and once more attained the level of 1929. In 1935 the price of silver increased by another 50 percent. Silver was sucked with a vengeance out of China, which then experienced a fierce deflation.[31] The Great Depression had caught up with this unfortunate country after all.

In other countries on the periphery, gold flowed out in torrents after Great Britain had left the gold standard in September 1931 and was floating the pound. This immediately increased the price of gold. Money lenders then forced their debtors to part with their gold and a stream of "distress gold" flowed from the periphery to the center of the world economy. This was of great advantage to the floating pound and the emerging "Sterling area."[32] It was the last instance in which the control over the colonies was useful for imperial powers. If countries like India had been independent at that time, they would have imposed a gold export embargo and used the gold for reflating their economy. But the colonial rulers saw to it that India had to disgorge its gold. They followed a deflationary policy that deepened the Depression and helped to squeeze out more gold.[33] In earlier times colonies were valued because they guaranteed access to raw materials and agricultural produce. The steep fall in commodity prices had deprived the colonial rulers of this benefit. They now held on to the colonies as creditors having their debtors in a tight grip. The trend toward decolonization emerged in the 1930s. The German economist Moritz Bonn, who taught at the London School of Economics, had coined the term "decolonization" in 1931 and in his book *The Crumbling of Empire* he stated, "A decolonization movement is sweeping over the continents. An age of empire-breaking is following an age of empire-making."[34] Anticolonial movements were growing in the 1930s as the Depression lingered on in the periphery after it had receded in the industrial countries of the West. Studies of the Depression have usually been concerned with the fate of the workers in the United States and Europe and not with that of the peasants of Asia, Africa, and South America. The peasants then benefited from a rise in prices caused by the onset of the Second World War.

Repeat Performance: The Drama of the Second World War

The Depression was one of the main causes of the Second World War. It had led to a deterioration of international relations due to the "beggar-thy-neighbor" policies followed by many countries. It had also caused severe unemployment in some countries, particularly in highly industrialized Germany where social unrest led to the rise of the National Socialist Party led by Adolf Hitler. In order to be able to honor its obligations to pay reparations, which have been mentioned earlier, the German government had stuck to the gold standard and had followed a deflationary policy that made the Depression much worse. The aim of this policy was to demonstrate that Germany was not in a position to pay the reparations any longer even if it tried very hard to do so. Hitler, however, wanted to abrogate the reparations and to get rid of the restrictions imposed on Germany by the Treaty of Versailles. After winning an election, he seized power in 1933 and put an end to parliamentary democracy. He was ably supported by Hjalmar Schacht, head of the German central bank (Reichsbank) who gradually reflated the German economy and practiced Keynesianism even before Keynes had published his *General Theory*. Schacht was a conservative nationalist who backed Hitler because he shared his desire to get rid of the restrictions of the Treaty of Versailles. But Hitler wanted to rearm Germany in order to win a Second World War. Initially Hitler was cautious and did not show his hand. He carefully watched the reactions of the British and the French to his moves. If they had stopped him early, they could have prevented the war. But they hardly ever saw eye to eye and did not coordinate their policies. When Hitler let his troops occupy the Rhineland in 1936, which was demilitarized due to the Treaty of Versailles, and got away with it, he felt encouraged to move on. His next aims were the annexation of Austria and reclaiming the predominantly German regions of Czechoslovakia. President Wilson's well-meaning emphasis on the self-determination of nations had saddled Europe with a problematic legacy. The boundaries of the nations emerging from the defunct Habsburg Empire were determined by the victorious powers and not by those nations themselves. The Germans in what was left of Austria were inclined to join Germany. Similarly the Germans of Czechoslovakia, whose settlements formed a ring around the Czech area, had their eyes on Germany. Hitler could thus appeal to their "self-determination," which would upset the order imposed by the Treaty of Versailles.

In November 1937 Hitler received an unexpected "private" visitor: Viscount Halifax.[35] This British nobleman was an influential member of the Conservative Party. When Anthony Eden resigned as head of the British Foreign Office in 1938 in protest against the appeasement policy of his government, Halifax became his successor. Actually, the visit was "private" only for diplomatic reasons. Halifax told Hitler that he had discussed his initiative with Prime Minister Chamberlain. He assured Hitler that the British agreed with him on the Czech and Austrian problems and would not obstruct a "solution," if it could be achieved without a war. It seems that Hitler convinced him of his "peaceful" intentions and that he assured him that he had no further territorial ambitions. Poland sided at that time with Germany, as it had also claims on Czech territory in Silesia. Both Hitler and Halifax could feel that their talks had been successful. This was the prelude to the Munich conference of 1938 in which "appeasement" triumphed. Halifax may not have been amused by some remarks Hitler made during their conversation. Hitler had recommended that the British should shoot Gandhi in order to keep ruling India. In his earlier career Halifax (then Lord Irwin) had been Viceroy of India and had concluded the Gandhi-Irwin Pact of 1931. He could have gauged Hitler's brutal instincts at that time, but he rather opted for appeasement as he was not sure of Great Britain's preparedness for a war. Although he would not have told this to Hitler, the Führer must have felt that his interlocutor was representing a weak adversary. After the "solution" of the Austrian and Czech problems he resolutely pursued his aim of starting a world war.

At this stage Hitler clashed with Schacht who had so far backed him, creating a veritable economic miracle. In January 1939 Schacht feared that Germany was heading for a serious inflation. Just like Keynes, Schacht was convinced that there was no harm of reflating an economy to achieve full employment if one stopped short of precipitating an inflation. He felt that this point had been reached in Germany due to excessive spending on rearmament. He could not see why this was necessary any longer as Hitler's aim of getting rid of the terms of the Treaty of Versailles had been reached; therefore he wrote a courageous letter to Hitler, which was signed by all members of the board of the Reichsbank. Hitler responded by sacking Schacht and his board.[36] He then went ahead with his preparations for the Second World War. While Germany had been wrongly blamed for starting the First World War, it was certainly at fault this time. There were no "sleepwalkers" now, only a determined warmonger and reluctant leaders of nations ill prepared for stopping him at the right time. But when the drama of the war unfolded, it appeared to be a repeat performance of the First World War, starting with a German invasion of France, followed by a prolonged war in the East and finally terminated by American intervention. But at this time the Americans had become vastly more powerful and decided to stay on in Europe, giving a new shape to world affairs.

The Irresistible Rise of the United States

The self-destruction of Europe in the First World War created an opening for the United States, which then began its irresistible rise to global power without really aiming at it. An important element of this rise was its financial strength, which enabled it to emerge from the First World War as the dominant creditor of Great Britain and France. The United States found the imposing of reparations on Germany inopportune and did not join in this demand, but it firmly insisted on the debt service for the war debts of the Allies. Any bracketing of war debts and reparations was rejected. But there was an awareness of the fact that the Allies needed the reparations in order to service the war debts. In spite of its isolationist withdrawal from Europe, the United States had to see to it that the cycle of reparation payments and servicing the war debts would continue. Two important American negotiators have to be mentioned in this context: Charles Dawes and Owen Young. Dawes had been a general in the First World War and became vice president of the United States in 1925. In 1924 he was sent to Germany in order to regularize the payment of reparations after Germany had just overcome a devastating hyperinflation. He saw to it that Germany became creditworthy again by inaugurating a flow of American capital. The Dawes Plan subjected Germany to a deflationary policy.[37] The Reichsbank was restored to its old position and half of its board members were nominated by the Americans. In addition, an American banker acted as a watchdog in Berlin in order to monitor the working of the Dawes Plan. This was a blow to German sovereignty, but Schacht, who headed the Reichsbank already at that time, did not see it that way. On the contrary, he welcomed the American presence, which shielded the Reichsbank against German political pressures.[38]

After 1924 the flow of American funds to Europe increased by leaps and bounds. Earlier European borrowers had come to the United States asking for credit, and now the agents of American banks swarmed all over Europe, offering bonds. The American public was eager to invest in such bonds. The 1920s were a "defaultless" era, and this encouraged American investment in foreign stocks and bonds. The total flow of funds amounted to $1.2 to 1.5 billion annually from 1924 to 1928; bonds had the lion's share, with stocks amounting to an average of $10 million annually, but increasing to $41 million in 1928. In 1929 this flow was reduced while the American stock market still attracted an enormous amount of funds until the crash stopped the merry-go-round. By 1930 the debt service on American loans abroad amounted to $900 million.[39] This was much more than the British had derived from their capital export before the war. The United States had replaced Great Britain with a vengeance as creditor of the world. But due to the impact of the Great Depression, the United States turned to a "New Deal" of internal consolidation rather than playing the role of a prudent creditor who must try to keep a debtor going so as to rely on its debt service.

The drying up of American credit after 1929 made it difficult for Germany to pay reparations and another American plan was required. Owen Young, who had already participated in the drafting of the Dawes Plan, was sent to Germany. Young was chairman of General Electric and the founder of the Radio Corporation of America. He was accompanied by the famous New York banker J. P. Morgan, Jr., so the Young Plan thus had the backing of the American banking community. This plan eased the burden of reparation payments by spreading them out over a longer period of time.[40] But by the time the plan was finalized in 1930, the Depression had set in and the German government was soon captured by Hitler.

Hitler's seizure of power was paralleled by the beginning of Roosevelt's long presidency in the United States. Much has been said about his New Deal, but actually Roosevelt's most important measure was going off the gold standard and initiating a devaluation of the US dollar in April 1933. Unlike Great Britain, which had been forced to go off gold in September 1931 due to a drain of its gold reserves, the United States had an enormous treasure of hoarded gold and could have very well retained the gold standard. But Roosevelt wanted to push up agricultural prices in order to help his voters, the American farmers. He did very well, as far as this was concerned, and he did not care about stabilizing the world at that time. He refused to attend the World Economic Conference in London in June 1933 and sent his "bombshell message," telling the Europeans to put their house in order.[41] His emphasis was on domestic consolidation rather than on external leadership.

The United States actually profited from exporting the Depression. This was, of course, not a deliberate act, but it certainly undermined the position of the colonial empires on which the United States had tried to impose an "open door" policy while at the same time clinging to protectionism. When the Second World War engulfed the European empires, these empires depended on American help. Once more, the United States entered the war late and decided its outcome. It then could dictate the terms of the future world order and secure a dominant position for the US dollar. The Fed could print money for the whole world and derive a "seigniorage" from this. The French Finance Minister, Valery Giscard d'Estaing, had called this an "exorbitant privilege."[42] It had been acquired at the end of the Second World War, when the United States accounted for more than half of the combined output of the Great Powers.[43] But it was retained even when the relative weight of the US economy declined. The sequence of war-depression-war had put the United States into the driver's seat for the world economy.

NOTES

1. Hardach, *Der Erste Weltkrieg*, 64.
2. König and Weber, *Netzwerke Stahl und Strom, 1849–1914*, 384.
3. Hardach, *Der Erste Weltkrieg*, 68.
4. Münkler, *Der Grosse Krieg*, 498.
5. Ibid., 507.
6. Ibid., 508.
7. Ibid., 459, 642.
8. Ibid., 526.
9. Hardach, *Der Erste Weltkrieg*, 115.
10. Ibid., 187.

11. Ibid., 160.

12. Ibid., 173.

13. Tipton and Aldrich, *An Economic and Social History of Europe, 1890–1939*, 177.

14. Ritschl, "International Capital Movements and the Onset of the Great Depression," 1–14.

15. Roberts, "Benjamin Strong, the Federal Reserve and the Limits to Interwar American Nationalism," diary entry of March 9, 1916, Strong Papers File 1000.2.

16. Rothermund, *The Global Impact of the Great Depression*, 21.

17. Ibid., 27.

18. Burk, "The House of Morgan in Financial Diplomacy, 1920–1939," 148.

19. James, "The Creation of a World Central Bank?"

20. Rothermund, *The Global Impact of the Great Depression*, 63.

21. Bernanke, *Essays on the Great Depression*, 43.

22. Ibid., 28.

23. Ibid., 256.

24. Topik and Wells, "Warenketten in einer globalen Welt," 713.

25. Ibid., 706.

26. Ibid., 698.

27. Rothermund, *The Global Impact of the Great Depression*, 40.

28. Rothermund, *India in the Great Depression, 1929–1939* (New Delhi: Manohar, 1992), 82, 87.

29. Ibid., 86.

30. Rothermund, "Currencies, Taxes and Credit," 15–34.

31. Rothermund, *The Global Impact of the Great Depression*, 113.

32. Drummond, *The Floating Pound and the Sterling Area 1931–1939*, 260.

33. Rothermund, *India in the Great Depression*, 54.

34. Bonn, *The Crumbling of Empire*, 101.

35. Tomaszewski, "Lord Edward Halifax Visiting Adolf Hitler."

36. Rothermund, *The Global Impact of the Great Depression*, 150.

37. Tipton and Aldrich, *An Economic and Social History of Europe, 1890–1939*, 205.

38. Rothermund, *The Global Impact of the Great Depression*, 35.

39. Mintz, *Deterioration in the Quality of Foreign Bonds Issued in the United States, 1920–1930*.

40. Rothermund, *The Global Impact of the Great Depression*, 67.

41. Clavin, "Explaining the Failure of the London World Economic Conference."

42. Eichengreen, *Exorbitant Privilege*, 4.

43. Ibid., 2.

14

World War I, the Rise of Hitler, and the Legacy of Dictatorship

Klaus Schwabe

As a German historian recently remarked, for Germany Adolf Hitler was the "offspring," the outstanding legacy, of World War I, and no one doubts that.[1] He himself started his political career in 1919 in the wake of a lost war and the crushing peace of Versailles. That treaty reduced Germany's territory by 14 percent and its population by 6.5 million citizens. It created for Germany large minorities outside its new borders and for the time being an unlimited reparations liability.[2] Hitler's rise to dictatorship is unthinkable without the humiliation and misery that resulted for the German people out of their defeat. And still: was he bound to become the war's nemesis in destroying the Weimar Republic? This essay thus asks the question whether Hitler's rise to power from Germany's defeat to the proclamation of the Third Reich was inevitable. For that purpose the ways in which Germans tried to come to terms with their defeat and the war's legacies will be discussed. As an illustration the article focuses on two highly popular political doctrines, both legacies of the war, and each in its own way denying the hopelessness of Germany's military situation at the end of the war. These were (1) the doctrine of the "stab-in-the-back" (*Dolchstoss*) and (2) the doctrine of the "war-guilt lie" (*Kriegsschuldlüge*). At its conclusion, this analysis will raise the question as to whether Hitler's exploitation of these two doctrines immediately led to his dictatorship.

The stab-in-the-back doctrine first was foreshadowed, when, on October 3, 1918, the German government requested an armistice with the Allies and peace negotiations on the basis of the peace program that President Woodrow Wilson had propagated. To the

German public this move was an absolutely shattering surprise. Until then the German High Command had failed to admit the increasing seriousness of Germany's military position resulting from strategic overstretch and military exhaustion.[3] Instead, all the public had perceived was that the German troops fighting in France had protected them against the direct experience of war and that, in the East, Germany's predominance extended as far as the Caucasus Mountains. How then could Germany's bid be explained?[4] Could it be that the million-fold sacrifice of lives had been in vain? The gap that throughout the war had yawned between far-flung popular hopes and the grim military reality thus deepened even further. Other, nonmilitary reasons, it was believed, must have been behind Germany's sudden giving up. The German military command concealed what it had confessed to the political leadership in Berlin—that it feared German troops in France were on the verge of being routed. To avoid a public loss of face, it claimed that nonmilitary reasons lay behind Germany's critical military situation. Ludendorff, the de facto highest commander of Germany's troops, concocted an explanation by inventing the stab-in-the-back doctrine. Germany had sued for an armistice, he asserted in a confidential talk with his officers, because it had become impossible to continue the war. This was due to the "poison" of Marxist–Socialist propaganda that had undermined the soldiers' resolution to go on fighting and made them "unreliable," although the chances of a successful defense, if not victory, continued to be good.[5] Ludendorff's statement initiated a lengthy process of political onus shifting between military and civil authorities, between the Right and the Left, regarding the responsibility for the military disaster that was threatening their country.[6]

Actually, the antecedents of this doctrine went further back—well into the fall of 1916. At that point, under the impression of a precarious military situation during the Battle of the Somme, the first doubts arose in Germany regarding the prospects of a victory. A heated controversy about the war's purpose and Germany's war aims broke out. The military leadership and the exponents of the nationalist right kept insisting that a total victory was indispensable that would ensure sizable annexations, improve Germany's geopolitical position, and entail a reward for the sacrifices the German people had made. Significantly, it was also held that only the perspective of a total victory would maintain morale at home and at the front.[7] The forces of the German Center and Left, not least Labor, on the other hand, pressed for a peace of accommodation based on a military tie as the only realistic way out of a war that Germany apparently could not win. The real reward of the war seemed to be liberal reforms in Prussia and the empire.[8] On July 19, 1917, a majority of the German Reichstag passed a resolution demanding just that.[9] To the rightist die-hards this amounted to outright treason subverting the public morale. According to the Right, internal reforms could not be a substitute for military victory.[10]

In October 1918, the German request for an armistice appeared as a victory of the defeatists. Within the military leadership, but even among some liberal political observers, portents of an imminent revolt in Germany conjured up the image of pernicious forces that launched an attack from behind against the fighting armies.[11] The German Revolution of early November 1918 was seen as a self-fulfilling prophecy. By paralyzing any further military resistance it seemed to finalize the German defeat and to prove what was soon called the stab-in-the-back doctrine.[12] The "organized treason" of the German Revolution, not the actual military balance, was made responsible for the collapse of Germany's military resistance.[13] Half a year later, the final German acceptance of the Treaty of Versailles was regarded as another stab in the back of those German patriots who pleaded for a rejection of the peace terms and renewed military resistance.[14] This variety of the stab-in-the-back doctrine reflected the disappointment over the peace terms shared by virtually all political groups in Germany, not only by the Right. The unanimous protest against the treaty even created hopes for a national revival like the one experienced at the outbreak of the war—the outburst of an all-compassing patriotism, which would strengthen the reputation of the new Republic. The acceptance of the treaty dashed such hopes.[15] Public opinion merged this final humiliation with the earlier ones. In that widened meaning, the image of a *Dolchstoss* became common currency in the public discourse. By implication, it indicted democracy as inadequate in dealing with military problems.

In the meantime, the doctrine had acquired two additional facets: anti-Semitism and an attack on American policies under Woodrow Wilson. Since the revolution, first, it went along with violent outbursts of anti-Semitism. In 1917, the nationalist Right ascribed the Reichstag's demand for a compromise of peace to Jewish influences (*Judenfrieden*).[16] The Armistice and the German Revolution then unleashed a most violent outburst of anti-Semitism, which merged with the stab-in-the-back doctrine. To the Right, the Versailles treaty appeared as the predicted *Judenfrieden*.[17] The other facet of the doctrine aimed at the United States under the leadership of Woodrow Wilson. The American president, so it was said, had inveigled the German Left by propagating the mirage of a lenient peace. He thus had induced it to appeal for an end of the hostilities, an end that in reality turned out to militarily cripple Germany. At Versailles then going back on his "promise" he signed a victors' peace. His "betrayal" was a crucial element held responsible for Germany's defeat.[18]

Soon after the Armistice, some of the very political leaders whom the Right accused of having incited the revolution indirectly helped to popularize these charges. Welcoming the German troops that returned to Berlin on December 10, 1918, Friedrich Ebert, the Social Democratic chairman of the provisional German government, declared: "Let me extend a cordial welcome to you soldiers, political as well as military comrades. . . . No enemy defeated you. It was only when the superior strength of the adversary grew overwhelming, we had to give up. . . . You are entitled to return with your heads held high." This halfway denial of Germany's defeat amounted to an indirect approval of the stabin-the-back doctrine. It confirmed the secret informal alliance that had been forged between the new Social Democratic German leadership and the military. In a situation that at times came close to a civil war it was part of a common carefully orchestrated strategy designed to uphold the troops' loyalty to the new government in fighting against its German Bolshevik foes.[19]

The term "stab in the back" was first used in this sense in mid-December 1918 by a Swiss newspaper that, erroneously, referred back to a British army officer who allegedly had invented it. This seemingly impartial assessment helped its German adherents, initially not only spokesmen of the Right but also more moderate personalities like Gustav Stresemann, to defend this doctrine. During the election of January 1919, the Conservative Party (DNVP) indiscriminately exploited it as a political weapon to discredit the communists, Social Democrats, and the bourgeois Left as well as the new republican form of government.[20] On the other hand, the Left countered by developing a stab-inthe-back doctrine of its own by blaming Imperial diplomacy, the military, and the reactionary nationalists for having torpedoed chances for a peace of compromise during the war and for deciding to launch an unrestricted submarine campaign that involved the United States in the war.[21]

After plans for legal action had been abandoned, the national parliament appointed a commission to investigate the mutual stab-in-the-back charges. The most prominent witness to appear before the commission was no one less than Field Marshall Paul von Hindenburg, the war hero and symbol of German nationhood. In a prepared statement he read on November 18, 1919, he pretended that if the German people had remained united the country would have won the war. Minimizing the effects of the American entry into the war, he blamed "the clandestine, systematic corruption of the fleet and the army" (*Zersetzung*)—a development of which the revolution and Germany's collapse merely represented the "consummation." He then expressly referred to the image of the stab in the back of the German troops, quoting the alleged remark of the British officer referred to above. In his memoirs he went so far as to speak of a crime.[22] His statements created a sensation and dealt a devastating blow to the reputation of the republic—as it turned out, the prelude to the right-wing military coup (*Kapp-Putsch*) attempted a few weeks later.[23]

The parliamentary investigations dealing with the political responsibilities for Germany's defeat lasted well into the late 1920s. They arrived at more balanced results assigning the responsibility for the revolution exclusively to the radical Left. Meanwhile, the stab-in-the-back doctrine had lost some of its appeal even to the DNVP, which had succeeded in distancing itself from its ultra-rightist and anti-Semitic wing and after the crisis of 1923 joined a coalition with the pro-republican moderate Left.[24] The only exception was the extreme Right, which remained vociferous, but relatively small, still succeeding in keeping the doctrine from being forgotten.[25]

As opposed to the disruptive effects of the stab-in-the-back propaganda, the defense of the German cause in World War I and specifically Germany's role regarding its outbreak integrated the German public. The consensus prevailing when Germany entered the war remained intact beyond the Armistice. It was the conviction that the German Empire had been the victim of a vicious attack on the part of its enemies and fought a war of self-defense—a consensus questioned only by the radical socialist Left and some pacifists.[26]

These forces had gained temporary prominence as the result of the revolution. In view of the impending peace conference, Kurt Eisner, the spokesman of the radical USPD (Unabhängige Sozialdemokratische Partei Deutschlands), had urged the new revolutionary government to fully admit Germany's war guilt. Soon to become one of the few remaining German Wilsonians, to him and his supporters this admission was a question of honesty as well as political expediency. Only if the new republic disassociated itself clearly from the monarchical regime and conceded Germany's responsibility for the war, he held, could it create a climate of trust between the former enemies and facilitate negotiations for a peace based on the lenient terms that Wilson had enunciated.[27] For this policy to become effective, Eisner and his followers like Eduard Bernstein advocated the opening of the German archives to compromise the old governmental forces. Under the supervision of Karl Kautsky, a historian and friend of Eisner's, a collection of relevant documents from the governmental offices was assembled. These efforts met violent opposition from the rest of the political spectrum. The term Kriegsschuldlüge—that is, the "lie" alleging Germany's responsibility for the outbreak of the war—originated.[28]

However, not only the political leadership in Berlin, including most Social Democrats, was opposed to Eisner's efforts, but also the Foreign Office. It declined to publish potentially compromising documents dealing with the former government's role in the outbreak of the war. Its reasons went back to the weeks immediately after the conclusion of the Armistice, when it had received information that led it to believe that Germany's presumed "war guilt" would provide the legal basis for the peace terms. Anticipating this situation, it urged the political representatives to prepare the ground for refuting this allegation.[29] This led to a momentous decision arrived at by the Berlin cabinet along with the Foreign Office in March 1919. On that occasion, Eduard David, a prominent member of the Social Democratic Party (SPD), endorsed the approach Eisner had urged: the German government should admit its war guilt and thus demonstrate that the revolutionary government had nothing to do with its monarchical predecessor, could not be held responsible for the war, and, therefore, was entitled to a lenient peace based on the American terms. In line with the Foreign Office, the cabinet was opposed to David's proposal on a technical legal ground: the Armistice, including its commitment to base the future peace on the American terms, it pointed out, still had been concluded by representatives of the old regime. For Germany to come out with a confession of war guilt disassociating itself from the Imperial Government would be counterproductive because legally it would blame itself and thus would forfeit the Wilsonian base of the coming peace treaty. In other words, only if Germany's peacemakers denied the result of the German Revolution would they maintain Germany's claim to obtain a Wilsonian peace. This was crucial. From then on, the German government and an overwhelming part of the public upheld the belief in Germany's innocence of any war guilt. Only the communists remained outside that national consensus.[30] The myth of Germany's total innocence in initiating World War I, another of the war's legacies, was born.

For the peace conference, though, the government instructed Germany's delegates, headed by Foreign Minister Ulrich Graf Brockdorff-Rantzau, to soft-pedal that issue. The foreign minister disagreed and felt vindicated after, on May 7, 1919, the draft treaty was presented to the German negotiators. It brought the German peace delegates face to face with what they had feared: Article 231, which introduced the reparation chapter and declared Germany's aggression responsible for the outbreak of the war and the resulting damage to the Allies. As is well known by now, that famous so-called war-guilt clause of the Versailles treaty had a rather technical background resulting from the big gap that existed between the Allies' demands and Germany's ability to pay. In that respect, the treaty represented a compromise: It did confirm Germany's moral liability, but in the following Article 232 it conceded that Germany's means were not unlimited. What counted in German eyes, however, was Germany's assumed moral liability based on its "aggression" in 1914.[31] To Brockdorff-Rantzau, the war-guilt issue represented the very essence of the victors' legal position. For that reason he urged that the rejection of the treaty text should focus on this very point. As a consequence, the German foreign minister defiantly rejected the accusation of Germany as the initiator of the war as an insult violating Germany's national dignity. He retorted by impugning the victors' honor, claiming that they had replaced their promise of a lenient Wilsonian peace by using the pretext of Germany's war guilt as a means to impose harsh peace terms.[32]

Insisting on Germany's immediate signature under the treaty, the victors' final covering note summarily condemned the German people and its wartime government as criminals. Their conduct in the war, it claimed, had been "almost unexampled in human history." The note culminated in calling the war "the greatest crime against humanity and the freedom of peoples that any nation, calling itself civilized, has ever consciously committed." To the British premier, this language was needed to revive the war spirit among the Allied troops in case the Germans refused to sign the treaty and hostilities resumed.[33]

To the German side this accusation was unacceptable, not least because it dismissed the democratic transformation Germany had undergone after the revolution: the Versailles verdict seemed to question the very legitimacy of the new German Republic. Despite all such protestations Germany had to accept the incriminating articles.[34] The stage was set for an extensive principled debate. After the signing of the treaty, all governments of the Weimar Republic were unanimous in insisting that Article 231 be annulled, that Germany's honor be restored, and that the reparations be reduced. The peace strategy Germany had pursued during the conference thus had to be carried on in the eye of the public. The victors had be forced to repudiate the "war-guilt lie" and, as a result, to revise the reparations terms. Germany had to be restored as an undisputed great power.[35]

As one of the first steps, historiography was to be mobilized. Ironically, this work had been begun by Eisner and Kautsky, although, as has been shown, with a different slant: Kautsky in his publications spared no efforts to distance the new Germany from the old, although he revised his original opinion according to which the former German government was primarily responsible for the outbreak of the war.[36] From early on the official publicity efforts aimed at fully exonerating Germany. They tried to establish a taboo around the monarchical regime and their policies, as well as to shift the blame to the victorious countries. To maintain close control of the ensuing campaign, the Foreign Office set up a special agency (Kriegsschuldreferat). For publicity purposes, two huge nationwide nonpartisan organizations were founded. Attempts by more open-minded collaborators to admit some German co-responsibility for the outbreak of the war were muted as unpatriotic.[37] They intended to act as a public sounding board in support of the more moderate official revisionist foreign policy conducted by Gustav Stresemann. The Foreign Office on its part published massive documentation covering Germany's foreign policy from Bismarck until 1914.[38] Stresemann saw in it the expression of Germany's "clear conscience" regarding the outbreak of the war. Not fully free from influences emanating from the Foreign Office and somewhat apologetic in its footnotes, this publication still attempted to observe scholarly standards to influence opinion outside Germany. Its rapidly published forty volumes received international praise.[39]

As in the case of the stab-in-the-back doctrine, the forum that appeared most suitable to produce an impartial assessment of Germany's war guilt was an investigation commission appointed by the German Parliament. Its deliberations dragged on until 1932. To an extent, the Foreign Office succeeded in "guiding" its work, making sure that it avoided compromising conclusions and excluded the issue of Germany's aims during the war from its inquiry.[40] Still, these organizations intended to act in support of the more moderate official revisionist policy conducted by Gustav Stresemann, leader of the DVP (Deutsche Volkspartei) and Germany's foreign minister since 1923. Stresemann, the outstanding representative of right-wing Liberalism in the Weimar Republic, single-mindedly pursued a pragmatic approach—he called it "responsible *Realpolitik*"—for Germany's foreign policy. His tactics were to seek compromises and accommodation with the West, thus enlisting American financial support. His goal was to peacefully revise the Versailles treaty, especially regarding Germany's border to Poland, and to restore the status of a great European power of equal rights to his country.[41]

The emotions that the domestic debate about the war-guilt issue had stirred up created a problem as to how Stresemann's foreign diplomacy could be made palatable to Parliament, which had to ratify its legal results. Initially, the right-wing parties refused to subscribe to any accommodation with France and Great Britain. As a prerequisite for supporting Stresemann, they insisted that the Allies first restore Germany's honor and renounce the "war-guilt clause" of the treaty. Differently from Stresemann, they largely adhered to the diplomatic approach, which Brockdorff-Rantzau, Stresemann's predecessor, had opted for at Versailles. They harbored the illusion that once the supposed legal cornerstone of the treaty was eliminated the whole edifice of the treaty text would crumble. Stresemann had ceased to share such illusions. In his mind, the issue of war guilt could only be brought up again after his "responsible Realpolitik" had succeeded.[42]

During the years' long debate about the basic approach of Germany's foreign policy, the merits of the case—the degree of a German responsibility for outbreak of the war—became immaterial. The all-important problem was for the foreign minister to maintain parliamentary support for his diplomacy of accommodation, which is where the American role entered into the war-guilt legacy. The Dawes Plan for a temporary settlement regarding the payment of German reparations (1924) was the first case in point. Stresemann needed the votes of the DNVP. By way of domestic concessions and cautiously backed up by American diplomats, he finally won one-half of the conservative deputies to ensure a majority.[43] Germany's accession to the Treaty of Locarno (1925), which mutually guaranteed France's and Germany's common borders and thus implied Germany's acceptance of the loss of Alsace-Lorraine, raised similar parliamentary problems.[44] In both instances, spokesmen of the DNVP and the parties of the extreme Right criticized that the victorious Allies had failed to revoke the war-guilt clause. The fundamental alternative for Germany's contemporary foreign policy was thus raised: a "responsible realpolitik" of mutual accommodation and gradual revision, as advocated by Stresemann, or confrontation.[45] For the Right and some military leaders like Hans von Seeckt, that meant an outright rejection of the Versailles treaty, especially the war-guilt cause, possibly a cooperation with Soviet Russia with the attendant risk of a civil war, if not, ultimately, even another military conflict with the victors.[46] It was not the least of Stresemann's accomplishments that despite the initial opposition of the DNVP he managed to form a governmental coalition with that powerful party and to induce its leadership to dampen their opposition to his diplomacy.[47]

In 1928, in the wake of an election and ensuing losses at the polls, the DNVP, under the leadership of Alfred Hugenberg, broke with Stresemann and resumed its aggressive opposition to his foreign policy. Its major target became an agreement to be negotiated between Germany and the Western Powers to arrive at a definite settlement of the reparation issue coupled with the withdrawal of French occupation troops from the Rhineland. Once again, American experts like Parker Gilbert, the official reparation agent, and Owen Young, mediated. Lengthy talks led on June 7, 1929, to the adoption of the Young Plan and an Allied agreement to evacuate the Rhineland. The Young Plan reduced Germany's annual payments but extended them until 1988.[48]

The conservative opposition viewed the impending agreement as a bonanza intensifying their propaganda to discredit Stresemann as well as the Versailles treaty and to regain lost political ground.[49] Their efforts culminated in the decision to submit the Young Plan to a plebiscite. For this campaign Hugenberg sought support by radical right-wing organizations like the veterans' organization (Stahlhelm) or the Pan-Germans and, significantly, also by Hitler's NSDAP.[50] The German voter was asked to endorse a law that would demand that Germany's admission of war guilt be revoked and that the reparations in Article 232 be abrogated, thus annulling any further reparation claims. If the Berlin government failed to comply with that law, for example, by acknowledging some German war guilt, the responsible persons were to be tried for treason. Hitler had made his continued cooperation dependent on the acceptance of this last drastic provision.[51]

Still, on the day of the referendum (December 22, 1929), only 5.8 million German voters (i.e., 14 percent of the total) approved. Once more, the extreme Right and Hitler himself had to admit that they represented only a small fraction of the German electorate.[52] In 1928, at the previous national election, the Nazi Party alone had done much worse. Then a mere 2.8 percent of the German electorate had voted for it, less than in the election before. What counted in 1929, however, was not the number of votes in favor of the referendum, but the rise to some national prominence Hitler owed to his alliance with the respectable conservative policymakers.[53]

What then was the program Hitler propagated, and how was it related to the stab-in-the-back and the war-guilt doctrines? There can be no doubt that Hitler's political creed both fused and vastly radicalized these two right-wing stereotypes. The literal term "stab-in-the-back" (Dolchstoss) does not appear in his autobiography Mein Kampf, but he referred to it in many of his speeches and publications, at times even verbally. It is needless to add that other Nazi publications abounded with references to the Dolchstoss. As Hitler alleged, a whole chain of events led to the abject misery of the Germany of his days, all to him parts of a "colossal crime" that had made Germany's defeat inevitable. The signing of the Versailles treaty, including the war-guilt article, which "sacrificed" "the German past" and finalized the "enslavement of the German people," sealed Germany's fall. As his speeches reveal, in Hitler's mind the stab-in-the-back and the war-guilt clauses merged in a pernicious whole the first as the cause of Germany's surrender, the second as its most important consequence. The Nazi leader did not only attack those who claimed or admitted a possible German responsibility for the war, but also reproached Imperial Germany for having been too peaceful to have launched a preventive war before 1914. To him, the personalities whom he held accountable for this syndrome were all November-Verbrecher (criminals of November 1918). To this category belonged not only much of Germany's wartime, more left-wing–oriented political leadership, but also the political decision makers who conducted Berlin's foreign policy after Versailles. Significantly, in the later 1920s, the prime object of his campaign of denigration was no one else than Stresemann. It was he, Hitler claimed, who had turned Germany into a "robbers' den" and was responsible for the "unspeakable sufferings" of the German people.[54]

Of course, Hitler's invectives revolved around the notorious racial anti-Semitism that he had preached since the beginning of his political career.[55] "The Jews' dominance" during the transition he had observed in Munich at the time of the Councils' Republic only reinforced his fixed idea of the pernicious role the Jews had played as instigators of the November Revolution. The German people had to make sure that there would not be another Dolchstoss and no other defeat in a war.[56] His fixation on the victors' *Kriegsschuldlüge* provided the frame of his propaganda against the Young Plan. To him it served the purposes of its frequently Jewish authors and of international high finance to "transform our people economically and mentally into global white negroes" (*Weisse Weltneger*).[57]

In hindsight, the reader of Hitler's speeches is struck by the thunderous applause this demagogue received for his hardly disguised call to arms in the not-too-distant future.[58] Were these cheers a part of a general "internal denial of peace" characteristic of the political climate in the Weimar Republic? In any event, Hitler's listeners did not regard their mother country as vanquished.[59] This observation raises the question as to his standing and his impact in contemporary Germany's public opinion. Actually, Hitler, in propagating his extremist views during the mid-1920s, belonged to the lunatic fringe on the right of Germany's political spectrum, even though in the contemporary public eye he enjoyed a somewhat more distinct social and intellectual respectability than would similar sorts of persons in present-day Germany. Still it is doubtful to what extent the Nazi leader at that time presented a challenge to the Weimar Republic.[60] It is true that in these years he managed to swallow up other right-wing extremist organizations and to submit the Nazi movement ideologically and structurally to his leadership. And yet, until 1929, despite some local successes, the Nazi movement was viewed as a more or less local Bavarian phenomenon. This changed, as we have seen, with Hitler's participation in the propaganda campaign against the Young Plan—which Hitler himself regarded as the turning point of his political fortunes. The basis of his power grew dramatically, however, during the roughly two years between the national elections of May 1928 and September 1930. In the election of September 14, 1930, the Nazi Party won a landslide victory rising from the 800,000 votes it had received in 1928 to 6.4 million votes, or 18.3 percent of the electorate. To Hitler himself this big victory came unexpectedly.[61] What had happened to explain this breakthrough?

There are indeed two factors that were not immediately related to the war that suggest an answer. The first of them was the crash in the American stock exchange of late October 1929, the following panic, and the beginning of the Great Depression. Scholarly research is unanimous in seeking the origins of this disaster in the United States, even though its repercussions were soon to be felt on the other side of the Atlantic. As to Germany, the ensuing global financial and economic crisis dried up American credits and discouraged further industrial investments. It exacerbated protectionism and increased structural problems in the agricultural sector. Last but not least, it reduced German exports and worsened unemployment. It is true that the "Big Crash" hit a

German economy that beginning with 1927 was already ailing. That earlier recession, however—and this is important—had not yet resulted in a general radicalization of German politics and in Hitler's rise to political prominence.[62]

After Black Friday, Hitler's party began to gain in some local and state elections. But all that was nothing in comparison to Hitler's electoral triumph of September 1930. What then had happened? Obviously, the American crash accelerated the deterioration of Germany's economic performance.[63] But how specifically did this downturn translate itself into the outcome of the 1930 election? A look at the German labor market provides the answer. It was here that the acceleration of Germany's slump presented the most perceptible and most devastating effects.[64] The official number of the unemployed rose from 1.9 million in 1929 to 3.7 million in 1930. Already in January 1930 the number had reached 3.2 million.[65] The actual number was still higher (up to 4.5 million), because a part of the unemployed was officially not recorded. The younger generation was particularly hard hit. Significantly the number of Nazi votes in that group was disproportionally high.[66] The significance of the problem of the unemployed was highlighted in March 1930 by the disruption of the last German government that rested on a parliamentary majority. The ruling Great Coalition resigned because it was unable to agree as to how to finance the deficit the National Employment Agency faced as a result of the rapid growth of unemployment insurance payments.

The steep growth of the number of unemployed was the point where Hitler struck in his campaign anticipating the election of September 1930. The Frankfurter Zeitung aptly called it an "election of resentment" (Verbitterungswahlen). Focused on Germany, as it was, Nazi propaganda hardly ever referred to the United States. The official party newspaper did not even bother to mention Black Friday.[67] Instead, Hitler repeatedly blamed an anonymous "unassailable and inaccessible" high finance for Germany's economic difficulties. But these forces were not the real target of his hate campaign; instead, it was the parties that so far dominated the Reichstag. Speaking of the majority of the German Reichstag, which had adopted the Young Plan, he went so far as to condemn the German Social Democratic Party for having acted as henchmen, if not "pimps," of international high finance in its effort to reduce the German people to helotry to international capitalists, and he never failed to blame the governing moderate Left for the growth of the army of the unemployed.[68]

In order to bolster his populist election campaign, Hitler constructed a connection between two events that were coincident but at that point still unrelated—the parliamentary adoption of the Young Plan on March 12, 1930, on the one hand, and the onset of the depression in Germany on the other.

In advertising the Young Plan as a recipe for a quick economic recovery, Stresemann had proved to be a swindler, Hitler contended. Hitler denigrated the Young Plan as the source of all the miseries that had visited the German people.[69]

All along Hitler kept predicting an economic disaster for Germany, blaming the moderate parties for their incapacity to avert it and for attempting to spread optimism at the same time—to Hitler the final proof of their dishonesty and corruption. He thus acted as a prophet of doom, and the deterioration of the economic situation as well as the slump in the labor market made his predictions self-fulfilling prophesies. This at least in part explains his political magnetism and his election victories in 1930 and beyond, and it is here that a causal link between the Wall Street crash and the rise of Hitler has to be sought.[70]

As far as the German electorate and its reaction to Hitler's propaganda are concerned, research of the past two decades has shown that people who were jobless and had nothing to lose mostly did in fact vote not for Hitler, but for the communists. Instead, those who flocked to Hitler's party, coming from all strata of society, and voting for him mostly had a modest or medium income. They had gone through the anxieties of a runaway inflation and had managed to rebuild a tolerable livelihood for themselves. They did have something to lose and were driven by the fear of being laid off and of having to face the utter misery of a minimal unemployed compensation. These people began to share Hitler's indictment of the Young Plan and the "policy of fulfillment" as the source of their misery. They hoped for a strong personality to protect them from poverty. They were attracted by Hitler's promise of renewed German greatness to replace the mediocrity of the Weimar Republic. All this made them susceptible to Hitler's propaganda and made them vote for him in 1930 and the years to come, when the initial business turned slump turned into a grim banking and financial crisis.[71]

So there does exist a clear link between the onset of the Depression in the United States, its impact on a shaky economy in Germany, especially on the labor market in Germany, and the underlying social and psychological anxieties of many German voters as well as the expansion of the Nazi electorate. Hitler, however, had every incentive to disguise the specific international aspects of the Depression, in order to divert public attention from it, and instead to place all the blame for the economic crisis on the democratic leadership of the Weimar Republic, to discredit it and pave the way to replace it by his own followers. To him all the achievements of the Young Plan, the easing of the reparations' burden and its political neutralization along with the termination of the French occupation of the Rhineland, did not alter its presumed quality as an instrument for enslaving the German people.[72] For a country like Germany that had not yet come to terms with its national and political identity this propaganda proved particularly effective.[73]

The other factor that contributed to Hitler's breakthrough in German politics can be dealt with more briefly. It goes back to Germany's earlier political culture as it was formed during the nineteenth century. As Stresemann repeatedly pointed out, old Imperial Germany lacked a tradition of responsible parliamentary government. This deficiency was carried over to the Weimar Republic. The public did not honor responsible political behavior, but rather punished it by not voting for parties that had participated in a government. Many politicians, therefore, were more comfortable on the side of the parliamentary opposition.[74] The Weimar constitution provided for government responsibility, but there continued to be a hesitancy of the parties to join governing coalitions and risk the support of their constituencies: in terms of votes, it did not pay to belong to a government. These reservations reflected the fact that democracy had taken but tenuous roots in the minds of many Germans. Hitler, on his part, had no qualms whatsoever to assume political responsibility and thus to gain power.[75] This was in stark contrast to the great coalition, which, eschewing responsibility, broke apart in 1930 for political reasons that today seem trivial— and yet that rupture, as the contemporaries learned, when it was too late, paved the way for governments that derived their legitimacy from the president (who was Hindenburg) and not from the Weimar "system."[76]

In summary, I agree with Jan Kershaw in believing that only World War I made Hitler possible.[77] At the same time, I subscribe to the view that Hitler, as a political power in Germany, was not an immediate product of World War I.[78] The Nazi leader provided and sharpened the instruments that discredited the Weimar Republic and prepared its downfall. These instruments can be derived from the ideology and the myths the German Right had introduced to the public discourse in Germany even before the end of the war. The application of these instruments to the political reality and their impact on it, however, depended on factors that were no longer directly related to the war. The course of German history from World War I to Hitler's dictatorship was not a one-way street, nor was it predetermined. World War I was a necessary, but not a sufficient, cause for the advent of Hitler to power and the collapse of the Weimar Republic.[79]

NOTES

1. Herbert, "Was haben die Nationalsozialisten aus dem Ersten Weltkrieg gelernt?," 21.

2. Winkler, *Weimar 1918–1933*, 91.

3. Deist, "Der militärische Zusammenbruch des Kaiserreiches," 117–122.

4. Herbert, "Was haben die Nationalsozialisten aus dem Ersten Weltkrieg gelernt?," 22.

5. Ludendorff, statement of October 1, 1918, quoted in Barth, *Dolchstoßlegenden und politische Desintegration*, 79; Leonhard, *Die Büchse der Pandora*, 1006.

6. Barth, *Dolchstoßlegenden und politische Desintegration*, 81–84.

7. Münkler, *Der grosse Krieg*, 272, 294, 621; Schwabe, *Wissenschaft und Kriegsmoral*, 96.

8. Krumeich, "Die Dolchstoßlegende," 587ff.

9. Münkler, *Der grosse Krieg*, 633ff.

10. Barth, *Dolchstoßlegenden und politische Desintegration*, 24.

11. Gaertringen, "'Dolchstoss'-Diskussion und 'Dolchstosslegende' im Wandel von vier Jahrzehnten," 124–126, 131.

12. Thimme, *Flucht in den Mythos*, 65.

13. "Evangelische Kirchenzeitung," October 27, 1918, quoted in Barth, *Dolchstoßlegenden und politische Desintegration*, 169; Hagenlücke, "Wie tot war die Vaterlandspartei 1919 wirklich," in Dülffer and Krumeich, *Der verlorene Friede*, 261; Cornelißen, "Die Frontgeneration deutscher Historiker und der Erste Weltkrieg," in Dülffer and Krumeich, *Der verlorene Friede*, 326; Krumeich, "Die Dolchstoßlegende," 593.

14. Gaertringen, "'Dolchstoss'-Diskussion und 'Dolchstosslegende' im Wandel von vier Jahrzehnten," 139.

15. Dülffer, "Frieden schließen nach einem Weltkrieg?," in Dülffer, *Der verlorene Friede*, 33; Hillgruber, "Unter dem Schatten von Versailles," 57ff.; Herbert, "Was haben die Nationalsozialisten aus dem Ersten Weltkrieg gelernt?," 22; Barth, *Dolchstoßlegenden und politische Desintegration*, 368, 447, 451.

16. Barth, *Dolchstoßlegenden und politische Desintegration*, 322; Zechlin, *Die Deutsche Politik und die Juden im Ersten Weltkrieg*, 517, 520ff., 524, 548ff., 558ff.; Wirsching, *Vom Weltkrieg zum Bürgerkrieg?*, 316; Leonhard, *Die Büchse der Pandora*, 1002ff.

17. "Kreuzzeitung," December 31, 1918, quoted in Thimme, *Flucht in den Mythos*, 65; Barth, *Dolchstoßlegenden und politische Desintegration*, 322–325; Dülffer, "Frieden schließen nach einem Weltkrieg?," in Dülffer, *Der verlorene Friede*, 33; Herbert, "Was haben die Nationalsozialisten aus dem Ersten Weltkrieg gelernt?," 21, 25, 30.

18. Adolf Hitler, speech, September 21, 1928, in Hitler, *Reden, Schriften, Anordnungen*, vol. 3.1, 101; Schwabe, "Anti-Americanism within the German Right, 1917–1933," 93ff.

19. Barth, *Dolchstoßlegenden und politische Desintegration*, 212ff., 214, 216.

20. Ibid., 148, 219, 322–325, 360ff., 428; Gaertringen, "'Dolchstoss'-Diskussion und 'Dolchstosslegende' im Wandel von vier Jahrzehnten," 128, 139; Schulze, *Weimar*, 273; Thimme, *Flucht in den Mythos*, 76–79.

21. Gaertringen, "'Dolchstoss'-Diskussion und 'Dolchstosslegende' im Wandel von vier Jahrzehnten," 129; Barth, *Dolchstoßlegenden und politische Desintegration*, 146, 149, 169, 223; Heinemann, *Die verdrängte Niederlage*, 19, 23, 26, 40ff., 162–165; Sammet, "Dolchstoß," 259–266.

22. Pyta, *Hindenburg*, 407ff.; Krumeich, "Die Dolchstoßlegende," 594.

23. Erger, *Der Kapp-Lüttwitz-Putsch*, 72; Barth, *Dolchstoßlegenden und politische Desintegration*, 510–515; Sammet, "*Dolchstoß*," 227–231.

24. Liebe, *Die Deutschnationale Volkspartei*, 64ff., 70ff.

25. Heinemann, *Die verdrängte Niederlage*, 175–188; Krumeich, "Die Dolchstoßlegende," 598; Barth, *Dolchstoßlegenden und politische Desintegration*, 354, 372; Sammet, "*Dolchstoß*," 227–231, 247, 254, 272ff.; Bookbinder, *Weimar Germany*, 115; Winkler, *Weimar 1918–1933*, 138ff.; Barth, *Dolchstoßlegenden und politische Desintegration*, 372–379.

26. Jäger, *Historische Forschung und politische Kultur in Deutschland*, 20ff.

27. Heinemann, *Die verdrängte Niederlage*, 19, 25, 28; Schwabe, *Woodrow Wilson, Revolutionary Germany, and Peacemaking, 1918–1919*, 131, 137ff., 179.

28. Jäger, *Historische Forschung und politische Kultur in Deutschland*, 15, 22–25.

29. Krüger, *Deutschland und die Reparationen 1918/19*, 46ff.; Dickmann, *Die Kriegsschuldfrage auf der Friedenskonferenz von Paris 1919*, 63ff., 75ff.; Schwabe, "Germany's Peace Aims and the Domestic and International Constraints," 47ff.

30. Richter, *Kriegsschuld und Nationalstolz*, 60, 66, 72, 74.

31. Burnett, *Reparation at the Paris Peace Conference*, 66ff., 142ff.; Dickmann, *Die Kriegsschuldfrage auf der Friedenskonferenz von Paris 1919*, 56ff.

32. Dickmann, *Die Kriegsschuldfrage auf der Friedenskonferenz von Paris 1919*, 89ff.; Schwabe, *Woodrow Wilson, Revolutionary Germany, and Peacemaking, 1918–1919*, 306, 343ff., 353, 404; Lentin, *Guilt at Versailles*, 88.

33. English-language original in *Foreign Relations of the United States: Paris Peace Conference 1919* (Washington, DC: Government Printing Office, 1946), vol. 6, 926ff.; Lentin, *Guilt at Versailles*, 103.

34. Walter Simons of the German peace delegation correctly predicted that, if unacceptable terms were imposed on Republican Germany, "the German Nationalist movement will immediately gain strength and a leader, as yet undiscovered, would be found to head a great popular uprising" (quoted in Schwabe, "Germany's Peace Aims and the Domestic and International Constraints," 64, 67).

35. Schwabe, *Woodrow Wilson, Revolutionary Germany, and Peacemaking, 1918–1919*, 305ff.; Jäger, *Historische Forschung und politische Kultur in Deutschland*, 26ff.; Heinemann, *Die verdrängte Niederlage*, 31ff.

36. Jäger, *Historische Forschung und politische Kultur in Deutschland*, 24, 34, 38.

37. Ibid., 24, 34, 44, 46; Heinemann, *Die verdrängte Niederlage*, 120–132.

38. Jäger, *Historische Forschung und politische Kultur in Deutschland*, 63–66.

39. Heinemann, *Die verdrängte Niederlage*, 86; Jäger, *Historische Forschung und politische Kultur in Deutschland*, 58–61, 225ff.; Thimme, *Friedrich Thimme 1968–1939*, 43–49.

40. Heinemann, *Die verdrängte Niederlage*, 95–97, 156ff., 174ff., 211ff.; Jäger, *Historische Forschung und politische Kultur in Deutschland*, 61.

41. Wright, *Gustav Stresemann*, 285 et passim, 354, 378–382.

42. Krüger, *Die Außenpolitik der Republik von Weimar*, 61, 215–225, 265; Wright, *Gustav Stresemann*, 267; Kraus, *Versailles und die Folgen*, 98.

43. Wright, *Gustav Stresemann*, 284ff., 290–296; Link, *Die amerikanische Stabilisierungspolitik in Deutschland, 1921–1931*, 306–309.

44. Wright, *Gustav Stresemann*, 306ff., 310, 317–322, 340–345, 367, 370–373, 390.

45. Ibid., 387.

46. Ibid., 295, 325, 387, 436, 440, 489, 504, 510, 512; Schulze, *Weimar*, 276, 288, 395; Mommsen, *Die verspielte Freiheit*, 213; Herbert, "Was haben die Nationalsozialisten aus dem Ersten Weltkrieg gelernt?," 23.

47. Wright, *Gustav Stresemann*, 294ff., 487.

48. Krüger, *Die Außenpolitik der Republik von Weimar*, 438ff., 453–455; Wright, *Gustav Stresemann*, 461–465.

49. Wright, *Gustav Stresemann*, 321, 329, 362, 365–368, 393–395.

50. Kershaw, *Hitler 1889–1936*, 169.

51. Winkler, *Weimar 1918–1933*, 354–358; Mommsen, *Die verspielte Freiheit*, 284ff.; Heinemann, *Die verdrängte Niederlage*, 250. A leading Nazi magazine demanded even the death penalty for people questioning the "war-guilt lie" (Sösemann, "Der Erste Weltkrieg im propagandistischen Kalkül von Joseph Goebbels," 57).

52. Wright, *Gustav Stresemann*, 515; Berg, *Gustav Stresemann*, 128ff.

53. Winkler, *Weimar 1918–1933*, 356; Schulze, *Weimar*, 303.

54. Hitler, *Reden, Schriften, Anordnungen*, vol. 3.1, 222 ("erdolcht"), ibid., 45, 101, 107, 109, 210, 218, 223; 227, 249, *et passim*; vol. 3.2, 266, 291; vol. 3.3, 416, 434, 436, 445. See also Sammet, "*Dolchstoß*," 117, 251f., 255; Hirschfeld, "Der Führer spricht vom Krieg," 42; Kershaw, *Hitler 1889–1936*, 161.

55. Deuerlein, "Hitlers Eintritt in die Politik und die Reichswehr," 203ff.; Weber, *Hitlers Erster Krieg*, 338.

56. Winkler, *Weimar 1918–1933*, 356; Kershaw, *Hitler 1889–1936*, 152, 168–171, 321, 369; Sammet, "*Dolchstoß*," 117, 166, 170, 279; Hirschfeld, "Der Führer spricht vom Krieg," 42; Herbert, "Was haben die Nationalsozialisten aus dem Ersten Weltkrieg gelernt?," 24–26.

57. Hitler, *Reden, Schriften, Anordnungen*, vol. 3.2, 445, also 301, 375, 421; Hitler, *Mein Kampf*, 212, 359, 585ff., 772; Kershaw, *Hitler 1889–1936*, 321, 395ff., 405; Herbert, "Was haben die Nationalsozialisten aus dem Ersten Weltkrieg gelernt?," 3, 24ff., 30; Fest, *Hitler*, 372.

58. Hitler, *Reden, Schriften, Anordnungen*, vol. 3.1, 45, 109; ibid., vol. 3.2, 417.

59. Bessel, *Germany after the First World War*, 283.

60. Sammet, "*Dolchstoß*," 282.

61. Hitler, Rede, July 24, 1930, in Hitler, *Reden, Schriften, Anordnungen*, vol. 3.3, 282; Fest, *Hitler*, 405ff.; Ulrich, *Hitler*, 261.

62. Galbraith, *The Great Crash 1929*, 29ff., 174ff., 182f.; Hesse, Köster, and Plumpe, *Die Große Depression*, 54ff., 60f.; Wirsching, *Vom Weltkrieg zum Bürgerkrieg?*, 447, 465; Winkler, *Weimar 1918–1933*, 357; Eichengreen, *Hall of Mirrors*, 58, 60.

63. James, *The German Slump*, 58f.

64. Winkler, *Weimar 1918–1933*, 357, 365ff.

65. Wehler, *Deutsche Gesellschaftsgeschichte*, 260.

66. Herbert, *Deutsche Geschichte*, 264f.; Winkler, *Weimar 1918–1933*, 357, 359; Kershaw, *Hitler 1889–1936*, 405; Fest, *Hitler*, 386, 403.

67. Kershaw, *Hitler 1889–1936*, 405. Hitler himself, in an article published on January 1, 1930, called "the expansive American" economic activities a "danger" to Europe (Hitler, *Reden, Schriften, Anordnungen*, vol. 3.3, 44). He also complained about Germany's being ousted from the world market (ibid., 8f.).

68. Hitler, *Politik der Woche*, October 26, 1929, in Hitler, *Reden, Schriften, Anordnungen*, vol. 3.2, 421; Hitler, speech, January 10, 1930, in Hitler, *Reden, Schriften, Anordnungen*, vol. 3.3, 36. In a speech delivered on August 12, 1930, he claimed that the socialist parties worked hand in hand with an international "financial spider." The official NSDAP election appeal talked of a "pact" concluded between the marxist parties and global capital (Hitler, *Reden, Schriften, Anordnungen*, vol. 3.3, 332; Hitler, *Aufruf an das deutsche Volk*, September 10, 1930, in Hitler, *Reden, Schriften, Anordnungen*, vol. 3.3, 395). See also Kershaw, *Hitler 1889–1936*, 419.

69. Hitler, speech, October 15, 1929, in Hitler, *Reden, Schriften, Anordnungen*, vol. 3.2, 419; Hitler, *Politik der Woche*, December 28, 1929, in *Reden, Schriften, Anordnungen*, vol. 3.2, 536; Hitler, *Politik der Woche*, January 25, 1930, in Hitler, *Reden, Schriften, Anordnungen*, vol. 3.3, 39; also 57; Hitler, *Aufruf an das deutsche Volk*, September 10, 1930, in Hitler, *Reden, Schriften, Anordnungen*, vol. 3.3, 401.

70. See, e.g., Hitler, speech, December 28, 1929, in Hitler, *Reden, Schriften, Anordnungen*, vol. 3.2, 535f.; also vol. 3, 3, 9, 39, 55, 141, 238, 282, 398ff.

71. Herbert, *Deutsche Geschichte*, 266, 282f.; Falter, *Hitlers Wähler*, 373. For the years following the election of 1930, see Rothermund, "War-Depression-War: The Fatal Sequence in a Global Perspective," in this volume.

72. See, e.g., Hitler, speech, October 25, 1929, in Hitler, *Reden, Schriften, Anordnungen*, vol. 3.2, 419. For the undisputable merits of the Young Plan, see Link, *Die amerikanische Stabilisierungspolitik in Deutschland, 1921–1931*, 469–473.

73. Wehler, *Deutsche Gesellschaftsgeschichte*, vol. 4, 259; Herbert, *Deutsche Geschichte*, 262f.

74. Wright, *Gustav Stresemann*, 450, 454; Bookbinder, *Weimar Germany*, 169ff.

75. Hitler, *Politik der Woche*, January 25, 1930, in Hitler, *Reden, Schriften, Anordnungen*, vol. 3.3, 41; also 55, 141, 233, 237, 282, *et passim*.

76. Schwabe, "Der Weg der Republik vom Kapp-Putsch bis zum Scheitern des Kabinetts Müller," in Bracher, Funke, and Jacobsen, *Die Weimarer Republik 1918–1933*, 128–133.

77. Kershaw, *Hitler 1889–1936*, 109.

78. Mommsen, *Die verspielte Freiheit*, 303–305; Schulze, *Weimar*, 313; Kershaw, *Hitler 1889–1936*, 404.

79. Schwabe, "Der Weg der Republik vom Kapp-Putsch bis zum Scheitern des Kabinetts Müller," 128–133.

15

International Law and World War I

A Pivotal Turn

Hatsue Shinohara

In 1966, Charles G. Fenwick, a US professor of international law and one of the most active members in the movement to reorient and reform international law in the first half of the twentieth century, contributed a leading article in the *American Journal of International Law*. In the article he claimed that international law had been steadily making progress in the previous half century. He argued that "a new world has now opened up" and that "the old international law of rights and duties" had been supplemented "by an international law of cooperation." For him, President Woodrow Wilson's proposals for collective responsibility and international cooperation, realized in the legal mechanisms and norms elaborated at the Paris Peace Conference, were a key turning point because they marked "a line, however inconclusively, between the old international law and the new."[1] Fenwick's anecdotal observation resonates with the legal historian Wilhelm Grewe's recent scholarly account on the history of international law, which has contended that the interwar years formed a pivotal period of transition for international law.[2]

This chapter will assess Fenwick's statement by highlighting the change and transformation of international law before and after World War I while touching on the legal discussions during the war itself. By contextualizing and examining what was happening in the realm of international law at the time, a broad picture of the fundamental normative transformation concerning interstate relations and the status of war emerges.[3] The chapter will sketch the features of pre–World War I international law in brief and then examine its wartime practice and discussion. Finally it will analyze the nature and features of the international legal order established in 1919 as well as its evolution in later decades.[4]

International Legal Order before World War I

The latter half of the nineteenth century witnessed frequent wars for national unification as well as wars over territorial disputes and competition among states. International law accommodated itself with the state practices of the time. Namely, nations were entitled to go to war, and during a war nonbelligerent countries were supposed to remain neutral. Hence, a system of neutrality gradually evolved that specified the duties and rights of nonbelligerent countries in time of war. At the same time, humanitarian concerns during times of war also began to surface. This resulted in the creation of the International Red Cross (1863) and the Geneva Convention for the Amelioration of the Condition of the Wounded and Sick (1864). On other occasions, when powers—especially those equipped with enough legal competency—had conflicts, arbitration was adopted to settle disputes. Such was the case with the Alabama Claims of 1872, a dispute involving American demands for compensation over Great Britain's role in constructing and supplying the Confederacy with warships during the American Civil War. Both sides agreed to the use of an international arbitration tribunal, which successfully resolved the dispute by awarding a financial settlement to the United States. On the other hand, when Western powers expanded their empires in other parts of the world, their claims were justified in the name of international law. They forced "unequal treaties" on what they considered noncivilized countries, based on the premise that international law was an indicator of civilization.[5]

The turn of the century brought with it the Hague Peace Conferences of 1899 and 1907. The participation of China, Japan, Persia, and Siam in these conferences indicated the regional expansion of the application of international law. More significantly, some important agreements were reached at these conferences. For example, the Hague Convention on the Law and Customs of War on Land and the Hague Convention for the Pacific Settlement of International Disputes were signed in 1899. Through the Hague Conferences countries sought to enhance the means to solve conflicts by peaceful measures, rather than by war. At the same time, they anticipated that war could still happen and established specific rules to regulate the conduct of belligerents in warfare.

In this regard the Hague Conferences made gradual progress in developing a code of civilized conduct in war. Thus, in the case of the Russo-Japanese War of 1904–1905, Japan followed the rules of war carefully, as could be observed in its dutiful treatment of Russian prisoners of war. The observation of international law was deemed as a necessary requirement for a state to be accepted as a member of the civilized society of nations. In addition, at the 1899 conference the establishment of the Permanent Court of Arbitration (PCA) was agreed upon, although it was only permanent in terms of the existence of its secretariat, not its judges. Encouraged by the fruits of the two conferences, advocates of a permanent world court called for a Third Hague Conference, which was scheduled for 1914 but ultimately canceled due to World War I.

Under these circumstances, knowledge of international law was gaining ascendance in many circles. Several notable national and international academic associations were established around this period. One was the International Law Association, which was established in Brussels in 1873 to promote the study of international law. This association was a private and transnational body that held meetings in major European cities. In the same year, the Institute of International Law was founded in Belgium. It was characterized by an elitist orientation that aimed to provide professional legal counsel to governments and organizations. Meanwhile, the increased importance of international law could be observed through the establishment of domestic organizations. Two examples include the American Society of International Law (ASIL), established in 1906,[6] and the Japanese Society of International Law, established in 1897.

Following the Second Hague Conference of 1907, more progressive and liberal views of international law began to emerge. Scholars in this camp straightforwardly advocated that the mission of international law was to build a peaceful international world. During this period, in 1911, Lassa Oppenheim, one of the most influential international law theorists of the time, published his book *Die Zukunft des Völkerrechts* (The future of international law), in which he stressed the importance of the concept of "the family of nations." Through this notion, Oppenheim advocated that nations should cooperate in enhancing common interests to move toward an international society. In the United States, a new generation of scholars—such as Fenwick—began to publish their works in line with Oppenheim's arguments.[7]

Through these developments it can be observed that international law on the eve of the war had a blend of a traditional orientation that supported imperialism—Western dominance and the legality of war—as well as a genesis of new elements: geographic expansion and the introduction of humanitarian concerns to the legal code.

International Law during World War I

Soon after the outbreak of war in August 1914, President Wilson proclaimed that the United States would maintain neutrality. His proclamation signified that the system of neutrality was believed to be in force. Within this system, nonbelligerent neutral nations were allowed to conduct trade with belligerents under certain regulations. On the other hand, belligerent nations were expected to respect the rules concerning neutrality, in addition to following the laws of war.

However, as the war dragged on, violations of international law were repeatedly reported. For instance, Germany was reported to have violated the Geneva Conventions by firing upon hospitals, ambulances, stretcher bearers, and dressing stations. In one such case on August 19, 1917, a hospital near Verdun was attacked by German warplanes and twenty nurses and ten soldiers were killed.[8] The observation of the rules of neutrality also proved to be lacking, with frequent violations taking place throughout the war. The very nature of a total war and the magnitude of destructiveness brought about by new technology, such as submarines and aircraft, appeared to reveal the limits of the pre-1914 legal mechanisms.

In US academic circles, international jurists were shocked by the outbreak of the war. In Fenwick's words, "a rude awakening came with the month of August 1914."[9] At the annual meeting of the ASIL held in April 1915, Elihu Root, the president of the Carnegie Endowment for International Peace,[10] remarked that the entire structure of international law had been "rudely shaken" and that nations "will observe law only when national interest prevails."[11] This sense of crisis was shared by other members of the ASIL and led to vigorous discussions about international law at the annual meetings of 1916 and 1917. As the war in Europe dragged on and the United States increased its trade with the Allies, the idea of neutrality was called into question. Under these circumstances, skepticism of the old rules of international law naturally emerged.

During a panel discussion on neutrality at the ASIL's annual meeting in 1916, both of the speakers were critical of the traditional concept of neutrality. James Wilford Garner of the University of Illinois raised questions about the ethics of this practice, charging that the United States was "a party to the war across the ocean" because it was furnishing arms.[12] From a different perspective, Philip Marshall Brown of Princeton University remarked that the system of neutrality contradicted the view that regarded the world as one body. Rather than sticking to the old view of neutrality, he recommended the principles enunciated by a newly established private organization, the League to Enforce Peace (LEP), which supported the collective use of force against aggressors.

Brown described this as "a frank abandonment of the idea of neutrality."[13] On the other hand, Root and James Brown Scott advocated the unchanging importance of traditional international law,[14] which was centered on judicial settlement of disputes and specification of concrete duties and rights between nations. They were critical of the LEP and in particular they did not endorse the notion of international sanctions.[15]

New perspectives on the role of international law in war were developing on the other side of the Atlantic as well. In Great Britain, the Grotius Society was founded in 1915 to advance the study of international law and promote peace, while Lord James Bryce founded the League of Nations Society that had close communication with the LEP. In France, the organization La Paix par le Droit (Peace through Law—established in 1886) formulated a program in 1915 that proposed to strengthen the Hague system of judicial settlement of international disputes.[16] Additionally, even before the official process of drafting the Covenant of the League of Nations had begun, numerous groups in the United States and Europe were actively engaging in postwar planning. International lawyers participated in this process in significant ways. It was lawyers who strongly pointed out the weakness of traditional international law by indicating its violation and impracticability in the actual conduct of total war.

An International Legal Order with a Janus Face

At the Paris Peace Conference, statesmen engaged in the task of crafting a postwar international order with professional help from legal experts. The drafting process of the Covenant of the League of Nations surpassed former initiatives of multilateral treaty making in terms of both the number of participants and the scope of the task involved. Although states were committed to negotiate over multilateral treaties at the Hague Peace Conferences, each treaty dealt with more narrow and specific aspects such as the treatment of prisoners of war. In Paris, drafting the Covenant entailed the more fundamental endeavor of designing an international order in which multiple actors—states, nongovernmental organizations, and some representatives from colonial regions— would interact with each other and work together to build a world without war.

The drafting process of the Covenant was primarily led by President Wilson under the dominance of the four major victorious powers. Wilson himself was unenthusiastic and not very supportive of a legalistic and judicial approach toward his postwar plan. Instead, he concentrated his efforts on establishing a legislative and administrative organization. Nonetheless, he strongly believed that the prewar order had failed and needed to be reformed and improved to build a peaceful world.[17] His priority lay in the establishment of an effective organization, and the foundational document of this organization, the Covenant of the League of Nations, took the form of a concrete multilateral agreement.

One of the most significant norms established in the Covenant was the principle of legal equality for each member state. This legal equality was embodied in the voting system at the Assembly of the League of Nations. In principle, once admitted as a member of the League, each country was assured as having legal equality with other member states. However, the Covenant created a double standard through its Council—the preeminent status of the great powers was legally assured in Article 4.1, which read that "the Council shall consist of Representatives of the Principal Allied and Associated Powers [the United States, the British Empire, France, Italy and Japan]," and these powers would become permanent members of the Council.

The Covenant put a heavy focus on creating a legal and institutional framework to prevent war based upon the notion of collective security. First of all, Article 8 proclaimed that member states would make efforts for disarmament. Following the assumption that disarmament would be worked out, and hence that security competition would be reduced, Article 10 stated that the territorial integrity of member states would be mutually assured. It called for member states to "undertake to respect and preserve as against external aggression the territorial integrity and existing political independence of all Members of the League." This was an innovative and revolutionary principle, because each member state would be committed to other states' territorial integrity, and as such it became a focal point for the US Senate's arguments against joining the League. In addition, Article 11 stated that "any war or threat of war, whether immediately affecting any of the Members of the League or not, is hereby declared a matter of concern to the whole League," which can be read as a challenge to the idea of neutrality because member states were not allowed to be indifferent toward any war. Finally, while Articles 12–15 stipulated means to solve disputes peacefully, Article 16 suggested that the Council recommend "armed forces to be used to protect the covenants of the League." Thus, the framers expected that the Covenant's system of collective security would replace the old interstate security system that rested on alliances.

Moreover, although the Covenant did not officially and clearly endorse the principle of self-determination as a concrete legal norm, its drafters created the mandate system.[18] Under the principle of "a sacred trust of civilization," some parts of former belligerents' colonies were entrusted to the governance of certain League members. Critics and skeptics regarded this measure as a product of political compromise and as colonialism under a different name, but it is important to note that the League endorsed the idea that new colonial expansion would not henceforth gain legal legitimacy.

At the very core of the Covenant was an emphasis on the concept of "international cooperation." This was clearly stated in the preamble, which declared that the high contracting parties agree to the Covenant in order "to promote international cooperation." More specifically, Article 23 stipulated that the League would work to improve cooperation in social, economic, and labor conditions, while Article 25 referred to the International Red Cross organization and to the prevention of disease. In a significant departure from the model of traditional international agreements that only set to regulate the particular rights and duties of states, the Covenant made it clear that respect for cooperation was a common purpose of the international body.

Regarding judicial aspects of international order, Article 14 of the Covenant stipulated that the Council would take necessary measures to establish the Permanent Court of International Justice (PCIJ). Thus, the Covenant did not completely abandon the Hague system of judicial settlement of international disputes. In addition, Article 18 stated that member states should register every treaty and international agreement with the Secretariat of the League.

In contrast to the progressive legal order created by the Covenant, the peace treaties between the Allied and Associated Powers and between Germany, Austria-Hungary, Bulgaria, and Turkey—namely, the Treaty of Versailles, the Treaty of Saint-Germain (Austria), the Treaty of Neuilly (Bulgaria), the Treaty of Trianon (Hungary), and the Treaty of Lausanne (Turkey)—contained sterner clauses and represented the typical nature of past peace treaties. The Treaty of Versailles largely deprived Germany of its territory, and Article 231 stated that Germany and its allies would be responsible for war damages, which would require an enormous amount of reparation payments from Germany. In a similar vein, Germany's responsibility for starting the war was also highlighted in Article 227—a clause that charged the German Kaiser with "a supreme offence against international morality and the sanctity of treaties"—although the Kaiser was never put on trial for such an offense.[19]

The leaders at the Paris Peace Conference also anticipated a new international landscape in which the disintegration of empires and territorial settlements would result in the birth of new states, a development that would produce issues concerning minority groups. In order to prepare for this possibility, five special treaties, the Minority treaties, were concluded between the Principal Allied and Associated Powers and Czechoslovakia, Greece, Poland, Rumania, and Yugoslavia. These international agreements created a system of minority protection under the auspices of the League, which opened the way to implement institutional protection of human rights.[20]

The postwar international order created at the Paris Peace Conference can be interpreted as having been based upon two kinds of international agreements that differed in purpose and orientation: the Covenant on the one hand, and the peace treaties signed between the Allied and Associated Powers and belligerent countries on the other hand. The former represented a more liberal and progressive international order that stressed the importance of international cooperation and created a system that aimed to prevent war. The latter was a more punitive order that placed traditional legal obligations on the losers of war.

The Covenant, Codification, and the PCIJ: Accomplishments in the 1920s

The signing and ratification of a legal agreement do not automatically guarantee its effectiveness. Even if a treaty has a binding and compulsory clause, if signatories do not observe the treaty it will die and fade out, ending up as no more than so many words on a piece of paper. This is especially true in the case of international law, because no central government exists in the international arena. Hence, after the war, the job of actualizing a legal order was left in the hands of statesmen, international jurists, and to a lesser degree civil society and the public of the respective states. In this process, international lawyers of the interwar years played a significant and remarkable role.

Some progressive international jurists rallied for and supported the Covenant, presenting an argument that the Covenant could be interpreted as equivalent to a constitution for the "society of nations." They sensed that a transformation was taking place from a "state of nature" to the emergence of a "society" in international relations. In Great Britain, Lassa Oppenheim noted the constitutionality of the Covenant, while Hersch Lauterpacht—another renowned international law professor at Cambridge University—presented the Covenant as "higher law"—higher than regular agreements and treaties among states. In France, Georges Scelle—a theorist of international law who later became a member of the International Law Commission of the United Nations—presented the argument that the Covenant created a "quasi-world order," because under the Covenant it was possible for the individual to become a legal subject.[21]

In the United States, Manley O. Hudson of Harvard Law School, Quincy Wright of the University of Chicago, and Garner of the University of Illinois joined the debate and presented progressive interpretations of the Covenant. Wright praised the Covenant, declaring that it indicated a fundamental change of international law through its "shifting of emphasis from rights of state to responsibilities of state."[22] Garner's interpretation of the Covenant was even more striking; in his 1922 publication *Recent Developments in International Law* he wrote that the Covenant had altered "some of the fundamental bases on which international law has heretofore rested." He argued that the Covenant established a new conception of international duty and "shifted emphasis more and more from the right of states to obligations and responsibilities." In addition, he noted that many of the Covenant's stipulations "fall within the category of what Oppenheim calls 'law-making' treaties," meaning that this type of treaty could serve as a universal legal standard and potentially have effects on nonsignatories.[23]

Around this time these liberal scholars in the US legal community often spoke of the "enlargement of law," even though they were not very clear about what this meant. The term seemed to imply several dimensions—an emphasis on the concept of law-making treaties, a tendency to regard the Covenant as the constitution of international society, and the idea that law should flexibly adapt to changes, a view held by Hudson and Wright in particular.[24]

Actual political developments in the 1920s seemed to confirm their perception that international law was undergoing a significant transformation. The Geneva Protocol (officially called the Protocol for the Pacific Settlement of International Disputes) of 1924 and the Kellogg-Briand Pact of 1928 underscored this. Even though the Geneva Protocol did not go into effect, contemporary jurists hailed it as a more elaborate and systematic approach to prevent war, combining collective security, disarmament, and the role of the PCIJ.

Above all, the Kellogg-Briand Pact of 1928, which officially renounced war as a national policy, was viewed as a milestone legal agreement. In political actuality, French desire for ensuring US commitment to their country's security resulted in a multilateral treaty instead of a bilateral one, as the United States was unwilling to make such an explicit commitment. Even during the time of negotiation some regarded the value of the treaty as merely political and symbolic, meant to satisfy American public opinion, which supported the movement to outlaw war. From its outset international lawyers realized that the Pact was not a perfect legal document due to its general nature, its lack of any sanction clause, and its ambiguity in allowing for self-defense. Nevertheless, they decided to devote their efforts to making the Pact legally meaningful. For instance, at the annual meeting of the ASIL in April 1929, the supporters of the Pact argued that it was legally effective and significant because it took the form of a multilateral treaty.

In the meantime, the relevance and feasibility of neutrality and the laws of war were questioned and discussed among international lawyers. Some liberal scholars raised the view that teaching of the laws of war in fact helped to justify the legality of war. Responding to the question of whether future textbooks should include sections on the laws of war, Hudson argued that authors should "leave it out."[25] In addition, Wright presented a skeptical view of neutrality, because now that any war would no longer be the concern of belligerents alone but of all signatories, signatories should abandon indifferent treatment toward belligerents.[26]

In line with scholars' efforts to present and elaborate supportive views of the Covenant and the Pact, the League took several significant steps in the realm of law development. One such effort was a codification project. For issues and areas where international regulations were desirable but absent, legal experts devoted their professional knowledge to making preliminary efforts toward codification before the official meetings and discussions between national delegates. To this end, the Committee of Experts for the Progressive Codification of International Law was appointed by the Council of the League in December 1924. The experts included representatives from Sweden, Italy, El Salvador, Holland, Portugal, Czechoslovakia, Japan, Poland, Germany, Belgium, China, and the United States. As a result, in March 1930 the Conference for the Codification of International Law was held in The Hague, attended by forty-seven states including eight non-member states of the League—the United States, Brazil, Egypt, Iceland, Mexico, Monaco, Turkey, and the Soviet Union. The conference included discussions on issues concerning nationality, territorial waters, and the responsibility of states.[27] This was remarkable in the sense that not just the League members but also most of the non-member states at that time came together to discuss the legal framework. In addition, women's legal status in international marriages was brought up during discussions of nationality issues, which can be interpreted as one of the first-ever discussions of gender equality at an official international body.

In other cases, too, the activities of League committees directly resulted in the formation of multilateral agreements. For instance, the control of opium traffic was deemed an important public health matter of global concern. To this end, the League set up the Advisory Committee on Traffic in Opium and Other Dangerous Drugs, which successfully led to the 1925 Geneva Convention on Opium and Other Drugs, an agreement that aimed to strictly limit the production of narcotic drugs to medical and scientific needs. Codification and the League committees' initiatives facilitated the promulgation of other important multilateral conventions and agreements, such as the Convention on Certain Questions Relating to the Conflict of Nationality Laws (1930). In light of these developments, Grewe pointed out that in this period the "techniques of treaty-making" were significantly improved.[28] In proportion to the increase of agreements, the number of treaties registered by the League rose remarkably, as Figure 15.1 indicates. Through these measures, the daily conduct of state affairs became more transparent for other parties.

Developments were also made regarding judicial settlement mechanisms. The PCIJ, launched in January 1922, was significantly different from its predecessor, the PCA, in that judges were exclusively nominated for the PCIJ and were in regular residence.[29] From 1922 to 1929, the PCIJ delivered sixteen judgments and sixteen advisory opinions, including the case of German minorities in Upper Silesia and the denunciation of the Sino-Belgian Treaty of 1865. One noteworthy case was the advisory opinion regarding the International Labor Organization (ILO). The French government denied that the ILO had competence in the international regulation of the conditions of agricultural laborers, and it appealed the case to the PCIJ. However, the PCIJ ruled in favor of the ILO.[30] From one perspective, it can be argued that the role of the PCIJ was limited in terms of the broader arena of international relations of the time, as states only voluntarily and selectively appealed cases to the PCIJ. However, over the long term, the practice and experience of the PCIJ opened the way to a more advanced judiciary system that would evolve after World War II.

Interestingly enough, even as these new forms of international law took shape, arbitration outside of multilateral institutions remained popular during the interwar years, particularly for the United States, which signed arbitration

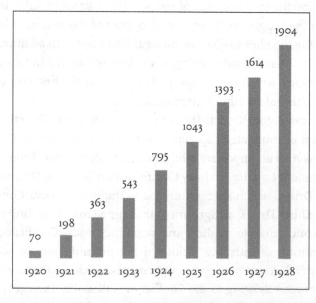

FIGURE 15.1 Cumulative number of international treaties registered by the League of Nations, 1920–1928. From *The League of Nations: A Pictorial History* (Geneva, 1929).

treaties in the inter-American system.[31] During the 1920s many such bilateral arbitration treaties were negotiated and signed: forty-six agreements in 1928 and forty-seven in 1930. This was partly because the United States preferred to adopt such an approach in its foreign policy toward Latin American countries.[32]

Legal Knowledge as *Zeitgeist* and Transnational Networks

During this period, international law was not merely the province of international institutions; there was also a growing interest in spreading the knowledge of international law as a reflection of the spirit of the time. One of the early pioneers of this movement was Lassa Oppenheim. The historian Mathias Schmoeckel has written that "Oppenheim hoped to propagate a common legal sense and thus to prevent international violence."[33] Similar expectations were shared by some reform-minded US international lawyers. Quincy Wright in particular held such hopes, and he repeatedly advocated the importance of developing an understanding of international law among nonprofessionals. This was made evident in his efforts to promote its teaching to college students. Furthermore, at the Conference of Teachers of International Law and Related Subjects in 1925, Wright proposed that even high school teachers should be given a chance to study international law at summer schools.[34]

Another notable feature of this period was the growth of a transnational academic community of international lawyers. The International Law Association met mostly in Europe, but moved to Buenos Aires in 1922 and New York City in 1930. When it met in Oxford in 1932 and in Budapest in 1934, its participants held important discussions on the changing concept of neutrality and the interpretation of the Kellogg-Briand Pact. At the latter meeting, the Budapest Articles of Interpretation of the Kellogg-Briand Pact were adopted. Even though the document was drafted by a private association of international lawyers, the Budapest Articles gained enough authority to attract some official attention.[35]

Furthermore, in 1923 the Hague Academy of International Law began its renowned summer program thanks to funding from the Carnegie Endowment for International Peace. Even before World War I, The Hague had been known as the center for the study of international law, symbolized by the impressive architecture of the Peace Palace, which was completed in 1913 with a donation from Andrew Carnegie. After World War I, the city solidified its position as the "Mecca of international law," not coincidentally hosting the PCIJ. Through the academy's summer program, professors, students, and judges gathered and exchanged their views, contributing to the vibrant intellectual milieu of the time.[36] The script of the summer lectures for the academy was published in full as *Recueil des Cours*, a practice that continues to this day.

In the intellectual milieu of the 1920s and 1930s, scholars travelled internationally to spread knowledge of international law. The American scholars Hudson and Garner visited Calcutta, India, to teach international law, while Westel W. Willoughby of Johns Hopkins University served as a legal counselor for the Chinese delegation at the League of Nations.[37] Nicholas Politis from Greece taught international law at the University of Paris from 1910 to 1914, although after the outbreak of the war he returned to his country and became Foreign Minister. Even after returning to Greece, he was an active participant at the League, and in 1933 he gave a series of lectures on neutrality at the University of Salamanca in Spain.[38] Likewise, Hudson pursued both teaching and practice in international law, becoming a judge at the PCIJ in 1936. These pioneers in international law were scholars and teachers as well as practitioners, serving as judges or counselors for official projects along with their work in education and academia. The résumés of active international lawyers around the time show they maintained an impressive scope of activities, both domestic and international and both academic and practical/political. In the years following World War I, the institutional building of international society started to take shape, and the efforts of such international lawyers in a range of official capacities and private endeavors reveal the high demand and respect for their legal expertise.

Peace through Law

Facing the destruction wrought by World War I and countless violations of international law, some international lawyers came to speculate about the validity of traditional international law and started to advocate for its transformation. In subsequent decades they sincerely and earnestly strived toward building an international legal order that could maintain peace. For them, "peace through law" appeared to be a feasible and promising endeavor. As the historian Randall Lesaffer has argued, the harbinger of this changing attitude toward an international legal order emerged in the late nineteenth century and early twentieth century, and thus this trend predated the war.[39] Nonetheless, World War I accelerated and vindicated it in an irrefutable way. Despite the fact that the legal order created at the Paris Peace Conference had both liberal and punitive aspects, the immediate postwar period witnessed the ascendance of a liberal force that helped achieve a significant transformation of international law.

The Covenant of the League of Nations served as a legal cornerstone for this transformative movement. Its progressive advocates promoted a view that the Covenant could and should be interpreted as the equivalent of a constitution for international society. In line with the Covenant, creative and progressive legal reasoning was elaborated in the interpretation of the Kellogg-Briand Pact. The process of this norm transformation, however, was neither automatic nor spontaneous, but rather reflected the culmination of conscientious work carried out by multiple actors: statesmen, international lawyers, academic organizations (the ASIL, the International Law Association), and such private foundations as the Carnegie Endowment for International Peace.

The movement to establish a new international law was not confined to the United States; there were also advocates among British and French jurists, as well as scholars, such as Nicolas Politis of Greece, from other countries. There were frequent and important exchanges of opinion among such scholars, including at the International Law Association regularly held in European cities, and the Hague Academy of International Law's summer programs. Throughout this period, however, American international lawyers were the leaders of the movement, forming a distinct group that worked tirelessly to advance the movement. The official US role in these developments was limited because it had declined to join the League and was not enthusiastic about international political commitments. Nonetheless, its role was more than merely symbolic, for the US government was a sponsor of the Kellogg-Briand Pact, which was crucial in establishing the framework of the new international law. It is true that the broad and general nature of these treaties, which did not stipulate specific obligations, was compatible with the official stance of the US government. But insofar as the treaties advanced the valuable and innovative norm of declaring war illegal, American involvement in the agreements was seen as an endorsement of the larger movement of building a peaceful world order. The active role played by American legal scholars demonstrates that internationalism had a voice in the United States during the interwar years.

Even though "peace through law" would soon face a major setback in its effort to achieve collective security, initially through Japan's launching of war in Manchuria, followed by the actions of Italy and Germany, the promulgation of the United Nations Charter in 1945 eventually reaffirmed and developed the legal norms established in the interwar years. This in turn demonstrated the fact that international law experienced a process of gradual change in the decades following World War I. In this process the change of the legal status of war was most important: to wage a war as a means of national policy was no longer permissible as it had been in the nineteenth century. Other significant changes took place regarding the emerging concept of an international society and the introduction of humanitarian principles, along with the establishment of an international organization. As the case of opium traffic control and the development of mandate systems demonstrated, "international cooperation" as a legal norm promulgated in the Covenant had evolved into actual practice. "Peace through law"—a political and intellectual program that came to the fore around the World War I years—was to be passed over in the progressive development of international norms and institution building in international society.[40]

NOTES

1. Fenwick, "International Law," 475.
2. Grewe, *The Epochs of International Law*, 575–636. For a recent work on the history of international law, see Neff, *Justice among Nations*.
3. In defining the notion of international law in this chapter, this author endorses a broad definition that follows recent scholarship. In this regard, Martti Koskenniemi argues that international law should not and cannot be limited to positivist claims of existing legal rules and state practices, but it should include lawyers' aspirations for and commitment to it. See Koskenniemi, *From Apology to Utopia*; Koskenniemi, *The Gentle Civilizer of Nations*. For a recent work on the importance of international lawyers' discourse, see Ohlin, *The Assault on International Law*.
4. In recent years a number of scholars have claimed that there is increasing academic attention to the historical investigation of international law. This chapter echoes the growing interest in this field. See Fassbender and Peters, "Introduction: Towards a Global History of International Law," in Fassbender and Peters, *The Oxford Handbook of the History of International Law*; Simpson, "International Law in Diplomatic History"; Janis, *America and the Law of Nations 1776–1939*. On international law and foreign policy during World War I and the following decades, see Zasloff, "Law and the Shaping of American Foreign Policy"; Zasloff, "Law and the Shaping of American Foreign Policy"; Kennedy, "When Renewal Repeats"; Coates, "Transatlantic Advocates"; Shinohara, *U.S. International Lawyers in the Interwar Years*.
5. For imperialism and international law, see Berman, *Passion and Ambivalence*.
6. For the history of the ASIL, see Kirgis, *The American Society of International Law's First Century 1906–2006*.
7. Oppenheim, *Die Zukunft des Völkerrechts*; Shinohara, *U.S. International Lawyers in the Interwar Years*, 17–21.
8. Garner, *International Law and World War*, vol. I, 498–500. For a comparative study on how Germany and Britain interpreted international law differently, see Hull, *A Scrap of Paper*.
9. Fenwick, "The Sources of International Law," 393.
10. On the Carnegie Endowment and the study of international law, see Rietzler, "Fortunes of a Profession," 8–23.

11. Root, "The Outlook for International Law."

12. Garner, "Some True and False Conceptions."

13. Brown, "Munitions and Neutrality."

14. On Root, Scott, and the LEP, see Coates, "Transatlantic Advocates," 377–388.

15. See Wertheim, "The League That Wasn't"; Wertheim, "The League of Nations."

16. Kuehl, *Seeking World Order*.

17. Miller, *The Drafting of the Covenant*; Patterson, "The United States and the Origins of the World Court"; Ambrosius, *Woodrow Wilson and American Diplomatic Tradition*; Knock, *To End All Wars*.

18. On the League's mandatory system, see Susan Pedersen's excellent work, *The Guardians*. As she cited, the legal basis of the mandatory system is Article 22 of the Covenant of the League of Nations.

19. Tomuschat, "The 1871 Peace Treaty and the 1919 Versailles Treaty."

20. Mazower, "Minorities and the League of Nations in Interwar Europe."

21. Schmoeckel, "Lassa Oppenheim and His Reaction to World War I"; Grewe, *The Epochs of International Law*, 604. For Scelle, see Oliver Deggelmann, "Georges Scelle," in Fassbender and Peters, *The Oxford Handbook of the History of International Law*, 1162–1166. For Lauterpacht, see Koskenniemi, *The Gentle Civilizer of Nations*, 353–412; Elihu Lauterpacht, *The Life of Hersch Lauterpacht* (Cambridge: Cambridge University Press, 2010).

22. Quincy Wright, "Effects of the League of Nations Covenant," *American Political Science Review* 13 (November 1919): 558.

23. Garner, *Recent Developments in International Law* (Calcutta: University of Calcutta, 1922), ix, 397–398. Oppenheim emphasized this notion. See Oppenheim, *International Law*, 3rd ed. (London: Longmans, Green and Co., 1920), 16–22.

24. Shinohara, *U.S. International Lawyers in the Interwar Years*, 62–63.

25. *Proceedings of the Second Conference of Teachers of International Law and Related Subjects* (1925), 80. This conference was held in 1914, 1925, 1928, 1929, 1938, 1941, and 1946, made possible by the support from the Carnegie Endowment for International Peace.

26. Shinohara, *U.S. International Lawyers in the Interwar Years*, 81.

27. League of Nations, *Ten Years of World Cooperation* (Geneva: League of Nations, Information Section, 1930), 168–170.

28. Grewe, *The Epochs of International Law*, 608.

29. For the PCIJ, see Ole Spiermann, *International Legal Argument in the Permanent Court of International Justice: The Rise of International Judiciary* (Cambridge: Cambridge University Press, 2005).

30. The League, *Ten Years of Cooperation*, 157.

31. Cornelis G. Roelofsen, "International Arbitration and Courts," in Fassbender and Peters, *The Oxford Handbook of the History of International Law*, 167.

32. Grewe, *The Epochs of International Law*, 612.

33. Schmoeckel, "Lassa Oppenheim," in Fassbender and Peters, *The Oxford Handbook of the History of International Law*, 1153.

34. Shinohara, *U.S. International Lawyers in the Interwar Years*, 56.

35. Ibid., 131–136.

36. Sacriste and Vauchez, "The Force of International Law."

37. Garner was elected to the Tagore Professorship of Law at the University of Calcutta. He was the first American to receive the appointment. See also Hudson, *Current International Co-operation.*

38. Politis, *Neutrality and Peace.*

39. Lesaffer, "Conclusion," in *Peace Treaties and International Law in European History*, 400.

40. On the change of international norms and international relations, see Finnemore, *The Purpose of Intervention*; Betts and Orchard, *Implementation and World Politics: How International Norms Change Practice* (Oxford: Oxford University Press, 2014).

Bibliography

PRIMARY AND CONTEMPORARY MATERIALS

Auswärtiges Amt [German Foreign Ministry], *Belgische Aktenstücke, 1905–1914: Berichte der belgischen Vertreter in Berlin, London und Paris an den Minister des Aeußeren in Brüssel* (Berlin: Auswärtiges Amt, 1915).

Newton D. Baker, *Why We Went to War* (New York: Harper and Bros., 1936).

Ernest Bicknell, *With the Red Cross in Europe, 1917–1922* (Washington, DC: American National Red Cross, 1938).

Philip Marshall Brown, "Munitions and Neutrality," *Proceedings, ASIL* (1916), 33–42.

John Bates Clark, "An Economic View of War and Arbitration: An Address before the Sixteenth Annual Lake Mohonk Conference," *International Conciliation* 1, no. 32 (1910): 531–538.

John Bates Clark Papers, Rare Book and Manuscript Library, Columbia University.

Irvin S. Cobb, *Paths of Glory: Impressions of War Written at or Near the Front* (New York: Grosset and Dunlap, 1918).

E. David Cronon, ed., *The Cabinet Diaries of Josephus Daniels, 1913–1921* (Lincoln: University of Nebraska Press, 1962).

Enoch H. Crowder, *Second Report of the Provost Marshal General to the Secretary of War on the Operations of the Selective Service System to December 20, 1918* (Washington, DC: Government Printing Office, 1919).

Henry P. Davison, *The American Red Cross in the Great War* (New York: Macmillan, 1919).

Charles G. Fenwick, "The Sources of International Law," *Michigan Law Review* 16 (April 1 1918): 393–401.

James Wilford Garner, *International Law and World War* (London: Longmans, Green, 1920).

James Wilford Garner, "Some True and False Conceptions Regarding the Duty of Neutrals in Respect to the Sale and Exportation of Arms and Munitions to Belligerents," *Proceedings, ASIL* (1916): 19–31.

Arthur Gleason, *Our Part in the Great War* (New York: Frederick Stokes, 1917).

Francis Whiting Halsey, *The Literary Digest History of the World War* (New York: Funk and Wagnalls, 1919), vol. 1, 233–234.

John L. Heaton, ed., *Cobb of "The World": A Leader in Liberalism* (New York: E. P. Dutton and Company, 1924).

John A. Hobson, *Imperialism: A Study* (London: Nabu, 1911).

Otto Kahn, "Americans of German Origin and the War," n.d. (Spring 1917?), National Library of Ireland, Dublin, P1003, 22.

Anne Wintermute Lane and Louise Herrick Wall, eds., *The Letters of Franklin K. Lane, Personal and Political* (Boston: Houghton Mifflin, 1922).

Robert Lansing, *War Memoirs of Robert Lansing, Secretary of State* (Indianapolis: Bobbs-Merrill, 1935).

Laymen's Foreign Missions Inquiry, Commission of Appraisal, *Re-Thinking Missions: A Laymen's Inquiry after One Hundred Years* (New York: Harper and Brothers, 1932).

League of Nations, *Ten Years of World Cooperation* (Geneva: League of Nations Information Section, 1930), 168–170.

Vladimir Lenin, *Imperialism: The Highest Stage of Capitalism* (London: Martino, 1911).

Life, August 20, 1914, 300.

Life, August 27, 1914, 344.

Nelson Lloyd, *How We Went to War* (New York: Charles Scribners Sons, 1919).

London Times, *The Times War Atlas* (London: The Times, 1914).

David Hunter Miller, *The Drafting of the Covenant* (New York: G. P. Putnam's Sons, 1928).

William (Billy) Mitchell, *Winged Defense: The Development and Possibilities of Modern Air Power—Economic and Military* (New York: G. P. Putnam's Sons, 1925).

Hugo Münsterberg, *The War and America* (New York: D. Appleton, 1914).

"National Board for Historical Service," *American Historical Review* 22, no. 4 (1917): 918–919.

New-York Historical Society. "Chinese-American: Inclusion/Exclusion" (exhibit).

Office of the Judge Advocate General of the Army, *Compilation of the War Laws of the Various States and Insular Possessions* (Washington, DC: Government Printing Office, 1919), 9–17.

Official German Documents Relating to the World War. Translated by the Carnegie Endowment for International Peace (New York: Carnegie Endowment for International Peace, 1923), reviewed by Herbert Adams Gibbons, *Yale Law Journal* 33, no. 5 (1924): 566–567.

Lassa F. Oppenheim, *Die Zukunft des Völkerrechts* (Leipzig: W. Engelmann, 1911).

Outbreak of the World War. German Documents Collected by Karl Kautsky and Edited by Max Montgelas and Walther Schücking. Translated by the Carnegie Endowment for International Peace (New York: Carnegie Endowment for International Peace, 1924).

Frederick Palmer, *Bliss, Peacemaker: The Life and Letters of Tasker H. Bliss* (New York: Dodd, Mead, and Company, 1934).
——, *My Year of the Great War* (New York: Dodd, Mead, and Company, 1915).
——, *Newton D. Baker, America at War* (New York: Dodd, Mead, and Company, 1931), vol. 1.
The Papers of Ray Stannard Baker, Library of Congress, Washington, DC.
John J. Pershing, *General Pershing's Story of the American Army in France* (New York: John H. Eggers, 1919).
Proceedings of the Second Conference of Teachers of International Law and Related Subjects (1925).
Mary Roberts Rinehart, *My Story* (New York: Farrar and Rinehart, 1931).
Elihu Root, "The Outlook for International Law," *Proceedings of the American Society of International Law* (1915): 2.
Samuel Rosenman, ed., *The Public Papers and Addresses of Franklin D. Roosevelt* (New York: Random House, 1938).
Charles Seymour, ed., *The Intimate Papers of Colonel House* (Boston: Houghton Mifflin, 1926–1928), 4 vols.
James T. Shotwell Papers, Rare Book and Manuscript Library, Columbia University.
William Roscoe Thayer, *Germany vs. Civilization: Notes on the Atrocious War* (Boston: Houghton Mifflin, 1916).
US Congress, Senate, Committee on Haiti and Santo Domingo, *Inquiry into the Occupation and Administration of Haiti and Santo Domingo, 1921–1922*, at http://books.google.com/books.
US Department of State, *Foreign Relations of the United States: The Lansing Papers* (Washington, DC: Government Printing Office, 1939), 2 vols.
Walter Weyl, *American World Policies* (New York: Macmillan, 1917).
The Papers of Woodrow Wilson, Library of Congress, Washington, DC.

ARTICLES, CONTRIBUTIONS, AND DISSERTATIONS

Matthew Lloyd Adams, "Herbert Hoover and the Organization of the American Relief Effort in Poland, 1919–1923," *European Journal of American Studies* [Online], 2 (2009). URL: http://ejas.revues.org/7627.
Michael Adas, "Contested Hegemony: The Great War and the Afro-Asian Assault on the Civilizing Mission Ideology," *Journal of World History* 15, no. 1 (2004): 31–63.
Sabri M. Akural, "Ziya Gökalp: The Influence of His Thought on Kemalist Reforms," Ph.D. thesis, Indiana University, 1979.
Al Jazeera, "World Leaders Join Gallipoli Commemoration in Turkey," *Al Jazeera*, April 24, 2015, http://www.aljazeera.com/news/2015/04/world-leaders-remember-gallipoli-centenary-150424060036088.html.
Sunil Amrith and Patricia Clavin, "Feeding the World: Connecting Europe and Asia, 1930–1945," *Past and Present* 218, Supplement 8 (2013): 29–50.
Leon E. Aylsworth, "The Passing of Alien Suffrage," *American Political Science Review* 25 (February 1931): 114–116.

William J. Barber, "British and American Economists and Attempts to Comprehend the Nature of War, 1910–1920," *History of Political Economy* 23, Supplement (1991): 61–67.

Charles A. Beard, "Who's to Write the History of the War?," *Saturday Evening Post*, October 4, 1947.

Amira K. Bennison, "Muslim Universalism and Western Globalization," in A. J. Hopkins, ed., *Globalization in World History* (New York: W. W. Norton, 2002), 74–97.

Robert C. Binkley, "*Social and Economic History of the World War* by James T. Shotwell," *American Historical Review* 44, no. 3 (1939): 629–632.

Thomas Boghardt, "Chasing Ghosts in Mexico," *Army History* 89 (Fall 2013): 11–15.

Selma Botman, "The Liberal Age, 1923–1952," in M. W. Daly, ed., *The Cambridge History of Egypt, Vol. II: Modern Egypt* (Cambridge: Cambridge University Press, 1998), 285–308.

Thomas A. Britten, "The Creek Draft Rebellion of 1918: Wartime Hysteria and Indian Baiting in WWI Oklahoma," *Chronicles of Oklahoma* 79 (Summer 2001): 200–215.

Stephen Broadberry and Mark Harrison, "The Economics of World War I: An Overview," in Stephen Broadberry and Mark Harrison, eds., *The Economics of World War I* (Cambridge: Cambridge University Press, 2005), 3–40.

Kathleen Burk, "The House of Morgan in Financial Diplomacy, 1920–1939," in Brian J. C. McKercher, ed., *Anglo-American Relations in the 1920s: The Struggle for Supremacy* (Edmonton: University of Alberta Press, 1990), 125–157.

Cara L. Burnidge, "The Business of Church and State: Social Christianity in Woodrow Wilson's White House," *Church History* 82 (September 2013): 659–666.

Christopher Capozzola, "The U.S. Empire," in Robert Gerwarth and Erez Manela, eds., *Empires at War, 1911–1923* (Oxford: Oxford University Press, 2014), 235–253.

Susan Carruthers, "Propaganda, Communications and Public Opinion," in Patrick Finney, ed., *Palgrave Advances in International History* (Basingstoke, UK: Palgrave Macmillan, 2005), 189–222.

Alain Chatriot, "Comprendre la guerre: L'histoire économique et sociale de la Guerre mondiale, les séries de la Dotation Carnegie pour la paix internationale," in Jean-Jacques Becker, ed., *Histoire culturelle de la Grande Guerre* (Paris: Collin, 2005), 33–44.

Patricia Clavin, "Explaining the Failure of the London World Economic Conference," in Harold James, ed., *The Interwar Depression in an International Context* (Munich: Oldenbourg, 2002), 77–98.

Benjamin Coates, "Transatlantic Advocates: American International Law and U.S. Foreign Relations, 1898–1919," Ph.D. dissertation, Columbia University, 2010.

John Milton Cooper, Jr., "The League Fight," in Ross Kennedy, ed., *A Companion to Woodrow Wilson* (New York: Wiley-Blackwell, 2013), 518–527.

Edward Cuddy, "Irish-Americans and the 1916 Election: An Episode in Immigrant Adjustment," *American Quarterly* 21, no. 2 (Summer 1969): 228–243.

Nick Cullather, "The Foreign Policy of the Calorie," *American Historical Review* 112 (2007): 337–364.

Silvia Álvarez Curbelo, "Puerto Rican Soldiers in the First World War: Colonial Troops for a New Empire," *World History Bulletin* 31 (Spring 2015): 18–22.

Wilhelm Deist, "Der militärische Zusammenbruch des Kaiserreiches. Zur Realität der Dolchstosslegende," in Ursula Büttner, ed., *Das Unrechtsregime* (Hamburg: Christians, 1986), 117–122.

François Denord, "French Neoliberalism and Its Divisions: From the Colloque Walter Lippmann to the Fifth Republic," in Philip Mirowski and Dieter Plehwe, eds., *The Road from Mont Pèlerin: The Making of the Neoliberal Thought Collective* (Cambridge, MA: Harvard University Press, 2009), 45–67.

Frances Densmore, "If the Red Man Can Fight, Why Can't He Vote?" *Literary Digest* 59 (December 21, 1918): 36–37.

———, "The Songs of Indian Soldiers during the World War," *Musical Quarterly* 20 (October 1934): 419–425.

Ernst Deuerlein, "Hitlers Eintritt in die Politik und die Reichswehr," *Vierteljahrshefte für Zeitgeschichte* 7 (1959): 177–227.

Paul Dumont, "The Origins of Kemalist Ideology," in Jacob M. Landau, ed., *Atatürk and the Modernization of Turkey* (Boulder, CO: Westview, 1984), 25–44.

Kathleen Duval, "We Have a President for a Reason: A History Lesson for the Republicans Who Wrote to Iran," *New York Times*, March 13, 2015.

Gordon East, "The Concept and Political Status of the Shatter Zone," in N. J. G. Pounds, ed., *Geographical Essays on Eastern Europe* (Bloomington: Indiana University Press, 1961), 1–27.

Julia Eichenberg, "The Dark Side of Independence: Paramilitary Violence in Ireland and Poland after the First World War," *Contemporary European History* 19 (2010): 231–248.

———, "Soldiers to Civilians, Civilians to Soldiers: Poland and Ireland after the First World War," in Robert Gerwarth and John Horne, eds., *War in Peace: Paramilitary Violence after the Great War* (Oxford: Oxford University Press, 2012), 184–199.

David Ekbladh, "'Wise as a Serpent and Harmless as a Dove': John F. Stevens and American Policy in Manchuria and Siberia, 1918–1924," *Prologue: The Magazine of the National Archives* (Winter 1995): 319–333.

Richard N. Ellis, "'Indians at Ibapah in Revolt': Goshutes, the Draft and the Indian Bureau, 1917–1919," *Nevada Historical Society Quarterly* 19 (Fall 1976): 163–170.

Charles G. Fenwick, "International Law: The Old and New," *American Journal of International Law* 60, no. 3 (July 1966): 475–483.

Martha Finnemore, "Constructing Norms of Humanitarian Intervention," in Peter Katzenstein, ed., *The Culture of National Security, Norms and Identity in World Politics* (New York: Columbia University Press, 1996), 153–185.

L. F. Fitzhardinge, "William Morris Hughes," in Bede Nairn and Geoffrey Serle, eds., *Australian Dictionary of Biography Vol. 9, 1891–1939* (Melbourne: Melbourne University Press, 1983), 393–400.

Stephen Garton, "Demobilization and Empire: Empire Nationalism and Soldier Citizenship in Australia after the First World War—in Dominion Context," *Journal of Contemporary History* 1, no. 50 (2015): 124–143.

Peter Gatrell, "Wars after the War: Conflicts, 1919–1923," in John Horne, ed., *A Companion to World War I* (Chichester, UK: Wiley-Blackwell, 2010), 558–575.

Robert Gerwarth and Ugur Ümit Üngör, "Imperial Apocalypse: The Collapse of the Ottoman and Habsburg Empires and the Brutalization of the Successor States," *Journal of Modern European History* 2, no. 13 (2015): 226–248.

Petra Goedde, "Global Cultures," in Akira Iriye, ed., *Global Interdependence: The World after 1945* (Cambridge, MA: Belknap Press of Harvard University Press, 2013), 537–678.

Jaclyn Granick, "Waging Relief: The Politics and Logistics of American Jewish War Relief in Europe and the Near East (1914–1918)," *First World War Studies* 5, no. 1 (2014): 55–68.

Erich J. C. Hahn, "The German Foreign Ministry and the Question of War Guilt in 1918–1919," in Carole Fink, Isabel V. Hull, and MacGregor Knox, eds., *German Nationalism and the European Response, 1890–1945* (Norman: University of Oklahoma Press, 1985), 43–70.

Karen Halttunen, "Humanitarianism and the Pornography of Pain in Anglo-American Culture," *American Historical Review* 100, no. 2 (1995): 303–334.

Robert T. Handy, "The American Religious Depression, 1925–1935," *Church History* 29 (March 1960): 3–16.

M. Şükrü Hanioğlu, "Garbcilar: Their Attitudes toward Religion and Their Impact on the Official Ideology of the Turkish Republic," *Studia Islamica* 86 (1997): 133–158.

John L. Harvey, "An American *Annales*? The AHA and the *Revue international d'histoire économique* of Lucien Febvre and Marc Bloch," *Journal of Modern History* 76, no. 3 (2004): 578–621.

Ulrich Herbert, "Was haben die Nationalsozialisten aus dem Ersten Weltkrieg gelernt?," in Gerd Krumeich, ed., *Nationalsozialismus und Erster Weltkrieg* (Essen: Klartext Verlagsges. Mbh, 2010), 21.

Holger Herwig, "Clio Deceived: Patriotic Self-Censorship after the Great War," in Keith M. Wilson, ed., *Forging the Collective Memory: Government and International Historians through Two World Wars* (Oxford: Berghahn, 1996), 90–91, 108–112.

Friedrich Frh. Hiller von Gaertringen, "'Dolchstoss'-Diskussion und 'Dolchstosslegende' im Wandel von vier Jahrzehnten," in Waldemar Besson et al., eds., *Geschichte und Gegenwartsbewusstsein* (Göttingen: Vandenhoeck and Ruprecht, 1963), 124–126, 131.

Andreas Hillgruber, "Unter dem Schatten von Versailles. Die außenpolitische Belastung der Weimarer Republic: Realität und Perzeption bei den Deutschen," in Karl Dietrich Erdmann and Hagen Schulze, eds., *Weimar. Selbstpreisgabe einer Demokratie* (Düsseldorf: Droste, 1980), 51–67.

Gerhard Hirschfeld, "Der Erste Weltkrieg in der deutschen und internationalen Geschichtsschreibung," *Aus Politik und Zeitgeschichte*, 29–30 (July 12, 2004), http://www.bpb.de/apuz/28194/der-erste-weltkrieg-in-der-deutschen-und-internationalen-geschichtsschreibung?p=all.

————, "Der Führer spricht vom Krieg: Der Erste Weltkrieg in den Reden Adolf Hitlers," in Gerd Krumeich, ed., *Nationalsozialismus und Erster Weltkrieg* (Essen: Klartext Verlagsges, 2010), 35–51.

David A. Hollinger, "The Realist-Pacifist Summit Meeting of March 1942 and the Political Reorientation of Ecumenical Protestantism in the United States," *Church History* 79 (September 2010): 654–677.

———, "The 'Secularization' Question and the United States in the Twentieth Century," *Church History* 70 (March 2001): 132–143.

John Horne, "The Great War at Its Centenary," in Jay Winter, ed., *The Cambridge History of the First World War* (Cambridge: Cambridge University Press, 2014), vol. 3, 618–639.

Ben Jackson, "At the Origins of Neo-Liberalism: The Free Economy and the Strong State 1930–47," *Historical Journal* 53, no. 1 (2010): 129–151.

James B. Jacobs and Leslie Ann Hayes, "Aliens in the U.S. Armed Forces: A Historico-Legal Analysis," *Armed Forces and Society* 7 (Winter 1981): 187–208.

Harold James, "The Creation of a World Central Bank? The Early Years of the Bank of International Settlements," in Harold James, ed., *The Interwar Depression in an International Context* (Munich: Oldenbourg, 2002), 159–170.

Moon-Ho Jung, "Seditious Subjects: Race, State, Violence, and the U.S. Empire," *Journal of Asian American Studies* 14 (June 2011): 221–247.

P. C. Kemeny, "Power, Ridicule, and the Destruction of Religious Moral Reform Politics in the 1920s," in Christian Smith, ed., *The Secular Revolution: Power, Interests, and Conflict in the Secularization of American Public Life* (Berkeley: University of California Press, 2003), 216–268.

David Kennedy, "When Renewal Repeats: Thinking against the Box," *New York University Journal of International Law and Politics* 32 (Winter 2000): 335–500.

Jack Temple Kirby, "The Southern Exodus, 1910–1960: A Primer for Historians," *Journal of Southern History* 49 (November 1983): 585–600.

Gerd Krumeich, "Die Dolchstoßlegende," in Etienne François and Hagen Schulze, eds., *Deutsche Erinnerungsorte* (Munich: C. H. Beck, 2001), 585–599.

Jonathan Kwan, "Nationalism and All That: Reassessing the Habsburg Monarchy and Its Legacies," *European History Quarterly* 41 (2011): 88–108.

Branden Little, "Band of Crusaders: American Humanitarians, the Great War, and the Remaking of the World," Ph.D. dissertation, University of California at Berkeley, 2009.

Walter Lippmann, "A Clue," *The New Republic*, April 14, 1917, 316–317.

Philip E. Lothyan, "A Question of Citizenship," *Prologue* 21 (Fall 1989): 267–273.

Sue Malvern, "War, Memory and Museums: Art and Artefact in the Imperial War Museum," *History Workshop Journal* 49 (2000): 177–203.

Mark Mazower, "Minorities and the League of Nations in Interwar Europe," *Daedalus* 126 (Spring 1997): 47–63.

Michael McGuire, "An Ephemeral Relationship: American Non-governmental Organizations, the Reconstruction of France, and Franco-American Relations, 1914–1924," Ph.D. dissertation, Boston University, 2012.

Alan McPherson, "World War I and US Empire in the Americas," in Andrew Tait Jarboe and Richard S. Fogarty, eds., *Empires in World War I: Shifting Frontiers and Imperial Dynamics in a Global Conflict* (London: I. B. Tauris, 2014), 328–350.

Allan R. Millet, "Cantigny, 28–31 May 1918," in C. E. Heller and W. A. Stofft, eds., *America's First Battles, 1776–1965* (Lawrence: University of Kansas Press, 1986), 149–185.

———, "Over Where? The AEF and the American Strategy for Victory, 1917–1918," in Kenneth J. Hagen and William R. Roberts, eds., *Against All Enemies: Interpretations of American Military History from Colonial Times to the Present* (New York: Greenwood, 1986), 235–256.

Walter Millis, "1939 Is Not 1914," *Life*, vol. 6, November 6, 1939.

E. P. de Monchy, "Commerce and Navigation," in *The Netherlands and the World War: Studies in the War History of a Neutral* (New Haven, CT: Yale University Press, 1928), 251–278.

Susanne Moranian, "The Armenian Genocide and American Missionary Relief Efforts," in Jay Winter, ed., *America and the Armenian Genocide of 1915* (Cambridge: Cambridge University Press, 2008), 185–213.

Timothy K. Nenninger, "The Army Enters the Twentieth Century, 1904–1917," in Kenneth J. Hagen and William R. Roberts, eds., *Against All Enemies: Interpretations of American Military History from Colonial Times to the Present* (New York: Greenwood, 1986), 219–234.

John Paul Newman, "Post-imperial and Post-war Violence in the South Slav Lands, 1917–1923," *Contemporary European History* 19 (2010): 249–265.

Arthur C. Parker, "Making Democracy Safe for the Indian," *Southern Workman* 47 (August 1918): 399.

David S. Patterson, "The United States and the Origins of the World Court," *Political Science Quarterly* 91 (Summer 1976): 279–295.

Susan Pedersen, "The Meaning of the Mandates System: An Argument," *Geschichte und Gesellschaft* 32, no. 4 (October–December 2006): 560–582.

Jennifer Polk, "Constructive Efforts: The American Red Cross and YMCA in Revolutionary and Civil War Russia, 1917–1924," Ph.D. dissertation, University of Toronto, 2012.

F. E. Posthuma, "Food Supply and Agriculture," in E. P. de Monchy, ed., *The Netherlands and the World War: Studies in the War History of a Neutral* (New Haven, CT: Yale University Press, 1928).

Andrew Preston, "Universal Nationalism: Christian America's Response to the Years of Upheaval," in Niall Ferguson, Charles S. Maier, Erez Manela, and Daniel J. Sargent, eds., *The Shock of the Global: The 1970s in Perspective* (Cambridge, MA: Harvard University Press, 2010), 306–318.

Alan Price, "Edith Wharton at War with the American Red Cross: The End of *Noblesse Oblige*," *Women's Studies* 20 (1991): 121–131.

Tammy Proctor, "An American Enterprise? British Participation in US Food Relief Programmes (1914–1923)," *First World War Studies* 5, no. 1 (2014): 29–42.

James W. Rainy, "The Questionable Training of the AEF in World War I," *Parameters* (Winter 1992–1993): 90–91.

Michael A. Reynolds, "Native Sons: Post-Imperial Politics, Islam, and Identity in the North Caucasus, 1917–1918," *Jahrbücher für Geschichte Osteuropas* 56 (2008): 221–247.

Katharina Rietzler, "Before the Cultural Cold Wars: American Philanthropy and Cultural Diplomacy in the Interwar Years," *Historical Research* 84, no. 223 (2011): 148–164.

————, "Fortunes of a Profession: American Foundations and International Law, 1919–1939," *Global Society* 28 (2014): 8–23.

————, "Philanthropy, Peace Research and Revisionist Politics: Rockefeller and Carnegie Support for the Study of International Relations in Weimar Germany," *Bulletin of the German Historical Institute, Washington D.C.*, Supplement 5 (2008): 61–79.

Albrecht Ritschl, "International Capital Movements and the Onset of the Great Depression: Some International Evidence," in Harold James, ed., *The Interwar Depression in an International Context* (Munich: Oldenbourg, 2002), 1–14.

Priscilla Roberts, "Benjamin Strong, the Federal Reserve and the Limits to Interwar American Nationalism," *Economic Quarterly* (Federal Reserve Bank of Richmond) 86, no. 2 (spring 2000): 61–98.

Davide Rodogno, "The American Red Cross and the International Committee of the Red Cross' Humanitarian Politics and Policies in Asia Minor and Greece (1922–1923)," *First World War Studies* 5, no. 1 (2014): 83–99.

Emily S. Rosenberg, "War and the Health of the State: The U.S. Government and the Communications Revolution during World War I," in Kenneth Osgood and Andrew Frank, eds., *Selling War in a Media Age: The Presidency and Public Opinion in the American Century* (Gainesville: University Press of Florida, 2010), 48–66.

Dietmar Rothermund, "Currencies, Taxes and Credit. Asian Peasants in the Great Depression," in Harold James, ed., *The Interwar Depression in an International Context* (Munich: Oldenbourg, 2002), 15–34.

Kevin Rozario, "'Delicious Horrors': Mass Culture, the Red Cross, and the Appeal of Modern American Humanitarianism," *American Quarterly* 55, no. 3 (2003): 417–455.

Shane Ryland, "Edwin Montagu in India, 1917–1918: Politics of the Montagu-Chelmsford Report," *South Asia* 3 (1973): 79–92.

Emmanuelle Saada, "The Empire of Law: Dignity, Prestige, and Domination in the 'Colonial Situation,'" *French Politics, Culture and Society* 20 (2002): 98–120.

Guillaume Sacriste and Antonine Vauchez, "The Force of International Law: Lawyers' Diplomacy on the International Scene in the 1920s," *Law and Social Inquiry* 32 (2007): 83–107.

Lucy E. Salyer, "Baptism by Fire: Race, Military Service, and U.S. Citizenship Policy, 1918–1935," *Journal of American History* 91 (December 2004): 847–876.

Priya Satia, "The Defense of Inhumanity: Air Control and the British Idea of Arabia," *American Historical Review* 111 (2006): 16–51.

Harold Scheub, "Soukeina and Isabelle—Senghor and the West," in Philip Curtin, ed., *The World and the West: The European Challenge and the Overseas Response in the Age of Empire* (Cambridge: Cambridge University Press, 2000), 189–230.

Mathias Schmoeckel, "Lassa Oppenheim and His Reaction to World War I," in Randall Lesaffer, ed., *Peace Treaties and International Law in European History: From the Late Middle Ages to World War One* (Cambridge: Cambridge University Press, 2007), 382–396.

Klaus Schwabe, "Anti-Americanism within the German Right, 1917–1933," *Amerika-Studien* 21 (1976): 89–107.

————, "Germany's Peace Aims and the Domestic and International Constraints," in Manfred Boemeke, Gerald Feldman, and Elisabeth Glaser, eds., *The Treaty of Versailles—A Reassessment after 75 Years* (Cambridge: Cambridge University Press, 1998), 37–68.

James T. Shotwell, preface to Albrecht Mendelssohn-Bartholdy, *The War and German Society: The Testament of a Liberal* (New Haven, CT: Yale University Press, 1937).

Gerry Simpson, "International Law in Diplomatic History," in James Crawford and Martti Koskenniemi, eds., *The Cambridge Companion to International Law* (Cambridge: Cambridge University Press, 2012), 25–46.

Bernd Sösemann, "Der Erste Weltkrieg im propagandistischen Kalkül von Joseph Goebbels," in Gerd Krumeich, ed., *Nationalsozialismus und Erster Weltkrieg* (Essen: Klartext Verlag, 2010), 53–75.

Gary C. Stein, "The Indian Citizenship Act of 1924," *New Mexico Historical Review* 47 (July 1972): 257–274.

Sunday Mercury, "152 Volumes of War History: Massive Task Now Finished," *Sunday Mercury* (Birmingham, UK), April 4, 1937.

Melanie Tanielian, "The War of Famine: Everyday Life in Wartime Beirut and Mount Lebanon (1914–1918)," Ph.D. dissertation, University of California at Berkeley, 2012.

Michael L. Tate, "From Scout to Doughboy: The National Debate over Integrating American Indians into the Military, 1891–1918," *Western Historical Quarterly* 17 (October 1986): 417–437.

Valérie Tesnière, "La BDIC dans le 'moment documentaire,'" *Matériaux pour l'histoire de notre temps* 100 (2010): 7–13.

Trygve Throntveit, "The Fable of the Fourteen Points: Woodrow Wilson and National Self-Determination," *Diplomatic History* 35 (June 2011): 445–481.

Times of India, "Post-war Germany," *Times of India*, March 25, 1938.

Jerzy Tomaszewski, "Lord Edward Halifax Visiting Adolf Hitler: The Antecedents of Munich," in Karl Hardach, ed., *Internationale Studien zur Geschichte von Wirtschaft und Gesellschaft* (Frankfurt: Peter Lang, 2012), 1119–1130.

Christian Tomuschat, "The 1871 Peace Treaty and the 1919 Versailles Treaty," in Randall Lesaffer, ed., *Peace Treaties and International Law in European History: From the Late Middle Ages to World War One* (Cambridge: Cambridge University Press, 2007), 382–396.

Steven C. Topik and Allen Wells, "Warenketten in einer globalen Wel," in Akira Iriye and Jürgen Osterhammel, eds., *Geschichte der Welt*, Bd. 5 (Munich: Beck, 2012).

Keith David Watenpaugh, "Humanitarianism in the Era of the First World War," Special Issue of *First World War Studies* 5, no. 1 (2014): 1–129.

————, "'A Pious Wish Devoid of All Practicability': Interwar Humanitarianism, the League of Nations and the Rescue of Trafficked Women and Children in the Eastern Mediterranean, 1920–1927," *American Historical Review* 115, no. 4 (October 2010): 1315–1339.

Paul Weindling, "The Role of International Organizations in Setting Nutritional Standards in the 1920s and 1930s," in Harmke Kamminga and Andrew

Cunningham, eds., *The Science and Culture of Nutrition, 1840–1940* (Amsterdam: Rodopi, 1995), 319–332.

Stephen Wertheim, "The League of Nations: A Retreat from International Law?," *Journal of Global History* 7 (2012): 210–232.

——, "The League That Wasn't: American Designs for a Legalist-Sanctionist League of Nations and the Intellectual Origins of International Organization, 1914–1920," *Diplomatic History* 35 (November 2011): 797–836.

Thomas Westerman, "Rough and Ready Relief: American Identity, Humanitarian Experience, and the Commission for Relief in Belgium, 1914–1917," Ph.D. dissertation, University of Connecticut, 2014.

John Sharp Williams, "War to Stop War," *Annals of the American Academy of Political and Social Science* 72 (July 1917): 180–181.

Jay Winter, "Cultural Divergences in Patterns of Remembering the Great War in Britain and France," in Robert Tombs and Emile Chabal, eds., *Britain and France in Two World Wars: Truth, Myth and Memory* (London: Bloomsbury, 2013), 161–177.

David L. Wood, "American Indian Farmland and the Great War," *Agricultural History* 55 (July 1981): 249–265.

Quincy Wright, "Effects of the League of Nations Covenant," *American Political Science Review* 13 (November 1919): 558.

Piotr Wróbel, "The Seeds of Violence: The Brutalization of an East European Region, 1917–1921," *Journal of Modern European History* 1 (2003): 125–149.

Jim Yardley and Arsu Sebnem, "Pope Calls Killings of Armenians 'Genocide,' Provoking Turkish Anger," *New York Times*, April 12, 2015, http://www.nytimes.com/2015/04/13/world/europe/pope-calls-killings-of-armenians-genocide-provoking-turkish-anger.html.

Ceylan Yeginsu, "Turkey's Focus Is Elsewhere on Anniversary of Armenian Genocide," *New York Times*, April 24, 2015, http://www.nytimes.com/2015/04/25/world/europe/turkey-armenian-genocide-gallipoli.html.

Jonathan Zasloff, "Law and the Shaping of American Foreign Policy: From the Gilded Age to the New Era," *New York University Law Review* 78 (April 2003): 239–371.

——, "Law and the Shaping of American Foreign Policy: The Twenty Years' Crisis," *California Law Review* 77 (2003–2004): 583–682.

Erik Zissu, "Conscription, Sovereignty, and Land: American Indian Resistance during World War I," *Pacific Historical Review* 64 (November 1995): 537–566.

Erik-Jan Zürcher, "The Ottoman Empire and the Armistice of Moudros," in Hugh Cecil and Peter H. Liddle, eds., *At the Eleventh Hour: Reflections, Hopes, and Anxieties at the Closing of the Great War, 1918* (Barnsley, UK: Leo Cooper, 1998), 266–275.

MONOGRAPHS AND EDITED VOLUMES

Michael Adas, *Dominance by Design: Technological Imperatives and America's Civilizing Mission* (Cambridge, MA: Harvard University Press, 2006).

———, *Machines as the Measure of Men: Science, Technology, and Ideologies of Western Dominance* (Ithaca, NY: Cornell University Press, 2014 [1989]).

Lloyd E. Ambrosius, *Woodrow Wilson and American Diplomatic Tradition* (Cambridge: Cambridge University Press, 1987).

Scott Anderson, *Lawrence in Arabia: War, Deceit, Imperial Folly and the Making of the Modern Middle East* (New York: Doubleday, 2013).

Kwame Anthony Appiah and Henry Louis Gates, Jr., eds., *Africana: The Encyclopedia of the African and African American Experience* (New York: Basic Civitas, 1999), 1st ed.

César J. Ayala and Rafael Bernabé, *Puerto Rico in the American Century: A History since 1898* (Chapel Hill: University of North Carolina Press, 2007).

Riccardo Bachi, *L'alimentazione e la politica annonaria in Italia* (Bari: Laterza, 1926).

Leo J. Bacino, *Reconstructing Russia: U.S. Policy in Revolutionary Russia, 1917–1922* (Kent, OH: Kent State University Press, 1999).

Ray Stannard Baker, *American Chronicle* (New York: Charles Scribners Sons, 1945).

Tony Ballantyne and Antoinette Burton, *Empires and the Reach of the Global, 1870–1945* (Cambridge, MA: Harvard University Press, 2014).

Arthur E. Barbeau and Florette Henri, *The Unknown Soldiers: African-American Troops in World War I* (New York: Da Capo, 1996).

Michael Barnett, *Empire of Humanity: A History of Humanitarianism* (Ithaca, NY: Cornell University Press, 2011).

———, ed., *Humanitarianism in Question: Politics, Power, Ethics* (Ithaca, NY: Cornell University Press, 2008).

Boris Barth, *Dolchstoßlegenden und politische Desintegration. Das Trauma der deutschen Niederlage im Ersten Weltkrieg 1914–1933* (Düsseldorf: Droste Verlag, 2003).

Omer Bartov and Eric D Weitz, eds., *Shatterzone of Empire: Coexistence and Violence in the German, Habsburg, Russian and Ottoman Borderlands* (Bloomington: Indiana University Press, 2013).

C. A. Bayly, *The Birth of the Modern World, 1780–1914: Global Connections and Comparisons* (Malden, MA: Blackwell, 2004).

Howard K. Beale, *Theodore Roosevelt and the Rise of America to World Power* (Baltimore, MD: Johns Hopkins University Press, 1956).

Charles A. Beard, *President Roosevelt and the Coming of the War, 1941: A Study in Appearances and Realities* (New Haven, CT: Yale University Press, 1948).

Mark Benbow, *Leading Them to the Promised Land: Woodrow Wilson, Covenant Theology, and the Mexican Revolution, 1913–1915* (Kent, OH: Kent State University Press, 2010).

Marcella Bencivenni, *Italian Immigrant Radical Culture: The Idealism of the Sovversivi in the United States, 1890–1940* (New York: New York University Press, 2011).

Geoffrey Bennet, *Naval Battles of the First World War* (London: Pan, 1974).

Manfred Berg, *Gustav Stresemann. Eine politische Karriere zwischen Reich und Republik* (Göttingen: Verlag Musterschmidt, 1992).

Nathaniel Berman, *Passion and Ambivalence: Colonialism, Nationalism and International Law* (Leiden: Brill-Nijhoff, 2012).

Ben Bernanke, *Essays on the Great Depression* (Princeton, NJ: Princeton University Press, 2004).

Léon Bernard, *La défense de la santé publique pendant la guerre* (Paris: Presses Universitaires de France, 1929).

Richard Bessel, *Germany after the First World War* (Oxford: Oxford University Press, 1993).

Alexander Betts and Phil Orchard, eds., *Implementation and World Politics: How International Norms Change Practice* (Oxford: Oxford University Press, 2014).

William Beveridge, *British Food Control* (London: H. Milford, Oxford University Press, 1928).

Camille Bloch, *Bibliographie méthodique de l'histoire économique et sociale de la France pendant la guerre* (Paris: Presses Universitaires de France, 1925).

Donald Bloxham, *The Final Solution: A Genocide* (Oxford: Oxford University Press, 2009).

Donald Bloxham and Robert Gerwarth, eds., *Political Violence in Twentieth-Century Europe* (Cambridge: Cambridge University Press, 2011).

Moritz Bonn, *The Crumbling of Empire: The Disintegration of World Economy* (London: George Allen and Unwin, 1938).

Paul Bookbinder, *Weimar Germany. The Republic of the Reasonable* (Manchester: Manchester University Press, 1996).

Sugata Bose and Kris Manjapra, eds., *Cosmopolitan Thought Zones: South Asia and the Global Circulation of Ideas* (Basingstoke, UK: Palgrave Macmillan, 2010).

R. J. B. Bosworth, *Mussolini* (London: Arnold, 2002).

Karl-Dietrich Bracher, Manfred Funke, and Hans-Adolf Jacobsen, eds., *Die Weimarer Republik 1918–1933* (Bonn: Bundeszentrale für Politische Bildung, 1998).

Paul Braim, *The Test of Battle: The American Expeditionary Forces in the Meuse-Argonne Campaign* (Newark: University of Delaware Press, 1987).

Candice Lewis Bredbenner, *A Nationality of Her Own: Women, Marriage, and the Law of Citizenship* (Berkeley: University of California Press, 1998).

Nancy Bristow, *Making Men Moral: Social Engineering during the Great War* (New York: New York University Press, 1997).

Vera Brittain, *Testament of Youth* (London: Victor Gollancz, 1933).

Thomas A. Britten, *American Indians in World War I: At Home and at War* (Albuquerque: University of New Mexico Press, 1997).

Ian Brownlie, *International Law and the Use of Force by States* (Oxford: Clarendon Press, 1964).

Hedley Bull, *Anarchical Society: A Study of Order in International Politics* (New York: Columbia University Press, 2002), 3rd ed.

Jane Burbank and Frederick Cooper, *Empires in World History: Power and the Politics of Difference* (Princeton, NJ: Princeton University Press, 2011).

Angus Burgin, *The Great Persuasion: Reinventing Free Markets since the Depression* (Cambridge, MA: Harvard University Press, 2012).

Peter Burke, *The French Historical Revolution: The Annales School, 1929–89* (Cambridge, UK: Polity, 1990).

Christina Duffy Burnett and Burke Marshall, eds., *Foreign in a Domestic Sense: Puerto Rico, American Expansion, and the Constitution* (Durham, NC: Duke University Press, 2001).

Philip Mason Burnett, *Reparation at the Paris Peace Conference. From the Standpoint of the American Delegation* (New York: Octagon, 1965), vol. 1.

Cara L. Burnidge, *A Peaceful Conquest: Woodrow Wilson, the League of Nations, and the Great War of American Protestantism* (Chicago: University of Chicago Press, 2016).

Bruno Cabanes, *The Great War and the Origins of Humanitarianism, 1918–1924* (Cambridge: Cambridge University Press, 2014).

Georges Cahen-Salvador, *Les prisonniers de guerre (1914–1919)* (Paris: Payot, 1929).

Bruce Calder, *The Impact of Intervention: The Dominican Republic during the U.S. Occupation of 1916–1924* (Austin: University of Texas Press, 1984).

Malcolm Campbell, *Ireland's New Worlds* (Madison: University of Wisconsin Press, 2008).

Margot Canaday, *The Straight State: Sexuality and Citizenship in Twentieth-Century America* (Princeton, NJ: Princeton University Press, 2009).

Vincent J. Cannato, *American Passage: The History of Ellis Island* (New York: Harper, 2009).

Christopher Capozzola, *Uncle Sam Wants You: World War I and the Making of the Modern American Citizen* (New York: Oxford University Press, 2008).

M. S. Careless, *Canada: A Story of Challenge* (Cambridge: Cambridge University Press, 1953).

Joel A. Carpenter, *Revive Us Again: The Reawakening of American Fundamentalism* (New York: Oxford University Press, 1997).

E. H. Carr, *The Twenty Years' Crisis 1919–1939* (London: Macmillan, 1939).

Martin Ceadel, *Living the Great Illusion: Sir Norman Angell, 1872–1967* (Oxford: Oxford University Press, 2009).

John Whiteclay Chambers, *To Raise an Army: The Draft Comes to Modern America* (New York: Free Press, 1987).

Charles Chatfield, *For Peace and Justice: Pacifism in America, 1914–1941* (Knoxville: University of Tennessee Press, 1971).

Roger Chickering, *Imperial Germany and the Great War* (Cambridge: Cambridge University Press, 2000).

Kathleen Christison, *Perceptions of Palestine: Their Influence on U.S. Middle East Policy* (Berkeley: University of California Press, 1999).

Christopher Clark, *The Sleepwalkers: How Europe Went to War in 1914* (New York: Harper Perennial, 2014).

John Maurice Clark, *The Costs of the World War to the American People* (New Haven, CT: Yale University Press, 1931).

Patricia Clavin, *Securing the World Economy: The Reinvention of the League of Nations, 1920–1946* (Oxford: Oxford University Press, 2013).

Kendrick Clements, *The Life of Herbert Hoover: Imperfect Visionary* (New York: Palgrave Macmillan, 2010).

Michael Clodfelter, *Warfare and Armed Conflicts: A Statistical Reference to Casualty and Other Figures, 1500–2000*, 2nd ed. (Jefferson, NC: McFarland, 2002).

Edward M. Coffman, *The War to End All Wars: The American Military Experience in World War I* (Madison: University of Wisconsin Press, 1986).

Warren Cohen, *American Revisionists: The Lessons of Intervention in World War I* (Chicago: University of Chicago Press, 1967).

G. D. H. Cole, *Labour in the Coal-mining Industry (1914–1921)* (Oxford: Clarendon Press, 1923).

———, *Trade Unionism and Munitions* (Oxford: Clarendon Press, 1923).

Wayne S. Cole, *Senator Gerald P. Nye and American Foreign Relations* (Minneapolis: University of Minnesota Press, 1962).

Matthew Connelly, *Fatal Misconception: The Struggle to Control World Population* (Cambridge, MA: Belknap Press of Harvard University Press, 2008).

James J. Cooke, *Billy Mitchell* (Boulder, CO: Lynne Rienner, 2002).

John Milton Cooper, Jr., *Breaking the Heart of the World: Woodrow Wilson and the Fight for the League of Nations* (New York: Cambridge University Press, 2001).

————, ed., *Reconsidering Woodrow Wilson: Progressivism, Internationalism, War, and Peace* (Washington, DC: Woodrow Wilson Center Press, 2008).

————, *Woodrow Wilson: A Biography* (New York: Cambridge University Press, 2009).

C. H. Cramer, *Newton D. Baker: A Biography* (Cleveland, OH: World Publishing, 1961).

Nick Cullather, *The Hungry World: America's Cold War Battle against Poverty in Asia* (Cambridge, MA: Harvard University Press, 2010).

Bruce Cumings, *Dominion from Sea to Sea: Pacific Ascendancy and American Power* (New Haven, CT: Yale University Press, 2009).

Hamid Dabashi, *The World of Persian Literary Humanism* (Cambridge, MA: Harvard University Press, 2012).

Joy Damousi, *The Labour of Loss: Mourning, Memory and Wartime Bereavement in Australia* (Cambridge: Cambridge University Press, 1999).

Lawrence Davidson, *America's Palestine: Popular and Official Perception from Balfour to Statehood* (Gainesville: University Press of Florida, 2001).

Belinda Davis, *Home Fires Burning: Food, Politics and Everyday Life in World War I Berlin* (Chapel Hill: University of North Carolina Press, 2000).

Donald E. Davis and Eugene P. Trani, *The First Cold War: The Legacy of Woodrow Wilson in U.S.-Soviet Relations* (Columbia: University of Missouri Press, 2002).

Carlo D'Este, *Patton: A Genius for War* (New York: HarperCollins, 1995).

Robert Divine, *The Illusion of Neutrality* (Chicago: University of Chicago Press, 1962).

Justus Doenecke, *Nothing Less Than War: A New History of America's Entry into World War I* (Lexington: University Press of Kentucky, 2011).

Ann Douglas, *Terrible Honesty: Mongrel Manhattan in the 1920s* (New York: Farrar, Straus, and Giroux, 1995).

Ian M. Drummond, *The Floating Pound and the Sterling Area 1931–1939* (Cambridge: Cambridge University Press, 1981).

Jost Dülffer and Gerd Krumeich, eds., *Der verlorene Friede. Politik und Kriegskultur nach 1918* (Essen: Klartext Verlagsgesellschaft, 2002).

Lynn Dumenil, *The Modern Temper: American Culture and Society in the 1920s* (New York: Hill and Wang, 1995).

Jonathan H. Ebel, *Faith in the Fight: Religion and the American Soldier in the Great War* (Princeton, NJ: Princeton University Press, 2010).

Myron Echenberg, *Colonial Conscripts: The Tirailleurs Sénégalais in French West Africa, 1857–1960* (London: J. Currey, 1991).

Astrid M. Eckert, *The Struggle for the Files: The Western Allies and the Return of German Archives after the Second World War*, translated by Dona Geyer (New York: Cambridge University Press, 2012).

Mark Thomas Edwards, *The Right of the Protestant Left: God's Totalitarianism* (New York: Palgrave Macmillan, 2012).

Paul R. Ehrlich, Loy Bilderback, and Anne H. Ehrlich, *The Golden Door: International Migration, Mexico, and the United States* (New York: Ballantine, 1979).

Barry Eichengreen, *Exorbitant Privilege. The Rise and Fall of the Dollar* (Oxford: Oxford University Press, 2011).

———, *Hall of Mirrors: The Great Depression, and the Uses—and Misuses of History* (Oxford: Oxford University Press, 2015).

David Ekbladh, *The Great American Mission: Modernization and the Construction of an American World Order* (Princeton, NJ: Princeton University Press, 2010).

Modris Eksteins, *Rites of Spring: The Great War and the Birth of the Modern Age* (Boston: Houghton Mifflin, 1989).

David Engerman, *Modernization from the Other Shore: American Intellectuals and the Romance of Russian Development* (Cambridge, MA: Harvard University Press, 2004).

Johannes Erger, *Der Kapp-Lüttwitz-Putsch* (Düsseldorf: Droste Verlag, 1967).

Edward J. Erickson, *Ordered to Die: A History of the Ottoman Army in the First World War* (Westport, CT: Greenwood, 2001).

Hubert Essame, *The Battle for Europe, 1918* (New York: Scribner's Sons, 1972).

Jürgen W. Falter, *Hitlers Wähler* (München: C. H. Beck Verlag, 1991).

Bardo Fassbender and Anne Peters, eds., *The Oxford Handbook of the History of International Law* (Oxford: Oxford University Press, 2012).

Didier Fassin, *Humanitarian Reason: A Moral History of the Present* (Berkeley: University of California Press, 2011).

Didier Fassin and Mariella Pandolfi, eds., *Contemporary States of Emergency: The Politics of Military and Humanitarian Interventions* (New York: Zone, 2013).

Leila Fawaz, *A Land of Aching Hearts: The Middle East in the Great War* (Cambridge, MA: Harvard University Press, 2014).

Niall Ferguson, *The Pity of War: Explaining World War I* (New York: Basic Books, 1999).

Robert H. Ferrell, *American Diplomacy: A History* (New York: W. W. Norton, 1975), 3rd ed.

Joachim C. Fest, *Hitler* (Frankfurt: Propyläen-Ullstein Verlag, 1973).

Martha Finnemore, *The Purpose of Intervention* (Ithaca, NY: Cornell University Press, 2003).

Fritz Fischer, *Germany's Aims in the First World War* (New York: W. W. Norton, 1967).

Harold H. Fisher, *The Famine in Soviet Russia, 1919–1923: The Operations of the American Relief Administration* (New York: Macmillan, 1927).

Lisa Pierce Flores, *The History of Puerto Rico* (Santa Barbara, CA: Greenwood, 2010).

Ronald B. Flowers, *To Defend the Constitution: Religion, Conscientious Objection, Naturalization, and the Supreme Court* (Lanham, MD: Scarecrow, 2003).

M. Ryan Floyd, *Abandoning Neutrality: Woodrow Wilson and the Beginning of the Great War, August, 1914–December, 1915* (London: Palgrave Macmillan, 2013).

Richard S. Fogarty, *Race and War in France: Colonial Subjects in the French Army, 1914–1918* (Baltimore, MD: Johns Hopkins University Press, 2008).

David Foglesong, *America's Secret War against Bolshevism: U.S. Intervention in the Russian Civil War, 1917–1920* (Chapel Hill: University of North Carolina Press, 1995).

Nancy Gentile Ford, *Americans All! Foreign-Born Soldiers in World War I* (College Station: Texas A&M University Press, 2001).

Carolyn Thomas Foreman, *Indians Abroad, 1493–1938* (Norman: University of Oklahoma Press, 1943).

Ernest Freeberg, *Democracy's Prisoner: Eugene V. Debs, The Great War, and the Right to Dissent* (Cambridge, MA: Harvard University Press, 2008).

Marcel Frois, *La santé et le travail des femmes pendant la guerre* (Paris: Presses Universitaires de France, 1926).

David Fromkin, *A Peace to End All Peace: The Fall of the Ottoman Empire and the Creation of the Modern Middle East* (New York: Henry Holt, 1989).

Paul Fussell, *The Great War and Modern Memory* (New York: Oxford University Press, 1975).

Donna R. Gabaccia, *Foreign Relations: American Immigration in Global Perspective* (Princeton, NJ: Princeton University Press, 2012).

John Kenneth Galbraith, *The Great Crash 1929* (Boston: Houghton Mifflin, 1961).

Marc Gallicchio, *The African American Encounter with Japan and China: Black Internationalism in Asia, 1895–1945* (Chapel Hill: University of North Carolina Press, 2000).

Richard Gamble, *The War for Righteousness: Progressive Christianity, the Great War, and the Rise of the Messianic Nation* (Wilmington, DE: ISI, 2003).

Lloyd C. Gardner, *Safe for Democracy: The Anglo-American Response to Revolution, 1913–1923* (New York: Oxford University Press, 1984).

Martha Gardner, *The Qualities of a Citizen: Women, Immigration, and Citizenship, 1870–1965* (Princeton, NJ: Princeton University Press, 2005).

Stephen Garton, *The Cost of War: Australians Return* (Melbourne: Oxford University Press, 1996).

Brett Gary, *The Nervous Liberals: Propaganda Anxieties from World War I to the Cold War* (New York: Columbia University Press, 1999).

Peter Gatrell, *Russia's First World War: A Social and Economic History* (Harlow: Pearson/ Longman, 2005).

Peter Gay, *My German Question: Growing Up in Nazi Berlin* (New Haven, CT: Yale University Press, 1998).

James L. Gelvin, *The Modern Middle East: A History* (New York: Oxford University Press, 2008), 2nd ed.

Gary Gerstle, *American Crucible: Race and Nation in the Twentieth Century* (Princeton, NJ: Princeton University Press, 2001).

Robert Gerwarth and John Horne, eds., *War in Peace: Paramilitary Violence after the Great War* (Oxford: Oxford University Press, 2012).

Robert Gerwarth and Erez Manela, eds., *Empires at War, 1911–1923* (New York: Oxford University Press, 2014).

Edward Gibbons and Floyd Gibbons, *Floyd Gibbons, Your Headline Hunter: A Biography* (New York: Exposition, 1953).

Mary C. Gillett, *The Army Medical Department, 1917–1941* (Washington, DC: Center of Military History, US Army, 2009).

Nils Gilman, *Mandarins of the Future: Modernization Theory in Cold War America* (Baltimore, MD: Johns Hopkins University Press, 2003).

Ryan Gingeras, *Sorrowful Shores: Violence, Ethnicity and the End of the Ottoman Empire, 1912–1923* (Oxford: Oxford University Press, 2009).

Julian Go, *Patterns of Empire: The British and American Empires, 1688 to the Present* (New York: Cambridge University Press, 2011).

David J. Goldberg, *Discontented America: The United States in the 1920s* (Baltimore, MD: Johns Hopkins University Press, 1999).

G. P. Gooch, *Recent Revelations of European Diplomacy* (London: Longmans, 1940), 4th ed.

Daniel Gorman, *The Emergence of International Society in the 1920s* (Cambridge: Cambridge University Press, 2012).

James N. Gregory, *The Southern Diaspora: How the Great Migrations of Black and White Southerners Transformed America* (Chapel Hill: University of North Carolina Press, 2005).

Wilhelm Georg Grewe, translated and revised by Michael Byers, *The Epochs of International Law* (Berlin: Walter de Gruyter, 2000).

Gerhard P. Gross, *Die vergessene Front—der Osten 1914/15: Ereignis, Wirkung Nachwirkung* (Paderborn: Schöningh, 2009), 2nd ed.

Mark Ethan Grotelueschen, *The AEF Way of War: The American Army and Combat in World War I* (New York: Cambridge University Press, 2007).

———, *Doctrine under Trial: American Artillery Employment in World War I* (Westport, CT: Greenwood, 2001).

Carol S. Gruber, *Mars and Minerva: World War I and the Uses of Higher Learning in America* (Baton Rouge: Louisiana State University Press, 1975).

Richard Hall, *The Balkan Wars, 1912–1913: Prelude to the First World War* (London: Routledge, 2000).

Philip Hamburger, *Separation of Church and State* (Cambridge, MA: Harvard University Press, 2002).

Robert T. Handy, *Undermined Establishment: Church-State Relations in America, 1880–1920* (Princeton, NJ: Princeton University Press, 1991).

Arlen Hansen, *Gentlemen Volunteers: The Story of the American Ambulance Drivers in the First World War* (New York: Arcade, 2006).

Gerd Hardach, *Der Erste Weltkrieg* (Munich: DTV, 1973).

Meirion Harries and Susie Harries, *The Last Days of Innocence: America at War, 1917–1918* (New York: Random House, 1997).

Ulrich Heinemann, *Die verdrängte Niederlage: Politische Öffentlichkeit und Kriegsschuldfrage in der Weimarer Republik* (Göttingen: Vandenhoeck and Ruprecht, 1983).

David Held et al., *Global Transformations: Politics, Economics, and Culture* (Stanford, CA: Stanford University Press, 1999).

Albert Henry, *Le ravitaillement de la Belgique pendant l'occupation allemande* (Paris: Presses Universitaires de France, 1924).

Kelly Lytle Hernández, *Migra! The History of the U.S. Border Patrol* (Berkeley: University of California Press, 2010).

Édouard Herriot, *Lyon pendant la guerre* (Paris: Presses Universitaires de France, 1925).

Hazel W. Hertzberg, *The Search for an American Indian Identity: Modern Pan-Indian Movements* (Syracuse, NY: Syracuse University Press, 1971).

Jan-Otmar Hesse, Roman Köster, and Werner Plumpe, *Die Große Depression. Weltwirtschaftskrise 1929–1939* (Frankfurt: Campus Verlag, 2014).

Walker Hines, *War History of American Railroads* (New Haven, CT: Yale University Press, 1928).

Izumi Hirobe, *Japanese Pride, American Prejudice: Modifying the Exclusion Clause of the 1924 Immigration Act* (Stanford, CA: Stanford University Press, 2001).

Adolf Hitler, *Mein Kampf* (Munich: Zentralverlag NSDAP, F. Eher, 1934).

———, *Reden, Schriften, Anordnungen*, edited by Institut für Zeitgeschichte (July 1928–February 1929) (Munich: Saur, 1994).

E. J. Hobsbawm, *The Age of Empire, 1875–1914* (New York: Vintage, 1987).

———, *The Age of Extremes: A History of the World, 1914–1991* (New York: Pantheon Books, 1994).

Godfrey Hodgson, *The Myth of American Exceptionalism* (New Haven, CT: Yale University Press, 2009).

———, *Woodrow Wilson's Right Hand: The Life of Colonel Edward M. House* (New Haven, CT: Yale University Press, 2006).

David A. Hollinger, *After Cloven Tongues of Fire: Protestant Liberalism in Modern American History* (Princeton, NJ: Princeton University Press, 2012).

C. Howard Hopkins, *John R. Mott, 1865–1955: A Biography* (Grand Rapids, MI: Eerdmans, 1979).

Gerald Horne, *The End of Empires: African Americans and India* (Philadelphia: Temple University Press, 2008).

John Horne, ed., *A Companion to World War I* (Malden, MA: Wiley-Blackwell, 2010).

Richard Hough, *The Great War at Sea 1914–1918* (New York: Oxford University Press, 1983).

Manley O. Hudson, *Current International Co-operation* (Calcutta: University of Calcutta, 1927).

Isabel V. Hull, *A Scrap of Paper: Breaking and Making International Law during the Great War* (Ithaca, NY: Cornell University Press, 2014).

Alfred Hurley, *Billy Mitchell: Crusader for Air Power* (Bloomington: Indiana University Press, 1975).

William R. Hutchison, *Errand to the World: American Protestant Thought and Foreign Missions* (Chicago: University of Chicago Press, 1987).

Richard H. Immerman, *Empire for Liberty: A History of American Imperialism from Benjamin Franklin to Paul Wolfowitz* (Princeton, NJ: Princeton University Press, 2010).

Luciano Iorizzo and Salvatore Mondello, *The Italian-Americans* (Boston: Twayne, 1980).

Akira Iriye, *Cultural Internationalism and World Order* (Baltimore, MD: Johns Hopkins University Press, 1997).

———, *Global and Transnational History: The Past, Present, and Future* (Basingstoke, UK: Palgrave Macmillan, 2013).

———, *Global Community: The Role of International Organizations in the Making of the Contemporary World* (Berkeley: University of California Press, 2002).

Julia F. Irwin, *Making the World Safe: The American Red Cross and a Nation's Humanitarian Awakening* (New York: Oxford University Press, 2013).

Matthew F. Jacobs, *Imagining the Middle East: The Building of an American Foreign Policy, 1919–1967* (Chapel Hill: University of North Carolina Press, 2011).

Matthew Frye Jacobson, *Barbarian Virtues: The United States Encounters Foreign Peoples at Home and Abroad, 1876–1917* (New York: Hill and Wang, 2000).

Wolfgang Jäger, *Historische Forschung und politische Kultur in Deutschland* (Göttingen: Vandenhoeck and Ruprecht, 1984).

Harold James, *The German Slump. Politics and Economics 1924–1936* (Oxford: Clarendon Press, 1986).

Mark Weston Janis, *America and the Law of Nations 1776–1939* (Oxford: Oxford University Press, 2010).

James Jankowski and Israel Gershoni, eds., *Rethinking Nationalism in the Arab Middle East* (New York: Columbia University Press, 1997).

Jean Noel Jeanneney, *Jours de Guerre, 1914–1918: Les trésors des archives photographiques du Journal Excelsior* (Paris: Arènes, 2013).

H. Paul Jeffers and Alan Axelrod, *Marshall: Lessons in Leadership* (New York: Palgrave Macmillan, 2010).

Philip Jenkins, *The Great and Holy War: How World War I Became a Religious Crusade* (New York: HarperCollins, 2014).

Hilary Jenkinson, *A Manual of Archive Administration Including the Problems of War Archive Making* (Oxford: Clarendon Press, 1922).

Joan M. Jensen, *Army Surveillance in America, 1776–1980* (New Haven, CT: Yale University Press, 1991).

Benjamin Heber Johnson, *Revolution in Texas: How a Forgotten Rebellion and Its Bloody Suppression Turned Mexicans into Americans* (New Haven, CT: Yale University Press, 2003).

Claudius O. Johnson, *Borah of Idaho* (Seattle: University of Washington Press, 1936).

Robert David Johnson, *The Peace Progressives and American Foreign Relations* (Cambridge, MA: Harvard University Press, 1995).

David T. Jones, *Rural Scotland during the War* (London: H. Milford, Oxford University Press, 1926).

Harold Josephson, *James T. Shotwell and the Rise of Internationalism in America* (Rutherford, NJ: Fairleigh Dickinson University Press, 1975).

Nagai Kafu, *Amerika monogatari* (American stories), translated by Mitsuko Iriye (New York: Columbia University Press, 2000).

Michael Kazin, *The War against War: The Americans Who Fought for Peace, 1914–1918* (New York: Simon and Schuster, 2017).

John Keegan, *The First World War* (New York: Alfred A. Knopf, 1999).

George F. Kennan, *Soviet-American Relations, 1917–1920: The Decision to Intervene* (Princeton, NJ: Princeton University Press, 1958).

David M. Kennedy, *Over Here: The First World War and American Society* (New York: Oxford University Press, 1980).

Paul Kennedy, *The Rise and Fall of the Great Powers: Economic Change and Military Conflict from 1500 to 2000* (New York: Random House, 1987).

Ross A. Kennedy, *The Will to Believe: Woodrow Wilson, World War I, and America's Strategy for Peace and Security* (Kent, OH: Kent State University Press, 2009).

Linda K. Kerber, *No Constitutional Right to Be Ladies: Women and the Obligations of Citizenship* (New York: Hill and Wang, 1998).

Jan Kershaw, *Hitler 1889–1936* (Munich: Deutsche Verlasgs-Anstalt, 2000).

John Maynard Keynes, *The End of Laissez-Faire* (London: Hogarth, 1927).

Barbara J. Keys, *Reclaiming American Virtue: The Human Rights Revolution of the 1970s* (Cambridge, MA: Harvard University Press, 2014).

Rashid Khalidi, *The Iron Cage: The Story of the Palestinian Struggle for Statehood* (Boston: Beacon, 2006).

———, *Palestinian Identity: The Construction of Modern National Consciousness, with a New Introduction by the Author* (New York: Columbia University Press, 2010).

Frederic L. Kirgis, *The American Society of International Law's First Century 1906–2006* (Leiden: Martinus Nijhoff, 2006).

Thomas J. Knock, *To End All Wars: Woodrow Wilson and the Quest for a New World Order* (Princeton, NJ: Princeton University Press, 1992).

Christian Koller, *"Von Wilden aller Rassen niedergemetzelt". Die Diskussion um die Verwendung von Kolonialtruppen in Europa zwischen Rassismus, Kolonial- und Militärpolitik (1914–1930)* (Stuttgart: Steiner, 2001).

Wolfgang König and Wolfhard Weber, *Netzwerke Stahl und Strom, 1849–1914*, Propyläen Technikgeschichte, Bd. 4 (Berlin: Propyläen, 1997).

Joseph Kip Kosek, *Acts of Conscience: Christian Nonviolence and Modern American Democracy* (New York: Columbia University Press, 2009).

Martti Koskenniemi, *From Apology to Utopia: The Structure of International Legal Argument* (Cambridge: Cambridge University Press, 2005).

———, *The Gentle Civilizer of Nations* (Cambridge: Cambridge University Press, 2001).

Alan Kramer, *Dynamics of Destruction: Culture and Mass Killing in the First World War* (Oxford: Oxford University Press, 2008).

Hans-Christof Kraus, *Versailles und die Folgen. Außenpolitik zwischen Revisionismus und Verständigung* (Berlin: be.bra Verlag, 2013).

Susan Applegate Krouse, *North American Indians in the Great War* (Lincoln: University of Nebraska Press, 2007).

Peter Krüger, *Deutschland und die Reparationen 1918/19* (Stuttgart: Deutsche Verlagsanstalt, 1973).

Warren Kuehl, *Seeking World Order: The United States and International Organization to 1920* (Nashville: Vanderbilt University Press, 1969).

Walter LaFeber, *The American Search for Opportunity, 1865–1913* (New York: Cambridge University Press, 2013).

Nicholas A. Lambert, *Planning Armageddon: British Economic Warfare and the First World War* (Cambridge, MA: Belknap Press of Harvard University Press, 2012).

William L. Langer, *The Diplomacy of Imperialism, 1890–1902* (New York: Alfred A. Knopf, 1951), 2nd ed.

William L. Langer and S. Everett Gleason, *The Challenge to Isolation, 1937–1940* (New York: Harper, 1952).

———, *The Undeclared War, 1940–1941* (New York: Harper, 1953).

Marina Larrson, *Shattered Anzacs: Living with the Scars of War* (Sydney: University of New South Wales Press, 2009).

David Laskin, *The Long Way Home: An American Journey from Ellis Island to the Great War* (New York: HarperCollins, 2010).

Michael E. Latham, *Modernization as Ideology: American Social Science and "Nation Building" in the Kennedy Era* (Chapel Hill: University of North Carolina Press, 2000).

——, *The Right Kind of Revolution: Modernization, Development, and U.S. Foreign Policy from the Cold War to the Present* (Ithaca, NY: Cornell University Press, 2010).

Elihu Lauterpacht, *The Life of Hersch Lauterpacht* (Cambridge: Cambridge University Press, 2010).

T. J. Jackson Lears, *No Place of Grace: Antimodernism and the Transformation of American Culture, 1880–1920* (New York: Pantheon, 1981).

Waldo G. Leland, *Introduction to the American Official Sources for the Economic and Social History of the World War* (New Haven, CT: Yale University Press, 1926).

Antony Lentin, *Guilt at Versailles: Lloyd George and the Pre-History of Appeasement* (London: Methuen, 1985).

Jörn Leonhard, *Die Büchse der Pandora. Geschichte des Ersten Weltkrieges* (Munich: C. H. Beck, 2014).

Richard Leopold, *The Growth of American Foreign Policy: A History* (New York: Alfred A. Knopf, 1962).

Johannes Lepsius, Albrecht Mendelssohn Bartholdy, and Friedrich Thimme, eds., *Die Große Politik der Europäischen Kabinette 1871–1914. Sammlung der Diplomatischen Akten des Auswärtigen Amtes* (Berlin: Deutsche Verlagsgesellschaft für Politik und Geschichte, 1922–1928), 40 vols.

Randall Lesaffer, ed., *Peace Treaties and International Law in European History: From the Late Middle Ages to World War One* (Cambridge: Cambridge University Press, 2007).

Heike Liebau et al., eds., *The World in World Wars: Experiences, Perceptions, and Perspectives from Africa and Asia* (Leiden: Brill, 2010).

Werner Liebe, *Die Deutschnationale Volkspartei* (Düsseldorf: Droste Verlag, 1956).

Arthur S. Link, *The Higher Realism of Woodrow Wilson* (Nashville, TN: Vanderbilt University Press, 1971).

——, ed., *The Papers of Woodrow Wilson* (Princeton, NJ: Princeton University Press, 1983), vol. 41.

Werner Link, *Die amerikanische Stabilisierungspolitik in Deutschland, 1921–1931* (Düsseldorf: Droste Verlag, 1970).

Walter Lippmann, *U. S. Foreign Policy: Shield of the Republic* (Boston: Little, Brown, 1943).

——, *U.S. War Aims* (Boston: Little, Brown, 1944).

Douglas Little, *American Orientalism: The United States and the Middle East since 1945* (Chapel Hill: University of North Carolina Press, 2008), 3rd ed.

Vejas Gabriel Liulevicius, *War Land on the Eastern Front: Culture, National Identity and German Occupation in World War I* (Cambridge: Cambridge University Press, 2000).

Charlotte Lorenz, *Die gewerbliche Frauenarbeit während des Krieges* (Stuttgart: Deutsche Verlagsanstalt, 1928).

D. A. Low, ed., *Congress and the Raj: Facets of the Indian Struggle, 1917–1947* (New Delhi: Oxford University Press, 2004), 2nd ed.

Hans Löwenfeld-Russ, *Die Regelung der Volksernährung im Kriege* (Vienna: Hölder-Pichler-Tempsky, 1926).

Joe Lunn, *Memoirs of the Maelstrom: A Senegalese Oral History of the First World War* (Portsmouth, NH: Heinemann, 1999).

Jay Luvaas, *The Military Legacy of the Civil War* (Chicago: University of Chicago Press, 1959).

Michael J. Lyons, *World War I: A Short History* (Upper Saddle River, NJ: Prentice Hall, 2000), 2nd ed.

Nancy K. MacLean, *Behind the Mask of Chivalry: The Making of the Second Ku Klux Klan* (New York: Oxford University Press, 1994).

Margaret MacMillan, *Paris 1919: Six Months That Changed the World* (New York: Random House, 2003).

———, *The War That Ended Peace* (New York: Random House, 2013).

Malcolm D. Magee, *What the World Should Be: Woodrow Wilson and the Crafting of a Faith-Based Foreign Policy* (Waco, TX: Baylor University Press, 2008).

Erez Manela, *The Wilsonian Moment: Self-Determination and the International Origins of Anticolonial Nationalism* (New York: Oxford University Press, 2007).

Gregory Mann, *Native Sons: West African Veterans and France in the Twentieth Century* (Durham, NC: Duke University Press, 2006).

C. Roland Marchand, *The American Peace Movement and Social Reform, 1898–1918* (Princeton, NJ: Princeton University Press, 1972).

George M. Marsden, *Fundamentalism and American Culture: The Shaping of Twentieth-Century Evangelicalism, 1870–1925* (New York: Oxford University Press, 1980).

———, ed., *The Fundamentals: A Testimony to Truth* (Chicago, 1910–1915; New York: Garland, 1988), 40 vols.

George Marshall, *Memoirs of My Services in the World War 1917–1918* (Boston: Houghton Mifflin, 1976).

Martin E. Marty, *Modern American Religion*, vol. 1, *The Irony of It All, 1893–1919* (Chicago: University of Chicago Press, 1986).

Ernest R. May, *The World War and American Isolation, 1914–1917* (Cambridge, MA: Harvard University Press, 1959).

Arno Mayer, *Politics and Diplomacy of Peacemaking: Containment and Counterrevolution at Versailles, 1918–1919* (New York: Alfred A. Knopf, 1967).

———, *Wilson vs. Lenin: Political Origins of the New Diplomacy* (New York: Meridian, 1969).

William B. McAllister, Joshua Botts, Peter Cozzens, and Aaron W. Marrs, *Toward "Thorough, Accurate, and Reliable": A History of the Foreign Relations of the United States Series*, Preview Edition, January 23, 2014 (Washington, DC: Office of the Historian, US Department of State, 2014).

Thomas J. McCormick, *China Market: America's Quest for Informal Empire, 1893–1901* (Chicago: Quadrangle, 1967).

John H. McNeill, *Something New Under the Sun: An Environmental History of the Twentieth-Century World* (New York: W. W. Norton, 2001).

Joseph M. McShane, *"Sufficiently Radical": Catholicism, Progressivism, and the Bishops' Program of 1919* (Washington, DC: Catholic University of America Press, 1986).

Albrecht Mendelssohn-Bartholdy, *The War and German Society: The Testament of a Liberal* (New Haven, CT: Yale University Press, 1937).

Suzanne Mettler, *The Submerged State: How Invisible Government Policies Undermine American Democracy* (Chicago: University of Chicago Press, 2011).

Walter Millis, *The Road to War: America, 1914–1917* (Boston: Houghton Mifflin, 1935).

Ministère des Sciènces et des Arts, *La Commission des archives de la guerre* (Brussels: Ministère des Sciènces et des Arts de Belgique, 1923).

Ilse Mintz, *Deterioration in the Quality of Foreign Bonds issued in the United States, 1920–1930* (New York: National Bureau of Economic Research, 1951).

David Mitrany, *The Land and the Peasant in Rumania: The War and Agrarian Reform (1917–21)* (London: H. Milford, Oxford University Press, 1930).

Annika Mombauer, *The Origins of the First World War: Controversies and Consensus* (London: Longmans, 2002).

Hans Mommsen, *Die verspielte Freiheit. Der Weg der Republik von Weimar in den Untergang 1918–1933* (Berlin: Verlag Ullstein, 1990).

John Monash, *The Australian Victories in France in 1918* (London: Imperial War Museum, 1920).

Max Montgelas and Walter Schücking, eds., *Die deutschen Dokumente zum Kriegsausbruch. Vollständige Sammlung der von Karl Kautsky zusammengestellten amtlichen Aktenstücke mit einigen Ergänzungen* (Charlottenburg: Deutsche Verlagsgesellschaft für Politik und Geschichte, 1919).

Samuel Taylor Moore, *America and the World War: A Narrative of the Part Played by the United States from the Outbreak to Peace* (New York: Greenberg, 1937).

James A. Morone, *Hellfire Nation: The Politics of Sin in American History* (New Haven, CT: Yale University Press, 2003).

Samuel Moyn, *The Last Utopia: Human Rights in History* (Cambridge, MA: Belknap Press of Harvard University Press, 2010).

Malik Mufti, *Sovereign Creations: Pan-Arabism and Political Order in Syria and Iraq* (Ithaca, NY: Cornell University Press, 1996).

John M. Mulder, *Woodrow Wilson: The Years of Preparation* (Princeton, NJ: Princeton University Press, 1978).

Herfried Münkler, *Der Grosse Krieg. Die Welt 1914–1918* (Berlin: Rowohlt, 2014).

Eli Nathans, *The Politics of Citizenship in Germany: Ethnicity, Utility and Nationalism* (New York: Berg, 2004).

Stephen C. Neff, *Justice among Nations: A History of International Law* (Cambridge, MA: Harvard University Press, 2014).

Mae M. Ngai, *Impossible Subjects: Illegal Aliens and the Making of Modern America* (Princeton, NJ: Princeton University Press, 2004).

Christopher McKnight Nichols, *Promise and Peril: America at the Dawn of a Global Age* (Cambridge, MA: Harvard University Press, 2011).

Gottfried Niedhart, *Die Außenpolitik der Weimarer Republik* (Munich: Oldenbourg, 1999).

Jonathan M. Nielson, *American Historians in War and Peace: Patriotism, Diplomacy and the Paris Peace Conference* (Bethesda, MD: Academica Press, 2012).

Anne Norton, *Leo Strauss and the Politics of the American Empire* (New Haven, CT: Yale University Press, 2004).

Peter Novick, *That Noble Dream: The "Objectivity Question" and the American Historical Profession* (Cambridge: Cambridge University Press, 1988).

John S. Nurser, *For All Peoples and All Nations: The Ecumenical Church and Human Rights* (Washington, DC: Georgetown University Press, 2005).

William Ochsenwald and Sydney Nettleton Fisher, *The Middle East: A History* (New York: McGraw-Hill, 2011), 7th ed.

Jens David Ohlin, *The Assault on International Law* (Oxford: Oxford University Press, 2015).

David Omissi, *The Sepoy and the Raj: The Indian Army, 1860-1940* (London: Macmillan, 1994).

Cynthia E. Orozco, *No Mexicans, Women, or Dogs Allowed: The Rise of the Mexican American Civil Rights Movement* (Austin: University of Texas Press, 2009).

George Orwell, *Inside the Whale* (Harmondsworth, UK: Penguin, 1968).

Richard Overy, *Why the Allies Won* (New York: W. W. Norton, 1995).

Bertrande Patenaude, *The Big Show in Bololand: The American Relief Expedition to Soviet Russia in the Famine of 1921* (Stanford, CA: Stanford University Press, 2002).

Frederic Paxson, *American Democracy and the World War: Prewar Years, 1913–1917* (Boston: Houghton Mifflin, 1936).

Susan Pedersen, *The Guardians: The League of Nations and the Crisis of Empire* (Oxford: Oxford University Press, 2015).

John J. Pershing, *My Experiences in the World War* (New York: Frederick A. Stokes Company, 1931).

H. C. Peterson and Gilbert C. Fite, *Opponents of War, 1917–1918* (Seattle: University of Washington Press, 1968 [1957]).

Pierre Pinot, *Le contrôle du ravitaillement de la population civile* (Paris: Presses Universitaires de France, 1925).

Robert F. Piper, Jr., *The American Churches in World War I* (Athens: Ohio University Press, 1985).

Henri Pirenne, *La Belgique et la guerre mondiale* (Paris: Presses Universitaires de France, 1928).

Clemens Pirquet, *Volksgesundheit im Krieg* (Vienna: Hölder-Pichler-Tempsky, 1926).

Forrest C. Pogue, *George C. Marshall: Education of a General* (New York: Viking, 1963).

Nicolas Politis, *Neutrality and Peace* (Washington, DC: Carnegie Endowment for International Peace, 1935).

Andrew Preston, *Sword of the Spirit, Shield of Faith: Religion in American War and Diplomacy* (New York: Alfred A. Knopf, 2012).

Tammy M. Proctor, *Civilians in a World at War, 1914–1918* (New York: New York University Press, 2010).

Jules Prudhommeaux, *Le Centre Européen de la Dotation Carnegie pour la Paix Internationale, 1911–1921* (Paris: Centre Européen de la Dotation Carnegie pour la Paix Internationale, 1921).

Ronald W. Pruessen, *John Foster Dulles: The Road to Power* (New York: Free Press, 1982).

Alexander V. Prusin, *The Lands Between: Conflict in the East European Borderlands, 1870–1992* (Oxford: Oxford University Press, 2010).

Wolfram Pyta, *Hindenburg. Herrschaft zwischen Hohenzollern und Hitler* (Munich: Pantheon Verlag, 2009).

José A. Ramirez, *To the Line of Fire! Mexican Texans and World War I* (College Station: Texas A&M University Press, 2009).

Mary Renda, *Taking Haiti: Military Occupation and the Culture of U.S. Imperialism, 1915–1940* (Chapel Hill: University of North Carolina Press, 2000).

Pierre Renouvin, *The Forms of War Government in France* (New Haven, CT: Yale University Press, 1927).

David Reynolds, *The Long Shadow: The Great War and the Twentieth Century* (London: Simon and Schuster, 2013).

Michael A. Reynolds, *Shattering Empires: The Clash and Collapse of the Ottoman and Russian Empires, 1908–1918* (Cambridge: Cambridge University Press, 2011).

Carl J. Richard, *When the United States Invaded Russia: Woodrow Wilson's Siberian Disaster* (Lanham, MD: Rowman and Littlefield, 2013).

Jörg Richter, *Kriegsschuld und Nationalstolz. Politik zwischen Mythos und Realität* (Tübingen: Verlag Katzmann, 1972).

Gerhard Ritter, *The Sword and the Scepter: The Problem of Militarism in Germany*, translated by Heinz Norden (Coral Gables, FL: University of Miami Press, 1972).

Craig Robertson, *The Passport in America: The History of a Document* (New York: Oxford University Press, 2010).

Davide Rodogno, *Against Massacre: Humanitarian Interventions in the Ottoman Empire, 1815–1914* (Princeton, NJ: Princeton University Press, 2012).

Emily S. Rosenberg, *Financial Missionaries to the World: The Politics and Culture of Dollar Diplomacy, 1900–1930* (Durham, NC: Duke University Press, 2003).

———, ed., *A World Connecting: 1870–1945* (Cambridge, MA: Belknap Press of Harvard University Press, 2012).

Jonathan Rosenberg, *How Far the Promised Land? World Affairs and the American Civil Rights Movement from the First World War to Vietnam* (Princeton, NJ: Princeton University Press, 2005).

Patricia Rosenfield, *A World of Giving: Carnegie Corporation's First Century of International Philanthropy* (New York: Public Affairs, 2014).

Aviel Roshwald, *Ethnic Nationalism and the Fall of Empires: Central Europe, Russia and the Middle East, 1914–1923* (London: Routledge, 2001).

Dorothy Ross, *The Origins of American Social Science* (New York: Cambridge University Press, 1991).

Dietmar Rothermund, *The Global Impact of the Great Depression* (London: Routledge, 1996).

———, *India in the Great Depression, 1929–1939* (New Delhi: Manohar, 1992).

Markku Ruotsila, *The Origins of Christian Anti-Internationalism: Conservative Evangelicals and the League of Nations* (Washington, DC: Georgetown University Press, 2008).

Emmanuelle Saada, *Empire's Children: Race, Filiation, and Citizenship in the French Colonies* (Chicago: University of Chicago Press, 2012).

Rainer Sammet, *"Dolchstoß." Deutschland und die Auseinandersetzung mit der Niederlage im Ersten Weltkrieg* (Berlin: Trafo Verlag, 2003).

Hans Schmidt, *The United States Occupation of Haiti, 1915–1934* (New Brunswick, NJ: Rutgers University Press, 1971).

Kevin M. Schultz, *Tri-Faith America: How Catholics and Jews Held Postwar America to Its Protestant Promise* (New York: Oxford University Press, 2011).

Hagen Schulze, *Weimar. Deutschland 1917–1933* (Berlin: Severin und Siedler, 1982).

Klaus Schwabe, *Wissenschaft und Kriegsmoral. Die deutschen Hochschullehrer und die politischen Grundfragen des Ersten Weltkrieges* (Göttingen: Musterschmidt, 1969).

———, *Woodrow Wilson, Revolutionary Germany, and Peacemaking, 1918–1919* (Chapel Hill: University of North Carolina Press, 1985).

David Sehat, *The Myth of American Religious Freedom* (New York: Oxford University Press, 2011).

Bernard Semmel, *Imperialism and Social Reform: English Social-Imperial Thought, 1893–1914* (Cambridge: Harvard University Press, 1960).

Ronald Shaffer, *America in the Great War* (New York: Oxford University Press, 1991).

Hatsue Shinohara, *U.S. International Lawyers in the Interwar Years: A Forgotten Crusade* (Cambridge: Cambridge University Press, 2012).

James T. Shotwell, *The Autobiography of James T. Shotwell* (Indianapolis, IN: Bobbs-Merrill, 1961).

Nathan D. Showalter, *The End of a Crusade: The Student Volunteer Movement for Foreign Missions and the Great War* (Lanham, MD: Scarecrow, 1998).

August Skalweit, *Die Deutsche Kriegsernährungswirtschaft* (Stuttgart: Deutsche Verlagsanstalt, 1927).

Nico Slate, *Colored Cosmopolitanism: The Shared Struggle for Freedom in the United States and India* (Cambridge, MA: Harvard University Press, 2002).

Glenda Sluga, *Internationalism in the Age of Nationalism* (Philadelphia: University of Pennsylvania Press, 2013).

Neil Smith, *American Empire: Roosevelt's Geographer and the Prelude to Globalization* (Berkeley: University of California Press, 2003).

Richard Smith, *Jamaican Volunteers in the First World War: Race, Masculitinty, and the Development of National Consciousness* (Manchester: Manchester University Press, 2004).

Rogers Smith, *Civic Ideals: Conflicting Visions of Citizenship in U.S. History* (New Haven, CT: Yale University Press, 1997).

Mark A. Snell, ed., *Unknown Soldiers: The American Expeditionary Forces in Memory and Remembrance* (Kent, OH: Kent State University Press, 2008).

Sarah Snyder, *Human Rights Activism and the End of the Cold War: A Transnational History of the Helsinki Network* (Cambridge: Cambridge University Press, 2011).

Seema Sohi, *Echoes of Mutiny: Race, Surveillance, and Indian Anticolonialism in North America* (New York: Oxford University Press, 2014).

Lawrence Sondhaus, *The Great War at Sea: A Naval History of the First World War* (New York: Cambridge University Press, 2014).

Susan Sontag, *Regarding the Pain of Others* (New York: Picador, 2003).

Bartholomew H. Sparrow, *The Insular Cases and the Emergence of American Empire* (Lawrence: University Press of Kansas, 2006).

Ole Spiermann, *International Legal Argument in the Permanent Court of International Justice: The Rise of International Judiciary* (Cambridge: Cambridge University Press, 2005).

Ronald Steel, *Walter Lippmann and the American Century* (Boston: Little, Brown, 1980).

Zara Steiner, *The Lights That Failed: European International History, 1919–1933* (Oxford: Oxford University Press, 2005).

Christopher M. Sterba, *Good Americans: Italian and Jewish Immigrants during the First World War* (New York: Oxford University Press, 2003).

Ann Laura Stoler, ed., *Haunted by Empire: Geographies of Intimacy in North American History* (Durham, NC: Duke University Press, 2006).

Mark A. Stoler, *George C. Marshall: Soldier-Statesman of the American Century* (Boston: Twayne, 1989).

Ralph J. Stone, *The Irreconcilables and the Fight against the League of Nations* (Lexington: University Press of Kentucky, 1971).

Petr Berngardovich Struve, *Food Supply in Russia during the World War* (New Haven, CT: Yale University Press, 1930).

Frank Surface and Raymond Bland, *American Food in the World War and Reconstruction Period* (Stanford, CA: Stanford University Press, 1931).

Matthew Avery Sutton, *American Apocalypse: A History of Modern Evangelicalism* (Cambridge, MA: Harvard University Press, 2014).

A. J. P. Taylor, *The Struggle for Mastery in Europe, 1848–1918* (Oxford: Clarendon Press, 1954).

John Terraine, *To Win a War: 1918, The Year of Victory* (Garden City, NY: Doubleday, 1981).

Annelise Thimme, *Flucht in den Mythos. Die deutschnationale Volkspartei und die Niederlage von 1918* (Göttingen: Vandenhoeck and Ruprecht, 1969).

———, *Friedrich Thimme 1968–1939. Ein politischer Historiker, Publizist und Schriftsteller in seinen Briefen* (Boppard: Harald Boldt Verlag, 1994).

Martin Thomas, *The French Empire between the Wars: Imperialism, Politics and Society* (Manchester: Manchester University Press, 2005).

John A. Thompson, *Woodrow Wilson* (London: Longmans, 2002).

Frank B. Tipton and Robert Aldrich, *An Economic and Social History of Europe, 1890–1939* (Houndsmill, UK: Macmillan, 1987).

Mark G. Toulouse, *The Transformation of John Foster Dulles: From Prophet of Realism to Priest of Nationalism* (Macon, GA: Mercer University Press, 1985).

David Trask, *The AEF and Coalition Warmaking, 1917–1918* (Lawrence: University Press of Kansas, 1993).

Michel-Rolph Trouillot, *Silencing the Past: Power and the Production of History* (Boston: Beacon, 1997).

Steven Trout, *On the Battlefield of Memory: The First World War and American Remembrance, 1919–1941* (Tuscaloosa: University of Alabama Press, 2010).

Volker Ulrich, *Hitler* (Frankfurt: S. Fischer Verlag, 2013), vol. 1.

Paul Umbreit, *Der Krieg und die Arbeitsverhältnisse: Die deutschen Gewerkschaften im Kriege* (Stuttgart: Deutsche Verlagsanstalt, 1928).

Stephen Vaughn, *Holding Fast the Inner Lines: Democracy, Nationalism, and the Committee on Public Information* (Chapel Hill: University of North Carolina Press, 1980).

Helen Zoe Veit, *Modern Food, Moral Food: Self Control, Science, and the Rise of Modern American Eating in the Early Twentieth Century* (Chapel Hill: University of North Carolina Press, 2013).

James Vernon, *Hunger: A Modern History* (Cambridge, MA: Harvard University Press, 2007).

Paul Vincent, *The Politics of Hunger: The Allied Blockade of Germany, 1915–1919* (Athens: Ohio University Press, 1985).

Robert Vitalis, *America's Kingdom: Mythmaking on the Saudi Oil Frontier* (Stanford, CA: Stanford University Press, 2007).

Joseph Frazier Wall, *Andrew Carnegie* (New York: Oxford University Press, 1970).

Richard Wall and J. M. Winter, eds., *The Upheaval of War: Family, Work, and Welfare in Europe, 1914–1918* (New York: Cambridge University Press, 1988).

Bernhard Walpen, *Die offenen Feinde und ihre Gesellschaft: eine hegemonietheoretische Studie zur Mont Pèlerin Society* (Hamburg: VSA-Verlag, 2004).

Keith David Watenpaugh, *Bread from Stones: The Middle East and the Making of Modern Humanitarianism* (Berkeley: University of California Press, 2015).

Thomas Weber, *Hitlers Erster Krieg* (Berlin: Verlag Ullstein, 2010).

Hans-Ulrich Wehler, *Deutsche Gesellschaftsgeschichte*, vol. 4: *1914–1949* (Munich: C. H. Beck, 2003).

Russell F. Weigley, *The American Way of War: A History of United States Military Strategy and Policy* (Bloomington: Indiana University Press, 1973).

Patrick Weil, *The Sovereign Citizen: Denaturalization and the Origins of the American Republic* (Philadelphia: University of Pennsylvania Press, 2013).

Barbara Young Welke, *Law and the Borders of Belonging in the Long Nineteenth-Century United States* (New York: Cambridge University Press, 2010).

Isabel Wilkerson, *The Warmth of Other Suns: The Epic Story of America's Great Migration* (New York: Random House, 2010).

Tim Wilson, *Frontiers of Violence: Conflict and Identity in Ulster and Upper Silesia, 1918–1922* (Oxford: Oxford University Press, 2010).

Heinrich August Winkler, *Weimar 1918–1933. Die Geschichte der ersten deutschen Demokratie* (Munich: C. H. Beck, 1998).

Jay Winter, ed., *The Cambridge History of the First World War* (Cambridge: Cambridge University Press, 2014).

Jay Winter and Antoine Prost, *The Great War in History: Debates and Controversies, 1914 to the Present* (Cambridge: Cambridge University Press, 2005).

Andreas Wirsching, *Vom Weltkrieg zum Bürgerkrieg? Politischer Extremismus in Deutschland und Frankreich 1918–1938/39* (Munich: Oldenbourg Wissensch.Vlg, 1999).

Jonathan Wright, *Gustav Stresemann: Weimar's Greatest Statesman* (Oxford: Oxford University Press, 2002).

Xu Guoqi, *Strangers on the Western Front: Chinese Workers in the Great War* (Cambridge, MA: Harvard University Press, 2011).

Serhy Yekelchyk, *Ukraine: Birth of a Modern Nation* (Oxford: Oxford University Press, 2007).

Daniel Yergin, *The Prize: The Epic Quest for Oil, Money, and Power* (New York: Simon and Schuster, 1992).

Mitchell A. Yockelson, *Borrowed Soldiers: Americans under British Command, 1918* (Norman: University of Oklahoma Press, 2008).

Marilyn B. Young, *The Rhetoric of Empire: American China Policy, 1895–1901* (Cambridge, MA: Harvard University Press, 1968).

Sacha Zala, *Geschichte unter der Schere politischer Zensur: Amtliche Aktensammlungen im internationalen Vergleich* (Munich: Oldenbourg, 2001).

Egmont Zechlin, *Die Deutsche Politik und die Juden im Ersten Weltkrieg* (Göttingen: Vandenhoeck and Ruprecht, 1969).

Susan Zeiger, *Entangling Alliances: Foreign War Brides and American Soldiers in the Twentieth Century* (New York: New York University Press, 2010).

Thomas W. Zeiler, *Free Trade, Free World: The Advent of GATT* (Chapel Hill: University of North Carolina Press, 1999).

David Zierler, *The Invention of Ecocide: Agent Orange, Vietnam, and the Scientists Who Changed the Way We Think about the Environment* (Athens: University of Georgia Press, 2011).

Aristide Zolberg, *A Nation by Design: Immigration Policy in the Fashioning of America* (Cambridge, MA: Harvard University Press, 2006).

Erik-Jan Zürcher, *The Unionist Factor: The Role of the Committee of Union and Progress in the Turkish National Movement 1905–1926* (Leiden: Brill, 1984).

Index

Page numbers in italics refer to figures.